CAMPAIGN FINANCE REFORM

CAMPAIGN FINANCE REFORM | A Sourcebook

ANTHONY CORRADO

THOMAS E. MANN

DANIEL R. ORTIZ

TREVOR POTTER

FRANK J. SORAUF

Editors

BROOKINGS INSTITUTION PRESS

Washington, D.C.

Copyright © 1997 by
THE BROOKINGS INSTITUTION
1775 Massachusetts Avenue, N.W., Washington, D.C. 20036

Library of Congress Cataloging-in-Publication data

Campaign finance reform : a sourcebook / editors, Anthony Corrado . . .
 [et al.].
     p.   cm.
   Includes index.
   ISBN 0-8157-1581-1 (pbk. : alk. paper)
   1. Campaign funds—United States. 2. Campaign funds—Law and
legislation—United States. I. Corrado, Anthony, 1957–   .
JK1991.C345   1997
324.7'8'0973—dc21   97-33765
                                                          CIP

The paper used in this publication meets the minimum requirements of the
American National Standard for Information Sciences—Permanence of Paper
for Printed Library Materials, ANSI Z39.48-1984

Typeset in Minion and Univers
Cynthia Stock
Silver Spring, Maryland

Interior design by Kathleen Sims
Bethesda, Maryland

Printed by R. R. Donnelley and Sons, Co.
Harrisonburg, Virginia

FOREWORD

The widely reported fund-raising abuses in the 1996 federal elections may have focused the attention of the political community on the need for campaign finance reform, but the obstacles to enacting constructive changes in the law remain daunting. Philosophical differences, partisan calculations, incumbent self-protection, and public disengagement have combined to frustrate recent efforts to patch the leaks that have sprung in our campaign finance system, and this round may prove as unproductive as the others. If progress is to be made, an essential first step is understanding how current campaign finance practices evolved from past decisions and what legal and administrative questions must be addressed in moving the system in a desired direction.

This book is an unusual one for Brookings in that it combines reprints of key documents shaping the statutory and administrative framework for campaign finance regulation with original essays that guide readers over an exceedingly complex legal terrain. The idea for the book originated with Trevor Potter, a former chairman of the Federal Election Commission and currently a partner in Wiley, Rein & Fielding, and Daniel Ortiz, a professor of law at the University of Virginia. They brought their idea to Thomas Mann, director of Governmental Studies at Brookings, who responded favorably and developed it into a Brookings project. Two additional experts on campaign finance—Anthony Corrado, an associate professor of government at Colby College, and Frank Sorauf, Regents' Professor Emeritus of Political Science at the University of Minnesota— were recruited to join the editorial team.

Many individuals and institutions contributed to the successful completion of this book. Tara

Adams Ragone was indispensable in managing the flow of materials among the editors, providing research assistance, obtaining reprint permissions, verifying the accuracy of the manuscript, and preparing it for posting on our website and for publication. In addition, Matthew Atlas verified chapters 3 and 4, Laurel Imig provided research assistance on chapter 2, Patricia Fowlkes and Kristen Lippert-Martin assisted with chapter 8, Steph Selice edited the manuscript, Marla Brown Fogelman, proofread it, and Julia Petrakis prepared the index.

Anthony Corrado wishes to thank Dawn DiBlasi and Katherine Charbonnier for their editorial and research assistance on chapters 6 and 9. Daniel Ortiz thanks Dianne Johnson for her invaluable administrative support. Trevor Potter is grateful for the generous support provided by the law firm of Wiley, Rein & Fielding to this project, in particular for the research assistance of Michael Toner, Allison Hayward, and Jason Cronic. Frank Sorauf is indebted to his research assistant, David Frisch, and to Bob Biersack of the Federal Election Commission, who has helped almost everyone in the country who is writing on campaign finance.

Financial support was provided by The Joyce Foundation and the Cissy Patterson Trust.

The views expressed in this book are those of the authors and should not be ascribed to the trustees, officers, or other staff members of the Brookings Institution.

MICHAEL H. ARMACOST
President

August 1997
Washington, D.C.

A NOTE ON THE DOCUMENTS

Some of the documents included in the *Sourcebook* were reprinted in their entirety, others were excerpted. When text in a document was elided or deleted, we used ellipses to indicate where we deleted words other than internal footnotes or citations, and brackets to indicate any editing or additions. Other than adding editorial comments, we made the minimum number of changes needed in these documents to conform them to the book's style. Notes, tables, and figures were renumbered within the documents so that the reader would not be confused by any deletions. We have provided complete references for all materials.

CONTENTS

LIST OF DOCUMENTS

CHAPTER 6

CHAPTER 7

CHAPTER 8

THOMAS E. MANN

Discussions of money in politics typically generate more heat than light, and the current controversy over fundraising abuses in the 1996 federal elections is no exception. News reports of White House coffees and Lincoln Bedroom sleepovers, of Buddhist nuns and Chinese conspiracies, provide titillating details of questionable and possibly criminal activity during the last campaign, but they leave most of us at a loss over how to place these revelations in perspective. It is difficult to understand the fundraising scandals of 1996 and to judge whether they involve primarily violations of existing laws (and thus indicate a problem of enforcement) or exploitation of legal loopholes (which can only be addressed by new legislative action to close them), without knowing the current state of campaign finance law and how it is being interpreted by the courts and enforced by the Federal Election Commission and other agencies.

This book is designed to help members of the press, interested citizens, students of American democracy, and would-be reformers understand how current campaign finance practices have evolved from previous decisions made by legislative, judicial, and executive bodies and what might be entailed in moving the system in a desired direction. It was conceived partly as a repository of key documents (statutes, court decisions, FEC advisory opinions, and reports) and scholarly articles that are essential references for an informed discussion of campaign finance reform, and partly as a series of original expositions of the state of the art in critical areas of campaign finance regulation. Unlike other treatments of the subject, which range from statistical analyses of the impact of campaign money on elections and policymaking to the politics of campaign finance reform, this book focuses on the statutory, legal, and administrative dimensions of the regulatory regime for financing federal elections, what might have contributed to its apparent collapse in 1996, and what legislative and judicial strategies are available for rehabilitating or replacing it.

Chapter 1 provides an overview of the current state of campaign finance law. Trevor Potter describes the regulated portion of the federal election finance system as well as those entities, funds, and activities that might influence federal elections from beyond the reach of the law. He specifies the legal standing of individuals, foreign nationals, corporations, unions, political action committees, political parties, and nonprofit organizations and what limits (if any) govern their contributions to candidates and parties, independent expenditures, and issue advocacy.

Efforts to restrain the role of money in U.S. elections have a long and checkered history. In chapter 2, Anthony Corrado traces how attempts early in this century to reduce the influence of corporations and wealthy individuals, to limit spending, and to disclose sources of campaign funds, though enacted into law, were frustrated by legal loopholes and woefully inadequate enforcement mechanisms. It was only after the Watergate scandal and reports of fundraising abuses in the 1972 Nixon campaign that Congress embraced a comprehensive approach to campaign finance regulation. Yet the system envisioned in the Federal Election Campaign Act Amendments of 1974 was never fully realized, as court decisions, subsequent amendments, and the resourceful actions of entrepreneurial politicians together reshaped it almost beyond recognition.

No single action had a greater impact in narrowing the reach of federal election law and in limiting the options of reformers than the Supreme Court's decision in *Buckley* v. *Valeo*. In chapter 3, Dan Ortiz describes how *Buckley*, which dealt with a challenge to the 1974 FECA amendments, created a framework that continues to define constitutional limitations on campaign finance regulation. *Buckley* gave Congress broad scope to regulate contributions in order to prevent corruption. However, it found no compelling state interest in limiting individual expenditures, which the Court took to be a form of political expression protected by the First Amendment. Subsequent decisions by the Supreme Court have introduced some confusion into the jurisprudence of campaign finance regulation, but the basic structure of *Buckley* remains intact.

Buckley and its progeny have precipitated a lively constitutional debate outside the confines of the U.S. Supreme Court. In chapter 4, Ortiz presents three prototypical positions. Ronald Dworkin argues that *Buckley* was wrongly decided and should be overruled. Bradley A. Smith celebrates the Court for vindicating the First Amendment and argues that the assumptions reformers make about money in politics are not supported by the evidence. He embraces a further deregulation of the system. Cass R. Sunstein criticizes *Buckley* on different grounds than Dworkin but agrees that it should be repudiated. At the same time, he is wary of the unintended consequences of campaign reform and counsels a searching review of regulatory proposals.

One of the most prominent sets of actors in the post-Watergate campaign finance arena, often the target of reformers, are political action committees (PACs). In chapter 5 Frank Sorauf provides documents and commentary that describe and explain the explosive growth of PACs in the 1970s and 1980s, the differences among PACs in their goals and strategies, and their impact on elections and policymaking. He questions the wisdom and constitutionality of efforts to eliminate or unduly restrict PACs, arguing they are important instruments of representation in contemporary American political life.

No aspect of campaign fundraising in the 1996 election cycle attracted more criticism than the aggressive efforts by President Bill Clinton, Vice President Al Gore, and other party officials to raise large "soft money" contributions for the nonfederal accounts of the Democratic party. The national parties raised $262.1 million in soft money contributions during the 1996 cycle, more than half by the Republicans. Outside the scope of federal law, soft money can be raised by national party organizations in unlimited amounts from individuals and from sources such as corporations and labor unions that are banned from contributing funds in federal elections. In chapter 6 Anthony Corrado reconstructs the sequence of events, including crucial advisory opinions of the Federal Election Commission, that provided the legal basis for the national parties moving beyond the limits on contributions to and expenditures by the parties contained in the Federal Election Campaign Act to initiate and then intensify soft money fundraising operations. Corrado also reviews the rules that have been developed for allocating hard and soft money funds for various party activities and considers reform proposals to eliminate or restrict soft money accounts.

If soft money allows parties to raise funds from sources that are illegal when used in connection with federal elections, issue advocacy provides the basis for parties and other groups to spend those otherwise prohibited funds to improve the political standing of their favored candidates and diminish that of their adversaries. So-called issue advocacy was central to President Clinton's reelection strategy during his battles with the Republican Congress in the winter of 1995–96; it was also crucial for keeping Senator Bob Dole visible in the months preceding the Republican convention when he had exhausted his presidential primary funds. And it was the means by which labor and business groups used union and corporate treasuries to finance hard-hitting advertisements in targeted districts and states. In chapter 7, Trevor Potter traces the evolution of issue advocacy, which has come to mean political speech which does not expressly advocate the election or defeat of a federal candidate, from the *Buckley* decision through subsequent actions by lower federal courts and the Federal Election Commission. Potter considers the current legal standing of issue advocacy communications that may have been coordinated with a candidate and identifies several approaches advocated to regulate the use of issue advocacy in federal elections.

Though weak enforcement has long plagued campaign finance law, the shortcomings of the Federal Election Commission were especially apparent during the 1996 campaign. In the face of extraor-dinary alleged violations involving fund-raising from foreign nationals, the use of soft money to circumvent spending limits of publicly funded presidential candidates, coordination of assertedly independent expenditures, and massive undisclosed expenditures on issue ads with an election message, the FEC was strikingly passive. In chapter 8, I discuss how and why Congress structured the FEC to ensure it would not develop into an aggressively independent enforcement agency and review various proposals for improving disclosure of campaign contributions and expenditures and for strengthening the enforcement machinery.

The final chapter, compiled by Anthony Corrado and Dan Ortiz, presents a summary of recent campaign finance reform innovations in the states, together with early responses by the courts, as well as two more ambitious plans for reshaping the financing and character of election campaigns—voluntary full public financing and free broadcast time for candidates and parties.

The Current State of Campaign Finance Law

TREVOR POTTER

The federal election laws were written broadly by Congress in 1971 and 1974 to cover all money spent "in connection with" or "for the purpose of influencing" federal elections. The intent of Congress was to regulate all funds which might be considered federal election related. However, the Supreme Court in *Buckley* v. *Valeo,* 424 U.S. 1 (1976) (see chapter 3), and subsequent cases, has defined these statutory phrases to have a much more limited reach. The Court held that the activity covered by the federal election laws must be narrowly and clearly defined so as not to "chill" speech protected by the First Amendment, and to provide notice of regulation to speakers. This chapter describes the regulated portion of the federal campaign finance system (contribution limits), and then the use of "soft" and "issue advocacy" money to influence federal elections from beyond the reach of the federal election laws. It also describes the many entities engaged in political speech and spending, from party committees to labor unions to 501(c)(3) and (c)(4) organizations. Much of the relevant statutory language and Federal Election Commission (FEC) regulations are reprinted in documents 6.1 and 6.2.

DIRECT CONTRIBUTIONS TO FEDERAL CANDIDATES AND NATIONAL COMMITTEES OF POLITICAL PARTIES

The Federal Election Campaign Act (FECA) defines "contribution" to include "anything of value" given to a federal candidate or committee. This encompasses not only direct financial contributions, loans, loan guarantees, and the like, but also in-kind contributions of office space, equipment, fundraising expenses, salaries paid to persons who assist a candidate, and the like; 2 U.S.C. § 431(8)(A). The act places limits on the amount individuals and other entities may contribute to candidates and federal committees, whether directly or in kind.

Individuals

The act permits individuals to contribute up to $1,000 to a candidate per election; § 441a(a)(1)(A). The term "election" under the act includes "a general, special, primary, or runoff election"; § 431(1)(A). An individual may therefore contribute up to $1,000 to a candidate's primary and another $1,000 to the general election campaign. Each individual has his or her own limit, so that a couple may give $4,000 in total per election cycle to each federal candidate. Additionally, minor children may give if it is their own money, under their own control, and voluntarily contributed by them—requirements sometimes ignored by politically active parents of infants and schoolchildren.

Individuals are also limited in the amounts that they can contribute to other political entities. Individuals are limited to $20,000 per year in contributions to the federal accounts of a national party committee, such as the Republican National Committee (RNC) or Democratic National Committee (DNC); § 441a(a)(1)(B). Additionally, individual contributions are limited to $5,000 per year to any other political committee, including a political action committee (PAC); § 441a(a)(1)(C). Contributions to state party committees are likewise limited to $5,000 per year. Local party committees are considered part of state party committees, so the $5,000 limit is a combined limit on the two.[1]

In addition to these specific limits to various candidates and committees, individuals have an *aggregate annual federal contribution limit* of $25,000 per year; § 441a(a)(3).[2] Thus, individuals who give to one or more party committees and several candidates may easily reach this limit for a given calendar year. The *Los Angeles Times* routinely runs a list of individuals who appear to have violated this limit, based solely on publicly available FEC records. Due to the complexity of the legal and accounting rules involved, there is often a factual dispute whether a violation has occurred. However, in many cases it appears that the ability to make unlimited "soft money" contributions to nonfederal committees and accounts has resulted in a general case of amnesia about the $25,000 annual federal limit.

The act and FEC regulations contain a host of exceptions from the definition of "contribution" applicable to individuals. Among the principal ones are the donation of personal time to a candidate (unless it is time paid for by someone else, such as an employer), home hospitality up to $1,000 per candidate per election, and costs of personal travel of up to $1,000 per candidate per election and up to $2,000 per year for party committees.

Political Committees

Whether an organization is a "political committee" required to register with the FEC and subject to the federal limitations on amounts and sources of contributions is a crucial question for any entity engaged in political activity. The act defines "political committee" as:

(A) any committee, club, association, or other group of persons which receives contributions aggregating in

excess of $1,000 during a calendar year or which makes expenditures aggregating in excess of $1,000 during a calendar year; or
(B) any separate segregated fund established under [the Federal Election Campaign Act]; or
(C) any local committee of a political party which receives contributions aggregating in excess of $5,000 during a calendar year, or makes payments exempted from the definitions of contribution or expenditure as defined [by the act] aggregating in excess of $5,000 during a calendar year, or makes contributions aggregating in excess of $1,000 during a calendar year or makes expenditures aggregating in excess of $1,000 during a calendar year.
2 U.S.C. § 431(4).

Whether an organization (such as GOPAC or the American Israel Public Affairs Committee) is a political committee, and thus subject to all the federal election laws, or is instead an entity completely unregulated by the federal campaign finance laws, has been the subject of much litigation. The question is whether merely spending $1,000 on express advocacy is sufficient to qualify a group as a political committee, or whether its political activity must be significantly more extensive and pervasive.[3] The current legal standard is unclear, as a result of several recent conflicting court decisions. This is a crucial issue for the coverage of the election laws and will likely continue to be hard fought, because groups that can successfully avoid qualifying as a federal political committee can spend unlimited sums, raised without restriction or disclosure, for activities often designed to influence federal elections.

Different forms of federal political committees face differing contribution limits. Political action committees are political committees that may qualify for *multicandidate committee* status. To so qualify, a PAC must demonstrate that it has been registered with the FEC for six months, receive contributions from at least fifty-one persons, and contribute to at least five federal candidates; 11 C.F.R. § 100.5(e)(3). A multicandidate committee may contribute up to $5,000 to a candidate per election, and up to $5,000 to other separate PACs each year. Additionally, a multicandidate committee can contribute up to $15,000 per year to a national party committee and has a combined limit of $5,000 per year to local and state party committees.

A PAC that does not qualify for multicandidate committee status is limited to contributions of $1,000 per candidate per election but may still contribute up to $5,000 to another PAC per year. Such PACs may contribute up to $20,000 per year to national party committees (more than multicandidate committees can) and have a combined limit of $5,000 per year to local and state party committees.

There are two types of noncandidate political committees: nonconnected (or independent) committees; and corporate or labor PACs, formally called separate segregated funds. Corporations and labor unions may pay all the administrative and solicitation costs of their committees, while nonconnected PACs must pay such costs out of the funds they raise. Corporate and labor PACs, however, have strict rules on who they may solicit, while nonconnected committees may solicit the general public.

Leadership PACs

Beginning in the 1980s, a number of political committees were established that had an "association" with a member of the congressional leadership. These "leadership PACs" usually use the name of a member of Congress in an honorific capacity such as "honorary chair," and the committee treasurer is a close associate of the congressional member (sometimes an employee of the congressional office). Members of Congress often personally solicit contributions to "their" leadership PACs, and the news media report contributions and expenditures by the committees as if they were a component of the member's campaign apparatus.

The advantage of leadership PACs for members of Congress is twofold. Such committees may qualify as "multicandidate" committees and accept contributions of up to $5,000 from individuals (as opposed to $1,000 for a candidate's campaign committee). In addition, since leadership PACs are not considered affiliated with their campaign accounts, members of Congress may obtain contributions from the same sources for both committees (so that a single PAC could give $20,000 in an election cycle: $5,000 each for the primary and general elections to the campaign committee and $5,000 per year to the leadership PAC). Members of Congress also have in some instances established *state* leadership PACs, which are not covered by any of the federal contribution limits or disclosure requirements. Such accounts may therefore be considered a new form of soft money: These state PACs may often accept contributions of corporate or labor funds, and unlimited personal funds, otherwise banned by federal election law.

Leadership PACs have traditionally been used by legislative leaders to contribute to the campaigns of other members of Congress as a way of gaining a party majority and earning the gratitude of their colleagues. Leadership PACs may not expend more than $5,000 to elect or defeat a federal candidate (including their "honorary chair"). However, these committees may not be subject to the FEC's personal use rules (which prohibit the conversion of campaign funds for a candidate's personal expenses) and are now increasingly serving as a source for travel and other expenses of a political nature. Press articles recently noted that Senator Ted Kennedy's (D.-Mass.) leadership PAC spent the vast majority of its funds for such purposes. This development is the latest in the forty-year cycle of regulating "office accounts" (pejoratively known as "slush funds"). Office accounts have historically allowed supporters of candidates to provide funds that can be used for a candidate's personal expenses related to political activity (member travel, and the care and feeding of supporters, potential donors, and constituents). House and Senate rules both now ban "unofficial office accounts" but exempt political committees from that ban.

Various reformers have urged the FEC to find leadership PACs to be under the control of the members of Congress with whom they are associated. The federal election laws state that all contributions made by committees "established," "maintained," or "controlled" by any person "shall be considered to have been made by a single political committee," because the committees are legally affiliated; 2 U.S.C. § 441a(a)(5). Thus, argue reformers, any contribution to a leadership PAC should also be considered a contribution to the candidate's campaign committee, subject to a common limit. However, the FEC has declined to adopt this approach to date.

Party Committees

FEC regulations define a party committee as "a political committee which represents a political party and is part of the official party structure at the national, state, or local level"; 11 C.F.R. § 100.5(e)(4). A party committee's contribution limits are the same as a multicandidate political committee's, with three major exceptions:

—For federal election law purposes (but not necessarily state law), party committees can transfer unlimited funds to other party committees, without such transfers being treated as contributions.

—A national party committee and the national senatorial committee may together contribute up to $17,500 to a candidate for U.S. Senate. This $17,500 limit is for the entire election cycle, rather than for each separate election within the cycle; 11 C.F.R. § 110.2(e).

—National and state party committees may spend an inflation-adjusted amount for coordinated spending supporting the party's House and Senate candidates, which differs by state depending on its voting age population.

In 1979, Congress amended the Federal Election Campaign Act to exempt from the definition of contribution and expenditure party spending on certain state party-building or volunteer activity, *provided* that it was paid for with funds raised under the act ("hard" or "federal" money) by state parties, and not from soft money or funds transferred from the national party committees (document 2.12). These exempted activities include yard signs, bumper stickers and pins, get-out-the-vote programs, and volunteer mailings, but not broadcast advertising or certain activities by paid staff. This exemption has generated years of FEC enforcement investigations and litigation—what is "volunteer" activity? what is a "mass mailing?" when is it paid for by a transfer of funds from a national party committee, using which accounting principles?—because such activity provides an important avenue for parties to support their federal candidates in priority races. (For a more detailed discussion of the rationale and effect of this 1979 volunteer and party-building exemption, please see chapter 6.)

EXPENDITURES

The act defines an *expenditure* to include "(i) any purchase, payment, distribution, loan, advance, deposit, or gift of money or anything of value, made by any person for the purpose of influencing any election for Federal office; and (ii) a written contract, promise, or agreement to make an expenditure"; 2 U.S.C. § 431(9). "Expenditure" thus encompasses virtually every payment made in connection with the federal election, including contributions. However, expenditures are only considered contributions when there is some connection with the recipient committee. This concept is explained more fully below in the section discussing "independent expenditures."

Party Committee Expenditures

Under the act, the national and state party committees may expend additional limited amounts for "coordinated" expenditures on behalf of their federal candidates. The amount is based on the population of the state (or, in the case of House candidates for states with more than one representative, is a fixed dollar amount). These expenditures may be made at any time, but only for the benefit of general election candidates; see 2 U.S.C. § 441a(d).

These expenditures can pay for goods and services for candidates, but payments cannot be made directly to the candidates' campaigns—that is, the party committees may not simply give a candidate money. However, it is important to understand that these expenditures are coordinated with the candidate: These are payments candidates can specifically request and direct. Where a committee makes expenditures independent of a candidate, they are not subject to limits, as explained below. The limits on coordinated party expenditures are being challenged in the *Colorado Republican Federal Campaign Committee* v. *Federal Election Commission* case on constitutional grounds (116 S. Ct. 2309 [1996], discussed below; see also document 3.4).

Independent Expenditures

"Independent expenditures" are just that—expenditures by individuals and committees involving elections for federal office that are not coordinated with the candidates seeking office. There are now no dollar limitations on independent expenditures, as *Buckley* v. *Valeo* established that the First Amendment protects the right of individuals and political committees to spend unlimited amounts of their own money on an independent basis to participate in the election process. Independent expenditures, however, must be publicly disclosed through the Federal Election Commission.

At one time, the Federal Election Commission presumed that party committees were incapable of making independent expenditures, reasoning that parties and their candidates were so intertwined that there could be no truly uncoordinated expenditures. However, in *Colorado Republican,* the Supreme Court ruled that party committees had the same right to make independent expenditures as

other committees, if the factual record demonstrates the actual independence of the activity. The remaining issue in that case—whether party committees may constitutionally be restricted in the amount they may spend on a *coordinated* basis to elect their candidates—is currently on remand to the lower courts.

The definition of what constitutes a "coordinated" expenditure is not clear at this time. The Federal Election Commission is currently in the midst of an administrative rulemaking to define more clearly what "coordination" means, and when the concept applies. Under current FEC regulations, there are several criteria to which the Commission looks in determining coordination. For instance, inside knowledge of a candidate's strategy, plans, or needs, consultation with a candidate or his or her agents about the expenditure, distribution of candidate-prepared material, or using vendors also used by a candidate may be considered by the FEC as evidence of coordination. See 11 C.F.R. § 109.1(d) (campaign literature); FEC Advisory Opinions 1982-30 and 1979-80 (vendors). For a discussion of the legal implications of coordinating issue advocacy advertising with candidates, see chapter 7.

PROHIBITED CONTRIBUTIONS AND EXPENDITURES

While most individuals and organizations are limited in their ability to make contributions in connection with federal elections, others are entirely prohibited by law from making contributions or expenditures. The Federal Election Campaign Act has four such prohibitions.

National Banks, Corporations, and Labor Organizations Prohibition

Section 441b of the act makes it unlawful for any national bank or any corporation organized by authority of any law of Congress, any other corporation, or any labor organization to make contributions in connection with a federal election, or for anyone to accept such contributions. Thus, corporations and unions cannot contribute their general treasury funds to a federal candidate (PAC funds, contributed voluntarily by individuals for these purposes, are not covered by this provision). This broad prohibition is subject to three significant exceptions.

Nonprofit issue-advocacy groups exemption. The Supreme Court has held that certain small, ideologically based nonprofit corporations should be exempt from the prohibition on independent expenditures by corporations in connection with federal elections; *Federal Election Commission* v. *Massachusetts Citizens for Life, Inc.*, 479 U.S. 238 (1986) (*MCFL*) (see document 7.4).

The FEC has adopted regulations containing criteria required for a corporation to be exempt under *MCFL*. According to the FEC, such a corporation:

(1) [must have as its only express purpose the promotion of political ideas];[4]
(2) cannot engage in business activities [other than fund-raising expressly describing the intended political use of donations];
(3) [can have:]

> (i) No shareholders or other persons, other than employees and creditors with no ownership interest, affiliated in any way that could allow them to make a claim on the [corporation's] assets or earnings; and
> (ii) No persons who are offered or who receive any benefit that is a disincentive for them to disassociate themselves with the corporation on the basis of the corporation's position on a political issue;[5]

(4) . . . [cannot be] established by a business corporation or labor organization [or accept anything of value from business corporations or labor organizations].[6]

If these criteria are satisfied, the corporation may make unlimited *independent expenditures* in connection with a federal election; 11 C.F.R. § 114.10.

If a qualified *MCFL* corporation makes independent expenditures aggregating more than $250 in a single year, it must report that expenditure to the FEC, as with any other independent expenditure. For *MCFL* corporations, this also involves filing a certification with the FEC that the corporation meets the qualifying criteria for the *MCFL* exemption.

The press exemption. The second major exception exempts certain press activities from the act's definition of expenditure; 2 U.S.C. § 431(9)(B)(i). The section provides that the term "expenditure" does not include " (i) any news story, commentary, or editorial distributed through the facilities of any broadcasting station, newspaper, magazine or other periodical publication, unless such facilities are owned or controlled by any political party, political committee, or candidate." According to the legislative history of this section, Congress included the provision to indicate that it did not intend the Act "to limit or burden in any way the first amendment freedoms of the press" and to assure "the unfettered right of the newspapers, TV networks, and other media to cover and comment on political campaigns"; H.R. Rep. No. 1239, 93rd Cong., 2d Sess., at 4.

Thus, any qualifying media organization can make expenditures in connection with federal elections provided the organization falls within the bounds of the exemption. However, exactly what is within the statute's protection remains unclear. The FEC has indicated that media entities may present debates or cablecast editorials, but the agency has challenged the distribution of printed materials endorsing a candidate as part of a cable company's billing process. The ultimate determination of that case remains pending. *See Federal Election Commission* v. *Multimedia Cablevision, Inc.*, No. 95-3280 (10th Cir. 1996).

Internal communications exemption. All corporations are permitted to communicate with their *restricted class* whenever they so choose, and labor unions may likewise communicate with their members. A corporation's restricted class is defined as its stockholders and its executive or administrative personnel and their families; 11 C.F.R. § 114.3(a). Thus, a corporation can send mailings to its restricted class, endorsing a particular candidate. Similarly, a corporation could invite a candidate to appear before its restricted class and endorse the candidate in connection with the event. However, the corporation must take steps to ensure that only its restricted class receive such communications. Communications with the restricted class are not generally regulated by the FEC, but internal communications of over $2,000 per election expressly advocating the election or defeat of a candidate must be reported; 2 U.S.C. § 431(9)(B)(iii).

The exemption for communications with members has been used by labor unions for voter registration drives, telephone banks to turn out the vote on election day, and candidate endorsements. Such communications may be completely partisan in nature but can only be made to the union's members or to the corporation's restricted class—not to the general public (see the discussion of general issue advocacy below and in chapter 7).

Foreign Contribution Prohibition

For many years there was no ban on foreign contributions. In 1938, in the face of evidence of Nazi German money spent to influence the U.S. political debate, Congress passed the Foreign Agents Registration Act. This law required agents of foreign entities engaged in publishing political "propaganda" to register and disclose their activities, but it did not regulate political contributions. In 1966, after congressional hearings in 1962–63 revealed campaign contributions to federal candidates by Philippine sugar producers and agents of Nicaraguan president Luís Somoza, Congress moved to prohibit political contributions in *any* U.S. election by any foreign government, political party, corporation, or individual (except foreign nationals who are permanent residents of the United States).

The act now prohibits foreign nationals, either directly or indirectly, from making contributions in connection with any election to political office, including state and local elections as well as federal; 2 U.S.C. § 441e.[7] The act defines "foreign national" as:

(1) a foreign principal, as such term is defined by section 611(b) of title 22, except that the term "foreign national" shall not include any individual who is a citizen of the United States; or[8]

(2) an individual who is not a citizen of the United States and who is not lawfully admitted for permanent residence, as defined by section 1101(a)(20) of title 8.[9]

This prohibition also operates to prevent domestic subsidiaries of foreign corporations from establishing PACs if the foreign parent finances the PAC's establishment, administration, or solicitation costs, or if individual foreign nationals within the corporation make decisions for the PAC, participate in its operation, or serve as its officers; 11 C.F.R. § 110.4(a)(2) and (3). Since federal law prohibits a foreign national from making contributions through another person or entity, a domestic subsidiary of a foreign parent corporation may only make contributions out of domestic profits. It may not make nonfederal contributions out of subsidies received from the foreign parent, nor may it use such funds to pay for the establishment, administration, or solicitation costs of its PAC. Similarly, foreign nationals may not participate in the selection of the individuals who run the PAC.

It is these provisions that are at the heart of much of the controversy about fund-raising activity in the 1996 election. One issue is whether this foreign national prohibition applies to the donation of "soft" or nonfederal money to a national party committee. The Department of Justice's stated view on this question has varied, and the matter is probably fact specific: Can the funds donated be said to have been used "in connection" with any election to political office, whether federal, state, or local, or were they only used for nonelection activities?[10]

Federal Contractors Prohibition

The act prohibits anyone who contracts with the United States or any of its departments or agencies to make any contribution to any political party, committee, or candidate for public office, nor may such a contribution be solicited from any person between the time of the negotiations and completion of the contract. However, federal contractors that are corporations can establish federal PACs; 2 U.S.C. § 441c.

Contributions in the Name of Another Prohibition

Section 441f of the act provides that "no person shall make a contribution in the name of another person or knowingly permit his name to be used to effect such a contribution, and no person shall knowingly accept a contribution made by one person in the name of another person." This section is often enforced in connection with other prohibitions. For example, where a foreign national gives money to a U.S. citizen to be contributed by such person to a federal candidate, there is both a violation of § 441e (foreign contributions) and § 441f (a contribution in the name of another).

THE PRESIDENTIAL SYSTEM

"Major" Parties (Democrats and Republicans)

The contribution and expenditure limits described above apply to all federal elections other than presidential campaigns. Presidential elections are partially publicly funded. That is, once a major party presidential candidate meets certain requirements, the general election campaign may choose to receive full U.S. government funding from the Treasury accounts funded from the $3 voluntary taxpayer checkoff.

Presidential primaries. Presidential primaries are funded through a combination of public and private funding. The partial public funding is provided in *matching* funds, public funds matching up to $250 of a single individual's contributions. To qualify for such matching funds, the candidate must demonstrate nationwide support through raising at least $5,000 in individual contributions of up to $250 each in at least twenty separate states. Candidates must also agree, among other things, to:

—Limit primary spending to an inflation-adjusted amount—approximately $31 million in 1996;
—Limit spending in each primary state to a specific amount (which increases with population); and
—Limit spending of personal funds to $50,000.

Once these requirements are met or agreed to, the candidate can receive matching payments. See generally 11 C.F.R. § 9033.1.

Private contributions for presidential candidates are still limited as in other federal elections. Individuals may contribute up to $1,000 to a presidential primary campaign committee, and qualified multicandidate PACs can contribute up to $5,000.

The general election. Once a candidate becomes the nominee for a major party, he or she becomes eligible for a public grant (which was $61.82 million per candidate in 1996). To receive these funds, however, the candidate must agree to spend no more than the grant received and must not accept private contributions.[11] Additionally, the two major party national committees may each spend a voting-age population adjusted amount ($12 million in 1996) in coordination with their presidential candidates; 2 U.S.C. § 441a(d)(2). This amount is separate from any get-out-the-vote or generic party-building activities the parties conduct. As noted below, the Republican and Democratic National Committees do not consider their "issue advocacy" advertising to be subject to this limit (whether or not coordinated with their presidential candidates).

Candidates not accepting public funds. Candidates are not required to accept public funds in either the primary or general elections. Candidates refusing such funds are permitted to spend as much of their own money in support of their campaigns as they wish. As a result, a candidate refusing public funding would have no per state spending limit or overall spending limit in the primary campaign (Steve Forbes in 1996) and no spending limit in the general election campaign (Ross Perot in 1992). Such a candidate could still accept private contributions in both the primary and general election campaigns, subject to the standard $1,000 per election contribution limit for individuals.

Convention funding. Each of the major parties' nominating conventions may also be paid for, in part, by public funding; *see* 26 U.S.C. § 9008. Each major party received a grant of $12.36 million in 1996 to finance its nominating convention. Minor parties may qualify for convention funding based on their presidential candidates' share of the popular vote in the preceding election.

Political parties accepting convention funding may spend in connection with the convention only the amount of public funds they receive. However, the host city and other sponsors support conventions in a variety of ways. The city, through its host committee (a federally registered committee created to support convention activities) may spend

money promoting itself as a convention location, may pay for the convention hall, and provide local transportation and related services to the convention; see 11 C.F.R. § 9008.52. Additionally, the host city itself may directly accept cash and in-kind contributions from local (but not other) businesses, which are often received by a tax-deductible entity. In some circumstances, corporations can also provide goods (such as automobiles) free to the conventions as part of a promotional program. These exemptions, as interpreted by the FEC, have in practice resulted in extensive convention-related fundraising by the host city and the political parties, usually raising individual, corporate, and labor funds for the convention far greater in total than the federal grant. Conventions now have "official" airlines, computer companies, car rental agencies, and the like, all in addition to the federal grants to the political parties.

"Third" and Minor Party Presidential Candidates

Minor parties (those which have received at least 5 percent but no more than 25 percent of the popular vote in the preceding presidential election) and new parties (a party that is not a major or minor party) may also receive partial public funding for the general election, in some instances. New and minor party candidates may accept private contributions, but only within the general limits on such contributions ($1,000 per election from individuals, and no corporate or labor contributions).

A candidate who agrees to abide by the restrictions applicable to publicly funded presidential candidates (including an FEC audit, and a $50,000 limit on the use of personal funds) and who then meets a threshold of 5 percent of the general election vote will receive public funding based on his or her share of the vote, but not until *after* the election; see 11 C.F.R. § 9004.3. Days after the 1980 general election, independent John Anderson became the first such candidate to receive "retroactive" funding, based on unofficial vote totals showing that he had received nearly 7 percent of the popular vote. In subsequent elections, an individual who has received 5 percent or more of the vote in a previous general election may be eligible to receive general election funding *before* the election. See 11 C.F.R. § 9004.2. The most prominent example is Ross Perot, who ran as an independent in 1992, then appeared on most state ballots as the nominee of the Reform Party in 1996. Even though Perot had not run under the Reform Party banner in 1992, he received public funding in 1996 based on his 1992 general election vote total.

Additionally, minor party candidates may be eligible for primary funding as well. Examples include Lyndon H. LaRouche, who appeared on the ballot in several states as the candidate of the U.S. Labor Party in 1976 but failed to qualify for public funding in that year's general election. Beginning in 1980, however, LaRouche sought the Democratic Party's nomination for president several times. He secured matching funds for most of those primary campaigns by receiving the necessary individual contributions to meet the statutory criteria for "nationwide support." Similarly, Lenora Fulani received matching funds when she sought the New Alliance Party nomination in 1988 and 1992. However, because of the 5 percent threshold, she failed to qualify for general election funding in either of those two years.

Once the FEC certifies a minor party or new party as a "national" party, then the party may contribute to its presidential candidate's campaign, subject to the same types of contribution limits that the major parties face. During the 1996 election, the Libertarian, Natural Law, and Taxpayers parties all had national recognition from the FEC. The Reform Party received no such recognition, in part because Ross Perot argued that the national organization was merely a collection of state parties. Without the national party designation, Perot could avoid federal limits in the personal funding he could provide for the Reform Party's convention. How-

ever, he could still only contribute a maximum of $50,000 to his own general election campaign because he accepted federal funding. Before and after the 1996 election, Reform Party members opposed to Perot sought federal recognition of state party organizations they controlled, both to limit Perot's influence and to gain control of the subsequent federal funding guaranteed by Perot's 8 percent showing in 1996. Had Perot not been the Reform Party's nominee in 1996, the party's presidential candidate would have had to meet the 5 percent vote threshold in the 1996 election before receiving any federal funding.

"SOFT MONEY"

The act prohibits party committees from accepting contributions in excess of individual or PAC limits, or from impermissible sources (corporations, unions, foreign nationals). In a series of Advisory Opinions, the FEC has allowed state and national party committees to accept funds from some sources and in amounts otherwise prohibited by federal election law, provided such funds are placed in separate "nonfederal" accounts and not used for federal election purposes. Those "soft money" accounts are discussed in detail in chapter 6.

The FEC has created a complex system of allocation formulas regulating the proportions of hard and soft money that party committees may use for generic party activity (administrative, overhead, get-out-the-vote, issue ads, and the like). National party committees (but not state or local) are also required to disclose soft money donations to the FEC.

RESTRICTIONS ON POLITICAL FUND-RAISING BY MEMBERS OF CONGRESS AND EXECUTIVE BRANCH OFFICIALS

There are several statutes that regulate the location and form of political fund-raising. Most of these are designed to protect federal employees from pressure to contribute to federal candidates and parties, but one simply prohibits any solicitation or receipt of a federal contribution in a federal workplace. These statutes carry criminal or civil penalties, and their intricacies have been the focus of much attention as a result of reported fundraising activities at the White House during the 1996 election.

A series of criminal provisions makes it unlawful to attempt to obtain a political contribution from a government employee by means of threats of firing (18 U.S.C. § 601); for a candidate for Congress or federal employee or officer to solicit a campaign contribution from any other federal employee or officer (18 U.S.C. § 602); for a federal officer or employee to contribute to his or her employer's campaign (18 U.S.C. § 603); for any person to solicit a political contribution from someone known to be entitled to funds for federal "work relief" (18 U.S.C. § 604); or to demote or threaten to demote a federal employee for giving or withholding a political contribution (18 U.S.C. § 606).

Additionally, 18 U.S.C. § 607 makes it a criminal offense (subject to a fine or three years in jail or both) to "solicit or receive any contribution . . . in any room or building occupied in the discharge of official duties" by any federal officer or employee. Congress is specifically exempted from the receipt portion of this provision, provided that any funds received are transferred within seven days to a federal political committee, and that the contributors were not *told* to send or deliver the money to the federal office building.

"Soft Money"

The most important limitation on the scope of these solicitation provisions was probably unintentional. In 1979, Congress amended each of these sections to replace language referring to "contributions for any political purpose" or "to be applied to the promotion of any political object" with the more precise "contribution" as "within the meaning of section 301(8) of the Federal Election Campaign Act of 1971." The result is that this new definition only reaches contributions "for the purpose of influencing" federal elections, thereby arguably leaving solicitations for nonfederal ("soft money") donations beyond the reach of the solicitation ban. (See chapter 6 for a definition and discussion of soft money.)

Thus, a key question for federal prosecutors becomes whether the money being solicited is hard or soft (a distinction unknown to Congress when the new definition of "contribution" was inserted in these laws in 1979). This in turn raises questions about contributions solicited by federal candidates or their agents explicitly for the purpose of influencing a federal election, but deposited in and spent out of a nonfederal account. Common Cause, among others, has argued that such donations should be considered "contributions" under the Federal Election Campaign Act of 1971, as amended.

A seldom used FEC regulation adopted in 1990 may be relevant to this debate:

Any party committee solicitation that makes reference to a federal candidate or a federal election shall be presumed to be for the purpose of influencing a federal election, and contributions resulting from that solicitation shall be subject to the prohibitions and limitations of the Act. This presumption may be rebutted by demonstrating to the Commission that the funds were solicited with express notice that they would not be used for federal election purposes. 11 C.F.R. §102.5(a)(3).

This provision has the potential to bring the solicitation of funds deposited in party soft money accounts within the federal definition of "contribution." Such a result would have significant implications for the interpretation of the criminal statutes banning solicitations of federal employees for campaign contributions, or the solicitation or receipt of such contributions in federal buildings.

Other Issues

Additional issues raised by 1996 events include which areas of the White House are exempt from the solicitation ban because they are not used "in the discharge of official duties" (in 1979, the Department of Justice issued an opinion to President Jimmy Carter that a luncheon with Democratic party fund-raisers held in the White House family quarters fell within the "private residence" exemption "implicit" in the law). Questions have also been raised about whether the prohibition on solicitation applies when the solicitation occurs through a phone call from a federal office but the recipient of the conversation is not in a federal building, and whether there is an exemption from the ban on "receiving" a contribution for "ministerial" acts (such as taking an envelope containing a contribution and delivering it to an authorized representative of a political committee).

Congress

As noted above, the prohibition on receiving contributions in a federal building does not apply to Congress, as long as certain conditions are met. However, the ban on solicitations from a federal workplace does apply to Congress.

The Committee on Standards of Official Conduct has recently reminded House members that, entirely aside from the criminal statute, the Rules of the House also regulate political fund-raising and "are quite specific, and quite restrictive"; "April 25, 1997 Memorandum for All Members, Officers and Employees." Under House rules, *Members and staff may not solicit political contributions in their office or elsewhere in the House buildings, whether in person, over the telephone, or otherwise* [emphasis in original]. Added the Committee, "The rule bars *all* political solicitations in these House buildings. Thus, a telephone solicitation would not be permissible merely because, for example, the call is billed to the credit card of a political organization or to an outside telephone number, or it is made using a cellphone in the hallway." Nor may House telephone numbers be left for a return call if the purpose is the solicitation of a political contribution, according to the Committee. This advice responds to claims that members of Congress were using cellular telephones in their offices, or fund-raising in the Capitol, instead of using the cubicles set aside for fund-raising telephone calls in office buildings near the Capitol owned by the Democratic and Republican campaign committees.

The Senate also has rules regulating campaign activity in Senate buildings and the Capitol and restricting the number of members of a Senator's staff who may handle campaign contributions.[12]

The Hatch Act

The Hatch Act, first passed by Congress in 1939 during President Franklin Roosevelt's second administration to protect federal employees from political pressure, bans all Executive Branch federal employees from knowingly soliciting, accepting, or receiving a political contribution from any person (see introduction to chapter 2); 5 U.S.C. § 7322. Although (unlike the criminal provisions) "political contribution" is still broadly defined as "any gift . . . made for any political purpose," the penalty for violations of the Hatch Act is either thirty days' suspension without pay or removal of the employee's position. The Hatch Act has no criminal penalties.

ISSUE ADVOCACY

As discussed in detail in chapter 7, issue advocacy is speech that does not "expressly advocate" the election or defeat of a federal candidate and is therefore not subject to any of the limits, prohibitions, or disclosure provisions of the federal election laws. As a result, corporations, unions, advocacy groups, and party committees may raise and spend funds for such speech without limit, and (except for party committees) without disclosure of sources or amounts. Three current issues concerning issue advocacy are the focus of legal attention:

—When does "issue advocacy" become "express advocacy"?;

—When is it "coordinated" with a candidate so as to make it a "contribution" subject to all of the federal election laws?; and

—Is some party committee issue advocacy exempt from the FEC's soft money allocation regulations, because it is unrelated to any election?

OTHER PLAYERS IN THE ARENA

In addition to those who contribute under the laws established by the act, there are other significant entities that play roles in political campaigns.

Unions

Although the act and FEC regulations treat corporate and union funds similarly, other considerations have made unions unique in the political landscape. Like corporations, they may not contribute directly to federal candidates, but may create and administer a PAC, may contribute to the nonfederal accounts of political parties, and may sponsor "issue" advertising to the general public.

As membership organizations, they may also communicate with their members (numbering in the millions) on any subject (including urging them to vote for specific candidates or parties) and may use union treasury funds to do so. In *Communications Workers of America* v. *Beck,* 487 U.S. 735 (1988), the Supreme Court determined that the National Labor Relations Act limited union uses of money raised from nonunion employees as a condition of employment to support collective bargaining ("agency agreements"). As a result, nonunion employees in closed-shop states cannot be required to fund political spending as a condition of their employment.

This decision potentially reduces the political use of funds paid involuntarily to unions by nonmembers. On April 13, 1992, President George Bush issued Executive Order 12800, which required government contractors to post notices informing their nonunion employees that they could object to use of their union dues for political purposes. On February 1, 1993, however, President Bill Clinton issued Executive Order 12836, rescinding Executive Order 12800, and referred the issue to the National Labor Relations Board for further consideration.

The broader question on the use of dues from union members themselves for political activity was not addressed in *Beck.* Republican party leaders argue that union members should be given some mechanism for authorizing or restricting the use of their dues for political purposes (perhaps including issue advertising), claiming that a substantial number of union members disagree with the political choices made by union leaders. Democrats and unions respond that union leaders are freely elected by the membership and are thus only exercising their representative authority. Besides, they add, corporate shareholders do not vote whether to approve corporate political spending on issue advocacy either. Member dues in any case provide only a portion of the funds available to unions for such communications, so union leaders could probably use other funds for these activities if necessary.

In 1996 the AFL-CIO announced a $35 million television advertising campaign, which ran in dozens of congressional districts with vulnerable Republican incumbents, attacking the members' congressional voting records on issues such as social security, medicare, and federal funding for education. These "issue" advertisements were paid for with union treasury funds, on the grounds that they did not "expressly advocate" the election or defeat of the member of Congress, but instead had end-

ings such as "tell your representatives to stop cutting medicare." This spending was in addition to
direct union PAC contributions to Democratic candidates and party committees, and the use of union
organizers in congressional districts. Additionally,
unions engaged in traditional voter registration
activity and election day get-out-the-vote telephone
banks directed to union members, and reportedly
assigned paid organizers to some congressional districts to coordinate communications activities.

Corporations

Corporations have been prohibited from contributing to federal candidates since the beginning of
this century, when the first federal campaign finance
restrictions were enacted by Congress (see chapter
2 for a detailed description of the history of this
ban). However, like unions, corporations still participate in the political process in a variety of ways.

Most visibly, corporations may establish and pay
the administrative costs of separate segregated
funds, known as PACs, and may encourage employees and stockholders to contribute personal funds
to those committees. (See chapter 5 for a description of PAC activity.) Additionally, corporations
may communicate with their executives and management personnel, urging them to support and
contribute to specific parties or candidates, and may
host visits by candidates at corporate facilities, subject to FEC rules. The most important aspect of such
internal corporate activity is the ability of corporate executives and PACs to raise funds for federal
candidates. The FEC has issued complicated new
regulations governing such corporate political activity, but fund-raising by corporate executives under these rules remains a substantial source of
money for federal candidates.

Corporations may also pay for "issue advocacy"
advertising, either directly or through donations to
other groups, such as industry associations or issue-oriented 501(c)(4)s that are engaged in public
advertising programs. Because issue advertising is

not defined as a campaign "expenditure," it does
not need to be disclosed, making it difficult to identify the sources or amounts of such spending. In
1996, "The Coalition" was formed by a group of
business associations, including the U.S. Chamber
of Commerce, to respond in kind to the labor
unions' televised issue advocacy ads. The Coalition
is reported to have raised some $3.5 million from
corporations for this activity and has announced
plans to continue such general public communications in the future. Additionally, corporations contribute substantial sums of "soft money" to the
nonfederal accounts of the national party committees, and directly to state parties (where permitted
by state law).

Finally, the Supreme Court has held that it is
unconstitutional to prohibit corporations from
spending funds to campaign for and against state
ballot measures. (See *First National Bank of Boston* v. *Bellotti*, 435 U.S. 765 [1978]; document 3.2.)
In states such as California, where ballot initiatives are often identified with particular candidates
or political parties, this can provide an avenue for
a significant direct expenditure of corporate funds
that may have the effect of influencing a federal
election.

501(c)(4) Organizations

Section 501(c)(4) of the Tax Code provides for the
establishment of "social welfare organizations" exempt from federal income tax. While these organizations must be operated exclusively for the
promotion of the public social welfare and cannot
be for profit, they still can engage in political activities, as long as these activities do not become
their primary purpose.

The Internal Revenue Service (IRS) interprets
this restriction to allow 501(c)(4) organizations to
participate in an election by doing such things as
rating candidates on a partisan basis; Rev. Rul. 67-
368, 1967-2 Cumulative Bulletin 194 (July 1967).
They also may promote legislation; Rev. Rul. 71-

530, 1971-2 Cumulative Bulletin 237 (July 1971); Rev. Rul. 67-293, 1967-2 Cumulative Bulletin 185 (July 1967). As long as its political activities do not become an organization's primary activity, a 501(c)(4) entity can engage in any activity consistent with state and federal laws. Under new FEC regulations, 501(c)(4)s that qualify as *MCFL* issue advocacy corporations (as discussed above and in document 7.4) may engage in independent political expenditures.

As the public becomes more aware of politically active 501(c)(4) organizations, there have been calls for limits on such activities by tax-exempt entities. For instance, the Christian Coalition, designed as a 501(c)(4) entity, has played a highly visible role in state and national Republican party politics, going so far as to claim credit for the Republican success in the 1994 elections and to create a multimillion-dollar war room at the 1996 Republican National Convention. The FEC has sued the group, claiming it has made illegal and unreported contributions to federal candidates, largely through its "voter guide" activities. Republicans argue that many other groups engage in similar (if smaller-scale) activities on behalf of Democrats.

Additionally, the IRS appears to be questioning whether some groups can become so partisan in nature or purpose that they advance a narrow private or partisan purpose, rather than the general social welfare, and thus are not entitled to a tax exemption. The IRS challenged the National Policy Forum, headed by former RNC Chairman Haley Barbour, on this basis. It may be raising similar objections to the Christian Coalition, which has apparently yet to receive IRS approval of its application for recognition of 501(c)(4) status after an unprecedented period of review. Both major parties have traditionally benefited from such organizations: the Democratic Leadership Council (DLC) is a 501(c)(4) organization that obtained its exemption in the 1980s and was once headed by President Clinton.

Another feature of the 1996 election year was the contribution of substantial sums by party committees to 501(c)(4) organizations, which then reportedly used those funds for issue advocacy activities. The advantage to the party committee is that the contribution can be entirely soft money, whereas if the same activity were done by the party entity, only 35 percent of it can be paid for with soft money, under FEC allocation regulations discussed above and in chapter 6.

501(c)(3) Organizations

Section 501(c)(3) organizations are tax-exempt entities organized for charitable and other similar purposes and are ostensibly prohibited from intervening in any political campaigns; Internal Revenue Code § 501(c)(3) of the Tax Code. Thus, these organizations cannot endorse candidates, contribute to campaigns, or organize a political action committee. However, they can conduct nonpartisan voter registration and get-out-the-vote efforts in accord with FEC regulations. See 11 C.F.R. § 114.4. Additionally, they may sponsor candidate forums on issues of public concern; Rev. Rul. 86-95, 1986-2 Cumulative Bulletin 73 (August 18, 1986). Candidates and party committees can (and do) raise money to enable such organizations to perform their "nonpartisan" tasks.

The FEC has recently gone to court to prevent party committees from funding 501(c)(3) voter registration activity solely with "soft" or nonfederal funds. *See Federal Election Commission* v. *California Democratic Party,* 97-0891 DFL PAN, Eastern Dist. Of Cal., filed May 9, 1997. The Commission argues that such voter registration activity can only be paid for by party committees pursuant to the FEC's allocation regulations and thus with a proportional use of "hard" and "soft" money. The FEC argues that party committees cannot avoid the allocation rules by "subcontracting" the voter registration activity out to a 501(c)(3) organization, as it alleges was done by the California Democratic Party.

Many well-known think tanks are 501(c)(3) organizations, including Brookings, the American Enterprise Institute, Heritage, Cato, the Family Research Council (Gary Bauer's group), and the Progressive Policy Institute (associated with the DLC). Some are genuinely nonpartisan, while others appear close to one party or group of candidates. Additionally, many organizations maintain a collection of entities under one umbrella, such as the Sierra Club, which has a 501(c)(3), a 501(c)(4), and a PAC. Many of the ethics charges against Newt Gingrich related to his use of just such a collection of organizations, including charitable and educational groups, for political purposes.

ENFORCEMENT

The Federal Election Commission

The federal campaign finance laws are enforced by the FEC in the case of civil violations, and by the Department of Justice when a criminal violation is charged. The FEC itself has no independent authority to impose penalties. If, after an investigation, the alleged violators are unwilling to sign a settlement agreement and pay a monetary penalty to the U.S. Treasury, then the FEC can vote to sue the offender in federal court, present the evidence to a judge, and ask the court to find a violation and impose a fine.

Penalties sought by the FEC range from a few hundred dollars to many thousands of dollars, depending on the size and nature of the violation. The act restricts penalties to $5,000 per violation, or the amount at issue, whichever is larger (and doubles these sums in the case of knowing and willful violations). For a detailed discussion of the FEC, see chapter 8.

Standing Issues—What if the FEC Deadlocks or Fails To Act?

The act contains a provision allowing parties whose complaints have been dismissed or otherwise not acted upon by the FEC to file suit against the FEC in federal court alleging that the FEC's failure to act was arbitrary and capricious. If successful, the party can obtain a court order requiring the FEC to act in accord with FECA on the complaint. If the FEC does not follow the court order within thirty days, the party may sue the alleged campaign law violator directly; 2 U.S.C. § 437g(a)(8). This provision of the act has almost never been used. For an example of a recent rare instance, see *Democratic Senatorial Campaign Committee* v. *Federal Election Commission,* Civil Action No. 96-2184 (JHG), (D.D.C. May 30, 1997), where a federal judge held that the FEC had failed in its statutory duty to investigate a Democratic complaint against Republican campaign activity in a number of Senate campaigns in 1992. The judge ruled that the Commission's inability to complete its investigative process after four and a half years was an abdication of its enforcement role, and as a result gave the Democratic Senatorial Campaign Committee the right to sue the National Republican Senatorial Committee directly in federal district court over the alleged violations.

The statutory right to challenge FEC action or nonaction is an unusual provision and has served as the basis for a number of successful challenges to FEC enforcement decisions in the past. However, this right to seek judicial review of FEC actions requires a high standard of proof (that the FEC decision was "arbitrary and capricious") and is in any case now being challenged and limited by the federal courts. As recent D.C. Circuit Court decisions make clear, complainants seeking judicial review of FEC action or nonaction must meet federal standing (right to file suit) requirements under Article III of the Constitution. They must suffer an "injury-in-fact" caused by the FEC's action (or failure to act) that may be redressed by the court's order. In what appear to be somewhat conflicting decisions, the D.C. Circuit has held that if complainants, as voters, were deprived of legally required information about contributions and expenditures, this is a sufficient injury to confer standing. *Akins v. Federal Election Commission,* 101 F.3d 731, 737 (D.C. Cir. 1996) (*en banc*) (*cert. granted,* 65 U.S.L.W. 3825 [U.S. June 16, 1997] [No. 96-1590]). However, the assertion that the FEC's acts deprived voters of information generally is not sufficient to convey standing; *Common Cause* v. *Federal Election Commission,* 108 F.3d 413, 418 (D.C. Cir. 1997). In that case, Common Cause was denied the right to challenge the FEC's conclusion of an investigation of Republican party spending in Montana, even though Common Cause had filed the original complaint with the FEC. The court held that Common Cause had not shown that it was injured by the FEC's decision (or that it would benefit from an FEC or judicial finding that the party activity violated the law), and thus could not bring the case. Since Common Cause has historically challenged numerous FEC enforcement decisions, this holding may significantly restrict the ability of such "public interest" organizations to seek court review of FEC decisions in the D.C. Circuit. The Supreme Court has also recently agreed to review the *Akins* decision. That review has the potential to result in the establishment of a clearer (and perhaps narrower) new nationwide standing rule, which could foreclose a significant amount of judicial review of FEC action or inaction.

The Justice Department—Criminal Prosecutions

The Justice Department pursues criminal violations of the campaign finance laws either after referral from the FEC or upon independent discovery. U.S. Attorneys or the Department's Public Integrity Section may investigate alleged violations, using FBI assistance and grand juries. Cases are tried in federal court, and allegations may include ancillary mail fraud/wire fraud or conspiracy violations. Penalties may include jail terms and substantial monetary penalties.

Aggravated and intentional campaign finance crimes may be prosecuted either as misdemeanor violations of the act or as felonies under the conspiracy and false statement provisions; 2 U.S.C. § 437g(d); 18 U.S.C. §§ 371 and 1001.[13] Prosecution under the mail or wire fraud statutes may also be available in some cases. See 18 U.S.C. §§ 1341 and 1343. The Department of Justice pursues campaign finance crimes involving $10,000 and under as FECA misdemeanors and considers for felony prosecution only those involving more than $10,000.[14]

Criminal prosecution of federal election law violations is pursued in cases demonstrating "willful violation of a core" FECA provision, involving "a substantial sum of money" ($2,000 or more) and resulting "in the reporting of false campaign information to the FEC."[15] The core provisions of FECA include the following:

—The contribution limits;
—The ban on corporation and labor contributions;
—The ban on contributions from federal contractors;
—The ban on contributions from foreign nationals;
—The prohibition against making contributions in the name of another; and
—The avoidance of FEC disclosure requirements.

Schemes used to disguise illegal contributions have also been prosecuted as violations of 18 U.S.C. § 371 (conspiracy to obstruct the lawful functioning of a government agency) and § 1001 (submitting false information to a federal agency).

Defendants convicted of FECA misdemeanors may receive sentences of imprisonment—*see United States* v. *Goland,* 959 F.2d 1449 (9th Cir. 1992) (ninety days)—and corporate defendants may receive large fines for misdemeanor FECA violations; *United States* v. *Fugi Medical Systems,* C.R. No. 90-288 (S.D.N.Y., sentencing proceedings, August 15, 1990).

Significant sentences have been applied to felony

Table 1-1.

Campaign Finance Law: A Summary

Contributors	May contribute to federal candidates	May contribute to party committees	May engage in independent expenditures	May engage in unlimited "issue advocacy"
Individuals	Yes—$1,000 per election to candidates	Yes—limited (unlimited soft money)	Yes	Yes
Foreign nationals	No	No, except "building funds"	No	Yes
Corporations	No	No, except unlimited soft money	No (except to "restricted class")	Yes
Unions	No	No, except unlimited soft money	No (except to members)	Yes
PACs (including corporate and union)	Yes—generally $5,000	Yes—limited	Yes	Yes
Party committees	Yes—variable limits	Unlimited transfers between committees	Yes	Yes
501(c)(4)s	No	No	In some cases	Yes
501(c)(3)s	No	No	No	Some IRS restrictions

campaign finance crimes prosecuted under §§ 371 (conspiracy) or 1001 (false statements). The theory behind conspiracy prosecutions is explained in the Justice Department's handbook on election law crimes: "A scheme to infuse patently illegal funds into a federal campaign, such as by using conduits or other means calculated to conceal the illegal source of the contribution, thus disrupts and impedes the FEC in the performance of its statutory duties."[16] To obtain a conviction under § 371, the evidence must show that the defendant intended to disrupt and impede the lawful functioning of the FEC (such as by causing false information to be provided to the FEC by the recipient committee, thereby "misleading the public as to the actual source of the contribution"). Causing another person to submit false information to the FEC may be prosecuted as a violation of 18 U.S.C. §§ 1001 and 2, which taken together criminalize acts that cause another person (that is, a campaign treasurer) to submit false information to the FEC; *see United States* v. *Curran,* 20 F.3d 560 (3d Cir. 1994).

Statute of Limitations Issues

FECA contains a three-year statute of limitation, which applies to prosecutions for criminal violations of Title 2; 2 U.S.C. § 455(a). However, it does not specify the statute of limitations for *civil* enforcement actions. A number of courts have concluded that the general federal default five-year statute of limitations applies to these civil actions; *Federal Election Commission* v. *Williams,* 104 F.3d 237, 240 (9th Cir. 1996); *Federal Election Commis-*

sion v. *National Right to Work Committee*, 916 F. Supp. 10 (D.D.C. 1996); and *Federal Election Commission* v. *National Republican Senatorial Committee*, 877 F. Supp. 15 (D.D.C. 1995). The statute of limitations for campaign finance violations prosecuted under 18 U.S.C. §§ 371 or 1001 is five years. See 18 U.S.C. § 3282. The Justice Department may prosecute under these ancillary criminal provisions (conspiracy, fraud, and so on) even though the three-year FEC statute of limitations has run, if the five-year statute applicable to the federal criminal statutes has not yet passed.

Some courts have found that the statute of limitations period commences when the violation is committed. In *Williams,* the court rejected the FEC's argument that the period should be "tolled" (with the clock not started) until the violation is discovered; *Williams,* 104 F.3d at 240. The FEC also contended that the period should be tolled or frozen under the doctrine of "equitable tolling" for fraudulent concealment. Tolling a limit under this theory requires a showing that the defendant fraudulently concealed operative facts, that the FEC failed to discover the facts in the limitations period, and that the FEC pursued the facts diligently until discovery of the facts. The court rejected this argument also, determining that the FEC had the facts it needed in FECA reports filed by recipient committees to discover the operative facts; *Williams,* 104 F.3d at 241. The practical effect of these decisions is to make it significantly more difficult for the FEC to pursue allegations of campaign finance violations, and to cause the Commission to close a number of high-profile investigations that were past or near the five-year limit. Especially in the case of presidential campaigns, which undergo a multiyear audit before the Commission even authorizes the opening of an enforcement matter, the combination of the FEC's current capabilities and the five-year statute of limitations means that many investigations will as a practical matter be aborted without a resolution.

NOTES

1. In certain circumstances, where a local committee can sufficiently demonstrate its independence, it will not be considered part of a state committee.

2. For purposes of calculating this limitation, a contribution to a candidate for an election in a year other than the year in which the contribution is made is considered to be made during the year in which that election is held. Thus, a $1,000 contribution made in 1997 to a candidate running for office in 1998 will count toward the contributor's annual limit for 1998. Contributions to multicandidate committees are always counted toward the limit of the year in which the contribution is made. 2 U.S.C. § 441a(a)(3).

3. The Federal Election Commission has required that a "committee, club, association, or other group of persons" as defined by section A of 2 U.S.C. § 431(4) have the "influencing of federal elections" as a major purpose in order to be considered a "political committee," based on the FEC's reading of Supreme Court rulings. However, the D.C. Circuit recently rejected this criterion, indicating that the $1,000 threshold for *contributions* is pertinent for evaluating political committee status (but "major purpose" is still the test if the group makes only expenditures). See *Akins* v. *FEC,* 101 F.3d 731 (D.C. Cir. 1996) (*en banc*), *cert. granted,* 65 U.S.L.W. 3825 (U.S. June 16, 1997) (No. 96-1590).

4. "Promotion of political ideas" is defined as "issue advocacy, election influencing activity, and research, training or educational activity that is expressly tied to the organization's political goals"; 11 C.F.R. § 114.10(b)(1).

5. Examples of such benefits are credit cards, insurance policies, savings plans, or training, education, or business information supplied by the corporation; 11 C.F.R. § 114.10(c)(3)(ii)(A) and (B).

6. A nonprofit corporation can show through its accounting records that this criterion is satisfied, or will meet this requirement if it is a qualified 501(c)(4) corporation and has a written policy against accepting

donations from business corporations or labor organizations; 11 C.F.R. § 114.10(c)(4)(iii).

7. Donations to a building fund of a national or state political party committee are specifically excepted from treatment as a "contribution" under the FECA. 2 U.S.C. § 431(8)(B)(viii), and thus seems likely not to be covered by the foreign money prohibition.

The statute states:

> any gift, subscription, loan, advance, or deposit of money or anything of value to a national or a State committee of a political party [is not a contribution if it is] specifically designated to defray any cost for construction or purchase of any office facility not acquired for the purpose of influencing the election of any candidate in any particular election for Federal office.

8. 22 U.S.C. § 611(b) provides:

> (b) The term "foreign principal" includes—
>
> (1) a government of a foreign country and a foreign political party;
>
> (2) a person outside of the United States, unless it is established that such person is an individual and a citizen of and domiciled within the United States, or that such person is not an individual and is organized under or created by the laws of the United States or of any State or other place subject to the jurisdiction of the United States and has its principal place of business within the United States; and
>
> (3) a partnership, association, corporation, organization, or other combination of persons organized under the laws of or having its principal place of business in a foreign country.

9. 8 U.S.C. § 1101(a)(20) provides:

> (20) The term "lawfully admitted for permanent residence" means the status of having been lawfully accorded the privilege of residing permanently in the United States as an immigrant in accordance with the immigration laws, such status not having changed.

10. Attorney General Janet Reno's testimony before the Senate Judiciary Committee on April 30, 1997, indicates that the Department of Justice may now interpret Section 441e to prohibit soft money contributions to party committees from foreign nationals. See Department of Justice Oversight, *Hearing of the Senate Judiciary Committee,* Federal News Service, April 30, 1997 (responses to questions from Senator Fred Thompson). Senator Thompson asserted in his questioning of Attorney General Reno that her interpretation that "soft money" was never a "contribution" under the act would make acceptance of soft money contributions from foreign sources legal. The attorney general disagreed, stating that "441e prohibits contributions from foreign nationals in connection with all elections, state and federal, and thus they can't use soft money from foreign sources for issue ads by political parties."

11. Individuals may still contribute to a special fund campaign committees may establish under FECA limits/restrictions to pay for legal and accounting compliance expenses.

12. See Select Committee on Ethics, U.S. Senate, *Senate Ethics Manual,* S. Pub. 104-44 (September 1996), pp. 178–88.

13. See generally Laura A. Ingersoll, ed., *Federal Prosecution of Election Offenses,* 6th ed. (Department of Justice, January 1995), pp. 133–35.

14. Ingersoll, *Federal Prosecution of Election Offenses,* p. 115.

15. Ingersoll, *Federal Prosecution of Election Offenses,* p. 93.

16. Ingersoll, *Federal Prosecution of Election Offenses,* p. 109.

A History of Federal Campaign Finance Law

CONTENTS

A History of Federal Campaign Finance Law

INTRODUCTION BY ANTHONY CORRADO

Controversy over the role of money in politics did not begin with Watergate. Nor did it start with the clamor over the high costs of campaigning that accompanied the growth of radio and television broadcasting in the postwar era. Money's influence on the political process has long been a concern, an outgrowth of our nation's continuing struggle to reconcile basic notions of political equality, such as the principle of "one person, one vote," with the unequal distribution of economic resources and the willingness of a relatively small group of citizens to participate financially in political campaigns. Though public criticism of the campaign finance system has been particularly acute in recent decades, the criticisms raised, and the consequent demand for campaign finance reform, can be traced back to almost every election since at least the Civil War.

The first major thrust for campaign finance legislation at the national level came during the progressive era as a result of a movement to eliminate the influence of big business in federal elections. By the end of the nineteenth century, lavish contributions by major corporations and wealthy "fat cat" donors had reached levels that alarmed progressive reformers. Money from corporations, banks, railroads, and other businesses had become a major source of political funds, and numerous corporations were reportedly making donations to national party committees in amounts of $50,000 or more to "represent their share in the nation's prosperity." In the elections of 1896 and 1900, Mark Hanna relied on such corporate largesse to raise millions of dollars for William McKinley's presidential cam-

paigns, most of which came from businesses or wealthy individuals with interests in government policy. Muckraking journalists and progressive politicians charged that these wealthy donors were corrupting government processes and gaining special favors and privileges as a result of their campaign gifts. They demanded regulation to prevent such abuses. Their calls went unheeded until the controversy surrounding the financing of the 1904 election led to the first organized movement for campaign finance reform.

In 1904, Judge Alton B. Parker, the Democratic presidential nominee, alleged that corporations were providing President Theodore Roosevelt with campaign gifts to buy influence with the administration. Roosevelt denied the charge; but in investigations conducted after the election, several major companies admitted making large contributions to the Republican campaign. The controversy led Roosevelt to include a call for campaign finance reform in his annual messages to Congress in 1905 and 1906. This spurred the formation of the National Publicity Law Organization (NPLO), a citizens' group dedicated to lobbying for the regulation of political finance and public disclosure of political spending.

Faced with increasing public sentiment in favor of reform, Congress finally acted in 1907. At the urging of Benjamin "Pitchfork Ben" Tillman, it took up a bill that had been introduced in an earlier Congress to restrict corporate giving in federal elections. The law, known as the Tillman Act, prohibited any contributions by corporations and national banks to federal political campaigns (document 2.1). This ban on corporate gifts to federal candidates remains in effect to this day, although it has been undermined in recent decades by the "soft [nonfederal] money" fundraising practices of national party committees (see chapter 6).

Though the Tillman Act constituted a landmark in federal law, its adoption did not quell the cries for reform. Eliminating corporate influence was only one of the ideas being advanced at this time to clean up political finance. Reducing the influence of wealthy individuals was also a concern, and some reformers pushed for limits on individual donations. Still others advocated even bolder ideas. The NPLO continued to press for disclosure of party campaign receipts and expenditures so that voters could know which interests were financing which campaigns. William Bourke Cockran, a Democratic representative from New York associated with Tammany Hall, had an even more radical idea. In 1904 he suggested that the problems caused by campaign funding might be relieved if the government paid for some or all of the expenses of a presidential election. This proposal was never considered by Congress. However, in his December 1907 message to Congress, President Roosevelt did suggest the possibility of public financing for party organizations. But few legislators were willing to pursue this idea.

The continuing pressure for reform produced additional legislation a few years later. On the eve of the 1910 elections, the Republican majority in Congress passed a bill initiated by the NPLO that required party committees "operating in two or more states" to report any contributions or expenditures made in connection with campaigns for the House of Representatives. As adopted, the Federal Corrupt Practices Act, more commonly known as the Publicity Act of 1910, required nothing more than postelection reports of the receipts and expenditures of national party committees or committees operating in two or more states (document 2.2). Consequently, the act only affected the national

party committees and their congressional campaign committees, and it did not require any disclosure prior to an election. Such a modest measure failed to appease the more vocal advocates of reform.

In the 1910 elections the Democrats took control of the House and picked up seats in the Senate. When the new Congress convened, the Democrats sought to revise the Publicity Act to include preelection reporting. House Republicans hoped to defeat the bill by adding provisions that would be unacceptable to Southern Democrats. Since Southerners favored states' rights and considered primaries the most important elections, House Republicans called for the regulation of committees operating in a single congressional district and the disclosure of primary campaign finances. Senate Republicans went even further, adopting a bill that included limits on campaign spending. But these tactics backfired; the Republican game of one-upmanship failed to defeat the bill. Instead, Congress ultimately agreed to reforms far more extensive than those originally proposed.

The 1911 Amendments to the Publicity Act improved disclosure and established the first spending limits for federal campaigns (document 2.3). The amendments extended disclosure in two ways. They required Senate as well as House campaigns to report receipts and expenditures. In addition, they required campaign committees to report their finances both before and after an election, in primary contests as well as general elections. The law also limited House campaign expenditures to a total of $5,000 and Senate campaign expenditures to $10,000 or the amount established by state law, whichever was less.

These spending limits quickly became controversial and were contested in court. Truman H. Newberry, a Michigan Republican who defeated Henry Ford in a fiercely contested Senate primary in 1918, was convicted of violating the spending limit in that race. His campaign committee reported spending close to $180,000 in its effort to secure the nomination, an amount almost 100 times the limit established by Michigan law. Newberry challenged the conviction, arguing that Congress had no authority to regulate primaries. Besides (the argument went), he and his codefendants had not violated the law, which applied to campaign committees, not to the candidate or individual supporters.

In 1921, the Supreme Court ruled in *Newberry v. United States* (256 U.S. 232) that the congressional authority to regulate elections did not extend to party primaries and nomination activities, thus striking down the spending limits. This narrow interpretation of congressional authority stood until 1941, when in *United States v. Classic* (313 U.S. 299), the Court ruled that Congress did have the authority to regulate primaries wherever state law made them part of the election process and wherever they effectively determined the outcome of the general election. But Congress did not reassert its authority to regulate the financing of primary campaigns until 1971, when it adopted the Federal Election Campaign Act (document 2.8; see discussion later in this chapter).

The Court's decision in *Newberry* was not the only event that highlighted the inadequacy of campaign finance reforms. Shortly after this ruling, the Teapot Dome scandal once again drew attention to the corruptive influence of large contributions. (In this case, the scandal involved gifts made by oil developers in a nonelection year to federal officials responsible for granting oil leases.) The scandal led Congress to act once again, this time passing the Federal Corrupt Practices Act of 1925, which stood as the basic legislation governing campaign finance until the 1970s (document 2.4).

The Federal Corrupt Practices Act of 1925 essentially followed the regulatory approach outlined by earlier legislation with little substantive change, except for the deletion of regulations governing primaries. The act revised the disclosure rules to account for the financial activity that led to the Teapot Dome scandal by requiring all multistate political committees (as well as House and Senate candidates) to file quarterly reports that included all contributions of $100 or more, even in nonelection years. The law also revised the spending limits. Senate campaigns would be allowed to spend up to $25,000 and House campaigns up to $5,000, unless state law called for a lower limit.

Despite these changes, an effective regulatory regime was never established. Though the law imposed clear reporting requirements, it provided for none of the publicity or enforcement mechanisms needed for meaningful disclosure. The law did not specify who would have access to the reports; it did not require that they be published; it did not even stipulate the penalties if committees failed to comply. As a result, many candidates did not file regular reports. When they did, the information was provided in various forms. Gaining access to the information through the Clerk of the House or Secretary of the Senate was difficult, and the reports were usually maintained for only two years and then destroyed.

The spending ceilings were even less effective and, in fact, were almost universally ignored. Because the limits were applicable to party committees, they were easily skirted by creating multiple committees for the same candidate or race. Each of these committees could then technically comply with the spending limit established for a particular race, while the total monies funneled into that race greatly exceeded the amount intended by the law. These multiple committees also facilitated evasion of disclosure. Donors could provide gifts of less than $100 to each committee without any reporting obligation, or give larger amounts to a variety of committees, thus obscuring the total given to any candidate.

Wealthy donors also contributed monies through family members, and there were widespread reports of corporations providing bonuses to employees, who passed these funds on to candidates. Yet in the history of the 1925 act, no one was prosecuted for failing to comply with the law. Only two people— Republicans William S. Vare of Pennsylvania and

Frank L. Smith of Virginia—were excluded from office for violating spending limits. And they were excluded in 1927 as a result of violations incurred in the first election in which the law was in place. Over the next forty-five years, no other candidates were punished under this act.

Even though it was well known that candidates and party committees were not complying with the dictates of federal law, Congress did not return to the issue of campaign financing until the success of Franklin Roosevelt's New Deal coalition led conservative Democrats and staunch Republicans to seek additional reforms. With the approach of the 1940 election, these opponents of Roosevelt's liberal politics became increasingly concerned that the rapidly expanding federal work force that arose under the New Deal would become a permanent political force in the Democratic Party. In an attempt to minimize this possibility, Congress passed the Hatch Act of 1939, named after its sponsor, Senator Carl Hatch, a Democrat from New Mexico. The Hatch Act extended the prohibitions on political activity by federal employees that were first established when the Pendleton Civil Service Act of 1883 created the civil service system. The Pendleton Act sought to restrain the influence of the spoils system in the selection of civil service workers and to reduce the reliance of party organizations on the assessment of federal officeholders as a source of campaign revenue. The law prohibited government civil service employees from soliciting political contributions and protected federal officeholders from forced campaign assessments.

Although the "classified" offices covered under the original legislation covered only about one-tenth of the civil service, subsequent administrations expanded the coverage. The 1939 Hatch Act, which was also called the Clean Politics Act, prohibited political activity by those federal workers who were not constrained by the Pendleton Act. It also specifically prohibited federal employees from soliciting campaign contributions, which removed a major source of revenue for state and local party organizations.

In 1940, Congress passed amendments to the Hatch Act to restrict the amount of money donated to political campaigns in another way (document 2.5). The revisions imposed a limit of $5,000 per year on individual contributions to federal candidates or national party committees and of $3 million on the total amount that could be received or spent by a party committee operating in two or more states. Like earlier regulations, these restrictions had little effect on political giving. Donors could still donate large sums by giving to multiple committees or by making contributions through state and local party organizations, which were not subject to the $5,000 limit.

Another change in political finance during the New Deal era was the rise of labor unions as a major source of campaign money. Roosevelt's policies, many of which were regarded as pro-labor, encouraged union membership and led to the growth of organized labor as a political force in national politics. Union funds became an important source of Democratic Party campaign money. This financial strength grew significantly in the early 1940s with the establishment of the Political Action Committee as the political arm of the Congress of Industrial Organizations (CIO). Republicans and Southern Democrats sought to reduce labor's influence by passing the Smith-Connally Act, or War Labor Disputes Act of 1943. This act prohibited labor unions from using their treasury funds to make political contributions to candidates for federal office.

The Smith-Connally Act, which was passed over President Roosevelt's veto, was adopted as a war measure and thus automatically expired six months after the end of the war. When the Republicans recaptured Congress in 1946, they made this ban permanent by including it as one of the provisions of the Taft-Hartley Act, or the Labor Management Relations Act of 1947 (document 2.6). This prohibition against the use of labor union treasury funds as a source of candidate contributions has been part of federal law ever since, matching the 1907 ban on corporate treasury funds.

In the decades after World War II, dramatic changes took place in the financing of political campaigns. Although party organizations remained an important source of revenue, campaigns became increasingly candidate based. Candidates for federal office established their own committees and raised funds independent of party efforts. At the same time, television was becoming an essential means of political communication, which significantly increased the costs of seeking federal office. Yet despite renewed concerns about the costs of campaigns and the role of wealth in national elections, Congress took no action. In fact, the only serious gesture made toward reform between World War II and the Vietnam War era was President John F. Kennedy's decision to form a Commission on Campaign Costs to explore problems in the system and develop legislative proposals. The Commission's 1962 report offered a comprehensive program of reform, including such innovative ideas as a system of public matching funds for presidential candidates. However, Congress was not receptive to the president's proposals, and no effort was made to resurrect these ideas after his assassination.

Congress did pass a related bill in 1966, but it never took effect. Campaign finance issues were once again in the news as a result of criticism of the Democratic "President's Club"—a group of donors, including some government contractors, who each gave $1,000 or more—and the censure of Senator Thomas Dodd (D.-Conn.) for using his political funds for personal purposes.

Under the leadership of Senator Russell Long (D.-La.), the powerful chair of the Senate Finance Committee, Congress passed the first major reform bill since 1925. Long hoped to reduce the potential influence of wealthy donors and ease the fundraising demands generated by the rising costs of elections by providing public subsidies to political parties to pay the costs of the presidential campaign. These subsidies would be appropriated from a "Presidential Election Campaign Fund," which would be financed by allowing taxpayers to use a federal tax checkoff to allocate $1 for this purpose. The proposal met with widespread criticism, but Long forced the Senate to approve the unusual measure by attaching it as a rider to the Foreign Investors Tax Act.

Long's victory was short-lived. In the spring of 1967, Senator Albert Gore, a Democrat from Tennessee, and Senator John Williams, a Republican from Delaware, sponsored an amendment to repeal the Long Act. Gore favored public financing, arguing that the Long plan discriminated against third parties and would do little to control campaign costs, since it simply added public money to the private funds already being raised. Others simply opposed the idea of using government funds to finance campaigns or argued that such a system of party subsidies would place too much power into the hands of the national party leaders. Eventually, after much legislative maneuvering, Congress decided to make the Long Act inoperative by voting to postpone the checkoff until guidelines could be developed governing disbursement of any funds collected through this device.

Even if the Long Act had been implemented, it would not have addressed the major problems that had emerged in the campaign finance system. By this time, it was obvious to most observers that the reporting requirements and spending limits set forth in the Federal Corrupt Practices Act had proven wholly ineffective and needed a complete overhaul. There was also increasing concern about the rising costs of campaigns. In the 1956 elections, total campaign spending was approximately $155 million, $9.8 million of which was used for radio and television advertising. By 1968, overall spending had nearly doubled to $300 million, while media expenditures had increased by almost 600 percent to $58.9 million.

This dramatic growth worried many members of Congress, who feared that they might be unable to raise the sums needed in future campaigns if costs kept escalating. Legislators also worried about wealthy challengers who might have access to the resources needed to defeat them in expensive media-based campaigns. Democrats were particularly concerned about the rising costs, since Republicans had demonstrated greater success at raising large sums and had spent more than twice as much as the Democrats in the 1968 presidential contest. Changing patterns of political finance thus sparked interest in further reform, and Congress responded by passing the Federal Election Campaign Act of 1971 (document 2.8).

The Federal Election Campaign Act (FECA) went into effect in 1972. It restricted rising campaign costs and strengthened national reporting and disclosure requirements. The legislation sought to address problems stemming from the Federal Corrupt Practices Act and cut rising campaign costs, thereby combining two approaches to reform. The first part of the law established contribution limits on the amount a candidate could give to his or her own campaign and set ceilings on the amount a campaign could spend on media. The second part imposed strict public disclosure procedures on federal candidates and political committees.

The FECA represented a departure from previous regulatory efforts by placing specific limits on the amounts candidates could spend on media advertising in both primaries and general elections. These limits may have helped to restrict media spending in 1972 but did little to slow the increase in campaign spending. The information gathered as a result of the new disclosure requirements revealed that total campaign expenses rose from an estimated $300 million in 1968 to $425 million in 1972. The growth in presidential campaign costs was especially significant: President Richard M. Nixon spent more than twice as much in 1972 as he did in 1968, while his Democratic opponent in 1972, George McGovern, spent more than four times what Hubert Humphrey did in 1968—and was still outspent by a substantial margin. These spending patterns suggested that more extensive expenditure limits would be needed if costs were to be brought under control. But before the new law could be tested in another election, the Watergate scandal broke and a more extensive system of regulation was adopted.

In 1974 Congress thoroughly revised the federal campaign finance system in response to the pressure for comprehensive reform in the wake of Watergate and other reports of financial abuse in the 1972 Nixon campaign. Detailed investigations into the Nixon campaign revealed an alarming reliance on large contributions, illegal corporate contributions, and undisclosed slush funds. They also raised questions about money's influence on the political process—it was alleged that contributors "bought" ambassadorships, gained special legislative favors, and enjoyed other special privileges. The scandals spurred Congress to change the law once again.

The FECA Amendments of 1974 represent the most comprehensive campaign finance legislation ever adopted (document 2.9). Although technically a set of amendments to the 1971 law, the 1974 act left few of the original provisions intact. It significantly strengthened the disclosure provisions of the 1971 law and enacted unprecedented limits on contributions and expenditures in federal elections. The law set specific limits on the amounts individuals, political committees, and party organizations could donate to federal campaigns. It also replaced the media expenditure ceilings adopted two years earlier with aggregate spending ceilings for presidential, senatorial, and congressional candidates. Limits on the amounts party organizations could spend on behalf of federal candidates were also established. To administer and enforce these provisions, the act created an independent agency, the Federal Election Commission (FEC), which was given primary authority for regulating political finance.

The most innovative aspect of the 1974 law was the creation of an optional program of full public financing for presidential general election campaigns and a voluntary system of public matching subsidies for presidential primary campaigns. As a result, it introduced the first program of public campaign funding at the national level. In general election campaigns, the presidential nominees for the major parties could receive an amount equal to the aggregate spending limit if they agreed to refrain from raising any additional private money. Qualified minor party or independent candidates could receive a proportional share of the subsidy. In prenomination campaigns, the candidates could qualify for matching subsidies on small contributions. The purpose was to reduce fund-raising pressures in national contests and encourage solicitation of small donations. The funding for this program came from a voluntary tax checkoff on federal income tax forms—funds deposited in the Presidential Election Campaign Fund, a separate account maintained by the U.S. Treasury.

This tax checkoff mechanism originated with the Revenue Act of 1971, the successor to Long's 1966 proposal, which laid the foundation for a less comprehensive system of public subsidies for presidential campaigns (document 2.7). This subsidy program had not yet been implemented when the 1974 legislation was passed. To avoid a threatened veto by President Nixon, Congress had to postpone any collection of revenues until 1973 for funds to be used in the 1976 election.

Another important feature of the Revenue Act was the creation of a federal income tax credit or tax deduction for small contributions to political candidates at all levels of government and to some political committees, including those associated with national party organizations. Like the matching funds program at the presidential level, this provision was designed to promote broad-based participation in elections. This tax benefit was modified by the Revenue Act of 1978, which eliminated the tax deduction option and doubled the maximum allowable tax credit (document 2.11). This credit was available until 1986, when it was repealed by the Tax Reform Act of 1986.

Like its 1971 predecessor, the 1974 law was substantially revised before it was ever fully implemented. As a result of the Supreme Court's findings in *Buckley* v. *Valeo* (424 U.S. 1 [1976]; see document 3.1), Congress was forced to adopt additional amendments in the midst of the 1976 primary elections. Most important, the Court ruled against the spending limits established for House and Senate candidates and the contribution limit for independent expenditures. This substantially weakened the potential efficacy of the act, because the only spending ceilings allowed to stand were those for publicly funded presidential campaigns. The Court also struck down the method of appointing Federal Election Commissioners. The 1976 amendments thus revised the means of appointing members of the Commission and made other changes in the public financing program, contribution limits, and disclosure procedures (document 2.10). But the law was not completed until May. This forced a two-month suspension of the public matching funds program, because the FEC was not allowed to exercise its powers until it was reconstituted in conformance with the Court's ruling.

Despite its shaky start, the new campaign finance system represented a major advancement over the patchwork of regulations it replaced. The disclosure and reporting requirements dramatically improved public access to financial information and regulators' ability to enforce the law. The contribution ceilings eliminated the large gifts that had tainted the process in 1972. Public financing quickly gained widespread acceptance among the candidates, and small contributions became a staple of presidential campaign financing.

But the new regime was not without its critics. Candidates and political committee operatives complained that the law's detailed reporting requirements forced them to engage in unnecessary and burdensome paperwork, which increased their administrative costs. State and local party leaders contended that the law reduced the level of spending on traditional party-building activities (such as voter registration and mobilization programs) and discouraged grass-roots volunteer efforts. Parties were limited in the amounts they could spend on behalf of candidates, and both presidential campaigns had chosen to concentrate their legally limited resources on media advertising rather than grass-roots political activities.

As a result of the initial experience with the FECA, Congress adopted additional revisions before the 1980 election. To ensure their quick passage, the Federal Election Campaign Act Amendments of 1979 centered on "noncontroversial" reforms acceptable to both houses of Congress (document 2.12). The 1979 law was thus designed primarily to revise the reporting and disclosure requirements, easing the paperwork required by participants and reducing the amount of financial information to be reported. But it also sought to address the concerns raised by state and local party officials regarding the diminished role of local party organizations in national elections. To this end, the 1979 law granted party organizations a limited exemption from the spending provisions of the 1976 act and allowed them to spend "federal" funds on certain grass-roots volunteer activities and on traditional activities such as voter registration and get-out-the-vote programs.

Although the parties still had to abide by the law's restrictions when raising these funds, the exemption from spending limits gave the local and state parties a much larger role in campaigns. This was especially so in Senate and presidential campaigns, where the parties are more likely to engage in such supplemental campaign activity. This exemption was designed to encourage volunteer activities and promote civic participation in the election process. Contrary to what is commonly believed, the 1979 amendments did not create soft money. They only allowed party committees to use "hard" dollars to fund certain narrowly specified activities for volunteers and for party-building purposes, without having those expenditures count against the party's contribution limitations to candidates.

With a "final" regulatory regime now in place, candidates and party organizations soon began to adapt to the new rules in ways both intended and unintended. Many of these responses undermined the efficacy of the regulations and raised further questions about the FECA's ability to control the flow of political money. Congressional campaign costs continued to rise, renewing concerns about the role money plays in federal races and how well challengers can compete financially against entrenched incumbents. Contributions and spending by political action committees (PACs) also became a big issue as the number of these committees increased and their resources were distributed in ways that provided substantial financial advantages to incumbents (see chapter 5). At the presidential level, candidates and party organizations looked for ways of circumventing the expenditure and contribution limits that accompanied public funding.

Most noteworthy among these new tactics was the aggressive exploitation of the exemption for party-related activities, and the rise of a phenomenon known as soft money. Soft money is the common name given to party funds that are not regulated by federal law (see chapter 6), but which the FEC has voted, through the Advisory Opinion process, to allow party committees to accept and spend on administrative expenses and for other allegedly nonfederal election-related purposes.

By the end of the 1980s, soft money funding had become a major component of national election financing, with both major national parties spending tens of millions of soft dollars. Most of this money was being raised through unlimited contributions from sources such as corporations and labor unions that had long been banned from participating in federal elections. Many critics therefore argued that the FECA had failed and that the FEC was incapable of fulfilling its responsibility to enforce the law (see chapter 8). Soft money is not a result of Congress's deliberation and action through the lawmaking process. Instead it is an almost inadvertent result of several FEC advisory opinions—approved without hearings, public comment, or much apparent thought for the enormous consequences for the federal campaign finance structure.

By 1986, Congress was once again confronting the issue of campaign finance reform. Although both houses of Congress have considered a number of different bills since 1986 and passed some version of reform on a couple of occasions, no new legislation has been adopted since 1979. Though there is consensus that the FECA is no longer working, there is wide disagreement as to how the problems should be fixed. Disagreements over the desirability and potential effects of such proposals as spending limits in House and Senate races, public subsidies at the congressional level, restrictions on PAC contributions, and the most effective means of eliminating soft money have produced more heat than light, often resulting in partisan gridlock or unresolvable differences between the upper and lower chambers of Congress.

History suggests that the best prospects for reform are when a new Congress faces some major financial controversy or scandal that has taken place in the previous election. The 105th Congress thus offers a new hope for reform. The unprecedented financial activities of 1996 have clearly demonstrated that the current regulatory scheme is broken; the allegations of illegal and improper fundraising at the national level have created the most notable controversy since the Watergate scandal twenty-five years ago. Whether this will produce a new system of regulation or further innovation in campaign funding remains to be seen. Regardless of what happens, history suggests that questions concerning the role of money and politics will continue to be a regularly recurring feature of our nation's political landscape.

The Tillman Act of 1907 was the first of the electoral reform acts aimed at reducing the growing influence of large donations in federal election campaigns. The act made it illegal for corporations and national banks to make financial contributions to candidates for federal office.

An Act to prohibit corporations from making money contributions in connection with political elections.

Be it enacted, That it shall be unlawful for any national bank, or any corporation organized by authority of any laws of Congress, to make a money contribution in connection with any election to any political office. It shall also be unlawful for any corporation whatever to make a money contribution in connection with any election at which Presidential and Vice-Presidential electors or a Representative in Congress is to be voted for or any election by any State legislature of a United States Senator. Every corporation which shall make any contribution in violation of the foregoing provisions shall be subject to a fine not exceeding five thousand dollars, and every officer or director of any corporation who shall consent to any contribution by the corporation in violation of the foregoing provisions shall upon conviction be punished by a fine of not exceeding one thousand and not less than two hundred and fifty dollars, or by imprisonment for a term of not more than one year, or both such fine and imprisonment in the discretion of the court.

The Publicity Act of 1910 was the first act to require disclosure of campaign receipts and expenditures in House elections. The law required national party committees and committees operating in two or more states to file postelection financial disclosure reports. Excerpts of the law follow.

An Act providing for publicity of contributions made for the purpose of influencing elections at which Representatives in Congress are elected.

Be it enacted, That the term "political committee" under the provisions of this Act shall include the national committees of all political parties and the national congressional campaign committees of all political parties and all committees, associations, or organizations which shall in two or more States influence the result or attempt to influence the result of an election at which Representatives in Congress are to be elected.

SEC. 2. That every political committee as defined in this Act shall have a chairman and a treasurer. It shall be the duty of the treasurer to keep a detailed and exact account of all money or its equivalent received by or promised to such committee or any member thereof, or by or to any person acting under its authority or in its behalf, and the name of every person, firm, association, or committee from whom received, and of all expenditures, disbursements, and promises of payment or disbursement made by the committee or any member thereof, or by any person acting under its authority or in its behalf, and to whom paid, distributed, or disbursed. No officer or member of such committee, or other person acting under its authority or in its behalf, shall receive any money or its equivalent, or expend or promise to expend any money on behalf of such committee, until after a chairman and treasurer of such committee shall have been chosen.

SEC. 3. That every payment or disbursement made by a political committee exceeding ten dollars in amount be evidenced by a receipted bill stating the particulars of expense, and every such record, voucher, receipt, or account shall be preserved for fifteen months after the election to which it relates.

SEC. 4. That whoever, acting under the authority or in behalf of such political committee, whether as a member thereof or otherwise, receives any contribution, payment, loan, gift, advance, deposit, or promise of money or its equivalent shall, on demand, and in any event within five days after the receipt of such contribution, payment, loan, gift, advance, deposit, or promise, render to the treasurer of such political committee a detailed account of the same, together with the name and address from whom received, and said treasurer shall forthwith enter the same in a ledger or record to be kept by him for that purpose.

SEC. 5. That the treasurer of every such political committee shall, within thirty days after the election at which Representatives in Congress were chosen in two or more States, file with the Clerk of the House of Representatives at Washington, District of Columbia, an itemized, detailed statement, sworn to by said treasurer and conforming to the requirements of the following section of this Act. The statement so filed with the Clerk of the House of Representatives shall be preserved by him for fifteen months, and shall be a part of the public records of his office, and shall be open to public inspection.

. . .

SEC. 10. That every person willfully violating any of the foregoing provisions of this Act shall, upon conviction, be fined not more than one thousand dollars or imprisoned not more than one year, or both.

The Publicity Act Amendments of 1911 extended financial disclosure and initiated the first spending limits for federal campaigns. Disclosure was extended to include primaries and conventions and the amendments required preelection as well as postelection disclosure of campaign finances by both Senate and House campaigns. In addition, it was the first law to limit House and Senate campaign expenditures. Excerpts of the amendments follow.

An Act to amend an act entitled "An act providing for publicity of contributions made for the purpose of influencing elections at which Representatives in Congress are elected" and extending the same to candidates for nomination and election to the offices of Representative and Senator in the Congress of the United States and limiting the amount of campaign expenses.

Be it enacted, That sections five, six, and eight of an Act entitled "An Act providing for publicity of contributions made for the purpose of influencing elections at which Representatives in Congress are elected," . . . be . . . amended to read as follows:

SEC. 5. That the treasurer of every such political committee shall, not more than fifteen days and not less than ten days next before an election at which Representatives in Congress are to be elected in two or more States, file in the office of the Clerk of the House of Representatives at Washington, District of Columbia, with said Clerk, an itemized detailed statement; and on each sixth day thereafter until such election said treasurer shall file with said Clerk a supplemental itemized detailed statement. Each of said statements shall conform to the requirements of the following section of this Act, except that the supplemental statement herein required need not contain any item of which publicity is given in a previous statement. Each of said statements shall be full and complete, and shall be signed and sworn to by said treasurer.

"It shall also be the duty of said treasurer to file a similar statement with said Clerk within thirty days after such election, such final statement also to be signed and sworn to by said treasurer and to conform to the requirements of the following section of this Act. The statements so filed with the Clerk of the House shall be preserved by him for fifteen months and shall be a part of the public records of his office and shall be open to public inspection.

. . .

SEC. 8. The word 'candidate' as used in this section shall include all persons whose names are presented for nomination for Representative or Senator in the Congress of the United States at any primary election or nominating convention, or for indorsement or election at any general or special election held in connection with the nomination or election of a person to fill such office, whether or not such persons are actually nominated, indorsed, or elected.

"Every person who shall be a candidate for nomination at any primary election or nominating convention, or for election at any general or special election, as Representative in the Congress of the United States, shall, not less than ten nor more than fifteen days before the day for holding such primary election or nominating convention, and not less than ten nor more than fifteen days before the day of the general or special election at which candidates for Representatives are to be elected, file with the Clerk of the House of Representatives at Washington, District of Columbia, a full, correct, and itemized statement of all moneys and things of value received by him or by anyone for him with his knowledge and consent, from any source, in aid or support of his candidacy together with the names of all those who have furnished the same in whole or in part; and such statement shall contain a true and itemized account of all moneys and things of value given, contributed, expended, used, or promised by such candidate, or by his agent, representative, or other person for and in his behalf with his knowledge and consent, together with the names of all those to whom any and all such gifts, contribution, payments, or promises were made, for the purpose of procuring his nomination or election.

"Every person who shall be a candidate for nomination at any primary election or nomination convention, or for indorsement at any general or special election or election by the legislature of any State, as Senator in the Congress of the United States, shall, not less than ten nor more than fifteen days before the day for holding such primary election or nominating convention, and not less than ten nor more than fifteen days before the day of the general or special election at which he is seeking indorsement, and not less than five nor more than ten days before the day upon which the first vote is to be taken in the two houses of the legislature before which he is a candidate for election as Senator, file with the Secretary of the Senate at Washington, District of Columbia, a full, correct, and itemized statement of all moneys and things of value received by him or by anyone for him with his knowledge and consent, from any source, in aid or support of his candidacy, together with the names of all those who have furnished the same in whole or in part; and such statement shall contain a true and itemized account of all moneys and things of value given, contributed, expended, used, or promised by such candidate, or by his agent, representative, or other person for and in his behalf with his knowledge and consent, together with the names of all those to whom any and all such gifts, contribution, payments, or promises were made for the purpose of procuring his nomination or election.

"Every such candidate for nomination at any primary election or nominating convention, or for indorsement or election at any general or special election, or for election by the legislature of any State, shall, within fifteen days after such primary election or nominating convention, and within thirty days after any such general or special election, and within thirty days after the day upon which the legislature shall have elected a Senator, file with the Clerk of the House of Representatives or with the Secretary of the Senate, as the case may be, a full, correct, and itemized statement of all moneys and things of value received by him or by anyone for him with his knowledge and consent, from any source, in aid or support of his candidacy, together with the names of all those who have furnished the same in whole or in part; and such statement shall contain a true and itemized account of all moneys and things of value given, contributed, expended, used, or promised by such candidate, or by his agent, representative, or other person for and in his behalf with his knowledge and consent, up to, on and after the day of such primary election, nominating convention, general or special election, or election by the legislature, together with the names of all those to whom any and all such gifts, contributions, payments, or promises were made for the purpose of procuring his nomination, indorsement, or election.

"Every such candidate shall include therein a statement of every promise or pledge made by him, or by any one for him with his knowledge and consent or to whom he has given authority to make any such promise or pledge, before the completion of any such primary election or nominating convention or general or special election or election by legislature, relative to the appointment or recommendation for appointment of any person to any position of trust, honor, or profit, either in the county, State, or Nation, or in any political subdivision thereof, or in any private or corporate employment, for the purpose of procuring the support of such person or of any person in his candidacy, and if any such promise or pledge shall have been made the name or names, the address or addresses, and the occupation or occupations, of the person or persons to whom such promise or pledge shall have been made, shall be stated, together with a description of the position relating to which such promise or pledge has been made. In the event that no such promise or pledge has been made by such candidate, that fact shall be distinctly stated.

"No candidate for Representative in Congress or for Senator of the United States shall promise any office or position to any person, or to use his influence or to give his support to any person for any office or position for the purpose of procuring the support of such person, or of any person, in his candidacy; nor shall any candidate for Senator of the United States give, contribute, expend, use, or promise any money or thing of value to assist in procuring the nomination of election of any particular candidate for the legislature of the State in which he resides, but such candidate may, within the limitation and restrictions and subject to the requirements of this act, contribute to political committees having charge of the disbursement of campaign funds.

"No candidate for Representative in Congress or for Senator of the United States shall give, contribute, expend, use, or promise, or cause to be given, contributed, expended, used, or promised, in procuring his nomination and election, any sum, in the aggregate, in excess of the amount which he may lawfully give, contribute, expend, or promise under the laws of the State in which he resides: *Provided*, That no candidate for Representative in Congress shall give, contribute, expend, use, or promise any sum, in the aggregate, exceeding five thousand dollars in any campaign for his nomination and election; and no candidate for Senator of the United States shall give, contribute, expend, use, or promise any sum, in the aggregate, exceeding ten thousand dollars in any campaign for his nomination and election: *Provided further*, That money expended by any such candidate to meet and discharge any assessment, fee, or charge made or levied upon candidates by the laws of the State in which he resides, or for his necessary personal expenses, incurred for himself alone, for travel and subsistence, stationery and postage, writing or printing (other than in newspapers), and distributing letters, circulars, and posters, and for telegraph and telephone service, shall not be regarded as an expenditure within the meaning of this section, and shall not be considered any part of the sum herein fixed as the limit of expense and need not be shown in the statements herein required to be filed. . . ."

The Federal Corrupt Practices Act of 1925 repealed and replaced provisions of the Publicity Acts of 1910 and 1911. The law broadened disclosure by requiring quarterly financial filings of House and Senate candidates and political committees operating in multiple states and districts. The law also raised campaign spending limits and limited the amount of expenditures that congressional candidates could spend on their campaigns. Due to the Supreme Court decision in 1921 (*Newberry* v. *United States*, 256 U.S. 232), which ruled that Congress did not have the authority to regulate primary election campaigns, the provisions regulating campaign expenditures in this 1925 act applied only to general elections.

SEC. 301. This title may be cited as the "Federal Corrupt Practices Act, 1925."

SEC. 302. When used in this title—

(a) The term "election" includes a general or special election, and, in the case of a Resident Commissioner from the Philippine Islands, an election by the Philippine Legislature, but does not include a primary election or convention of a political party;

(b) The term "candidate" means an individual whose name is presented at an election for election as Senator or Representative in, or Delegate or Resident Commissioner to, the Congress of the United States, whether or not such individual is elected;

(c) The term "political committee" includes any committee, association, or organization which accepts contributions or makes expenditures for the purpose of influencing or attempting to influence the election of candidates or presidential and vice presidential electors (1) in two or more States, or (2) whether or not in more than one State if such committee, association, or organization (other than a duly organized State or local committee of a political party) is a branch or subsidiary of a national committee, association, or organization;

(d) The term "contribution" includes a gift, subscription, loan, advance, or deposit, of money, or anything of value, and includes a contract, promise, or agreement, whether or not legally enforceable, to make a contribution;

(e) The term "expenditure" includes a payment, distribution, loan, advance, deposit, or gift, of money, or any thing of value, and includes a contract, promise, or agreement, whether or not legally enforceable, to make an expenditure;

(f) The term "person" includes an individual, partnership, committee, association, corporation, and any other organization or group of persons;

(g) The term "Clerk" means the Clerk of the House of Representatives of the United States;

(h) The term "Secretary" means the Secretary of the Senate of the United States;

(i) The term "State" includes Territory and possession of the United States;

SEC. 303. (a) Every political committee shall have a chairman and a treasurer. No contribution shall be accepted, and no expenditure made, by or on behalf of a political committee for the purpose of influencing an election until such chairman and treasurer have been chosen.

(b) It shall be the duty of the treasurer of a political committee to keep a detailed and exact account of—

(1) All contributions made to or for such committee;

(2) The name and address of every person making any such contribution, and the date thereof;

(3) All expenditures made by or on behalf of such committee; and

(4) The name and address of every person to whom any such expenditure is made, and the date thereof.

(c) It shall be the duty of the treasurer to obtain and keep a receipted bill, stating the particulars, for every expenditure by or on behalf of a political committee exceeding $10 in amount. The treasurer shall preserve all receipted bills and accounts required to be kept by this section for a period of at least two years from the date of the filing of the statement containing such items.

SEC. 304. Every person who receives a contribution for a political committee shall, on demand of the treasurer, and in any event within five days after the receipt of such contribution, render to the treasurer a detailed account thereof, including the name and address of the person making such a contribution, and the date on which received.

SEC. 305. (a) The treasurer of a political committee shall file with the Clerk between the 1st and 10th days of March, June, and September, in each year, and also between the 10th and 15th days, and on the 5th day, next preceding the date on which a general election is to be held, at which candidates are to be elected in two or more States, and also on the 1st day of January, a statement containing, complete as of the day next preceding the date of filing—

(1) The name and address of each person who has made a contribution to or for such committee in one or more items of the aggregate amount or value, within the calendar year, of $100 or more, together with the amount and date of such contribution;

(2) The total sum of the contributions made to or for such committee during the calendar year and not stated under paragraph (1);

(3) The total sum of all contributions made to or for such committee during the calendar year;

(4) The name and address of each person to whom an expenditure in one or more items of the aggregate amount or value, within the calendar year, of $10 or more has been made by or on behalf of such committee, and the amount, date, and purpose of such expenditure;

(5) The total sum of all expenditures made by or on behalf of such committee during the calendar year and not stated under paragraph (4);

(6) The total sum of expenditures made by or on behalf of such committee during the calendar year.

. . .

(c) The statement filed on the 1st day of January shall cover the preceding calendar year.

SEC. 306. Every person (other than a political committee) who makes an expenditure in one or more items, other than by contribution to a political committee, aggregating $50 or more within a calendar year for the purpose of influencing in two or more States the election of candidates, shall file with the Clerk an itemized detailed statement of such expenditure in the same manner as required of the treasurer of a political committee by section 305.

SEC. 307. (a) Every candidate for Senator shall file with the Secretary and every candidate for Representative, Delegate, or Resident Commissioner shall file with the Clerk not less than ten nor more than fifteen days before, and also within thirty days after, the date on which an election is to be held, a statement containing, complete as of the day next preceding the date of filing—

(1) A correct and itemized account of each contribution received by him or by any person for him with his knowledge or consent, from any source, in aid or support of his candidacy for election, or for the purpose of influencing the result of the election, together with the name of the person who has made such contribution;

(2) A correct and itemized account of each expenditure made by him or by any person for him with his knowledge or consent, in aid or support of his candidacy for election, or for the purpose of influencing the result of the election, together with the name of the person to whom such expenditure was made; except that only the total sum of expenditures for items specified in subdivision (c) of section 309 need be stated;

(3) A statement of every promise or pledge made by him or by any person for him with his consent, prior to the closing of the polls on the day of the election, relative to the appointment or recommendation for appointment of any person to any public or private position or employment for the purpose of procuring support in his candidacy, and the name, address, and occupation of every person to whom any such promise or pledge has been made, together with the description of any such position. If no such promise or pledge has been made, that fact shall be specifically stated.

(b) The statements required to be filed by subdivision (a) shall be cumulative, but where there has been no change in an item reported in a previous statement only the amount need be carried forward.

(c) Every candidate shall inclose with his first statement a report, based upon the records of the proper State official, stating the total number of votes cast for all candidates for the office which the candidate seeks, at the general election next preceding the election at which he is a candidate.

SEC. 308. A statement required by this title to be filed by a candidate or treasurer of a political committee or other person with the Clerk or Secretary, as the case may be—

(a) Shall be verified by the oath or affirmation of the person filing such statement, taken before any officer authorized to administer oaths;

(b) Shall be deemed properly filed when deposited in an established post office within the prescribed time, duly stamped, registered, and directed to the Clerk or Secretary at Washington, District of Columbia, but in the event it is not received, a duplicate of such statement shall be promptly filed upon notice by the Clerk or Secretary of its nonreceipt;

(c) Shall be preserved by the Clerk or Secretary for a period of two years from the date of filing, shall constitute a part of the public records of his office, and shall be open to public inspection.

SEC. 309. (a) A candidate, in his campaign for election, shall not make expenditures in excess of the amount which he may lawfully make under the laws of the state in which he is a candidate, nor in excess of the amount which he may lawfully make under the provisions of this title.

(b) Unless the laws of his State prescribe a less amount as the maximum limit of campaign expenditures, a candidate may make expenditures up to—

(1) The sum of $10,000 if a candidate for Senator, or the sum of $2,500 if a candidate for Representative, Delegate, or Resident Commissioner; or

(2) An amount equal to the amount obtained by multiplying three cents by the total number of votes cast at the last general elections for all candidates for the office which the candidate seeks, but in no event exceeding $25,000 if a candidate for Senator or $5,000 if a candidate for Representative, Delegate, or Resident Commissioner.

(c) Money expended by a candidate to meet and discharge any assessment, fee, or charge made or levied upon candidates by the laws of the State in which he resides, or expended for his necessary personal, traveling, or subsistence expenses, or for stationery, postage, writing, or printing (other than for use on billboards or in newspapers), for distributing letters, circulars, or posters, or for telegraph or telephone service, shall not be included in determining whether his expenditures have exceeded the sum fixed by paragraph (1) or (2) of subdivision (b) as the limit of campaign expenses of a candidate.

SEC. 310. It is unlawful for any candidate to directly or indirectly promise or pledge the appointment, or the use of his influence or support for the appointment of any person to any public or private position or employment, for the purpose of procuring support in his candidacy.

SEC. 311. It is unlawful for any person to make or offer to make an expenditure, or to cause an expenditure to be made or offered, to any person, either to vote or withhold his vote, or to vote for or against any candidate, and it is unlawful for any person to solicit, accept, or receive any such expenditure in consideration of his vote or the withholding of his vote.

SEC. 312. Section 118 of the act entitled "An Act to codify, revise, and amend the penal laws of the United States," approved March 4, 1909 is amended to read as follows:

"SEC. 118. It is unlawful for any Senator or Representative in, or Delegate or Resident Commissioner, or any officer or employee of the United States, or any person receiving any salary or compensation for services from money derived from the Treasury of the United States, to directly or indirectly solicit, receive, or be in any manner concerned in soliciting or receiving, any assessment, subscription, or contribution for any political purpose whatever, from any other such officer, employee, or person."

SEC. 313. It is unlawful for any national bank, or any corporation organized by authority of any law of Congress, to make a contribution in connection with any election to any political office, or for any corporation whatever to make a contribution in connection with any election at which presidential and vice presidential electors or a Senator or Representative in, or a Delegate or Resident Commissioner to, Congress are to be voted for, or for any candidate, political committee, or other person to accept or receive any contribution prohibited by this section. Every corporation which makes any contribution in violation of this section shall be fined not more than $5,000; and every officer or director of any corporation who consents to any contribution by the corporation in violation of this section shall be fined not more than $1,000, or imprisoned not more than one year, or both.

SEC. 314. (a) Any person who violates any of the foregoing provisions of this title, except those for which a specific penalty is imposed by sections 312 and 313, shall be fined not more than $1,000 or imprisoned not more than one year, or both.

    (b) Any person who willfully violates any of the foregoing provisions of this title, except those for which a specific penalty is imposed by section 312 and 313, shall be fined not more than $10,000 and imprisoned not more than two years.

SEC. 315. This title shall not limit or affect the right of any person to make expenditures for proper legal expenses in contesting the results of an election.

SEC. 316. This title shall not be construed to annul the laws of any State relating to the nomination or election of candidates, unless directly inconsistent with the provisions of this title, or to exempt any candidate from complying with such State laws.

SEC. 317. If any provision of this title or application thereof to any person or circumstance is held invalid, the validity or the remainder of the Act and of the application of such provision to other persons and circumstances shall not be affected thereby.

SEC. 318. The following Acts and parts of Acts are hereby repealed: the Act entitled "An Act providing for publicity of contributions made for the purpose of influencing elections at which Representatives in Congress are elected," approved June 25, 1910 (chapter 392, Thirty-sixth Statutes, page 822), and the Acts amendatory thereof, approved August 19, 1911 (chapter 33, Thirty-seventh Statutes, page 25) and August 23, 1912 (chapter 349, Thirty-seventh Statutes, page 360); the Act entitled "An Act to prevent corrupt practices in the election of Senators, Representatives, or Delegates in Congress," approved October 16, 1918 (chapter 187, Fortieth Statutes, page 1013); and section 83 of the Criminal Code of the United States, approved March 4, 1909 (chapter 321, Thirty-fifth Statutes, page 1088).

SEC. 319. This title shall take effect thirty days after its enactment.

The Hatch Act Amendments of 1940 imposed the first yearly limit on individual contributions to federal candidates or national party committees. The amendments also placed a limit on the total amount that a national party committee operating in two or more states could receive or spend in a year.

An Act to extend to certain officers and employees in the several States and the District of Columbia the provisions of the Act entitled "An Act to prevent pernicious political activities," approved August 2, 1939.

Be it enacted, That . . . the Act entitled "an Act to prevent pernicious political activities," approved August 2, 1939, is amended to read as follows: . . .

"**SEC. 13.** (a) It is hereby declared to be a pernicious political activity, and it shall hereafter be unlawful, for any person, directly or indirectly, to make contributions in an aggregate amount in excess of $5,000, during any calendar year, or in connection with any campaign for nomination or election, to or on behalf of any candidate for an elective Federal office (including the offices of President of the United States and Presidential and Vice Presidential electors), or to or on behalf of any committee or other organization engaged in furthering, advancing or advocating the nomination or election of any candidate for any such office or the success of any national political party. This subsection shall not apply to contributions made to or by a State or local committee or other State or local organization.

"(b) For the purposes of this section—

"(1) The term 'person' includes an individual, partnership, committee, association, corporation, and any other organization or group of persons.

"(2) The term 'contribution' includes a gift, subscription, loan, advance, or deposit of money, or anything of value, and includes a contract, promise, or agreement, whether or not legally enforceable, to make a contribution.

"(c) It is further declared to be a pernicious political activity, and it shall hereafter be unlawful for any person, individual, partnership, committee, association, corporation, and any other organization or group of persons to purchase or buy any goods, commodities, advertising, or articles of any kind or description where the proceeds of such a purchase, or any portion thereof, shall directly or indirectly inure to the benefit of or for any candidate for an elective Federal office (including the offices of President of the United States, and Presidential and Vice Presidential electors) or any political committee or other political organization engaged in furthering, advancing, or advocating the nomination or election of any candidate for any such office or the success of any national political party: *Provided,* That nothing in this sentence shall be construed to interfere with the usual and known business, trade, or profession of any candidate.

"(d) Any person who engages in a pernicious political activity in violation of any provision of this section, shall upon conviction thereof be fined not more than $5,000 or imprisoned for not more than five years. In all cases of violations of this section by a partnership, committee, association, corporation, or other organization or group of persons, the officers, directors, or managing heads thereof who knowingly and willfully participate in such violation, shall be subject to punishment as herein provided.

"(e) Nothing in this section shall be construed to permit the making of any contribution which is prohibited by any provision of law in force on the date this section takes effect. Nothing in this Act shall be construed to alter of amend any provisions of the Federal Corrupt Practices Act of 1925, or any amendments thereto. . . .

SEC. 6. Such Act of August 2, 1939, is further amended by adding at the end thereof the following new section:

"SEC. 20. No political committee shall receive contributions aggregating more than $3,000,000, or make expenditures aggregating more than $3,000,000, during any calendar year. For the purposes of this section, any contributions received and any expenditures made on behalf of any political committee with the knowledge and consent of the chairman or treasurer of such committee shall be deemed to be received or made by such committee. Any violation of this section by any political committee shall be deemed also to be a violation of this section by the chairman and the treasurer of such committee and by any other person responsible for such violation. Terms used in this section shall have the meaning assigned to them in section 302 of the Federal Corrupt Practices Act, 1925, and the penalties provided in such Act shall apply to violations of this section."

The Taft-Hartley Act of 1947 made permanent the ban on labor union contributions to federal election campaigns.

An Act to amend the National Labor Relations Act, to provide additional facilities for the mediation of labor disputes affecting commerce, to equalize legal responsibilities of labor organizations and employers, and for other purposes. . . .

SEC. 304. Section 313 of the Federal Corrupt Practices Act, 1925 (U.S.C., 1940 edition, title 2, sec. 251; Supp. V, title 50, App., sect. 1509), is amended to read as follows:

"**SEC. 313.** It is unlawful for any national bank, or any corporation organized by authority of any law of Congress, to make a contribution or expenditure in connection with any election to any political office, or in connection with any primary election or political convention or caucus held to select candidates for any political office, or for any corporation whatever, or any labor organization to make a contribution or expenditure in connection with any election at which Presidential and Vice Presidential electors or a Senator or Representative in, or a Delegate or Resident Commissioner to Congress are to be voted for, or in connection with any primary election or political convention or caucus held to select candidates for any of the foregoing offices, or for any candidate, political committee, or other person to accept or receive any contribution prohibited by this section. Every corporation or labor organization which makes any contribution or expenditure in violation of this section shall be fined not more than $5,000; and every officer or director of any corporation, or officer of any labor organization, who consents to any contribution or expenditure by the corporation or labor organization, as the case may be, in violation of this section shall be fined not more than $1,000 or imprisoned for not more than one year, or both. For the purposes of this section 'labor organization' means any organization of any kind, or any agency or employee representation committee or plan, in which employees participate and which exists for the purpose, in whole or in part, of dealing with employers concerning grievances, labor disputes, wages, rates of pay, hours of employment, or conditions of work. . . ."

The Revenue Act of 1971 (Public Law 92-178) was signed into law by President Richard Nixon on December 10, 1971 (document 2.8). This legislation, along with the Federal Election Campaign Act of 1971 (document 2.8), laid the foundation for the modern system of presidential campaign finance. The Revenue Act revived the tax checkoff and campaign fund provisions of the 1966 Presidential Election Campaign Fund Act, which was adopted as an amendment to the Foreign Investors Tax Act of 1966 (Public Law 89-809) but was effectively terminated before becoming operative in 1967. As enacted, the act allowed a taxpayer to earmark a checkoff contribution to the candidate of a specified party or direct that it be placed in a nonpartisan general account. To avoid a threatened veto by President Nixon, implementation of this tax checkoff provision was delayed until the 1972 tax year. This postponed the collection of revenues until 1973 and made the law's public subsidy program effective for the 1976 presidential campaign. But the Federal Election Campaign Act of 1974 (document 2.9) changed the terms of the program before it was fully implemented.

The 1971 Revenue Act created the Presidential Election Campaign Fund, a separate account in the U.S. Treasury, and established a voluntary checkoff provision on individual federal income tax returns to allow individuals to designate $1 of their tax payments (or $2 for married couples filing jointly) to the fund. Monies from the fund would be used to provide public subsidies to the campaigns of presidential candidates who met certain eligibility requirements. The act also provided for a system of federal income tax credits for political contributions to candidates for federal, state, and local office, and to some political committees, including national, state, and local committees of a national political party. Individuals who make a financial contribution to a candidate for federal, state, or local office could claim a federal income tax credit for 50 percent of their contribution, up to a maximum of $12.50 on a single return and $25 on a joint return. Alternatively, a political contributor could claim a tax deduction for the full amount of any contributions, up to a maximum of $50 on an individual return and $100 on a joint return.

The act also established the requirements for determining public subsidies to presidential general election campaigns in accordance with the provisions of the Federal Election Campaign Act of 1971. Presidential candidates were eligible to receive subsidies from the Presidential Election Campaign Fund if they agreed to abide by the act's statutory restrictions. The principal restrictions were that candidates adhere to an overall spending limit of $0.15 multiplied by the voting-age population of the United States and, for major party candidates (defined as those whose party received more than 25 percent of

---

Documents 2.7 through 2.12 were prepared by Anthony Corrado, in part from his essays that appeared in L. Sandy Maisel, ed., *Political Parties and Elections in the United States: An Encyclopedia,* vols. 1 and 2 (New York: Garland Publishing, 1991).

the popular vote in the previous presidential election), that they not accept contributions beyond the public subsidy. These candidates were eligible for a grant equal to the overall spending limit. Minor party candidates (defined as those whose party received between 5 and 25 percent of the popular vote in the previous presidential election) were eligible for a fraction of the major party grant, based on the party's vote in the previous election compared with the average vote received by the major parties. Candidates of new parties or of minor parties who reached the eligibility threshold in the current election were entitled to postelection subsidies based on their share of the vote compared with the average vote for the major party candidates. If the balance in the fund was insufficient for the full costs allowed under the law, funds would be distributed to the candidates on a prorated basis. The act granted the Comptroller General the responsibility of certifying payments from the fund, receiving and publishing disclosure reports, and enforcing the law.

Since its adoption the act has been amended a number of times. In a 1973 amendment to legislation continuing a temporary debt ceiling, Congress made two changes to the checkoff provision to simplify its implementation and promote public participation: the option of earmarking the contribution to a specific party was repealed, and the Internal Revenue Service was directed to place the checkoff in a visible location on tax forms. The allowable tax credit for political contributions was increased to $25 on an individual return and $50 on a joint return by the Tariff Schedules Amendments of 1975, doubled again by the Revenue Act of 1978 (document 2.11), and repealed by the Tax Reform Act of 1986. The tax deductions allowed under the law were doubled under the 1974 Federal Election Campaign Act Amendments and repealed by the Revenue Act of 1978.

The public financing program and the statutory provisions governing the Presidential Election Campaign Fund have undergone a number of modifications as a result of the 1974 Federal Election Campaign Act Amendments, the subsequent amendments of 1976 and 1979 (documents 2.10 and 2.12), and legislation concerning the public financing of national nomination conventions (Public Law 98-355). The thrust of these legislative amendments has been to expand the public subsidy program to include presidential primaries and nominating conventions and to alter the formula for determining general election subsidies.

The Federal Election Campaign Act of 1971 (Public Law 92-225) was signed into law by President Richard Nixon on February 7, 1972, and went into effect sixty days later, on April 7, 1972. The legislation sought to restrict rising campaign costs and strengthen the campaign reporting requirements of federal law. It therefore combined two different approaches to reform. The first part of the law established detailed spending limits for all federal campaigns, while the second part imposed strict public disclosure procedures on federal candidates and political committees.

The Federal Election Campaign Act's major provisions limited personal contributions, established specific ceilings for media expenditures, and required full public disclosure of campaign receipts and disbursements. The act imposed ceilings on personal contributions by candidates and their immediate families of $50,000 for presidential and vice presidential candidates, $35,000 for Senate candidates, and $25,000 for House candidates. It limited the amounts candidates for federal office could spend on radio, television, cable television, newspapers, magazines, and automated telephone systems in any primary, runoff, special, or general election to $50,000 or $0.10 times the voting-age population of the jurisdiction covered by the election, whichever was greater. In addition, the act declared that no more than 60 percent of a candidate's overall media spending could be devoted to radio and television advertising. These limits were to apply separately to primary and general elections and were indexed to reflect increases in the Consumer Price Index.

These ceilings governed all media spending in the 1972 primaries and general elections. As practiced, House candidates could spend no more than $52,150 for all media outlays in an election and a maximum of $31,290 on radio and television. Because of the differences in state voting populations, the limits for Senate candidates varied, ranging from $52,150 in sparsely populated states such as Alaska and Montana (of which $31,290 could be spent on radio and television) to $1.4 million in California (of which $850,000 could be spent on radio and television). Presidential candidates were limited to $14.3 million in overall expenditures, of which no more than $8.58 million could be spent on radio and television.

In the area of disclosure, the act required every candidate or political committee active in a federal campaign to file a quarterly report of receipts and expenditures. These reports were to list any contribution or expenditure of $100 or more and include the name, address, occupation, and principal place of business of the donor or recipient. During election years, additional reports had to be filed fifteen days and five days before an election, and any contribution of $5,000 or more had to be reported within forty-eight hours of its receipt. The reports were to be filed with the secretary of state of the state in which campaign activities took place and with the appropriate federal officer, as established under the act. For the latter purpose, House candidates filed with the Clerk of the House, Senate candidates with the Secretary of the Senate, and presidential candidates with the General Accounting Office. All reports had to be made available for public inspection within forty-eight hours of being received.

The Federal Election Campaign Act Amendments of 1974 (Public Law 93-443), were signed into law by President Gerald Ford on October 15, 1974. Though technically a set of amendments to the 1971 Federal Election Campaign Act (FECA) (document 2.8), this legislation stands as the most comprehensive reform of the campaign finance system ever adopted. It significantly strengthened the disclosure provisions of the 1971 law and enacted unprecedented limits on contributions and expenditures in federal elections. It introduced the first use of public financing at the national level by establishing optional public funding in presidential general election campaigns and a system of federal matching grants in presidential primary campaigns. It also created an independent agency, the Federal Election Commission, to administer and enforce campaign finance regulations.

The 1974 law was a direct result of the experience in the 1972 elections. The abuses revealed by the investigations surrounding the Watergate scandal and the continuing increase in campaign costs convinced the Congress that a more extensive regulatory scheme than that adopted in 1971 was necessary. Accordingly, the media spending ceilings established by the 1971 act were abolished and replaced with stringent limits on campaign expenditures. Under the new provisions, Senate candidates could spend no more than $100,000 or $0.08 times the voting-age population of the state in a primary election, whichever was greater, and no more than $150,000 or $0.12 times the voting-age population in a general election, whichever was greater. House candidates in multidistrict states were limited to total expenditures of $70,000 in each primary and general election. Those in states with a single representative were subject to the ceilings established for Senate candidates.

Presidential candidates were restricted to $10 million in a nomination campaign and $20 million in a general election. The amount they could spend in a state primary election was also limited to no more than twice the sum that a Senate candidate in that state could spend. All of these ceilings were indexed to reflect increases in the Consumer Price Index, and candidates were allowed to spend up to an additional 20 percent of the spending limit for fundraising costs. This latter provision was instituted in recognition of the added fundraising burden placed on candidates as a result of the contribution limits imposed by the act, which required that they finance their campaigns through small contributions.

The amendments also set limits on the amounts national party committees could expend on behalf of candidates. These organizations were allowed to spend no more than $10,000 per candidate in House general elections; the greater of $20,000 or $0.02 times the voting-age population for each candidate in Senate general elections; and $0.02 times the voting-age population (approximately $2.9 million) for their presidential candidate. The amount a party committee could spend on its national nominating convention was also restricted. Each of the major parties (defined as a party whose candidates received more than 25 percent of the popular vote in the previous election) was limited to $2 million in convention expenditures. Minor parties (defined as parties whose candidates received between 5 and 25 percent of the popular vote in the previous election) were limited to lesser amounts.

The legislation retained the contribution limits placed on candidates and their immediate families by the FECA and established additional restrictions designed to eliminate the potentially corruptive influence of large donors. An individual was allowed to contribute no more than $1,000 per candidate in any primary, runoff, or general election and could not exceed $25,000 in annual aggregate contributions to all federal candidates. Donations by political committees—in particular, the political action committees that the law sanctioned for use by labor unions and other groups of individuals—were limited to $5,000 per election for each candidate, with no aggregate limit. Independent expenditures made on behalf of a candidate were limited to $1,000 a year, and cash donations in excess of $100 were prohibited.

The most innovative aspect of the 1974 law was the creation of a public financing system for presidential election campaigns financed from the tax checkoff receipts deposited in the Presidential Election Campaign Fund. The legislation established a program of voluntary public financing for presidential general elections in which major party candidates could receive the full amount authorized by the spending limit ($20 million) if they agreed to eschew private donations. Minor party candidates could receive a proportionate share of this amount, with the size of their subsidy determined on the basis of the proportion of the vote they received in the previous election compared with the average vote of the major parties. New parties and minor parties could also qualify for postelection funds on the same proportional basis if their percentage of the vote in the current election entitled them to a larger subsidy than the grant generated by their vote in the previous election.

In the primary election, presidential candidates were eligible for public matching funds if they fulfilled certain fundraising requirements. To qualify, a candidate had to raise at least $5,000 in contributions of $250 or less in at least twenty states. Eligible candidates would then receive public monies on a dollar-for-dollar basis for the first $250 contributed by an individual, provided that the contribution was received after January 1 of the year before the election year. The maximum amount a candidate could receive in such payments was half of the spending limit, or $5 million under the original terms of the act. In addition, national party committees were given the option of financing their nominating conventions with public funds. Major parties could receive the entire amount authorized by the spending limit ($2 million), while minor parties were eligible for lesser amounts based on their proportion of the vote in the previous election.

Finally, the bill included a number of amendments designed to strengthen the disclosure and enforcement procedures of the 1971 act. The most important of these was the provision creating the Federal Election Commission, a six-member, full-time, bipartisan agency responsible for administering election laws and implementing the public financing program. This agency was empowered to receive all campaign reports, promulgate rules and regulations, make special and regular reports to Congress and the president, conduct audits and investigations, subpoena witnesses and information, and seek civil injunctions to ensure compliance with the law.

To assist the Commission in its task, the amendments tightened the FECA's disclosure and reporting requirements. All candidates were required to establish one central campaign committee through which all contributions and expenditures had to be reported. They were also required to disclose the bank depositories authorized to receive campaign funds. The reporting procedures mandated that each campaign file a complete report of its financial activities with the Federal Election Commission within ten days of the close of each quarter and ten days before and thirty days after every election, unless the committee received or spent less than $1,000 in the quarter. In nonelection years, each committee had to file a year-end report of its receipts and expenditures. Furthermore, contributions of $1,000 or more received within fifteen days of an election had to be reported to the Commission within forty-eight hours.

The initial implementation of the act was complicated first by President Ford's delay in appointing members to the Federal Election Commission and then by the Supreme Court's decision in *Buckley* v. *Valeo,* 424 U.S. 1 (1976) (document 3.1), which deemed certain provisions unconstitutional and forced Congress to adopt further amendments in the midst of the 1976 elections. In particular, the Court ruled against the spending limits established for House and Senate candidates and the contribution limit for independent expenditures, which substantially weakened the potential efficacy of the act. The decision also struck down the original method of appointing members of the Federal Election Commission. Under the 1974 legislation, the president, the Speaker of the House, and the president pro tempore of the Senate each appointed two of the six commissioners. The Court ruled that this method was unconstitutional since four of the six members were appointed by Congress but exercised executive powers. As a result, the Federal Election Commission was prohibited from enforcing the law or certifying public matching fund payments until it was reconstituted under a constitutional appointment process. The law was changed to provide for appointment by the president with confirmation by the Senate. In May 1976, the Commission was reconstituted and resumed full activity.

In January 1976, the Supreme Court issued its opinion in *Buckley* v. *Valeo,* 424 U.S. 1 (1976) (document 3.1), which ruled unconstitutional several major provisions of the Federal Election Campaign Act Amendments of 1974 (document 2.9). The Court's decision forced Congress to reconsider the campaign finance legislation it had enacted less than two years earlier. Since the 1976 election was already under way, President Gerald Ford asked for a bill that simply reconstituted the Commission. But the Congress, still in the grips of a climate of reform, decided to draft a more extensive bill that included revisions in the public financing program, contribution limits, and disclosure procedures established under the 1974 amendments. As a result, the bill President Ford signed into law in May 1976 (Public Law 94-283) did more than revise the regulations to accommodate the Court's ruling.

The law's basic provision changed the method of appointing Federal Election Commissioners. The original process gave the President, Speaker of the House, and President pro tempore of the Senate the right to appoint two members apiece, each of different parties, subject to congressional approval. The new legislation called for the appointment of all six members by the President, subject to Senate confirmation. The act also increased the Commission's ability to enforce the law by granting it the exclusive authority to prosecute civil violations of the law and jurisdiction over violations previously covered only in the criminal code. But, at the same time, it placed checks on the Commission's ability to act by requiring an affirmative vote of four members to issue regulations and initiate civil actions, by restricting advisory opinions to specific fact situations, and by giving Congress the power to disapprove proposed regulations.

The Court also ruled that limits on contributions by candidates and members of their immediate families to their own campaigns were unconstitutional, unless a candidate had accepted public funding. The Congress therefore placed a new ceiling of $50,000 on such contributions, which applied only to presidential and vice presidential candidates who had received public funds. It also established limits on political contributions that were not considered in their previous legislation. The ceilings on individual contributions enacted under the 1974 act were retained and new limits of $5,000 per year on the amount an individual could donate to a political action committee and of $20,000 per year on the amount that could be given to a national party committee were adopted. The amount a political action committee could donate to a national party committee was set at $15,000 a year, and the Democratic and Republican Senatorial Campaign Committees were restricted to giving no more than $17,500 per year to a federal candidate. The act further stipulated that all political action committees created by a company or international union would be treated as a single committee for the purpose of determining compliance with contribution limits, to prevent these organizations from circumventing the law by creating multiple committees.

Since the Court struck down the 1974 law's limit on independent expenditures, the 1976 amendments included a number of reporting procedures designed to ensure the disclosure of independent spending. Any committee or individual spending more than $100 independently to advocate the election or defeat of a candidate was required to file a report of this spending with the Commission and declare, under penalty of perjury, that the expenditure was not made in collusion with a candidate. Labor unions, corporations, and membership organizations were required to report expenditures of more than $2,000 per election for communications to their stockholders or members that advocated the election or defeat of a specific candidate. In addition, any independent expenditure of $1,000 or more made within fifteen days of an election had to be reported to the Commission within twenty-four hours.

Other important changes affected the spending limits and public financing program enacted by the 1974 amendments. Congress created a minor loophole in the spending limits by exempting payments by candidate committees or national party committees for legal and accounting costs incurred through complying with the law. But each committee had to list these payments in its disclosure reports. The act also modified the provisions of the matching funds program in order to ensure that these subsidies did not encourage a losing candidate to remain in the race. Under the new provisions, a presidential candidate who received less than 10 percent of the vote in two consecutive primaries in which he or she ran would be ineligible for additional matching payments. These subsidies would be restored if that candidate received 20 percent of the vote in a later primary. The law further required that candidates who withdraw from the primary contest after receiving matching funds return any remaining public monies to the Treasury.

The Revenue Act of 1978 (Public Law 95-600) was signed into law by President Jimmy Carter on November 6, 1978. It altered the tax deductions and credits for political contributions established by the Revenue Act of 1971 (document 2.7) as modified by the Tariff Schedules Amendments of 1975. It eliminated the deduction for political giving and doubled the maximum tax credit to $50 on an individual return and $100 on a joint return. The credit was later repealed by the Tax Reform Act of 1986.

This change in the tax provisions for political contributions was adopted as a minor amendment to an $18.7 billion tax relief bill designed to offset social security and other tax increases anticipated for 1979. It was formed by a House-Senate compromise that sought to maintain an incentive for political giving while simplifying taxes and reducing the overall amount of the tax cut to meet administration budget objectives. The initial bill approved by the House repealed the deduction and retained the credit so as to provide some tax simplification, reduce tax liabilities, and maintain an incentive for political participation. The Senate amended the bill to retain the deduction and double the maximum tax credit "to further expand individual participation in the electoral process" by encouraging contributions. But members of the committee agreed to repeal the deduction if the House would accept the increase in the credit. The conference committee adopted this suggestion and included it in the bill that became law. The amendment helped to reduce the overall amount of the tax package by increasing tax revenues by a projected $3 million annually.

The Federal Election Campaign Act Amendments of 1979 (Public Law 96-187) were enacted in response to the criticisms levied against the campaign finance regulations after the 1976 and 1978 elections. Critics charged that the detailed reporting requirements forced candidates and political committees to engage in unnecessary and burdensome paperwork. They also noted that the law reduced the role of state and local party committees in presidential elections, since both 1976 candidates had chosen to concentrate their legally limited resources on media advertising rather than grass-roots political activities. The 1979 legislation was therefore designed to ease the reporting requirements imposed on candidates and political committees and to increase volunteer and grass-roots party activity in presidential campaigns. To ensure the legislation's quick passage, Congress considered only "noncontroversial" reforms acceptable to both Houses. The final bill, which was signed into law by President Jimmy Carter on January 8, 1980, contained fewer substantive changes than the previous revisions of the act.

Many of the act's provisions were directed toward streamlining disclosure procedures. The maximum number of reports a federal candidate had to file in a two-year election cycle was reduced from twenty-four to nine. The maximum number of reports required of a Senate candidate over the six-year election cycle was reduced from twenty-eight to seventeen. The law eliminated reporting requirements for candidates who spend or receive less than $5,000. It also eliminated these requirements for those local party committees receiving less than $5,000 a year; spending less than $1,000 a year in connection with a federal election; or spending less than $5,000 a year on certain voluntary activities, such as the purchase of buttons and bumper stickers or voter registration drives. Previously, all candidates and committees involved in federal elections had been required to file reports with the Federal Election Commission. For those candidates and committees not exempted from the disclosure provisions, the threshold amount for reportable contributions and expenditures was increased from $100 to $200. This increase substantially reduced the amount of information they were required to provide to the Commission. The threshold for disclosing independent expenditures was also increased, from $100 to $250.

To enhance the role of political parties in presidential general elections, the law exempted certain types of party-related spending from the expenditure ceilings. State and local party committees were allowed to spend unlimited amounts on voter registration and get-out-the-vote activities, provided such activities were primarily conducted on behalf of the party's presidential nominee. These committees were also allowed to spend unlimited amounts on materials related to grass-roots or volunteer activities (such as buttons, bumper stickers, posters, and brochures), provided the funds used were not drawn from contributions designated for a particular candidate (see chapter 6). The amendments sought to encourage volunteer activities further by increasing the amount a volunteer could spend on travel or home entertainment on behalf of a candidate without having to report the expenses from $500 to

$1,000 and from $1,000 to $2,000 for expenses incurred through activities undertaken on behalf of a political party.

The act also included a number of miscellaneous changes. It modified the Federal Election Commission Advisory Opinion procedures and clarified certain compliance and enforcement actions. It increased the public subsidy a major political party could receive to finance its national nominating convention from $2 million to $3 million. More important, it prohibited conversion of excess campaign funds to personal use by any federal candidate or officeholder except for members of Congress in office at the time the amendments were adopted. This was already prohibited by Senate rules, which disallowed the personal use of campaign funds by both sitting and retired members of the Senate. House rules only disallowed this use of campaign funds for retired members. Individuals serving in the Congress at the time the act was proposed were concerned that the redistricting that would occur after the 1980 election might increase their chances of defeat. Some members were therefore unwilling to extend this prohibition to their own campaign funds; they apparently looked forward to receiving excess campaign funds should they lose their bid for reelection. The House version of the bill thus exempted incumbent members from this prohibition, and this provision survived in the compromise version of the bill that was finally adopted. This exemption was finally abolished in 1995 when the Federal Election Commission promulgated "personal use" regulations to govern the expenditure of leftover campaign monies.

THE FIRST AMENDMENT AT WORK

CHAPTER 3

Constitutional Restrictions on Campaign Finance Regulation

CONTENTS

Constitutional Restrictions on Campaign Finance Regulation

INTRODUCTION BY DANIEL R. ORTIZ

One would search the Constitution in vain for any mention of "campaign finance," let alone "contributions," "expenditures," "soft money," or any of the other specialized terms in the campaign finance vocabulary. Yet despite this silence, the U.S. Supreme Court has firmly and repeatedly held that the Constitution greatly limits what Congress and the states can do. Believing that campaign finance regulations restrict political expression and so implicate the First Amendment, which says only that "Congress shall make no law . . . abridging the freedom of speech," the Court has subjected them to searching review.

In *Buckley* v. *Valeo* (424 U.S. 1 [1976]; document 3.1), the first and most important of the campaign finance cases, the Supreme Court created a framework that still guides analysis in this area. *Buckley* concerned a challenge to many of the 1974 amendments to the Federal Election Campaign Act (document 2.9). The challengers attacked, among other things, the amendments' limitations on various forms of election spending. In deciding this group of challenges, the Court distinguished between contributions and expenditures—a distinction that, although widely criticized at the time (and since), has remained the most important feature of the legal landscape.

As defined by *Buckley* and the later cases, a contribution represents money completely given over to another entity, whether to a party, candidate campaign, or political action committee (PAC). In other words, the donor retains no control over the use of the money; the entity receiving it decides how it

will be spent. An expenditure, on the other hand, represents money controlled and spent directly by the spender. It may be spent on someone else's behalf, of course, and usually is, but the spender makes all the decisions over its use. If the spender should coordinate its use with a campaign, however, it will be treated as a contribution.

In *Buckley,* the Supreme Court found that these two different forms of campaign spending reflected quite different First Amendment concerns. In the Court's view, contributions conveyed only the fact that a donor supports a candidate, not why the donor supports him or her. As a result, Congress could broadly limit these contributions. So long as Congress did not restrict contributions so severely that it starved campaigns or blocked the basic signal of support, Congress had great freedom to regulate. By contrast, the Court found that regulating expenditures raised more serious First Amendment concerns. Since, to the Court's mind, expenditures (unlike contributions) did convey *why* a spender supports or opposes a candidate, limiting them would necessarily restrict the quantity and quality of political discourse. The Court therefore subjected expenditure limitations to the most searching constitutional review. Finding no governmental interest sufficient to justify them, the Court struck them down.

This finding that no sufficient state interest justified limiting individual expenditures has greatly shaped this whole area of law. In fact, this one small part of the discussion in *Buckley* has by itself doomed many reform proposals. In upholding individual contribution limitations, the Court said that Congress could somewhat burden political expression in the name of preventing "corruption and the appearance of corruption spawned by the real or imagined coercive influence of large financial contributions on candidates' positions and on their actions if elected to office." This interest was strong enough to justify some expressive burdens. But the Court thought that expenditures posed a much more remote and speculative danger of quid pro quo corruption. This same goal—no matter how weighty in general—could not therefore justify expenditure limitations.

Congress had to find an interest more directly related to expenditures, and it did: "to equalize the relative ability of [individuals and groups] to affect the outcome of elections." The Court, however, found this interest troubling too—this time for a different reason. Although such equalization might well bear a direct relationship to expenditure limitations, the equalization goal itself was faulty. It was constitutionally impermissible. As the Court put it: "the concept that government may restrict the speech of some elements of our society in order to enhance the relative voice of others is wholly foreign to the First Amendment." This stinging rejection of equality concerns has made the First Amendment an insurmountable bar to many forms of campaign finance regulation. Congress, of course, can still regulate campaign finance, but it can do so only in the pursuit of other goals. But these permissible goals, particularly preventing corruption, cannot accomplish all the work reformers typically want.

One other move in *Buckley* has greatly shaped law in this area: the Court's emphasis on the need for clear rules. Worried that vagueness in some of the Federal Election Campaign Act's definitions might lead citizens to steer clear of speech that would be constitutionally permitted, the Court found it necessary to interpret these statutory provisions quite specifically. Moreover, since the clear, sharp definitions had to avoid any potential con-

stitutional problems in application, the Court "erred" on the side of free expression. As a result, the Court narrowed the statute's coverage quite dramatically. For example, the Court interpreted the Act's central provision limiting "any expenditure . . . relative to a clearly identified candidate" to require mention of "explicit words of advocacy of election or defeat,'" such as "vote for," "elect," "vote against," and "defeat." Requiring these magic words protected free speech, to be sure. But requiring them also meant that much spending clearly intended to benefit or harm particular candidates would escape regulation.

The next major case in this area, *First National Bank of Boston* v. *Bellotti* (435 U.S. 765 [1978]; document 3.2), followed *Buckley* by two years. It asked whether a state could treat corporations differently. That is, could a state prohibit corporations from making expenditures, even though under *Buckley* it could not prohibit individuals from doing so? The Court answered no: a state could bar neither individual nor corporate expenditures. But the Court's holding was limited by the facts of the case: *Bellotti* concerned a *referendum*, not a *candidate*, election. Since a corporation cannot seek a quid pro quo from a ballot measure, the Court held, states did not need to ban corporate expenditures in referendum elections to prevent the one type of corruption *Buckley* had identified as a constitutionally permissible concern.

Not until 1986 did the Court begin to address the issue *Bellotti* left open: the extent to which government could regulate corporate expenditures in *candidate* elections. In two cases, *Federal Election Commission* v. *Massachusetts Citizens for Life*, 479 U.S. 238 (1986) (*MCFL*; see document 7.4) and *Austin* v. *Michigan State Chamber of Commerce* (494 U.S. 652 [1990]; document 3.3), the Court developed some complex rules. In *MCFL*, which is discussed extensively in the excerpts from *Austin*, the Federal Election Commission (FEC) sued Massachusetts Citizens for Life (MCFL), a nonprofit corporation organized to oppose abortion. The FEC claimed that by spending directly from its treasury to publish and widely distribute a list of candidates for state and federal office who supported its views MCFL had made an illegal corporate expenditure. The Court disagreed. At least as applied to "ideological," noneconomic corporations like MCFL, the federal prohibition against spending from the corporate treasury violated the First Amendment. The Court left open the question of whether the First Amendment similarly barred prohibiting expenditures by everyday "business" corporations.

In *Austin*, the Court took up this larger question. The Michigan Chamber of Commerce challenged a Michigan state law prohibiting corporations from making expenditures in support of state candidates. Although the Supreme Court found that the prohibition burdened expressive activity and thus needed a "compelling state interest" to withstand constitutional scrutiny, the state law passed muster. The surprise lay in the compelling interest the Court found at work: preventing corruption or the appearance of corruption. *Buckley*, of course, had held this interest compelling. Indeed, it found it the only permissible interest at work there. But *Buckley* had also found this interest insufficiently related to expenditures to justify their restriction. Why was corruption now sufficiently related to expenditures?

The difference sprang from a change in the notion of corruption. The *Austin* Court radically expanded it. Instead of covering just the danger of a quid pro quo—the exchange of spending in an election for later support on legislation—corruption grew to include "the corrosive and distorting effects of immense aggregations of wealth that are accumulated with the help of the corporate form and that have little or no correlation to the public's support for the corporation's political ideas." Corporate expenditures, the Court found, definitely pose the danger of corruption in this broader sense. The problem, though, as Justice Antonin Scalia argued forcefully in his dissent, is that this change undermines a critical feature of *Buckley*. Such a broad interpretation of corruption effectively rehabilitates

the equalization rationale rejected in *Buckley* as "wholly foreign to the First Amendment." *Austin* seems to say that in some cases Congress may legislate to equalize, just so long as it describes itself as doing something else. At the very least this move introduces great tension and some confusion into the jurisprudence.

The most recent campaign finance case, *Colorado Republican Federal Campaign Committee* v. *Federal Election Commission* (116 S. Ct. 2309 [1996]; document 3.4), considered the extent to which the First Amendment allows Congress to regulate political party spending on behalf of or against candidates. Because the Court splintered four ways, the case raises more issues than it answers. It also reveals the great differences of opinion over fundamental questions still present after all these years. Justice Stephen G. Breyer, joined by Justices Sandra Day O'Connor and David H. Souter, decided the case in such a way as to avoid the important First Amendment issue entirely. Finding (despite a presumption to the contrary) that the political party's expenditures were truly independent of its candidates, Justice Breyer held that a straightforward application of *Buckley* barred their limitation. However, he left open the question of whether the First Amendment would bar limiting party expenditures that were actually coordinated with a candidate.

By contrast, Justice John Paul Stevens together with Justice Ruth Bader Ginsberg held that Congress could limit this type of party expenditure. Congress and the FEC, they thought, could reasonably presume that party expenditures like this were not truly independent and could constitutionally regulate them as coordinated spending. Justice Anthony M. Kennedy, with Chief Justice William H. Rehnquist and Justice Scalia, came to exactly the opposite legal conclusion. They held that the First Amendment prevents Congress from limiting party spending on behalf of or against candidates, even when the expenditures are actually coordinated. They found no meaningful difference between party spending coordinated with a candidate and the candidate's own spending, and, since *Buckley* barred limiting the latter, they believed it should bar limiting the former as well.

Justice Clarence Thomas's opinion proved the most provocative. He found the limit unconstitutional on two different grounds. First, together with Chief Justice Rehnquist and Justice Scalia, Justice Thomas found that regulating party expenditures on behalf of or against candidates failed to prevent corruption—the single goal that *Buckley* had held permissible. Party spending on behalf of a candidate, he argued, represents about the least corrupting form of political spending there can be. Second, in a part of the opinion representing his own views only, Justice Thomas argued that the Court should discard *Buckley*'s central distinction between contributions and expenditures. Believing that expenditures and contributions promote the same kinds of political expression and that Congress has no better reason for regulating one than the other, he would prohibit limitations on both.

The *Colorado Republican* case represents a troubling last word on the constitutionality of campaign finance regulation. Although the case did answer the narrowest possible construction of the question before it, it left unsettled the larger issue of whether Congress could regulate political party expenditures actually coordinated with the party's candidates. Even more important, the Court's deep fragmentation of opinion as to first principles created much uncertainty about the future of campaign finance reform. It is now somewhat less clear than before which reforms will pass constitutional muster.

There is also now some question as to the Court's capacity to guide in this area. In the earlier cases, the justices disagreed but they at least produced majority opinions whose reasoning bound and guided lower courts. In the *Colorado Republican* case, however, disagreement ran so deep that an authoritative majority opinion proved impossible to reach. Are the justices still capable of laying down rules, as in *Buckley*, or only of producing widely disharmonious individual opinions that provide little general guidance for the future? Few areas of modern constitutional law have produced such confusion.

In 1974, Congress extensively amended the Federal Election Campaign Act (document 2.9). The amendments, among other things, tightened disclosure requirements and limited contributions and expenditures in federal elections, provided public financing for presidential general and, to a lesser extent, primary elections, and created the Federal Election Commission to administer and enforce most federal campaign finance requirements. The major provisions of the law were quickly challenged and the Supreme Court ruled on them in the following case. Because the case is so long, exceeding 290 pages in the official reports, it has been heavily excerpted and includes only that portion discussing contribution and expenditure limitations. It is the shadow of this part of the opinion that stretches so far over subsequent cases.

PER CURIAM.

[This case] present[s] constitutional challenges to the key provisions of the Federal Election Campaign Act . . . as amended in 1974.

[The chief provisions provide that] . . . individual political contributions are limited to $1,000 to any single candidate per election, with an overall annual limitation of $25,000 by any contributor; independent expenditures by individuals and groups "relative to a clearly identified candidate" are limited to $1,000 a year; [and] campaign spending by candidates for various federal offices and spending for national conventions by political parties are subject to prescribed limits. . . .

I. CONTRIBUTION AND EXPENDITURE LIMITATIONS

. . .

A. General Principles

The Act's contribution and expenditure limitations operate in an area of the most fundamental First Amendment activities. Discussion of public issues and debate on the qualifications of candidates are integral to the operation of the system of government established by our Constitution.

. . .

A restriction on the amount of money a person or group can spend on political communication during a campaign necessarily reduces the quantity of expression by restricting the number of issues discussed, the depth of their exploration, and the size of the audience reached.[1] This is because virtually every means of communicating ideas in today's mass society requires the expenditure of money. The distribution of the humblest handbill or leaflet entails printing, paper, and circulation costs. Speeches and rallies generally necessitate hiring a hall and publicizing the event. The electorate's increasing dependence on television, radio, and other mass media for news and information has made these expensive modes of communication indispensable instruments of effective political speech.

The expenditure limitations contained in the Act represent substantial, rather than merely theoretical, restraints on the quantity and diversity of political speech. The $1,000 ceiling on spending "relative to a clearly identified candidate," would appear to exclude all citizens and groups except candidates, political parties, and the institutional press from any significant use of the most effective modes of communication. Although the Act's limitations on expenditures by campaign organizations and political parties provide substantially greater room for discussion and debate, they would have required restrictions in the scope of a number of past congressional and Presidential campaigns and would operate to constrain campaigning by candidates who raise sums in excess of the spending ceiling.

By contrast with a limitation upon expenditures for political expression, a limitation upon the amount that any one person or group may contribute to a candidate or political committee entails only a marginal restriction upon the contributor's ability to engage in free communication. A contribution serves as a general expression of support for the candidate and his views, but does not communicate the underlying basis for the support. The quantity of communication by the contributor does not increase perceptibly with the size of his contribution, since the expression rests solely on the undifferentiated, symbolic act of contributing. At most, the size of the contribution provides a very rough index of the intensity of the contributor's support for the candidate. A limitation on the amount of money a person may give to a candidate or campaign organization thus involves little direct restraint on his political communication, for it permits the symbolic expression of support evidenced by a contribution but does not in any way infringe the contributor's freedom to discuss candidates and issues. While contributions may result in political expression if spent by a candidate or an association to present views to the voters, the transformation of contributions into political debate involves speech by someone other than the contributor.

Given the important role of contributions in financing political campaigns, contribution restrictions could have a severe impact on political dialogue if the limitations prevented candidates and political committees from amassing the resources necessary for effective advocacy. There is no indication, however, that the contribution limitations imposed by the Act would have any dramatic adverse effect on the funding of campaigns and political associations. The overall effect of the Act's contribution ceilings is merely to require candidates and political committees to raise funds from a greater number of persons and to compel people who would otherwise contribute amounts greater than the statutory limits to expend such funds on direct political expression, rather than to reduce the total amount of money potentially available to promote political expression.

---

1. Being free to engage in unlimited political expression subject to a ceiling on expenditures is like being free to drive an automobile as far and as often as one desires on a single tank of gasoline.

The Act's contribution and expenditure limitations also impinge on protected associational freedoms. Making a contribution, like joining a political party, serves to affiliate a person with a candidate. In addition, it enables like-minded persons to pool their resources in furtherance of common political goals. The Act's contribution ceilings thus limit one important means of associating with a candidate or committee, but leave the contributor free to become a member of any political association and to assist personally in the association's efforts on behalf of candidates. And the Act's contribution limitations permit associations and candidates to aggregate large sums of money to promote effective advocacy. By contrast, the Act's $1,000 limitation on independent expenditures "relative to a clearly identified candidate" precludes most associations from effectively amplifying the voice of their adherents, the original basis for the recognition of First Amendment protection of the freedom of association. . . .

In sum, although the Act's contribution and expenditure limitations both implicate fundamental First Amendment interests, its expenditure ceilings impose significantly more severe restrictions on protected freedoms of political expression and association than do its limitations on financial contributions.

B. Contribution Limitations

1. The $1,000 Limitation on Contributions by Individuals and Groups to Candidates and Authorized Campaign Committees. Section 608 (b) provides, with certain limited exceptions, that "no person shall make contributions to any candidate with respect to any election for Federal office which, in the aggregate, exceed $1,000." The statute defines "person" broadly to include "an individual, partnership, committee, association, corporation or any other organization or group of persons." The limitation reaches a gift, subscription, loan, advance, deposit of anything of value, or promise to give a contribution, made for the purpose of influencing a primary election, a Presidential preference primary, or a general election for any federal office. The $1,000 ceiling applies regardless of whether the contribution is given to the candidate, to a committee authorized in writing by the candidate to accept contributions on his behalf, or indirectly via earmarked gifts passed through an intermediary to the candidate. The restriction applies to aggregate amounts contributed to the candidate for each election—with primaries, runoff elections, and general elections counted separately and all Presidential primaries held in any calendar year treated together as a single election campaign.

Appellants contend that the $1,000 contribution ceiling unjustifiably burdens First Amendment freedoms, employs overbroad dollar limits, and discriminates against candidates opposing incumbent officeholders and against minor-party candidates in violation of the Fifth Amendment. We address each of these claims of invalidity in turn.

(a). As the general discussion in Part I-A, *supra*, indicated, the primary First Amendment problem raised by the Act's contribution limitations is their restriction of one aspect of the contributor's freedom of political association.

. . .

Appellees argue that the Act's restrictions on large campaign contributions are justified by three governmental interests. According to the parties and *amici*, the primary interest served by the limitations and, indeed, by the Act as a whole, is the prevention of corruption and the appearance of corruption spawned by the real or imagined coercive influence of large financial contributions on candidates' positions and on their actions if elected to office. Two "ancillary" interests underlying the Act are also allegedly furthered by the $1,000 limits on contributions. First, the limits serve to mute the voices of affluent persons and groups in the election process and thereby to equalize the relative ability of all citizens to affect the outcome of elections. Second, it is argued, the ceilings may to some extent act as a brake on the skyrocketing cost of political campaigns and thereby serve to open the political system more widely to candidates without access to sources of large amounts of money.

It is unnecessary to look beyond the Act's primary purpose—to limit the actuality and appearance of corruption resulting from large individual financial contributions—in order to find a constitutionally sufficient justification for the $1,000 contribution limitation. Under a system of private financing of elections, a candidate lacking immense personal or family wealth must depend on financial contributions from others to provide the resources necessary to conduct a successful campaign. The increasing importance of the communications media and sophisticated mass-mailing and polling operations to effective campaigning make the raising of large sums of money an ever more essential ingredient of an effective candidacy. To the extent that large contributions are given to secure political *quid pro quo's* from current and potential office holders, the integrity of our system of representative democracy is undermined. Although the scope of such pernicious practices can never be reliably ascertained, the deeply disturbing examples surfacing after the 1972 election demonstrate that the problem is not an illusory one.

Of almost equal concern as the danger of actual *quid pro quo* arrangements is the impact of the appearance of corruption stemming from public awareness of the opportunities for abuse inherent in a regime of large individual financial contributions. . . . Congress could legitimately conclude that the avoidance of the appearance of improper influence "is also critical . . . if confidence in the system of representative Government is not to be eroded to a disastrous extent."

Appellants contend that the contribution limitations must be invalidated because bribery laws and narrowly drawn disclosure requirements constitute a less restrictive means of dealing with "proven and suspected *quid pro quo* arrangements." But laws making criminal the giving and taking of bribes deal with only the most blatant and specific attempts of those with money to influence governmental action. And while disclosure requirements serve the many salutary purposes discussed elsewhere in this opinion, Congress was surely entitled to conclude that disclosure was only a partial measure, and that contribution ceilings were a necessary legislative concomitant to deal with the reality or appearance of corruption inherent in a system permitting unlimited financial contributions, even when the identities of the contributors and the amounts of their contributions are fully disclosed.

The Act's $1,000 contribution limitation focuses precisely on the problem of large campaign contributions—the narrow aspect of political association where the actuality and potential for corruption have been identified—while leaving persons free to engage in independent political expression, to associate actively through volunteering their services, and to assist to a limited but nonetheless substantial extent in supporting candidates and committees with financial resources. Significantly, the Act's contribution limitations in themselves do not undermine to any material degree the potential for robust and effective discussion of candidates and campaign issues by individual citizens, associations, the institutional press, candidates, and political parties.

We find that, under the rigorous standard of review established by our prior decisions, the weighty interests served by restricting the size of financial contributions to political candidates are sufficient to justify the limited effect upon First Amendment freedoms caused by the $1,000 contribution ceiling.

. . .

C. Expenditure Limitations

The Act's expenditure ceilings impose direct and substantial restraints on the quantity of political speech. The most drastic of the limitations restricts individuals and groups, including political parties that fail to place a candidate on the ballot to an expenditure of $1,000 "relative to a clearly identified candidate during a calendar year." Other expenditure ceilings limit spending by candidates, their campaigns, and political parties in connection with election campaigns. It is clear that a primary effect of these expenditure limitations is to restrict the quantity of campaign speech by individuals, groups, and candidates. The restrictions, while neutral as to the ideas expressed, limit political expression "at the core of our electoral process and of the First Amendment freedoms."

1. The $1,000 Limitation on Expenditures "Relative to a Clearly Identified Candidate." Section 608 (e)(1) provides that "No person may make any expenditure . . . relative to a clearly identified candidate during a calendar year which, when added to all other expenditures made by such person during the year advocating the election or defeat of such candidate, exceeds $1,000." The plain effect of § 608 (e)(1) is to prohibit all individuals, who are neither candidates nor owners of institutional press facilities, and all groups, except political parties and campaign organizations, from voicing their views "relative to a clearly identified candidate" through means that entail aggregate expenditures of more than $1,000 during a calendar year. The provision, for example, would make it a federal criminal offense for a person or association to place a single one-quarter page advertisement "relative to a clearly identified candidate" in a major metropolitan newspaper.

Before examining the interests advanced in support of § 608 (e)(1)'s expenditure ceiling, consideration must be given to appellants' contention that the provision is unconstitutionally vague. Close examination of the specificity of the statutory limitation is required where, as here, the legislation imposes criminal penalties in an area permeated by First Amendment interests. . . .

The key operative language of the provision limits "any expenditure . . . relative to a clearly identified candidate." Although "expenditure," "clearly identified," and "candidate" are defined in the Act, there is no definition clarifying what expenditures are "relative to" a candidate. The use of so indefinite a phrase as "relative to" a candidate fails to clearly mark the boundary between permissible and impermissible speech, unless other portions of § 608 (e)(1) make sufficiently explicit the range of expenditures covered by the limitation. The section prohibits "any expenditure . . . relative to a clearly identified candidate during a calendar year which, *when added to all other expenditures . . . advocating the election or defeat of such candidate,* exceeds $1,000." (Emphasis added.) This context clearly permits, if indeed it does not require, the phrase "relative to" a candidate to be read to mean "advocating the election or defeat of" a candidate.

But while such a construction of § 608 (e)(1) refocuses the vagueness question, the Court of Appeals was mistaken in thinking that this construction eliminates the problem of unconstitutional vagueness altogether. For the distinction between discussion of issues and candidates and advocacy of election or defeat of candidates may often dissolve in practical application. Candidates, especially incumbents, are intimately tied to public issues involving legislative proposals and governmental actions. Not only do candidates campaign on the basis of their positions on various public issues, but campaigns themselves generate issues of public interest. In an analogous context, this Court in *Thomas* v. *Collins,* 323 U.S. 516 (1945) observed:

Whether words intended and designed to fall short of invitation would miss that mark is a question both of intent and of effect. No speaker, in such circumstances, safely could assume that anything he might say upon the general subject would not be understood by some as an invitation. In short, the supposedly clear-cut distinction between discussion, laudation, general advocacy, and solicitation puts the speaker in these circumstances wholly at the mercy of the varied understanding of his hearers and consequently of whatever inference may be drawn as to his intent and meaning.

Such a distinction offers no security for free discussion. In these conditions it blankets with uncertainty whatever may be said. It compels the speaker to hedge and trim.

The constitutional deficiencies described in *Thomas* v. *Collins* can be avoided only by reading § 608 (e)(1) as limited to communications that include explicit words of advocacy of election or defeat of a candidate, much as the definition of "clearly identified" in § 608 (e)(2) requires that an explicit and unambiguous reference to the candidate appear as part of the communication. This is the reading of the provision suggested by the nongovernmental appellees in arguing that "[f]unds spent to propagate one's views on issues without expressly calling for a candidate's election or defeat are thus not covered." We agree that, in order to preserve the provision against invalidation on vagueness grounds, § 608 (e)(1) must be construed to apply only to expenditures for communications that in express terms advocate the election or defeat of a clearly identified candidate for federal office.[2]

We turn then to the basic First Amendment question—whether § 608 (e)(1) even as thus narrowly and explicitly construed, impermissibly burdens the constitutional right of free expression. . . .

The discussion in Part I-A, *supra,* explains why the Act's expenditure limitations impose far greater restraints on the freedom of speech and association than do its contribution limitations. The markedly greater burden on basic freedoms caused by § 608 (e)(1) thus cannot be sustained simply by invoking the interest in maximizing the effectiveness of the less intrusive contribution limitations. Rather, the constitutionality of § 608 (e)(1) turns on whether the governmental interests advanced in its support satisfy the exacting scrutiny applicable to limitations on core First Amendment rights of political expression.

We find that the governmental interest in preventing corruption and the appearance of corruption is inadequate to justify § 608 (e)(1)'s ceiling on independent expenditures. First, assuming, *arguendo,* that large independent expenditures pose the same dangers of actual or apparent *quid pro quo* arrangements as do large contributions, § 608 (e)(1) does not provide an answer that sufficiently relates to the elimination of those dangers. Unlike the contribution limitations' total ban on the giving of large amounts of

---

2. This construction would restrict the application of § 608 (e)(1) to communications containing express words of advocacy of election or defeat, such as "vote for," "elect," "support," "cast your ballot for," "Smith for Congress," "vote against," "defeat," "reject."

money to candidates, § 608 (e)(1) prevents only some large expenditures. So long as persons and groups eschew expenditures that, in express terms advocate the election or defeat of a clearly identified candidate, they are free to spend as much as they want to promote the candidate and his views. The exacting interpretation of the statutory language necessary to avoid unconstitutional vagueness thus undermines the limitation's effectiveness as a loophole-closing provision by facilitating circumvention by those seeking to exert improper influence upon a candidate or officeholder. It would naively underestimate the ingenuity and resourcefulness of persons and groups desiring to buy influence to believe that they would have much difficulty devising expenditures that skirted the restriction on express advocacy of election or defeat but nevertheless benefited the candidate's campaign. Yet no substantial societal interest would be served by a loophole-closing provision designed to check corruption that permitted unscrupulous persons and organizations to expend unlimited sums of money in order to obtain improper influence over candidates for elective office.

Second, quite apart from the shortcomings of § 608 (e)(1) in preventing any abuses generated by large independent expenditures, the independent advocacy restricted by the provision does not presently appear to pose dangers of real or apparent corruption comparable to those identified with large campaign contributions. The parties defending § 608 (e)(1) contend that it is necessary to prevent would-be contributors from avoiding the contribution limitations by the simple expedient of paying directly for media advertisements or for other portions of the candidate's campaign activities. They argue that expenditures controlled by or coordinated with the candidate and his campaign might well have virtually the same value to the candidate as a contribution and would pose similar dangers of abuse. Yet such controlled or coordinated expenditures are treated as contributions rather than expenditures under the Act. Section 608 (b)'s contribution ceilings rather than § 608 (e)(1)'s independent expenditure limitation prevent attempts to circumvent the Act through prearranged or coordinated expenditures amounting to disguised contributions. By contrast, § 608(e)(1) limits expenditures for express advocacy of candidates made totally independently of the candidate and his campaign. Unlike contributions, such independent expenditures may well provide little assistance to the candidate's campaign and indeed may prove counterproductive. The absence of prearrangement and coordination of an expenditure with the candidate or his agent not only undermines the value of the expenditure to the candidate, but also alleviates the danger that expenditures will be given as a *quid pro quo* for improper commitments from the candidate. Rather than preventing circumvention of the contribution limitations, § 608 (e)(1) severely restricts all independent advocacy despite its substantially diminished potential for abuse.

While the independent expenditure ceiling thus fails to serve any substantial governmental interest in stemming the reality or appearance of corruption in the electoral process, it heavily burdens core First Amendment expression. . . . Advocacy of the election or defeat of candidates for federal office is no less entitled to protection under the First Amendment than the discussion of political policy generally or advocacy of the passage or defeat of legislation.

It is argued, however, that the ancillary governmental interest in equalizing the relative ability of individuals and groups to influence the outcome of elections serves to justify the limitation on express advocacy of the election or defeat of candidates imposed by § 608 (e)(1)'s expenditure ceiling. But the concept that government may restrict the speech of some elements of our society in order to enhance the relative voice of others is wholly foreign to the First Amendment, which was designed "to secure 'the widest possible dissemination of information from diverse and antagonistic sources,'" and "to assure unfettered interchange of ideas for the bringing about of political and social changes desired by the people." The First Amendment's protection against governmental abridgment of free expression cannot properly be made to depend on a person's financial ability to engage in public discussion.

. . .

For the reasons stated, we conclude that § 608 (e)(1)'s independent expenditure limitation is unconstitutional under the First Amendment.

2. Limitation on Expenditures by Candidates from Personal or Family Resources. The Act also sets limits on expenditures by a candidate "from his personal funds, or the personal funds of his immediate family, in connection with his campaigns during any calendar year." § 608 (a)(1). These ceilings vary from $50,000 for Presidential or Vice Presidential candidates to $35,000 for senatorial candidates, and $25,000 for most candidates for the House of Representatives.

The ceiling on personal expenditures by candidates on their own behalf, like the limitations on independent expenditures contained in § 608 (e)(1), imposes a substantial restraint on the ability of persons to engage in protected First Amendment expression. The candidate, no less than any other person, has a First Amendment right to engage in the discussion of public issues and vigorously and tirelessly to advocate his own election and the election of other candidates. Indeed, it is of particular importance that candidates have the unfettered opportunity to make their views known so that the electorate may intelligently evaluate the candidates' personal qualities and their positions on vital public issues before choosing among them on election day. . . . Section 608 (a)'s ceiling on personal expenditures by a candidate in furtherance of his own candidacy thus clearly and directly interferes with constitutionally protected freedoms.

The primary governmental interest served by the Act—the prevention of actual and apparent corruption of the political process—does not support the limitation on the candidate's expenditure of his own personal funds. As the Court of Appeals concluded: "Manifestly, the core problem of avoiding undisclosed and undue influence on candidates from outside interests has lesser application when the monies involved come from the candidate himself or from his immediate family." Indeed, the use of personal funds reduces the candidate's dependence on outside contributions and thereby counteracts the coercive pressures and attendant risks of abuse to which the Act's contribution limitations are directed.

The ancillary interest in equalizing the relative financial resources of candidates competing for elective office, therefore, provides the sole relevant rationale for § 608 (a)'s expenditure ceiling. That interest is clearly not sufficient to justify the provision's infringement of fundamental First Amendment rights. First, the limitation may fail to promote financial equality among candidates. A candidate who spends less of his personal resources on his campaign may nonetheless outspend his rival as a result of more successful fundraising efforts. Indeed, a candidate's personal wealth may impede his efforts to persuade others that he needs their financial contributions or volunteer efforts to conduct an effective campaign. Second, and more fundamentally, the First Amendment simply cannot tolerate § 608 (a)'s restriction upon the freedom of a candidate to speak without legislative limit on behalf of his own candidacy. We therefore hold that § 608 (a)'s restriction on a candidate's personal expenditures is unconstitutional.

3. Limitations on Campaign Expenditures. Section 608 (c) places limitations on overall campaign expenditures by candidates seeking nomination for election and election to federal office.

. . .

No governmental interest that has been suggested is sufficient to justify the restriction on the quantity of political expression imposed by § 608 (c)'s campaign expenditure limitations. The major evil associated with rapidly increasing campaign expenditures is the danger of candidate dependence on large contributions. The interest in alleviating the corrupting influence of large contributions is served by the Act's contribution limitations and disclosure provisions, rather than by § 608 (c)'s campaign expenditure ceilings. The Court of Appeals' assertion that the expenditure restrictions are necessary to reduce the incentive to circumvent direct contribution limits is not persuasive. There is no indication that the substantial criminal penalties for violating the contribution ceilings, combined with the political repercussion of such violations, will be insufficient to police the contribution provisions. Extensive reporting, auditing, and disclosure requirements applicable to both contributions and expenditures by political campaigns are designed to facilitate the detection of illegal contributions. Moreover, as the Court of Appeals noted, the Act permits an officeholder or successful candidate to retain contributions in excess of the expenditure ceiling and to use these funds for "any other lawful purpose." This provision undercuts whatever marginal role the expenditure limitations might otherwise play in enforcing the contribution ceilings.

The interest in equalizing the financial resources of candidates competing for federal office is no more convincing a justification for restricting the scope of federal election campaigns. Given the limitation on the size of outside contributions, the financial resources available to a candidate's campaign, like the number of volunteers recruited, will normally vary with the size and intensity of the candidate's support. There is nothing invidious, improper, or unhealthy in permitting such funds to be spent to carry the candidate's message to the electorate. Moreover, the equalization of permissible campaign expenditures might serve not to equalize the opportunities of all candidates but to handicap a candidate, who lacked substantial name recognition or exposure of his views before the start of the campaign.

The campaign expenditure ceilings appear to be designed primarily to serve the governmental interests in reducing the allegedly skyrocketing costs of political campaigns. . . . [However,] the mere growth in the cost of federal election campaigns in and of itself provides no basis for governmental restrictions on the quantity of campaign spending and the resulting limitation on the scope of federal campaigns. The First Amendment denies government the power to determine that spending to promote one's political views is wasteful, excessive, or unwise. In the free society ordained by our Constitution, it is not the government but the people—individually as citizens and candidates and collectively as associations and political committees—who must retain control over the quantity and range of debate on public issues in a political campaign.

For these reasons we hold that § 608 (c) is constitutionally invalid.

. . .

DISSENT: MR. CHIEF JUSTICE [Warren E.] BURGER, concurring in part and dissenting in part.

. . .

CONTRIBUTION AND EXPENDITURE LIMITS

I agree fully with that part of the Court's opinion that holds unconstitutional the limitations the Act puts on campaign expenditures which "place substantial and direct restrictions on the ability of candidates, citizens, and associations to engage in protected political expression, restrictions that the First Amendment cannot tolerate." Yet when it approves similarly stringent limitations on contributions, the Court ignores the reasons it finds so persuasive in the context of expenditures. For me contributions and expenditures are two sides of the same First Amendment coin.

By limiting campaign contributions, the Act restricts the amount of money that will be spent on political activity—and does so directly. Appellees argue, as the Court notes, that these limits will "act as a brake on the skyrocketing cost of political campaigns." In treating campaign expenditure limitations, the Court says that the "First Amendment denies government the power to determine that spending to promote one's political views is wasteful, excessive, or unwise." Limiting contributions, as a practical matter, will limit expenditures and will put an effective ceiling on the amount of political activity and debate that the Government will permit to take place. The argument that the ceiling is not, after all, very low as matters now stand gives little comfort for the future, since the Court elsewhere notes the rapid inflation in the cost of political campaigning.

The Court attempts to separate the two communicative aspects of political contributions—the "moral" support that the gift itself conveys, which the Court suggests is the same whether the gift is $10 or $10,000, and the fact that money translates into communication. The Court dismisses the effect of the limitations on the second aspect of contributions: "[T]he transformation of contributions into political debate involves speech by someone other than the contributor." On this premise—that contribution limitations restrict only the speech of "someone other than the contributor"—rests the Court's justification for treating contributions differently from expenditures. The premise is demonstrably flawed; the contribution limitations will, in specific instances, limit exactly the same political activity that the expenditure ceilings limit, and at least one of the "expenditure" limitations the Court finds objectionable operates precisely like the "contribution" limitations.

The Court's attempt to distinguish the communication inherent in political contributions from the speech aspects of political expenditures simply "will not wash." We do little but engage in word games unless we recognize that people—candidates and contributors—spend money on political activity because they wish to communicate ideas, and their constitutional interest in doing so is precisely the same whether they or someone else utters the words.

. . .

MR. JUSTICE [Byron] WHITE, concurring in part and dissenting in part.

. . .

The . . . limitations on contributions and expenditures are challenged as invalid abridgments of the right of free speech protected by the First Amendment. I would reject these challenges. . . . I am . . . in agreement with the Court's judgment upholding the limitations on contributions. I dissent, however, from the Court's view that the expenditure limitations of 18 U.S.C. §§ 608 (c) and (e) violate the First Amendment.

. . .

In the interest of preventing undue influence that large contributors would have or that the public might think they would have, the Court upholds the provision that an individual may not give to a candidate, or spend on his behalf if requested or authorized by the candidate to do so, more than $1,000 in any one election. This limitation is valid although it imposes a low ceiling on what individuals may deem to be their most effective means of supporting or speaking on behalf of the candidate—i. e., financial support given directly to the candidate. The Court thus accepts the congressional judgment that the evils of unlimited contributions are sufficiently threatening to warrant restriction regardless of the impact of the limits on the contributor's opportunity for effective speech and in turn on the total volume of the candidate's political communications by reason of his inability to accept large sums from those willing to give.

. . .

It would make little sense to me, and apparently made none to Congress, to limit the amounts an individual may give to a candidate or spend with his approval but fail to limit the amounts that could be spent on his behalf. Yet the Court permits the former while striking down the latter limitation. No more than $1,000 may be given to a candidate or spent at his request or with his approval or cooperation; but otherwise, apparently, a contributor is to be constitutionally protected in spending unlimited amounts of money in support of his chosen candidate or candidates.

. . .

After *Buckley* (document 3.1), several large questions remained unsettled, most notably, the extent to which the First Amendment restricted regulation of corporate and labor spending on campaigns. In *Bellotti*, the Supreme Court took up this issue in the context of a referendum (not a candidate) election.

MR. JUSTICE [Lewis F.] POWELL Jr. delivered the opinion of the Court.

. . .

I

[A Massachusetts statute prohibits] . . . corporations, from making contributions or expenditures "for the purpose of . . . influencing or affecting the vote on any question submitted to the voters, other than one materially affecting any of the property, business or assets of the corporation." The statute further specifies that "[no] question submitted to the voters solely concerning the taxation of the income, property or transactions of individuals shall be deemed materially to affect the property, business or assets of the corporation." . . .

Appellants[, several national banking associations and banking corporations,] wanted to spend money to publicize their views on a proposed constitutional amendment that was to be submitted to the voters as a ballot question at a general election on November 2, 1976. The amendment would have permitted the legislature to impose a graduated tax on the income of individuals.

. . .

III

The court below framed the principal question in this case as whether and to what extent corporations have First Amendment rights. We believe that the court posed the wrong question. The Constitution often protects interests broader than those of the party seeking their vindication. The First Amendment, in particular, serves significant societal interests. The proper question therefore is not whether corporations "have" First Amendment rights and, if so, whether they are coextensive with those of natural persons. Instead, the question must be whether [the statute] abridges expression that the First Amendment was meant to protect. We hold that it does.

A

The speech proposed by appellants is at the heart of the First Amendment's protection.

. . .

If the speakers here were not corporations, no one would suggest that the State could silence their proposed speech. It is the type of speech indispensable to decisionmaking in a democracy, and this is no less true because the speech comes from a corporation rather than an individual. The inherent worth of the speech in terms of its capacity for informing the public does not depend upon the identity of its source, whether corporation, association, union, or individual.

. . .

The question in this case, simply put, is whether the corporate identity of the speaker deprives this proposed speech of what otherwise would be its clear entitlement to protection. We turn now to that question.

. . .

[Footnote in original: . . . In cases where corporate speech has been denied the shelter of the First Amendment, there is no suggestion that the reason was because a corporation rather than an individual or association was involved. . . .]

. . .

C

We . . . find no support in the First or Fourteenth Amendment, or in the decisions of this Court, for the proposition that speech that otherwise would be within the protection of the First Amendment loses that protection simply because its source is a corporation that cannot prove, to the satisfaction of a court, a material effect on its business or property. The "materially affecting" requirement is not an identification of the boundaries of corporate speech etched by the Constitution itself. Rather, it amounts to an impermissible legislative prohibition of speech based on the identity of the interests that spokesmen may represent in public debate over controversial issues and a requirement that the speaker have a sufficiently great interest in the subject to justify communication.

[The Massachusetts statute] permits a corporation to communicate to the public its views on certain referendum subjects—those materially affecting its business—but not others. It also singles out one kind of ballot question—individual taxation—as a subject about which corporations may never make their ideas public. The legislature has drawn the line between permissible and impermissible speech according to whether there is a sufficient nexus, as defined by the legislature, between the issue presented to the voters and the business interests of the speaker.

In the realm of protected speech, the legislature is constitutionally disqualified from dictating the subjects about which persons may speak and the speakers who may address a public issue. If a legislature may direct business corporations to "stick to business," it also may limit other corporations—religious, charitable, or civic—to their respective "business" when addressing the public. Such power in government to channel the expression of views is unacceptable under the First Amendment. Especially where, as here, the legislature's suppression of speech suggests an attempt to give one side of a debatable public question an advantage in expressing its views to the people, the First Amendment is plainly offended. Yet the State contends that its action is necessitated by governmental interests of the highest order. We next consider these asserted interests.

IV

The constitutionality of [the statute's] prohibition of the "exposition of ideas" by corporations turns on whether it can survive the exacting scrutiny necessitated by a state-imposed restriction of freedom of speech. Especially where, as here, a prohibition is directed at speech itself and the speech is intimately related to the process of governing, "the State may prevail only upon showing a subordinating interest which is compelling." Even then, the State must employ means "closely drawn to avoid unnecessary abridgment."

. . . Appellee . . . advances two principal justifications for the prohibition of corporate speech. The first is the State's interest in sustaining the active role of the individual citizen in the electoral process and thereby preventing diminution of the citizen's confidence in government. The second [, discussion of which is omitted,] is the interest in protecting the rights of shareholders whose views differ from those expressed by management on behalf of the corporation. However weighty these interests may be in the context of partisan candidate elections, they either are not implicated in this case or are not served at all, or in other than a random manner, by the prohibition in [the statute].

A

Preserving the integrity of the electoral process, preventing corruption, and "[sustaining] the active, alert responsibility of the individual citizen in a democracy for the wise conduct of government" are interests of the highest importance. . . .

Appellee advances a number of arguments in support of his view that these interests are endangered by corporate participation in discussion of a referendum issue. They hinge upon the assumption that such participation would exert an undue influence on the outcome of a referendum vote, and—in the end—destroy the confidence of the people in the democratic process and the integrity of government. According to appellee, corporations are wealthy and powerful and their views may drown out other points of view. If appellee's arguments were supported by record or legislative findings that corporate advocacy threatened imminently to undermine democratic processes, thereby denigrating rather than serving First Amendment interests, these arguments would merit our consideration. But there has been no showing that the relative voice of corporations has been overwhelming or even significant in influencing referenda in Massachusetts or that there has been any threat to the confidence of the citizenry in government.

Nor are appellee's arguments inherently persuasive or supported by the precedents of this Court. Referenda are held on issues, not candidates for public office. The risk of corruption perceived in cases involving candidate elections simply is not present in a popular vote on a public issue. To be sure, corporate advertising may influence the outcome of the vote; this would be its purpose. But the fact that advocacy may persuade the electorate is hardly a reason to suppress it: The Constitution "protects expression which is eloquent no less than that which is unconvincing." We noted only recently that "the concept that government may restrict the speech of some elements of our society in order to enhance the relative voice of others is wholly foreign to the First Amendment. . . ." *Buckley* [v. *Valeo*]. Moreover, the people in our democracy are entrusted with the responsibility for judging and evaluating the relative merits of conflicting arguments. They may consider, in making their judgment, the source and credibility of the advocate. But if there be any danger that the people cannot evaluate the information and arguments advanced by appellants, it is a danger contemplated by the Framers of the First Amendment.

. . .

In *Austin,* the Supreme Court again directly faced the question raised in *Bellotti* (document 3.2): to what extent does the First Amendment restrict government regulation of corporate and labor spending in elections? This time, however, the issue arose in the context of a candidate election, not an issue referendum, and the Supreme Court issued some clear guidance.

JUSTICE [Thurgood] MARSHALL delivered the opinion of the Court.

. . .

I

Section 54(1) of the Michigan Campaign Finance Act prohibits corporations from making contributions and independent expenditures in connection with state candidate elections. The issue before us is only the constitutionality of the State's ban on independent expenditures. The Act defines "expenditure" as "a payment, donation, loan, pledge, or promise of payment of money or anything of ascertainable monetary value for goods, materials, services, or facilities in assistance of, or in opposition to, the nomination or election of a candidate." An expenditure is considered independent if it is "not made at the direction of, or under the control of, another person and if the expenditure is not a contribution to a committee." The Act exempts from this general prohibition against corporate political spending any expenditure made from a segregated fund. A corporation may solicit contributions to its political fund only from an enumerated list of persons associated with the corporation.

The Chamber, a nonprofit Michigan corporation, challenges the constitutionality of this statutory scheme. The Chamber comprises more than 8,000 members, three-quarters of whom are for-profit corporations. The Chamber's general treasury is funded through annual dues required of all members. Its purposes, as set out in the bylaws, are to promote economic conditions favorable to private enterprise; to analyze, compile, and disseminate information about laws of interest to the business community and to publicize to the government the views of the business community on such matters; to train and educate its members; to foster ethical business practices; to collect data on, and investigate matters of, social, civic, and economic importance to the State; to receive contributions and to make expenditures for political purposes and to perform any other lawful political activity; and to coordinate activities with other similar organizations.

In June 1985 Michigan scheduled a special election to fill a vacancy in the Michigan House of Representatives. Although the Chamber had established and funded a separate political fund, it sought to use its general treasury funds to place in a local newspaper an advertisement supporting a specific candidate. As the Act made such an expenditure punishable as a felony, the Chamber brought suit in District Court for injunctive relief against enforcement of the Act, arguing that the restriction on expenditures is unconstitutional under both the First and the Fourteenth Amendments.

. . .

II

To determine whether Michigan's restriction on corporate political expenditures may constitutionally be applied to the Chamber, we must ascertain whether it burdens the exercise of political speech and, if it does, whether it is narrowly tailored to serve a compelling state interest. Certainly, the use of funds to support a political candidate is "speech"; independent campaign expenditures constitute "political expression 'at the core of our electoral process and of the First Amendment freedoms.'" The mere fact that the Chamber is a corporation does not remove its speech from the ambit of the First Amendment.

A

This Court concluded in *FEC* v. *Massachusetts Citizens for Life, Inc.*[(*MCFL*); document 7.4] that a federal statute requiring corporations to make independent political expenditures only through special segregated funds burdens corporate freedom of expression. The Court reasoned that the small nonprofit corporation in that case would face certain organizational and financial hurdles in establishing and administering a segregated political fund. For example, the statute required the corporation to appoint a treasurer for its segregated fund, keep records of all contributions, file a statement of organization containing information about the fund, and update that statement periodically. In addition, the corporation was permitted to solicit contributions to its segregated fund only from "members," which did not include persons who merely contributed to or indicated support for the organization. These hurdles "impose[d] administrative costs that many small entities [might] be unable to bear" and "create[d] a disincentive for such organizations to engage in political speech."

Despite the Chamber's success in administering its separate political fund Michigan's segregated fund requirement still burdens the Chamber's exercise of expression because "the corporation is not free to use its general funds for campaign advocacy purposes." The Act imposes requirements similar to those in the federal statute involved in *MCFL*: a segregated fund must have a treasurer and its administrators must keep detailed accounts of contributions and file with state officials a statement of organization. In addition, a nonprofit corporation like the Chamber may solicit contributions to its political fund only from members, stockholders of members, officers or directors of members, and the spouses of any of these persons. Although these requirements do not stifle corporate speech entirely, they do burden expressive activity. Thus, they must be justified by a compelling state interest.

B

The State contends that the unique legal and economic characteristics of corporations necessitate some regulation of their political expenditures to avoid corruption or the appearance of corruption. State law grants corporations special advantages—such as limited liability, perpetual life, and favorable treatment of the accumulation and distribution of assets—that enhance their ability to attract capital and to deploy their resources in ways that maximize the return on their shareholders' investments. These state-created advantages not only allow corporations to play a dominant role in the Nation's economy, but also permit them to use "resources amassed in the economic marketplace" to obtain "an unfair advantage in the political marketplace." As the Court explained in *MCFL*, the political advantage of corporations is unfair because

The resources in the treasury of a business corporation . . . are not an indication of popular support for the corporation's political ideas. They reflect instead the economically motivated decisions of investors and customers. The availability of these resources may make a corporation a formidable political presence, even though the power of the corporation may be no reflection of the power of its ideas.

We therefore have recognized that "the compelling governmental interest in preventing corruption support[s] the restriction of the influence of political war chests funneled through the corporate form."

The Chamber argues that this concern about corporate domination of the political process is insufficient to justify a restriction on independent expenditures. Although this Court has distinguished these expenditures from direct contributions in the context of federal laws regulating individual donors it has also recognized that a legislature might demonstrate a danger of real or apparent corruption posed by such expenditures when made by corporations to influence candidate elections. Regardless of whether this danger of "financial quid pro quo" corruption may be sufficient to justify a restriction on independent expenditures, Michigan's regulation aims at a different type of corruption in the political arena: the corrosive and distorting effects of immense aggregations of wealth that are accumulated with the help of the corporate form and that have little or no correlation to the public's support for the corporation's political ideas. The Act does not attempt "to equalize the relative influence of speakers on elections"; rather, it ensures that expenditures reflect actual public support for the political ideas espoused by corporations. We emphasize that the mere fact that corporations may accumulate large amounts of wealth is not the justification for § 54; rather, the unique state-conferred corporate structure that facilitates the amassing of large treasuries warrants the limit on independent expenditures. Corporate wealth can unfairly influence elections when it is deployed in the form of independent expenditures, just as it can when it assumes the guise of political contributions. We therefore hold that the State has articulated a sufficiently compelling rationale to support its restriction on independent expenditures by corporations.

. . .

III

The Chamber contends that even if the Campaign Finance Act is constitutional with respect to for-profit corporations, it nonetheless cannot be applied to a nonprofit ideological corporation like a chamber of commerce. In *MCFL*, we held that the nonprofit organization there had "features more akin to voluntary political associations than business firms, and therefore should not have to bear burdens on independent spending solely because of [its] incorporated status." In reaching that conclusion, we enumerated three characteristics of the corporation that were "essential" to our holding. Because the Chamber does not share these crucial features, the Constitution does not require that it be exempted from the generally applicable provisions of § 54(1).

The first characteristic of Massachusetts Citizens for Life, Inc., that distinguished it from ordinary business corporations was that the organization "was formed for the express purpose of promoting political ideas, and cannot engage in business activities." Its articles of incorporation indicated that its purpose was "[t]o foster respect for human life and to defend the right to life of all human beings, born and unborn, through educational, political and other forms of activities," and all of the organization's activities were "designed to further its agenda." MCFL's narrow political focus thus "ensure[d] that [its] political resources reflect[ed] political support."

In contrast, the Chamber's bylaws set forth more varied purposes, several of which are not inherently political. For instance, the Chamber compiles and disseminates information relating to social, civic, and economic conditions, trains and educates its members, and promotes ethical business practices. Unlike MCFL's, the Chamber's educational activities are not expressly tied to political goals; many of its seminars, conventions, and publications are politically neutral and focus on business and economic issues. The Chamber's president and chief executive officer stated that one of the corporation's main purposes is to provide "service to [its] membership that includes everything from group insurance to educational seminars, and . . . litigation activities on behalf of the business community." The Chamber's nonpolitical activities therefore suffice to distinguish it from MCFL in the context of this characteristic.

We described the second feature of MCFL as the absence of "shareholders or other persons affiliated so as to have a claim on its assets or earnings. This ensures that persons connected with the organization will have no economic disincentive for disassociating with it if they disagree with its political activity." Although the Chamber also lacks shareholders, many of its members may be similarly reluctant to withdraw as members even if they disagree with the Chamber's political expression, because they wish to benefit from the Chamber's nonpolitical programs and to establish contacts with other members of the business community. The Chamber's political agenda is sufficiently distinct from its educational and outreach programs that members who disagree with the former may continue to pay dues to participate in the latter. . . . Thus, we are persuaded that the Chamber's members are more similar to shareholders of a business corporation than to the members of MCFL in this respect.

The final characteristic upon which we relied in *MCFL* was the organization's independence from the influence of business corporations. On this score, the Chamber differs most greatly from the Massachusetts organization. MCFL was not established by, and had a policy of not accepting contributions from, business corporations. Thus it could not "serv[e] as [a] condui[t] for the type of direct spending that creates a threat to the political marketplace." In striking contrast, more than three-quarters of the Chamber's members are business corporations, whose political contributions and expenditures can constitutionally be regulated by the State. As we read the Act, a corporation's payments into the Chamber's general treasury would not be considered payments to influence an election, so they would not be "contributions" or "expenditures," and would not be subject to the Act's limitations. Business corporations therefore could circumvent the Act's restriction by funneling money through the Chamber's general treasury. Because the Chamber accepts money from for-profit corporations, it could, absent application of § 54(1), serve as a conduit for corporate political spending. In sum, the Chamber does not possess the features that would compel the State to exempt it from restriction on independent political expenditures.

IV

The Chamber also attacks § 54(1) as underinclusive because it does not regulate the independent expenditures of unincorporated labor unions. Whereas unincorporated unions, and indeed individuals, may be able to amass large treasuries, they do so without the significant state-conferred advantages of the corporate structure; corporations are "by far the most prominent example of entities that enjoy legal advantages enhancing their ability to accumulate wealth." The desire to counterbalance those advantages unique to the corporate form is the State's compelling interest in this case; thus, excluding from the statute's coverage unincorporated entities that also have the capacity to accumulate wealth "does not undermine its justification for regulating corporations."

Moreover, labor unions differ from corporations in that union members who disagree with a union's political activities need not give up full membership in the organization to avoid supporting its political activities. Although a union and an employer may require that all bargaining unit employees become union members, a union may not compel those employees to support financially "union activities beyond those germane to collective bargaining, contract administration, and grievance adjustment." *Communications Workers [of America]* v. *Beck,* 487 U.S. 735 (1988)]. An employee who objects to a union's political activities thus can decline to contribute to those activities, while continuing to enjoy the benefits derived from the union's performance of its duties as the exclusive representative of the bargaining unit on labor-management issues. As a result, the funds available for a union's political activities more accurately reflects members' support for the organization's political views than does a corporation's general treasury. Michigan's decision to exclude unincorporated labor unions from the scope of § 54(1) is therefore justified by the crucial differences between unions and corporations.

. . .

VI

Michigan identified as a serious danger the significant possibility that corporate political expenditures will undermine the integrity of the political process, and it has implemented a narrowly tailored solution to that problem. By requiring corporations to make all independent political expenditures through a separate fund made up of money solicited expressly for political purposes, the Michigan Campaign Finance Act reduces the threat that huge corporate treasuries amassed with the aid of favorable state laws will be used to influence unfairly the outcome of elections. The Michigan Chamber of Commerce does not exhibit the characteristics identified in *MCFL* that would require the State to exempt it from a generally applicable restriction on independent corporate expenditures. . . .

Colorado Republican Federal Campaign Committee v. *Federal Election Commission,* 116 S. Ct. 2309 (1996)

In its prior cases, the Supreme Court had mostly considered the constitutionality of government restrictions on candidate and private party spending. In *Colorado Republican Federal Campaign Committee,* the Court had to consider the extent to which Congress and the FEC can regulate political party spending on behalf of candidates. The result was a very splintered opinion.

JUSTICE [Stephen G.] BREYER announced the judgment of the Court and delivered an opinion, in which JUSTICE [Sandra Day] O'CONNOR and JUSTICE [David H.] SOUTER join.

[Section 441a(d)(3) of the Federal Election Campaign Act limits political party expenditures in senatorial campaigns. Before both the 1986 Democratic primary and Republican convention, the Colorado Republican Federal Campaign Committee bought radio ads attacking one of the Democratic primary candidates. The State Democratic Party complained that the purchase exceeded the Republican Party limits under the Act and the Federal Election Commission charged a violation.]

. . .

II

The summary judgment record indicates that the expenditure in question is what this Court in *Buckley* [v. *Valeo,* 424 U.S. 1 (1976)] called an "independent" expenditure, not a "coordinated" expenditure that other provisions of FECA treat as a kind of campaign "contribution." . . .

So treated, the expenditure falls within the scope of the Court's precedents that extend First Amendment protection to independent expenditures. Beginning with *Buckley,* the Court's cases have found a "fundamental constitutional difference between money spent to advertise one's views independently of the candidate's campaign and money contributed to the candidate to be spent on his campaign." This difference has been grounded in the observation that restrictions on contributions impose "only a marginal restriction upon the contributor's ability to engage in free communication," because the symbolic communicative value of a contribution bears little relation to its size and because such limits leave "persons free to engage in independent political expression, to associate actively through volunteering their services, and to assist to a limited but nonetheless substantial extent in supporting candidates and committees with financial resources." At the same time, reasonable contribution limits directly and materially advance the Government's interest in preventing exchanges of large financial contributions for political favors.

In contrast, the Court has said that restrictions on independent expenditures significantly impair the ability of individuals and groups to engage in direct political advocacy and "represent substantial . . . restraints on the quantity and diversity of political speech." And at the same time, the Court has concluded that limitations on independent expenditures are less directly related to preventing corruption, since "the absence of prearrangement and coordination of an expenditure with the candidate not only undermines the value of the expenditure to the candidate, but also alleviates the danger that expenditures will be given as a *quid pro quo* for improper commitments from the candidate."

Given these established principles, we do not see how a provision that limits a political party's independent expenditures can escape their controlling effect. A political party's independent expression not only reflects its members' views about the philosophical and governmental matters that bind them together, it also seeks to convince others to join those members in a practical democratic task, the task of creating a government that voters can instruct and hold responsible for subsequent success or failure. The independent expression of a political party's views is "core" First Amendment activity no less than is the independent expression of individuals, candidates, or other political committees.

We are not aware of any special dangers of corruption associated with political parties that tip the constitutional balance in a different direction. When this Court considered, and held unconstitutional, limits that FECA had set on certain independent expenditures by political action committees, it reiterated Buckley's observation that "the absence of prearrangement and coordination" does not eliminate, but it does help to "alleviate," any "danger" that a candidate will understand the expenditure as an effort to obtain a "quid pro quo." The same is true of independent party expenditures.

. . .

We therefore believe that this Court's prior case law controls the outcome here. We do not see how a Constitution that grants to individuals, candidates, and ordinary political committees the right to make unlimited independent expenditures could deny the same right to political parties. . . .

DISSENT: JUSTICE [John Paul] STEVENS, with whom JUSTICE [Ruth Bader] GINSBURG joins, dissenting.

In my opinion, all money spent by a political party to secure the election of its candidate for the office of United States Senator should be considered a "contribution" to his or her campaign. . . .

I am persuaded that three interests provide a constitutionally sufficient predicate for federal limits on spending by political parties. First, such limits serve the interest in avoiding both the appearance and the reality of a corrupt political process. A party shares a unique relationship with the candidate it sponsors because their political fates are inextricably linked. That interdependency creates a special danger that the party—or the persons who control the party—will abuse the influence it has over the candidate by virtue of its power to spend. The provisions at issue are appropriately aimed at reducing that threat. . . .

Second, these restrictions supplement other spending limitations embodied in the Act, which are likewise designed to prevent corruption.

Individuals and certain organizations are permitted to contribute up to $1,000 to a candidate. Since the same donors can give up to $5,000 to party committees if there were no limits on party spending, their contributions could be spent to benefit the candidate and thereby circumvent the $1,000 cap. . . .

Finally, I believe the Government has an important interest in leveling the electoral playing field by constraining the cost of federal campaigns. As Justice [Byron] White pointed out in his opinion in *Buckley*, "money is not always equivalent to or used for speech, even in the context of political campaigns." It is quite wrong to assume that the net effect of limits on contributions and expenditures—which tend to protect equal access to the political arena, to free candidates and their staffs from the interminable burden of fund-raising, and to diminish the importance of repetitive 30-second commercials—will be adverse to the interest in informed debate protected by the First Amendment.

. . .

JUSTICE [Anthony M.] KENNEDY, with whom THE CHIEF JUSTICE [William H. Rehnquist] and JUSTICE [Antonin] SCALIA join, concurring in the judgment and dissenting in part.

. . .

The First Amendment embodies a "profound national commitment to the principle that debate on public issues should be uninhibited, robust, and wide-open." Political parties have a unique role in serving this principle; they exist to advance their members' shared political beliefs. . . .

We have a constitutional tradition of political parties and their candidates engaging in joint First Amendment activity; we also have a practical identity of interests between the two entities during an election. Party spending "in cooperation, consultation, or concert with" a candidate therefore is indistinguishable in substance from expenditures by the candidate or his campaign committee. We held in *Buckley* that the First Amendment does not permit regulation of the latter and it should not permit this regulation of the former. Congress may have authority, consistent with the First Amendment, to restrict undifferentiated political party contributions which satisfy the constitutional criteria we discussed in *Buckley*, but that type of regulation is not at issue here.

. . .

JUSTICE [Clarence] THOMAS, concurring in the judgment and dissenting in part, with whom THE CHIEF JUSTICE and JUSTICE SCALIA join in Parts I and III.

. . .

I would reject the framework established by *Buckley* v. *Valeo* for analyzing the constitutionality of campaign finance laws and hold that § 441a(d)(3)'s limits on independent and coordinated expenditures fail strict scrutiny. But even under *Buckley*, [these limits] cannot stand, because the anti-corruption rationale that we have relied upon in sustaining other campaign finance laws is inapplicable where political parties are the subject of such regulation.

. . .

II

A

Critical to JUSTICE BREYER's reasoning is the distinction between contributions and independent expenditures that we first drew in *Buckley* v. *Valeo*. Though we said in *Buckley* that controls on spending and giving "operate in an area of the most fundamental First Amendment activities," we invalidated the expenditure limits of FECA and upheld the Act's contribution limits. The justification we gave for the differing results was this: "The expenditure limitations . . . represent substantial rather than merely theoretical restraints on the quantity and diversity of political speech," whereas "limitations upon the amount that any one person or group may contribute to a candidate or political committee entail only a marginal restriction upon the contributor's ability to engage in free communication." This conclusion was supported mainly by two assertions about the nature of contributions: first, though contributions may result in speech, that speech is by the candidate and not by the contributor; and second, contributions express only general support for the candidate but do not communicate the reasons for that support. Since *Buckley*, our campaign finance jurisprudence has been based in large part on this distinction between contributions and expenditures.

In my view, the distinction lacks constitutional significance, and I would not adhere to it. . . . Contributions and expenditures both involve core First Amendment expression because they further the "discussion of public issues and debate on the qualifications of candidates . . . integral to the operation of the system of government established by our Constitution." When an individual donates money to a candidate or to a partisan organization, he enhances the donee's ability to communicate a message and thereby adds to political debate, just as when that individual communicates the message himself. Indeed, the individual may add more to political discourse by giving rather than spending, if the donee is able to put the funds to more productive use than can the individual. The contribution of funds to a candidate or to a political group thus fosters the "free discussion of governmental affairs," just as an expenditure does. Giving and spending in the electoral process also involve basic associational rights under the First Amendment. As we acknowledged in *Buckley*, "'effective advocacy of both public and private points of view, particularly controversial ones, is undeniably enhanced by group association'" Political associations allow citizens to pool their resources and make their advocacy more effective, and such efforts are fully protected by the First Amendment. If an individual is limited in the amount of resources he can contribute to the pool, he is most certainly limited in his ability to associate for purposes of effective advocacy. And if an individual cannot be subject to such limits, neither can political associations be limited in their ability to give as a means of furthering their members' viewpoints. As we have said, "any interference with the freedom of a party is simultaneously an interference with the freedom of its adherents."

Turning from similarities to differences, I can discern only one potentially meaningful distinction between contributions and expenditures. In the former case, the funds pass through an intermediary—

some individual or entity responsible for organizing and facilitating the dissemination of the message—whereas in the latter case they may not necessarily do so. But the practical judgment by a citizen that another person or an organization can more effectively deploy funds for the good of a common cause than he can ought not deprive that citizen of his First Amendment rights. Whether an individual donates money to a candidate or group who will use it to promote the candidate or whether the individual spends the money to promote the candidate himself, the individual seeks to engage in political expression and to associate with likeminded persons. A contribution is simply an indirect expenditure; though contributions and expenditures may thus differ in form, they do not differ in substance. . . .

In sum, unlike the *Buckley* Court, I believe that contribution limits infringe as directly and as seriously upon freedom of political expression and association as do expenditure limits. The protections of the First Amendment do not depend upon so fine a line as that between spending money to support a candidate or group and giving money to the candidate or group to spend for the same purpose. In principle, people and groups give money to candidates and other groups for the same reason that they spend money in support of those candidates and groups: because they share social, economic, and political beliefs and seek to have those beliefs affect governmental policy. I think that the *Buckley* framework for analyzing the constitutionality of campaign finance laws is deeply flawed. Accordingly, I would not employ it. . . .

III

Were I convinced that the *Buckley* framework rested on a principled distinction between contributions and expenditures, which I am not, I would nevertheless conclude that § 441a(d)(3)'s limits on political parties violate the First Amendment. Under *Buckley* and its progeny, a substantial threat of corruption must exist before a law purportedly aimed at the prevention of corruption will be sustained against First Amendment attack. Just as some of the monetary limits in the *Buckley* line of cases were held to be invalid because the government interest in stemming corruption was inadequate under the circumstances to justify the restrictions on speech, so too is § 441a(d)(3) invalid.

The Government asserts that the purpose of § 441a(d)(3) is to prevent the corruption of candidates and elected representatives by party officials. The Government does not explain precisely what it means by "corruption," however; the closest thing to an explanation the Government offers is that "corruption" is "'the real or imagined coercive influence of large financial contributions on candidates' positions and on their actions if elected to office.'" We so defined corruption in *Buckley* for purposes of reviewing ceilings on giving or spending by individuals, groups, political committees (PACs), and candidates. But we did not in that case consider the First Amendment status of FECA's provisions dealing with political parties.

As applied in the specific context of campaign funding by political parties, the anti-corruption rationale loses its force. What could it mean for a party to "corrupt" its candidate or to exercise "coercive" influence over him? The very aim of a political party is to influence its candidate's stance on issues and, if the candidate takes office or is reelected, his votes. When political parties achieve that aim, that achievement does not, in my view, constitute "a subversion of the political process." For instance, if the Democratic Party spends large sums of money in support of a candidate who wins, takes office, and then implements the Party's platform, that is not corruption; that is successful advocacy of ideas in the political marketplace and representative government in a party system. . . .

The structure of political parties is such that the theoretical danger of those groups actually engaging in *quid pro quos* with candidates is significantly less than the threat of individuals or other groups doing so. American political parties, generally speaking, have numerous members with a wide variety of interests features necessary for success in majoritarian elections. Consequently, the influence of any one person or the importance of any single issue within a political party is significantly diffused. For this reason, . . . campaign funds donated by parties are considered to be some of "the cleanest money in politics." And, as long as the Court continues to permit Congress to subject individuals to limits on the amount they can give to parties, and those limits are uniform as to all donors, there is little risk that an individual donor could use a party as a conduit for bribing candidates.

In any event, the Government, which bears the burden of "demonstrating that the recited harms are real, not merely conjectural," has identified no more proof of the corrupting dangers of coordinated expenditures than it has of independent expenditures. And insofar as it appears that Congress did not actually enact § 441a(d)(3) in order to stop corruption by political parties "but rather for the constitutionally insufficient purpose of reducing what it saw as wasteful and excessive campaign spending," the statute's ceilings on coordinated expenditures are as unwarranted as the caps on independent expenditures.

In sum, there is only a minimal threat of "corruption," as we have understood that term, when a political party spends to support its candidate or to oppose his competitor, whether or not that expenditure is made in concert with the candidate. Parties and candidates have traditionally worked together to achieve their common goals, and when they engage in that work, there is no risk to the Republic. To the contrary, the danger to the Republic lies in Government suppression of such activity. Under *Buckley* and our subsequent cases, § 441a(d)(3)'s heavy burden on First Amendment rights is not justified by the threat of corruption at which it is assertedly aimed.

. . .

To conclude, I would find § 441a(d)(3) unconstitutional not just as applied to petitioners, but also on its face. . . .

THE REFORM DEBATE

Politics and the First Amendment

CONTENTS

Politics and the First Amendment

INTRODUCTION BY DANIEL R. ORTIZ

Few recent constitutional decisions have raised as much commentary as *Buckley* v. *Valeo* (424 U.S. 1 [1976]; document 3.1), and its progeny. On the one side, reformers attack the Supreme Court for misunderstanding both the First Amendment and how money works in politics. They read these cases as constitutional mistakes, as wrongheaded judicial meddling that magnifies the power of the rich. On the other side, deregulationists celebrate the Court for vindicating the First Amendment against strong public opinion. In their eyes, the Court has acted bravely to save the American political system from misguided (albeit popular) reform. Many commentators, of course, see some wisdom in both positions and seek to defend a view in between.

Ronald Dworkin presents a strong version of the reform argument. In his article, "The Curse of American Politics," Dworkin begins by asking whether *Buckley* was wrongly decided and ends by calling for the Court to overrule it (document 4.1). Cutting through to the Court's central justification, he finds that *Buckley* stands on an "individual-choice" model of politics. By this he means that its overall stance, which is deeply suspicious of government regulation, rests ultimately on the view that the First Amendment allows people to hear whatever they want, at least in the realm of politics. Although this notion may be attractive (especially to people who believe in a bustling, free marketplace of ideas) Dworkin thinks it fundamentally mistaken. To his mind, it misunderstands not only free speech, but also "what it really means for free people to govern themselves." The result is not just legal error but the weakening of democratic politics.

The mistake Dworkin finds in this view is that it sees equality as necessary to only one part of democracy. Although the individual-choice model gives each voter one vote and thus makes each an equally powerful judge of competing candidates and positions, the model ignores equality among citizens in another important respect. It allows some people more power than others as participants in the contest of forming political opinion. Wealthy individuals can "command [more] attention for their own candidates, interests, and convictions" than can others. As Dworkin puts it:

When the Supreme Court said, in the *Buckley* case, that fairness to candidates and their convictions is "foreign" to the First Amendment, it denied that such fairness was required by democracy. That is a mistake because the most fundamental characterization of democracy—that it provides self-government by the people as a whole—supposes that citizens are equals not only as judges but as participants as well.

According to Dworkin, we must have equal power not only to judge among the views presented—as the rule of "one person, one vote" seeks to guarantee—but also to command the attention of others to our own views. Such equality does not, of course, require that others find our arguments persuasive, but it does demand that each citizen be able to compete on equal terms for every other citizen's attention.

Dworkin believes this type of equality justifies regulating some spending in elections and thus necessitates overruling *Buckley*. But he sees little prospect of that—at least soon. In fact, as he notes, if the *Colorado Republican* case is any indication (*Colorado Republican Federal Campaign Committee* v. *Federal Election Commission,* 116 S.Ct. 2309 [1996]; document 3.4), more justices now seem inclined to extend *Buckley* than to overrule it. Instead, Dworkin argues a more realistic strategy: we should simply declare *Buckley* a mistake, even if the Supreme Court will not admit it, and do everything we can to avoid its implications. He thus advocates reform that pursues this second type of equality to the full extent *Buckley* permits and urges us to challenge *Buckley* whenever we can.

Bradley A. Smith's article, "Faulty Assumptions and Undemocratic Consequences of Campaign Finance Reform" (document 4.2), takes a quite different approach to *Buckley.* Although Smith does not address the constitutional question directly, he does, like Dworkin, try to uncover and then question the fundamental assumptions of one side of the debate—in his case, the reformers' assumptions. Unlike Dworkin, Smith does not find one overarching normative theory of politics holding together the side he attacks. He believes instead that the case for reform rests on many different faulty descriptive theories about how money works in our political system. But his discussion, no less than Dworkin's, holds quite deep implications for both the constitutionality and wisdom of reform.

Smith begins by laying out four major descriptive assumptions reformers make about money in politics: that too much money is spent, that smaller contributions are better than larger ones, that money buys elections, and that money corrupts politicians. All four, he argues, are wrong or at least unsupported. Smith argues against the first by comparing political and product advertising. As large as the amounts spent in political advertising may be, he points out, they are dwarfed by the amounts spent in advertising products. When considered per voter, moreover, the costs look reasonably small. Smith challenges the second assumption—that when it comes to contributions smaller is better—

by pointing out that too few Americans actually make contributions to support adequate political debate. Moreover, those candidates who can garner widespread small contributions are usually those who excite the passions of supporters on the extremes of the political debate. The mainstream appears poorly stocked with small contributors. Smith contests the third assumption—that money buys elections—by arguing that money may follow success more than success does money. And, finally, he uses empirical arguments to fight the view that money corrupts candidates. Money affects few votes in the legislature, he claims, and "the available evidence simply does not show a meaningful, causal relationship between campaign contributions and legislative voting patterns." This empirical claim, of course, has quite far-reaching implications for the anticorruption rationale *Buckley* upheld.

Smith does not rest there. He goes on to argue that the consequences of reform are just as bad as its assumptions. To his mind, the reformers have it exactly backwards. Far from shoring up democracy, reform undermines it in several particular ways. First, Smith argues that campaign finance reform entrenches the status quo. It necessarily favors incumbents by making it harder for challengers to raise money. Second, he believes that campaign finance reform promotes influence-peddling in the legislature. By restricting contributions, reform restricts people's ability to monitor their representatives and so keep them from shirking. Bad enough by itself, decreased monitoring also makes bribery, which Smith sees as a "substitute" for contributions, more likely.

Third, Smith argues that campaign finance reform favors "select elites." To the extent that reform decreases the power of money to influence elections, it increases the power of elite attributes (like name recognition and celebrity status) to influence them. This change simply redistributes power from wealthy individuals to select elites without making its overall distribution more equitable. In addition, Smith contends that campaign finance reform favors wealthy candidates. Additional regulation only increases the advantage *Buckley* gave to such candidates when it struck down restrictions on candidates contributing to their own campaigns. Finally, Smith argues that campaign finance reform favors special interest over grass-roots activity. Because it requires lawyers and others with specialized knowledge to navigate through the shoals of legal requirements, regulation "professionalizes" politics and thus distances it from ordinary citizens. To the extent Smith's arguments are sound, even reformers should worry.

In "Political Equality and Unintended Consequences," Cass R. Sunstein tries to steer a course between the reform and deregulation extremes (document 4.3). With *Buckley*'s foes he believes that equality should extend beyond the vote itself. Democracy demands that equality play a much wider role in politics. With *Buckley*'s supporters, on the other hand, he believes that regulation should be subject to searching review. To him, "money is speech" because it serves to communicate ideas. As the title of Sunstein's article suggests, moreover, he also agrees with Smith that campaign finance regulation can have many unwanted consequences.

Sunstein criticizes *Buckley* and, in particular, its hostility to equality concerns by placing the case in historical-legal perspective. The *Buckley* regime, under which Congress cannot restrict individual expenditures, should be familiar to us, he argues. It is a regime of economic laissez-faire, just like the regime the Supreme Court enforced during the early part of this century under *Lochner* v. *New York*, 198 U.S. 45 (1905), a case striking down state maximum hour and minimum wage legislation. In both cases, he explains, the Court viewed regulation as unjust because it disturbed some deeply held baseline of entitlement—of free speech in *Buckley* and of property in *Lochner*—that was thought to be natural and unrelated to society's political decisions.

Sunstein argues that this feeling, although deeply held, is wrong. The baselines the Court used in both cases are neither natural nor pre-political. Both reflect the existing distribution of legal entitlements and seem natural only because we are so used to them. The familiar, in a sense, blinds us. Furthermore, he argues, just as the Supreme Court ultimately recognized this fact about *Lochner* and repudiated that case as one of the great mistakes of our constitutional history, so too it should repudiate *Buckley*. They both rest on the same mistaken foundations.

The second part of Sunstein's piece takes a different tack and discusses reform's unintended consequences. He agrees with Smith on some details. Reform may, for example, entrench incumbents. More importantly, he argues that we should analyze reforms dynamically. When we contemplate a reform, we should take into account the different actors' likely reactions. Often regulated parties will respond in ways that thwart the regulator's original intentions or indeed make the situation worse. Sunstein argues, for example, that limiting individual expenditures might lead to more numerous and more influential political action committees (PACs) and that limiting hard money might increase soft money—both consequences most reformers would hate. If we do not take these dynamic reactions into account when setting policy and interpreting the First Amendment, our own good motives may defeat us.

These three writers offer a fair sample of the many different positions political and legal commentators take in this area. The great differences of opinion spring not just from different notions of what the Constitution requires, but also from different normative and descriptive assumptions about democratic politics. The debate is complex and fascinating, and so long as we all have such robust and differing ideas about how democracy should and does function it will remain unresolvable.

Ronald Dworkin, "The Curse of American Politics," *New York Review of Books,* October 17, 1996, pp. 19–24

Ronald Dworkin, one of the most prominent champions of reform, argues that *Buckley* v. *Valeo* (document 3.1) was wrongly decided and should be overturned or, barring that, simply ignored to the extent possible. He finds that it rests on a faulty normative assumption: that democracy requires equality only in voting, not in helping form the political opinions of others. To him, we must regulate much campaign spending in order to ensure that we can each equally compete for everyone else's political attention.

. . .

Was the *Buckley* decision right? The Constitution's First Amendment declares that Congress "shall make no law . . . abridging the freedom of speech." These abstract words cannot mean that government must pass no law that prevents or punishes *any* form of speech—that would rule out laws against blackmail and fraud. Free speech must mean the freedom to speak or publish when denying that freedom would damage some other individual right that free speech protects, or when it would impair democracy itself. It is a premise of democracy, for example, that the people as a whole must have final authority over the government, not vice versa. That principle is compromised when official censorship limits the character or diversity of political opinion the public may hear or the range of information it may consider, particularly—though not exclusively—when the censorship is designed to protect government from criticism or exposure. So the Supreme Court has ruled, as in the Pentagon Papers case, that government may not prohibit the publication of material pertinent to judging its own performance. It is another premise of democracy that citizens must be able, as individuals, to participate on equal terms in both formal politics and in the informal cultural life that creates the moral environment of the community. That principle is compromised when government prohibits speech on the ground that the convictions or tastes or preferences it expresses are unworthy or degraded or offensive, or that they would be dangerous if others were persuaded to embrace them. So, particularly in recent decades, the Court has been zealous in protecting neo-Nazis, pornographers, and flagburners from censorship inspired by such judgments.

Neither of these two principles of democracy is violated, however, by a legal restriction on campaign expenditures. Expenditure limits do not protect government from criticism—incumbents, as we saw, benefit more than challengers from unlimited spending—and they do not presuppose that any political opinion is less worthy or more dangerous than any other. Nor would such limits seriously risk keeping from the public any argument or information it would otherwise have: media advertising of rich candidates and campaigns is now extremely repetitive, and the message would not change if the repetitions were fewer.

In the *Buckley* decision, however, the Court claimed another, more general, principle of democracy. It declared that since effective speech requires money in the television age, any legal limit on how much politicians can spend necessarily diminishes the overall *quantity* of political speech, and violates the First Amendment for that reason. The Court conceded that capping expenditures would permit poor candidates to compete more effectively with rich ones. But, it said, "the concept that government may restrict the speech of some elements of our society in order to enhance the relative voice of others is wholly foreign to the First Amendment." What reason might we have for accepting that view?

Two arguments are often made. The first supposes, in the spirit of John Stuart Mill's famous defense of free speech, that a community is more likely to reach wise political decisions the more political argument or appeal its citizens are able to hear or read. It is certainly true that expenditure caps would limit the quantity of political speech. If a rich politician or a well-financed campaign is prevented from broadcasting as many television ads as he or it would like, then the sum total of political broadcasts is, by hypothesis, less than it would otherwise be. Some citizens would indeed be prevented from hearing a message they might have deemed pertinent.

But since the curtailed broadcasts would almost certainly have repeated what the candidate had said on other occasions, it seems unlikely that the repetition would have improved collective knowledge. Nothing in the history of the many democracies that do restrict electoral expense suggests that they have sacrificed wisdom by doing so. In any case, the argument that curtailing political expenditure would hinder the search for truth and justice seems so speculative—and the potential cost in those values so meager even if the argument is right—that it hardly provides a reason for forgoing the conceded gains in fairness that restricting electoral expenses would bring.

A second familiar argument is very different. It insists that the freedom of speech that really is essential to democracy—the freedom to criticize government or to express unpopular opinions, for example—is best protected from official abuse and evasion by a blanket rule that condemns any and all regulation of political speech—except, perhaps, to avoid immediate and serious violence or a national disaster. It is better for a community to forgo even desirable gains than to run the risk of abuse, and the censorship of genuinely important speech, that a less rigid rule would inevitably pose. But this argument overlooks the fact that, in this case, what we risk in accepting a rigid rule is not just inconvenience but a serious loss in the quality of the very democracy we supposedly thereby protect. It seems perverse to suffer the clear unfairness of allowing rich candidates to drown out poor ones, or powerful corporations to buy special access to politicians by making enormous gifts, in order to prevent speculative and unnamed dangers to democracy that have not actually occurred and that no one has shown are likely to occur. We would do better to rely on our officials—and ultimately on our courts—to draw lines and make distinctions of principle, as they do in all other fields of constitutional law.

But though these two familiar arguments are easily countered, the *Buckley* decision cited another, more profound, argument—I shall call it the "individual-choice" argument—which I believe has been very influential among those who support the decision even though it is rarely articulated in full. "In the free society ordained by our Constitution," the Court said, "it is not the government, but the people individually as citizens and candidates and collectively as associations and political committees who must retain control over the quantity and range of debate on public issues in a political campaign." We must take some care to appreciate the force of that argument. I said that much of First Amendment law is grounded in the ideal of democratic self-government—that the ultimate governors of a society should be the people as a whole, not the officials they have elected. That principle does not seem to apply in the case of expenditure limitations, I said, because those limits are designed not to prevent the public from learning any particular kind of information or hearing any particular kind of appeal but, on the contrary, to enhance the diversity and fairness of the political debate.

But the individual-choice argument insists that instead of that apparently admirable goal justifying the constraint, it explains what is *wrong* with it, because any attempt to determine the character of the political debate by legislation violates an important democratic right—the right of each individual citizen to make up his own mind about what information or message is pertinent to his decision how to use his vote. Should he watch as much of his favorite candidate or party as possible, to solidify or reinforce convictions he holds intuitively, or in order to arm himself for political arguments with other citizens? Or should he watch all candidates, including those whose personality or views he knows he detests, when he would rather do something else? Should he take an interest in negative ads that deride an opponent's character? Or should he try to follow complex political argument crammed full of statistics he knows can be manipulated?

Some people, including many who now press for expenditure limits and other reforms, have their own clear answer to such questions. They endorse a high-minded, "civic republican" ideal of democratic discourse. They imagine a nation of informed citizens giving equal time and care to all sides of important issues, and deliberating thoughtfully about the common good rather than their own selfish interests. But the individual-choice argument insists that those who accept that ideal have no right to impose it on others, and are therefore wrong to appeal to it as justification for coercive measures, like expenditure caps, that deny people the right to listen to whatever political message they want, as often as they want. In a genuine democracy, it insists, the structure, character, and tone of the public political discourse must be determined by the combined effect of individual choices of citizens making political decisions for themselves, not by the edicts of self-styled arbiters of political fairness and rationality. If we want to bring American politics closer to civic republican ideals, we must do so by example and persuasion, not by the coercive force of expenditure caps or other majoritarian rules.

It might seem natural to object to this argument that, in the real world we live in, people cannot make their own decisions about which political messages to watch or listen to anyway because those decisions are made for them by rich or well-financed candidates whose advertisements dominate programming. But that objection is less powerful than it might at first seem. There is little evidence that citizens who take an active interest in politics could not discover the statements and positions of any serious candidate—that is, of any candidate who would have any significant chance of winning if every voter knew his views in great detail—if they were willing to make the effort to do so. Of course it is true, as Senator [Bill] Bradley said, that voters are much more likely to be convinced by advertisements constantly shown during commercial breaks in popular programming than by the less expensive campaigning that poorer candidates can afford. If that were *not* true, then candidates who spent fortunes on such advertising would be wasting their money. But it does not decrease the freedom of a voter to choose for himself which candidate to watch when one candidate is on television constantly and another only rarely, provided that the voter can find the latter's message if he searches. And it would be unacceptably paternalistic to argue that a voter should not be allowed to watch what he wants to because he is too likely to be convinced by it.

It is also true, as I said, that many potential candidates decide not to run because they are likely to lose when money dominates politics. But we must distinguish between two reasons a poor candidate might have for that decision. He might fear that voters would not learn of his existence or policies, because he has too little money to spend on publicizing them, or he might fear that even if voters did learn, he would lose anyway, because the weight of money and advertisement on the other side would make his good ideas seem terrible ones.

The appropriate remedy for the first danger, according to the individual-choice argument, is some form of subsidy for poorer candidates—direct grants to those whose opponents spend more than a specified limit, for example, or free television time for poorer candidates on special cable channels created or used for that purpose, or in specified network slots paid for from a national fund. (Nothing in the Supreme Court's decisions would bar such government subsidies.) And according to the individual-choice argument, the second danger—that even candidates subsidized in such a way could not match the advertising power of those with enormous resources—is not one that a democracy can address through expenditure limits, because government would then be denying citizens the broadcasts they wished to watch on the ground that they should not want to watch them, or that they are too likely to be persuaded by them. Once again, these are obviously impermissible grounds for any constraints on speech.

I emphasize the apparent strength of the individual-choice argument not to support that argument, but to make its structure plainer, and to suggest that we must confront it at a more basic level, by rejecting the conception of democratic self-government on which it is based. Citizens play two roles in a democracy. As voters they are, collectively, the final referees or judges of political contests. But they also participate, as individuals, in the contests they collectively judge: they are candidates, supporters, and political activists; they lobby and demonstrate for and against government measures, and they consult and argue about them with their fellow citizens. The individual-choice argument concentrates exclusively on citizens in the first role and neglects them in the second. For when wealth is unfairly distributed and money dominates politics, then, though individual citizens may be equal in their vote and their freedom to hear the candidates they wish to hear, they are not equal in their own ability to command the attention of others for their own candidates, interests, and convictions. When the Supreme Court said, in the *Buckley* case, that fairness to candidates and their convictions is "foreign" to the First Amendment, it denied that such fairness was required by democracy. That is a mistake because the most fundamental characterization of democracy—that it provides self-government by the people as a whole—supposes that citizens are equals not only as judges but as participants as well.

Of course no political community can make its citizens literally their own governors one by one. I am not my own ruler when I must obey a law that was enacted in spite of my fierce opposition. But a community can supply self-government in a more collective sense—it can encourage its members to see themselves as equal partners in a cooperative political enterprise, together governing their own affairs in the way in which the members of a college faculty or a fraternal society, for example, govern themselves. To achieve that sense of a national partnership in self-government, it is not enough for a community to treat citizens only as if they were shareholders in a company, giving them votes only in periodic elections of officials. It must design institutions, practices, and conventions that allow them to be more engaged in public life, and to make a contribution to it, even when their views do not prevail. Though the question of what that means in practice is a complex one, it seems evident that at least two conditions must be met for any community fully to succeed in the ambition.

First, each citizen must have a fair and reasonably equal opportunity not only to hear the views of others as these are published or broadcast, but to command attention for his own views, either as a candidate for office or as a member of a politically active group committed to some program or conviction. No citizen is entitled to demand that others find his opinions persuasive or even worthy of attention. But each citizen is entitled to compete for that attention, and to have a chance at persuasion, on fair terms, a chance that is now denied almost everyone without great wealth or access to it. Second, the tone of public discourse must be appropriate to the deliberations of a partnership or joint venture rather than the selfish negotiations of commercial rivals or military enemies. This means that when citizens disagree they must present their arguments to one another with civility, attempting rationally to support policies they take to be in the common interest, not in manipulative, slanted, or mendacious pitches designed to win as much of the spoils of politics as possible by any means. These two requirements—of participant equality and civility—are parts of the civic republican ideal I described. But we can now defend them, not just as features of an attractive society that perceptive statesmen have the right to impose on everyone, but as essential conditions of fair political engagement, and hence of self-government, for all.

If we embraced that attractive account of the conditions of self-government, we would have to accept that democracy—self-government by the people as a whole—is always a matter of degree. It will never be perfectly fulfilled, because it seems incredible that the politics of a pluralistic contemporary society could ever become as egalitarian in access and as deliberative in tone as the standards I just described demand. We would then understand democracy not as a pedigree a nation earns just by adopting some constitutional structure of free elections, but as an ideal toward which any would-be democratic society must continually strive.

We would also have to accept not only that America falls short of important democratic ideals, but that in the age of television politics the shortfall has steadily become worse. The influence of wealth unequally distributed is greater, and its consequences more profound, than at any time in the past, and our politics seem daily more rancorous, ill-spirited, and divisive. So this analysis of democracy as self-government confirms—and helps to explain—the growing sense of despair about American politics that I began this essay by trying to describe. How should we respond to that despair? We must understand the First Amendment as a challenge, not a barrier to improvement. We must reject the blanket principle the Supreme Court relied on in *Buckley*, that government should never attempt to regulate the public political discourse in any way, in favor of a more discriminating principle that condemns the constraints that do violate genuine principles of democracy—that deny citizens information they need for political judgment or that deny equality of citizenship for people with unpopular beliefs or tastes, for example— but that nevertheless permits us to try to reverse our democracy's decline.

Is it realistic to hope that the Supreme Court will soon overrule or modify the *Buckley* decision? If I am right, the decision was a mistake, unsupported by precedent and contrary to the best understanding of prior First Amendment jurisprudence. It is internally flawed as well: its fundamental distinction between regulating any citizen's or group's contributions to someone else's campaign, which the Court allowed, and regulating the expenditures of individuals or groups on their own behalf, which it did not, is untenable. Justice [Clarence] Thomas remarked in his concurring opinion in the *Colorado Republican* [document 3.4] case last June that there is no difference in principle between these two forms of political expression. Thomas was right—why should [Ross] Perot be free to spend a great fortune promoting his views in the most effective way he can—by running for president and spending a fortune on television—while one of his passionate supporters is not free to promote his own views in the most effective way he can—by contributing what he can afford to Perot's campaign.

In retrospect, at least, this untenable distinction seems a compromise designed to split the difference, allowing Congress to achieve one of its purposes—preventing the corruption that almost inevitably accompanies large-scale contributions—while still insisting on the sanctity of political speech. If so, the Court's compromise has failed, because without a direct limit on spending, any system of regulation of contributions, no matter how elaborate, will collapse, as ours has. When politics desperately needs money, and money desperately seeks influence, money and politics cannot be kept far apart.

Therefore, the case for overruling *Buckley* is a strong one. The prospects for doing so are much less strong. Justices [Ruth Bader] Ginsburg and [John Paul] Stevens made plain, in a dissenting opinion by the latter, their doubts that the First Amendment really does bar expenditure limits. But though Justice Thomas even more openly announced himself ready to revise *Buckley*, he would revise it by forbidding contribution limits as well as expenditure limits, not by allowing limits on expenditures; and, as I said, he and three other Justices argued for an even stronger ban on regulating expenditures than *Buckley* imposed.

But the American public is becoming increasingly angered by the political role of money. Even in 1992, before the new explosion in campaign contributions, a poll of registered voters likely to vote showed that 74 percent agreed that "Congress is largely owned by the special interest groups," and that 84 percent endorsed the statement that "special interest money buys the loyalty of candidates." If that dissatisfaction continues to grow, and the public understands that the *Buckley* decision prevents the most direct attack on the problem, the pressure for overruling it would intensify. If the decision were overruled, the way might be opened for a new system of regulation banning, for example, political commercials in breaks in ordinary programming, as other democracies do, and providing free television time, out of public funds, for longer statements by the candidates themselves.

In any case, even if *Buckley* remains, we should feel no compunction in declaring the decision a mistake, and in attempting to avoid its consequences through any reasonable and effective device we can find or construct. The decision did not declare a valuable principle that we should hesitate to circumvent. On the contrary, it misunderstood not only what free speech really is but what it really means for free people to govern themselves.

DOCUMENT 4.2 Bradley A. Smith, "Faulty Assumptions and Undemocratic Consequences of Campaign Finance Reform," *Yale Law Journal,* vol. 105 (January 1996), pp. 1049–91

Bradley Smith lays out many different arguments against reform. In sum, he believes that the assumptions behind it are mistaken and the consequences perverse. Although he does not address the constitutional issues directly, his argument runs right to the policy matters at the heart of that debate.

. . .

III. FAULTY ASSUMPTIONS OF CAMPAIGN FINANCE REFORMERS

Four general assumptions underlie the arguments made in favor of campaign finance regulation: First, there is too much money being spent in political campaigns; second, campaigns based on small contributions are, in some sense, more democratic, more in touch with the "people," than campaigns financed through large contributions; third, money buys elections, presumably in a manner detrimental to the public good; and fourth, money is a corrupting influence on the legislature. Given these assumptions, it is believed that the end result of an unregulated finance system will be a political process increasingly dominated by wealthy individuals whose interests are at odds with those of ordinary citizens. But are these assumptions warranted? This part of the Essay will examine each of them in turn and conclude that each one is seriously flawed.

A. Assumption One: Too Much Money Is Spent on Campaigns

One often hears that too much money is spent on political campaigns. The language in which campaigns are described in the general press constantly reinforces that perception. Candidates "amass war chests" with the help of "special interests" that "pour" their "millions" into campaigns. "Obscene" expenditures "career" out of control or "skyrocket" upwards. This language notwithstanding, there is actually good cause to believe that we do not spend enough on campaigns.

The assertion that too much money is spent on campaigning essentially begs the question: Compared to what? Compared to yogurt or potato chips? Americans spend more than twice as much money each year on yogurt, and two to three times as much on the purchase of potato chips, as they do on political

Reprinted by permission of The Yale Law Journal Company and Fred B. Rothman & Company from the *Yale Law Journal,* vol. 105 (1996), pp. 1049–91.

campaigns. In the two-year election cycle culminating in the elections of November 1994, approximately $590 million was spent by all congressional general-election candidates combined. Although this set a new record for spending in congressional races, the amount is hardly exorbitant, amounting to roughly $3 per eligible voter spent over the two-year period between elections. Total direct campaign spending for all local, state, and federal elections, including congressional elections, over the same period can be reasonably estimated as between $1.5 billion and $2.0 billion, or somewhere between $7.50 and $10 per eligible voter over the two-year cycle. When one considers that this per-voter figure is spread over several candidates for which that voter is eligible to cast a ballot, it is hard to suggest that office seekers are spending "obscene" sums attempting to get their messages through to voters.

Comparisons to levels of corporate spending on product advertising help to illustrate that spending on political campaigns is minimal. The sum of the annual advertising budgets of Procter & Gamble and Philip Morris Company, the nation's two largest advertisers, is roughly equal to the amount spent by all federal and state political candidates and parties in a two-year election cycle. The value of such comparisons can be disputed: If one views the problem as the allegedly corrupting effect of campaign money, then the suggestion that it may take less to buy politicians than to sell soap and tobacco provides little comfort. But such numbers are useful to put political spending into perspective when it is the raw levels of spending that are challenged, and to consider the probable effect on political communication of reform measures that would limit spending.

Increased campaign spending translates into a better-informed electorate. Gary Jacobson's extensive studies have shown that "the extent and content of information [voters] . . . have has a decisive effect on how they vote." Voters' understanding of issues increases with the quantity of campaign information received. In short, spending less on campaigns will result in less public awareness and understanding of issues.

. . .

There are no objective criteria by which to measure whether "too much" is spent on political campaigns. What is spent on campaigns, one might fairly suggest, is the amount that individuals feel it is worthwhile to contribute and that candidates find it is effective to raise and spend. Considering the importance of elections to any democratic society, it is hard to believe that direct expenditures of approximately $10 per voter for all local, state, and national campaigns, over a two-year period, constitutes a crisis requiring limitations on spending.

B. Assumption Two: Campaigns Funded with Small Contributions Are More Democratic

Within the reform movement lies a deep-rooted belief that democratic political campaigns should be financed by small contributions. This position is motivated by the belief that large contributions corrupt either or both the electoral and legislative systems. Such a belief suggests that a campaign funded through small contributions will in the end lead to less corruption. However, small contributions are often seen as an end in themselves, on the notion that even if money were not corrupting, small contributions epitomize the American belief in self-government and participatory democracy. This notion of the campaign funded through small contributions as the embodiment of representative democracy is unrealistic.

First, this vision appears to be based on an idealized image of democratic politics. . . . The burden of financing political campaigns has always fallen on a small minority of the American public. Today, as many as eighteen million Americans make some financial contribution to a political party, candidate, or PAC in a given election cycle. . . . Yet this "broad base of support" amounts to only some 10% of the voting-age population. With the exception of the occasional race with a candidate who can whip up an ideological fervor on the fringe of mainstream politics, such as George McGovern or Oliver North, Americans are simply unwilling, individually, to contribute enough money in small amounts to run modern campaigns.

It is a mistake to assume that a broad base of contributors necessarily makes a campaign in some way more representative or more attuned to the popular will. Though the eighteen million who contribute to campaigns constitute a far broader base of financial contributors than existed in the eighteenth and nineteenth centuries, few would argue that this has made the political system more democratic or more responsive. Indeed, it is an article of faith in reformist literature that our system has grown less responsive to popular will in the last century. In fact, however, those candidates who have been best able to raise campaign dollars in small contributions have often been those who were most emphatically out of the mainstream of their time. Barry Goldwater's 1964 presidential campaign, for example, raised $5.8 million from 410,000 small contributors, before going down in a landslide defeat. On his way to an even more crushing defeat in 1972, George McGovern raised almost $15 million from small donors, at an average of approximately $20 per contributor. And if we assume that reliance on numerous small contributions makes a campaign in some way more "democratic," then the most "democratic" campaign of 1994 was the U.S. Senate campaign of Oliver North. North raised approximately $20 million, almost entirely from small contributors, and actually outspent his nearest rival by nearly 4 to 1. Yet he still lost to an unpopular opponent plagued by personal scandal. All of these campaigns were among the most prominent extremist candidacies in recent decades. This suggests that the ability to raise large sums in small amounts is a sign of fervent backing from a relatively small minority, rather than a sign of broad public support. At the same time, truly mass-based political movements have historically relied on a relatively small number of large contributors for "seed money," if not for the bulk of their funding.

Campaign finance reform efforts tend to overlook the significant collective action problem that prevents most voters from giving financially to candidates. Even if large contributions were totally banned, thereby increasing the relative importance of small contributions, no single contribution would be likely to have a significant impact on an election. Voters, therefore, still have little rational incentive to make contributions. This collective action problem may be overcome by a radical campaign in which donors are motivated by ideology rather than rational, utility-maximizing calculations. However, in most instances, there will not be sufficient funds available to finance campaigns at a level that informs the electorate unless a resort is made to public funds. Thus, a system of private campaign finance will almost inevitably come to rely on large individual donors who believe that their substantial gift can make a difference, and on interest groups (i.e., PACs) that overcome voter inertia by organizing voters to address particular concerns.

C. Assumption Three: Money Buys Elections

The third assumption of campaign finance reform is that money "buys" elections in some manner incompatible with a functioning democracy. It seems axiomatic that a candidate with little or no money to spend is unlikely to win most races. Furthermore, the candidate who spends more money wins more often than not. But correlation is not the same as cause and effect, and one must be careful not to make too much of such simple numbers. The correlation between spending and victory may stem simply from the desire of donors to contribute to candidates who are likely to win, in which case the ability to win attracts money, rather than the other way around. Similarly, higher levels of campaign contributions to, and spending by, a candidate may merely reflect a level of public support that is later manifested at the polls. Generally speaking, the same attributes that attract voters to a candidate will attract donations, and those that attract donations will attract voters. In other words, the candidate who is able to raise more money would usually win even if that candidate could not spend the added money: The ability to raise money is evidence of political prowess and popularity that would normally translate into votes, regardless of spending.

At the same time, higher spending does not necessarily translate into electoral triumph. . . . One need only look at recent elections to prove this point. In the 1994 U.S. House elections, for example, many incumbents won while spending considerably less than their opponents. More pointedly, the thirty-four Republican challengers who defeated Democratic incumbents spent, on average, only two-thirds of the amounts expended by their opponents, and one spent less than one-twentieth as much as did his incumbent opponent. Given the inherent advantages of incumbency, this is powerful evidence that a monetary advantage alone does not mean electoral success.

. . .

The assumption that money buys elections is based on simple correlation: The candidate who spends the most usually wins. However, it would be surprising if this were not the case, as contributions flow naturally to those candidates who are popular and are perceived as having a good chance of winning. It seems clear that many candidates win despite spending less than their opponents, and that the correlation between spending and success is not as strong as other indicators, such as the correlation between incumbency and success. The problem, if it exists, is not that some candidates "buy" elections by spending too much, but that other candidates spend too little to reach the mass of voters.

D. Assumption Four: Money Is a Corrupting Influence on Candidates

A fundamental tenet of the reform movement is that money has corrupted the legislative process in America. Large numbers of Americans have come to view legislative politics as a money game, in which campaign contributions are the dominant influence on policymaking.

In many respects, this would seem to be the most sound of the fundamental reformist assumptions. Experience and human nature tell us that legislators, like most people, are influenced by money, even when it goes into their campaign funds rather than directly into their pockets. Many legislators themselves have complained of the influence of money in the legislature.

In fact, however, a substantial majority of those who have studied voting patterns on a systematic basis agree that campaign contributions affect very few votes in the legislature. The primary factors determining a legislator's votes, these studies conclude, are party affiliation, ideology, and constituent views and needs. Where contributions and voting patterns intersect, they do so largely because donors contribute to those candidates who are believed to favor their positions, not the other way around.

. . .

If campaign contributions have any meaningful effect on legislative voting behavior, it is on a limited number of votes, generally related to specialized or narrow issues arousing little public interest. A legislator is unlikely to accept a campaign contribution, which can be used only to attempt to sway voters, in exchange for an unpopular vote, which definitely alienates voters. Therefore, specialized issues provide the best opportunity to trade votes for money. On these issues, prior contributions may provide the contributor with access to the legislator or legislative staff. The contributor may then be able to shape legislation to the extent that such efforts are not incompatible with the dominant legislative motives of ideology, party affiliation and agenda, and constituent views. Whether or not the influence of campaign contributions on these limited issues is good or bad depends on one's views of the resulting legislation. The exclusion of knowledgeable contributors from the legislative process can just as easily lead to poor legislation with unintended consequences as can their inclusion. In any case, it must be stressed that such issues are few.

. . .

The available evidence simply does not show a meaningful, causal relationship between campaign contributions and legislative voting patterns. While campaign contributions may influence votes in a few limited cases, this would not seem to justify wholesale regulation.

The pressure for campaign finance regulation has been based on assumptions that are, at best, questionable, and, at worst, seriously flawed. Not surprisingly, then, campaign finance reform efforts enacted into law have had negative consequences for our political system.

IV. THE UNDEMOCRATIC CONSEQUENCES OF CAMPAIGN FINANCE REGULATION

Campaign finance reform has generally focused on three specific tactics for promoting change: limiting contributions, whether by individuals, corporations, or PACs; limiting campaign spending; and, ultimately, using public funding for campaigns. These reform tactics have several negative consequences, which can be broadly labeled "undemocratic." Specifically, campaign finance reform efforts entrench the status quo; make the electoral system less responsive to popular opinion; strengthen the power of select elites; favor wealthy individuals; and limit opportunities for "grass-roots" political activity. This part discusses each of these consequences in turn, assuming that any regulation exists within a system of private campaign funding. . . .

A. Campaign Finance Reform Entrenches the Status Quo

Campaign finance reform measures, in particular limits on contributions and overall spending, insulate the political system from challenge by outsiders, and hinder the ability of challengers to compete on equal terms with those already in power.

Contribution limits tend to favor incumbents by making it harder for challengers to raise money and thereby make credible runs for office. The lower the contribution limit, the more difficult it becomes for a candidate to raise money quickly from a small number of dedicated supporters. The consequent need to raise campaign cash from a large number of small contributors benefits those candidates who have in place a database of past contributors, an intact campaign organization, and the ability to raise funds on an ongoing basis from PACs. This latter group consists almost entirely of current officeholders. Thus, contribution limits hit political newcomers especially hard because of the difficulties candidates with low name recognition have in raising substantial sums of money from small contributors. . . .

Beyond making it harder for challengers to raise cash, contribution limits also tend to decrease overall spending, which further works against challengers. Incumbents begin each campaign with significant advantages in name recognition. They are able to attract press coverage because of their office, and they often receive assistance from their staffs and send constituents postage-free mailings using their franking privilege. Through patronage and constituent favors, they can further add to their support. One way for challengers to offset these advantages is to spend money to make their names and positions known. Those few studies that have attempted to isolate and quantify the effect of campaign spending on votes have found that, once a candidate spends the minimal amount needed to penetrate the public consciousness, additional spending affects a very limited number of votes. However, the positive effect of added spending is significantly greater for challengers than for incumbents. In fact, studies show an inverse relationship between high levels of incumbent spending and incumbent success. Heavy spending by an incumbent indicates that the incumbent is in electoral trouble and facing a well-financed challenger. Because an incumbent's added spending is likely to have less of an effect on vote totals than the additional spending of a challenger, limits on total campaign spending will hurt challengers more than incumbents. By lowering overall campaign spending, therefore, contribution limits further lock into place the advantages of incumbency and disproportionately harm challengers.

Absolute spending ceilings, whether "mandatory" or "voluntary," have the potential to exacerbate this problem considerably. Set low enough, they may make it impossible for challengers to attain the critical threshold at which they can reach enough voters to run a credible race. Overall spending caps also prevent challengers from ever spending more than incumbents. While spending more than one's opponent is not necessary to win an election, a challenger's ability to outspend an incumbent can help to offset the advantages of incumbency. Efforts to limit spending, whether mandatory or through incentive-based "voluntary" caps, should therefore not be viewed as benign or neutral.

B. Campaign Finance Reform Promotes Influence Peddling and Reduces Accountability

Limits on contributions increase the incentives for contributors to seek "influence" rather than the election of like-minded legislators, and reduce the effectiveness of legislative-monitoring efforts. We have previously seen that, though the argument is overstated, campaign contributions may affect legislative votes on a limited number of issues. Many reformers have been more concerned about contributors who adopt a "legislative" strategy, attempting to influence legislative votes, than with donors who adopt an "electoral" strategy, aimed at influencing election outcomes. Yet strangely enough, contribution limits, the most popular reform measure, encourage PACs and other monied interests to adopt legislative strategies. This results in the representative system being less responsive to public opinion.

Campaign contributors must weigh the costs and benefits of pursuing an electoral strategy versus a legislative strategy. Money given to a losing challenger is not merely money wasted, it is money spent counterproductively, as it will probably increase the enmity of, and decrease access to, the incumbent. With incumbents winning in excess of 90% of House races, an electoral strategy of supporting challengers has very high risks. Even in close races, so long as a contributor is limited to a maximum contribution of $10,000 (or some other amount), the contributor's campaign donation is unlikely to increase significantly the odds of a victory for the challenger. The low-risk alternative is to contribute to incumbents in the hope that a legislative strategy might succeed, at least by minimizing otherwise hostile treatment aimed at the contributor's interests. Thus, because the risk of an electoral strategy is so high, contribution limits tend to lock the rational contributor into a legislative strategy. To the extent, then, that campaign contributions influence legislative voting behavior, campaign finance regulation in the form of contribution limits is likely to make the problem worse.

. . .

PACs perform a valuable monitoring function in the current campaign regime, a function that would be lost were private funding to be eliminated. It has been suggested that the real issue that the campaign reform movement attempts to address is "shirking," or the tendency of elected officials to betray their public trust in favor of their own or other interests. In most cases, it will not be rational for individuals to devote considerable time to monitoring the performance of elected officials. However, by banding together with others having similar concerns, individuals can perform the monitoring function at a reasonable cost. Interest groups, and the PACs they spawn, thus play an important role in monitoring officeholders' performances so as to prevent shirking. Therefore, measures that would limit or eliminate the role of PACs are likely to reduce legislative monitoring, leading to a legislature ever more isolated from the people.

Finally, there is always the possibility that limiting private contributions will simply increase the value of a more corrupting alternative: outright bribery. It is naive to think that when the government is heavily involved in virtually every aspect of economic life in the country (and quite a few noneconomic spheres as well), people affected by government actions will accept whatever comes without some kind of counterstrategy. In this way, too, contribution limits may make the electoral system less responsive to public opinion and, therefore, less democratic.

C. Campaign Finance Regulation Favors Select Elites

Campaign finance reform is usually sold as a populist means to strengthen the power of "ordinary" citizens against dominant, big-money interests. In fact, campaign finance reform has favored select elites and further isolated individuals from the political process.

There are a great many sources of political influence. These include direct personal attributes, such as speaking and writing ability, good looks, personality, time and energy, and organizational skills, as well as acquired attributes, such as wealth, celebrity, and access to or control of the popular press. In any society, numerous individuals will rise to the top of their professions to become part of an "elite." Both as a prerequisite to their success and as a reward for it, such individuals will have certain abilities that they can use for political ends. For example, Hollywood celebrities, by virtue of their fame, may gain audiences for their political views that they would not otherwise obtain. They may be invited to testify before Congress, despite their lack of any particular expertise, or they may use their celebrity to assist campaigns through appearances at rallies. Similarly, successful academics may write powerful articles that change the way people think about issues. Labor organizers may have at their disposal a vast supply of human resources that they can use to support favored candidates. Media editors, reporters, and anchors can shape not only the manner, but also the content, of news reporting. Those with marketing skills can apply their abilities to raise funds or to produce advertising for a candidate or cause. Successful entrepreneurs may amass large sums of money that they can use for political purposes. . . .

The common response to this argument is that money can buy other sources of power: It can purchase labor, marketing know-how, media access, even speaking coaches and improved physical appearance. Not only does this response not justify the prejudice against money, however, but it is simply incorrect, insofar as it sees this as a unique feature of money. A winning personality, the ability to forge political alliances, and the time to devote to politics can, like money, be used to gain access to the media, labor, and other prerequisites to political success. Moreover, these skills, like the ability to produce moving television ads or to write effective campaign literature and speeches, are themselves convertible into money. For example, money can be raised through slick direct mail pitches, operation of phone banks, advertisements, speeches at rallies, booths at county fairs, and countless other means. The trick to effective electoral politics is to take the assets with which one begins and to use them to obtain additional assets that one lacks. Money is no different.

Once we accept the fact that different individuals control different sources of political power, it becomes apparent that attempts to exclude a particular form of power—money—from politics only strengthen the position of those whose power comes from other, nonmonetary, sources, such as time or media access. For example, though the Supreme Court has allowed states to limit even independent expenditures by nonmedia corporations in candidate races, newspapers, magazines, and TV and radio corporations can spend unlimited sums to promote the election of favored candidates. Thus, Donald Graham, the publisher of the *Washington Post*, has at his disposal the resources of a media empire to promote his views, free from the campaign finance restrictions to which others are subjected. ABC News anchor Peter Jennings is given a nightly forum on national television in which to express his views.

Media elites are not the only group whose influence is increased by campaign spending and contribution limits. Restricting the flow of money into campaigns also increases the relative importance of in-kind contributions and so favors those who are able to control large blocks of human resources. Limiting contributions and expenditures does not particularly democratize the process, but merely shifts power from those whose primary contribution is money to those whose primary contribution is time, organization, or some other resource—for example, from small business groups to large labor unions. Others who benefit from campaign finance limitations include political middlemen, public relations firms conducting "voter education" programs, lobbyists, PACs such as EMILY's List that "bundle" large numbers of $1000 contributions, and political activists. These individuals and groups may or may not be more representative of public opinion than the wealthy philanthropists and industrialists who financed so many past campaigns.

. . .

D. Campaign Finance Limitations Favor Wealthy Candidates

Though campaign finance restrictions aim to reduce the role of money in politics, they have helped to renew the phenomenon of the "millionaire candidate"—with Michael Huffington and Ross Perot as only the most celebrated recent examples. In the *Buckley* [document 3.1] decision, the Supreme Court held that Congress could not limit the amount that a candidate could spend on his or her own campaign. Contribution limits, however, force candidates to raise funds from the public only in small amounts. The ability to spend unlimited amounts, coupled with restrictions on raising outside money, favors those candidates who can contribute large sums to their own campaigns from personal assets. A Michael Huffington, Herb Kohl, or Jay Rockefeller becomes a particularly viable candidate precisely because personal wealth provides a direct campaign advantage that cannot be offset by a large contributor to the opposing candidate. These candidates represent an array of views across the political spectrum. The point is not that these "rich" candidates hold uniform views but, more simply, that a system favoring personal wealth in candidates will restrict the number of viable candidates, potentially limiting voter choice. While most reformers have criticized *Buckley* for creating precisely this situation, it seems a mistake to exacerbate the problem through added regulation as long as *Buckley* remains law.

At the same time that contribution limits help independently wealthy candidates, they may harm working-class political interests. Historically, candidates with large constituencies among the poor and the working class have obtained their campaign funds from a small base of wealthy donors. By limiting the ability of wealthy individuals such as Stewart Mott to finance these efforts, regulations may harm working-class constituencies. Supporters of these candidates simply do not have the funds to compete with other constituencies and candidates.

. . .

E. Campaign Finance Regulation Favors Special Interests over Grassroots Activity

Campaign finance regulation is also undemocratic in that it favors well-organized special interests over grassroots political activity. Limitations on contributions and spending, by definition, require significant regulation of the campaign process, including substantial reporting requirements as to the amounts spent and the sources of funds. Typically, regulation favors those already familiar with the regulatory machinery and those with the money and sophistication to hire the lawyers, accountants, and lobbyists needed to comply with complex filing requirements. Such regulation will naturally disadvantage newcomers to the political arena, especially those who are themselves less educated or less able to pay for professional services. Efforts to regulate campaigns in favor of small contributors thus have the perverse effect of professionalizing politics and distancing the system from "ordinary" citizens.

Regulation also creates opportunities to gain an advantage over an opponent through use of the regulatory process, and litigation has now become "a major campaign tactic." Again, one can expect such tactics to be used most often by those already familiar with the rules. Indeed, there is some evidence that campaign enforcement actions are disproportionately directed at challengers, who are less likely to have staff familiar with the intricacies of campaign finance regulation. . . .

Campaign finance regulation has been packaged as a means of returning power to "ordinary people." In truth, however, such regulation acts to exclude ordinary people from the political process in a variety of ways: It insulates incumbents from the voting public, in both the electoral and legislative spheres; it increases the ability of certain elites to dominate the debate by eliminating competing voices; it places a renewed premium on personal wealth in political candidates; and it hampers grassroots political activity. These problems are not the result of a poorly designed regulatory structure, but rather the inevitable result of a regulatory structure built on faulty assumptions.

Cass R. Sunstein, "Political Equality and Unintended Consequences," *Columbia Law Review*, vol. 94 (May 1994), pp. 1390–1414

DOCUMENT 4.3

Cass Sunstein steers something of a middle-course between the reform and deregulationist camps. On the one hand, he argues that *Buckley* (document 3.1) was wrongly decided. To him, it repeats the mistake of the Supreme Court's interventions in the economic and social realms early in this century. On the other hand, he believes reform poses many potential pitfalls, like entrenching incumbents. In the end, he calls for some regulation but asks that it proceed carefully and cautiously.

It is a familiar point that government regulation that is amply justified in principle may go terribly wrong in practice. Minimum wage laws, for example, appear to reduce employment. Stringent regulation of new sources of air pollution may aggravate pollution problems, by perpetuating the life of old, especially dirty sources. If government closely monitors the release of information, there may be less information. Unintended consequences of this kind can make regulation futile or even self-defeating. By futile regulation, I mean measures that do not bring about the desired consequences. By self-defeating regulation, I mean measures that actually make things worse from the standpoint of their strongest and most public-spirited advocates. We do not lack examples of both of these phenomena. It is unfortunate but true that current campaign finance laws may well provide more illustrations.

Some campaign finance regulation is amply justified in principle. As we will see, there is no good reason to allow disparities in wealth to be translated into disparities in political power. A well-functioning democracy distinguishes between market processes of purchase and sale on the one hand and political processes of voting and reason-giving on the other. Government has a legitimate interest in ensuring not only that political liberties exist as a formal and technical matter, but also that those liberties have real value to the people who have them. The achievement of political equality is an important constitutional goal. Nonetheless, many imaginable campaign finance restrictions would be futile or self-defeating. To take a familiar example, it is now well-known that restrictions on individual expenditures—designed to reduce influence-peddling—can help fuel the use of political action committees (PACs), and thus increase the phenomenon of influence-peddling. This is merely one of a number of possible illustrations.

I can venture no exhaustive account here, and I attempt to describe possibilities rather than certainties. But one of my principal goals is to outline some of the harmful but unintended consequences of campaign finance restrictions.

. . .

I. CAMPAIGN FINANCE REFORM: JUSTIFICATIONS AND THE JUDICIAL RESPONSE

A. Arguments for Campaign Finance Reform

In principle, the case for campaign finance regulation is very strong. We can identify at least three central grounds for such regulation. First and most obvious, perhaps, is the need to protect the electoral process from both the appearance and the reality of "quid pro quo" exchanges between contributors and candidates. Such exchanges occur whenever contributors offer dollars in return for political favors. The purchase of votes or of political favors is a form of corruption—a large issue in recent campaigns. Corruption is inconsistent with the view that public officials should act on the basis of the merits of proposals, and not on the basis of their personal economic interest, or even the interest in increasing their campaign finances. Of course consideration of the merits will often involve people's preferences, and of course a willingness to pay cash may reflect preferences. But the link between particular cash payments and any responsible judgment about the merits is extremely weak. Laws should not be purchased and sold; the spectre of *quid pro quo* exchanges violates this principle.

The second interest, independent of corruption, involves political equality. This is a time-honored goal in American constitutional thought. People who are able to organize themselves in such a way as to spend large amounts of cash should not be able to influence politics more than people who are not similarly able. Certainly economic equality is not required in a democracy; but it is most troublesome if people with a good deal of money are allowed to translate their wealth into political influence. It is equally troublesome if the electoral process translates poverty into an absence of political influence. Of course economic inequalities cannot be made altogether irrelevant for politics. But the link can be diminished between wealth or poverty on the one hand and political influence on the other. The "one person-one vote" rule exemplifies the commitment to political equality. Limits on campaign expenditures are continuous with that rule.

The third interest is in some ways a generalization of the first two. Campaign finance laws might promote the goal of ensuring political deliberation and reason-giving. Politics should not simply register existing preferences and their intensities, especially as these are measured by private willingness to pay. In the American constitutional tradition, politics has an important deliberative function. The constitutional system aspires to a form of "government by discussion." Grants of cash to candidates might compromise that goal by, for example, encouraging legislatures to vote in accordance with private interest rather than reasons.

The goals of political equality and political deliberation are related to the project of distinguishing between the appropriate spheres of economic markets and politics. In democratic politics, a norm of equality is important: disparities in wealth ought not lead to disparities in power over government. Similarly, democracy requires adherence to the norm of reason-giving. Political outcomes should not be based only on intensities of preferences as these are reflected in the criterion of private willingness to pay. Taken together, the notions of equality and reason-giving embody a distinctive conception of political respect. Markets are operated on the basis of quite different understandings. People can purchase things because they want them, and they need not offer or even have reasons for their wants. Markets embody their own conception of equality insofar as they entail a principle of "one dollar–one 'vote'"; but this is not the conception of equality appropriate to the political sphere.

To distinguish between the market and politics is not to deny that an expenditure of money on behalf of a candidate or a cause qualifies as "speech" for first amendment purposes. Such an expenditure might well be intended and received as a contribution to social deliberation. Many people give money in order to promote discussion of a position that they favor. Indeed, we might see the ability to accumulate large sums of money as at least a rough indicator that large numbers of people are intensely interested in a candidate's success. If a candidate can accumulate a lot of money, it is probable that many people like what she has to say, or that even if the number of supporters is not so great, their level of enthusiasm is high indeed. In this way we might take the ability to attract a large amount of money to reveal something important—if not decisive—in a deliberative democracy. If and because political dissenters are able to attract funds, they might be able to do especially well in the political "marketplace." This possibility should hardly be disparaged.

In this regard, it is perhaps insufficiently appreciated that a system without limits on financial contributions favors people who can attract money without, however, simply favoring the rich over the poor. In theory, at least, some poor people may be able to attract a lot of money if their political commitments find broad support—from, say, a lot of relatively poor people, or from a smaller but intensely interested number of rich ones. Of course it is hardly unusual for a rich candidate to find it impossible to obtain sufficient funds, because other people are not at all interested in providing support. Many candidates with large personal fortunes have failed for just this reason.

These points are not decisive in favor of a system of laissez-faire for political expenditures and contributions. The correlation between public enthusiasm and the capacity to attract money is crude. There is a large disparity between donations and intensity of interest in a candidate. Candidate A might, for example, attract large sums of money from wealthy people; but A's supporters may be less interested in her success than Candidate B's poorer supporters are interested in B's success, even though B's supporters donate less money. Moreover, as I have emphasized, a democracy is concerned with much more than numbers and intensities of preferences.

At the very least, however, an expenditure of money is an important means by which people communicate ideas, and the First Amendment requires a strong justification for any government regulation of an important means of communication. We might therefore think of campaign finance laws as viewpoint-neutral and even content-neutral restrictions on political speech. At least if the laws are fair, the particular content of the speech—the message that is being urged—is irrelevant to whether the campaign finance restriction attaches. The area is especially difficult because while these restrictions can be severe, the government can point to strong reasons in their support.

. . .

C. *Lochner*, Redistribution, and *Buckley*

Let us put these various complexities to one side and return to the basic issue of political equality. In rejecting the claim that controls on financial expenditures could be justified as a means of promoting political equality, *Buckley* seems highly reminiscent of the pre–New Deal period. Indeed *Buckley* might well be seen as the modern-day analogue of the infamous and discredited case of *Lochner* v. *New York*, in which the Court invalidated maximum hour laws.

A principal problem with the pre–New Deal Court was that it treated existing distributions of resources as if they were prepolitical and just, and therefore invalidated democratic efforts at reform. In a key *Lochner* era case, *Adkins* v. *Children's Hospital*, [261 U.S.525, 56062(1923)] for example, the Court invalidated minimum wage legislation. In so doing, it said:

To the extent that the sum fixed by [the minimum wage statute] exceeds the fair value of the services rendered, it amounts to a compulsory exaction from the employer for the support of a partially indigent person, for whose condition there rests upon him no peculiar responsibility, and therefore, in effect, arbitrarily shifts to his shoulders a burden which, if it belongs to anybody, belongs to society as a whole.

The language of compulsory subsidy—of taking from some for the benefit of others—was central in the *Lochner* period. Regulatory adjustment of market arrangements was seen as interference with an otherwise law-free and unobjectionable status quo. It was a state-mandated transfer of funds from one group for another, and this kind of mandate was constitutionally illegitimate.

To compress a long and complex story: This whole approach became unsustainable in 1937, when the legal culture came to think that existing distributions were a product of law, were not sacrosanct, and could legitimately be subject to governmental correction. Throughout the legal system, it was urged that property rights were a function of law rather than nature, and ought not to be immunized from legal change. Such changes would not be banned in principle, but would be evaluated on the basis of the particular reasons brought forward on their behalf. In President Roosevelt's words: "We must lay hold of the fact that economic laws are not made by nature. They are made by human beings." And the Supreme Court, overruling *Lochner* itself, offered an uncanny reversal of the *Adkins* dictum, arguing that "the community is not bound to provide what is in effect a subsidy for unconscionable employers."

In its essential premises, *Buckley* is quite similar to the pre-1937 cases. Recall that the Court announced that "the concept that government may restrict the speech of some elements of our society in order to enhance the relative voice of others is wholly foreign to the First Amendment." It added that the "First Amendment's protection against governmental abridgement of free expression cannot properly be made to depend on a person's financial ability to engage in public discussion." The *Buckley* Court therefore saw campaign expenditure limits as a kind of "taking," or compulsory exaction, from some for the benefit of others. The limits were unconstitutional for this very reason. Just as the due process clause once forbade government "interference" with the outcomes of the economic marketplace, so too the First Amendment now bans government "interference" with the political marketplace, with the term "marketplace" understood quite literally. In this way *Buckley* replicates *Lochner*.

On the view reflected in both *Buckley* and *Lochner*, reliance on free markets is government neutrality and government inaction. But in the New Deal period, it became clear that reliance on markets simply entailed another—if in many ways good—regulatory system, made possible and constituted through law. We cannot have a system of market ordering without an elaborate body of law. For all their beneficial qualities, markets are legitimately subject to democratic restructuring—at least within certain limits—if the restructuring promises to deliver sufficient benefits. This is a constitutional truism in the post–New Deal era. What is perhaps not sufficiently appreciated, but what is equally true, is that elections based on existing distributions of wealth and entitlements also embody a regulatory system, made possible and constituted through law. Here as elsewhere, law defines property interests; it specifies who owns what, and who may do what with what is owned. The regulatory system that we now have for elections is not obviously neutral or just. On the contrary, it seems to be neither insofar as it permits high levels of political influence to follow from large accumulations of wealth.

Because it involves speech, *Buckley* is in one sense even more striking than *Lochner*. As I have noted, the goal of political equality is time-honored in the American constitutional tradition, as the goal of economic equality is not. Efforts to redress economic inequalities, or to ensure that they are not turned into political inequalities, should not be seen as impermissible redistribution, or as the introduction of government regulation into a place where it did not exist before. A system of unlimited campaign expenditures should be seen as a regulatory decision to allow disparities in resources to be turned into disparities in political influence. That may be the best decision, all things considered; but why is it unconstitutional for government to attempt to replace this system with an alternative? The Court offered no answer. Its analysis was startlingly cavalier. Campaign finance laws should be evaluated not through axioms, but pragmatically in terms of their consequences for the system of free expression.

II. THE PROBLEM OF UNINTENDED CONSEQUENCES

In principle, then, there are good arguments for campaign finance restrictions. Insofar as *Buckley* rejects political equality as a legitimate constitutional goal, it should be overruled. Indeed, the decision probably ranks among the strongest candidates for overruling of the post-World War II period. But there are real limits on how much we can learn from abstract principles alone. Many of the key questions are insistently ones of policy and fact. Was the system at issue in *Buckley* well-designed? How might it be improved? What will be the real-world consequences of different plans? Will they fulfill their intended purposes? Will they be self-defeating? Might they impair democratic processes under the guise of promoting them?

My goal here is to offer a brief catalogue of ways in which campaign finance legislation may prove unhelpful or counterproductive. My particular interest lies in the possibility that campaign finance legislation may have perverse or unintended consequences. The catalogue bears directly on a number of proposals now receiving attention in Congress and in the executive branch. Of course it would be necessary to look at the details in order to make a final assessment. I am describing possibilities, not certainties, and a good deal of empirical work would be necessary to come to terms with any of them.

A general point runs throughout the discussion. Although I have criticized what the Court said in *Buckley*, considerable judicial suspicion of campaign finance limits is justified by a simple point: Congressional support for such limits is especially likely to reflect congressional self-dealing. Any system of campaign finance limits raises the special spectre of governmental efforts to promote the interests of existing legislators. Indeed, it is hard to imagine other kinds of legislation posing similarly severe risks. In these circumstances, we might try to avoid rigid, command-and-control regulation, which poses special dangers, and move instead toward more flexible, incentive-based strategies.

A. Unintended Consequences in Particular

1. Campaign Finance Limits May Entrench Incumbents. Operating under the rubric of democratic equality, campaign finance measures may make it hard for challengers to overcome the effects of incumbency. The problem is all the more severe in a period in which it is extremely difficult for challengers to unseat incumbents. . . .

The risk of incumbent self-dealing becomes even more troublesome in light of the fact that dissidents or challengers may be able to overcome the advantages of incumbency only by amassing enormous sums of money, either from their own pockets or from numerous or wealthy supporters.

Consider in this regard the candidacy of Ross Perot. The Perot campaign raises many questions, but it is at least notable that large sums of money proved an indispensable mechanism for enabling an outsider to challenge the mainstream candidates. One lesson seems clear. Campaign finance limits threaten to eliminate one of the few means by which incumbents can be seriously challenged.

There is particular reason to fear self-dealing in some of the proposals now attracting considerable enthusiasm in Congress. For example, incumbent senators tend to have less difficulty in raising money than do members of the House of Representatives. Members of the House are therefore more dependent on PAC contributions. It should be unsurprising that while Senate bills propose a complete ban on multicandidate PACs, the leading House bill proposes a much less draconian contribution limit of $2,500 per candidate. More generally, the current proposals do nothing to decrease the benefits of incumbency, and they may well increase those benefits.

Whether campaign finance limits in general do entrench incumbents is an empirical question. There is some evidence to the contrary. Usually the largest amounts are spent by incumbents themselves; usually incumbents have an advantage in accumulating enormous sums, often from people who think that they have something to gain from a financial relationship with an officeholder. In these circumstances, one of the particular problems for challengers is that they face special financial barriers by virtue of the ability of incumbents to raise large sums of money. Probably the fairest generalization is that campaign finance limits in general do not entrench incumbents, but that there are important individual cases in which such limits prevent challengers from mounting serious efforts. In any case, any campaign finance reforms should be designed so as to promote more electoral competition.

2. Limits on Individual Contributions Will Produce More (and More Influential) PACs. The early regulation of individual contributions had an important unintended consequence: It led directly to the rise of the political action committee. When individuals were banned from contributing to campaigns, there was tremendous pressure to provide a mechanism for aggregating individual contributions. The modern PAC is the result. . . .

The post-*Buckley* rise of PACs has a general implication. If individual contributions are controlled while PACs face little or no effective regulation, there could be a large shift of resources in the direction of PACs. Of course a combination of PAC limits and individual contribution limits could counteract this problem. But limits of this kind create difficulties of their own.

3. Limits on "Hard Money" Encourage a Shift to "Soft Money." In the 1980s, the tightening of individual contribution limits—"hard money"—helped increase the amount of "soft money," consisting of gifts to political parties. It should not be surprising to see that in recent years there has been an enormous increase in fund-raising by political parties, which dispense contributions to various candidates. In 1980, the two parties raised and spent about $19 million; in 1984, the amount rose to $19.6 million; in 1988, it increased to $45 million. . . .

In some ways the shift from hard to soft money has been a salutary development. It is more difficult for soft money contributors to target particular beneficiaries, and perhaps this reduces the risk of the *quid pro quo* donation. Reasonable people could believe that soft money poses lower risks to the integrity of the political process while also exemplifying a legitimate form of freedom of speech and association. But the substitution, if it occurs, means that any contribution limits are easily evaded. Candidates know, moreover, the identity of the large contributors to the party, and for this reason soft money can produce risks of corruption as well.

4. Limits on PACs Lead to an Increase in Individual Expenditures. In the next few years, Congress may well impose limits on PACs, or even eliminate them altogether. If it does so, there will be pressure for more in the way of both individual contributions and individual expenditures. Limits or bans on PAC expenditures will increase the forms of financial help that Congress' original efforts in 1971 were specifically designed to limit. It is ironic but true that new legislation designed to counteract PACs will spur the very activity against which Congress initially sought to guard.

For reasons suggested above, this development, even if ironic, may improve things overall. There is a good argument that PAC contributions are especially harmful to democratic processes, because they are particularly likely to be given with the specific purpose of influencing lawmakers. It is also the case that candidates who receive individual contributions are often unaware of the particular reason for the money, whereas PAC beneficiaries know exactly what reasons underlie any donation. For all these reasons, a shift from PACs to individual expenditures may be desirable.

On the other hand, PACs have some distinctive benefits as well. They provide a method by which individuals may band together in order to exercise political influence. Sometimes they offer a helpful aggregative mechanism of the kind that is plausibly salutary in a democracy. A shift from PACs to individual expenditures may be unfortunate insofar as it diminishes the power of politically concerned people to organize and pool their resources on behalf of their favored causes.

On balance, individual expenditures do seem preferable to PACs, because the most severe threats to the "*quid pro quo*" and public deliberation come from PAC money. Restrictions on PACs that move people in the direction of individual expenditures and contributions are therefore desirable. My point is only that there is a trade-off between the two.

5. Limits on PACs Can Hurt Organized Labor and Minority Candidates. Sometimes minority candidates can succeed only with the help of PACs specifically organized for their particular benefit. For this reason, PAC limits will in some circumstances diminish the power of minority candidates. The Congressional Black Caucus has expressed concerns over campaign finance regulation on this ground. Similar results are possible for PACs organized to benefit women. PAC restrictions may also hurt organized labor. Currently labor PACs spend most of their money on individual candidates, especially incumbent Democrats. By contrast, corporate PACs contribute about equally to Democrats and Republicans, and give substantial sums to the parties rather than to individual candidates. A ban on PACs may therefore diminish the influence of labor unions without materially affecting corporate PACs. Perhaps these effects are good or justified on balance. But many people who favor campaign finance regulation might be disturbed to see this effect.

6. Limits on PACs May Increase Secret Gifts. Many current interest groups appear unconcerned about PAC limits, even though their interests would appear to be jeopardized by the proposed limits. Perhaps it will be easy for them to evade any such limits, especially by offering "soft money" and also by assembling large amounts as a result of contributions from unidentifiable sources. We lack detailed evidence on this issue, but there is reason to think that the concern is legitimate. It is possible that limits on PACs will make it harder to identify sources of money without materially decreasing special interest funding. The current proposals do not respond to this risk.

7. Limits on Both PACs and Contributions Could Hinder Campaign Activity. Most of the discussion thus far has been based on the assumption that campaign finance reform proposals would limit either PACs or individual contributions. In either case, limitations on one could lead to increased spending through the other. A third option might be to limit both PACs and individual contributions. But this option could quite possibly lead to a number of negative effects. If the limits were successful, campaign activity might be sharply limited as a whole. Any such limit would raise First Amendment problems and perhaps compromise democratic government. Alternatively, resources could be funneled into campaigns through "soft money," secret gifts, or other loopholes in the reforms. . . .

CONTENTS

INTRODUCTION BY FRANK J. SORAUF

Nothing symbolizes the funding of campaigns after the post-Watergate reforms of 1974 as aptly as political action committees (PACs). And nothing better typifies the discontent that regulatory system has generated. For the central fact is that, while PACs existed as early as the 1940s, they reached their maturity and full flowering in the 1970s and 1980s. In the first counting in 1974 there were 608 registered with the Federal Election Commission (FEC), but by the end of 1984 there were 4,009. Within the same ten-year span their contributions to all congressional candidates rose from $12.5 million to $105.3 million. In short, PACs have become the most visible icons of this generation's campaign finance.

The first American PAC was called the Political Action Committee, a name that quickly became the generic term for all of its successors. It was founded in 1943 as a political arm of the Congress of Industrial Organizations (CIO), largely in response to Congress's outlawing of direct campaign contributions from the treasuries of labor unions. (Congress had outlawed direct contributions by corporations thirty-six years earlier [document 2.1].) Its purpose—to raise money in voluntary individual contributions for a separate political fund from which to support the interests of the sponsoring organization with campaign contributions—is still the chief purpose of most PACs.

PACs proliferated slowly and somewhat silently until their sudden growth coincided with the first years of the post-Watergate reforms. The connection was clear and direct. Congress in the Federal Election Campaign Act of 1974 (FECA; document 2.9) set the limit on contributions by individuals at $1,000 per candidate per election and that for PACs at $5,000. Primaries and general elections each were a separate election; thus the effective limits were $2,000 and $10,000 for the two-year election cycle. In 1974 Congress wanted above all to curb the giving of wealthy individuals (the so-called "fat cats"); W. Clement Stone, a Chicago insurance executive, had set a record in 1968 with $2.8 million in contributions, most of it to Richard Nixon's campaign for the presidency. In its zeal to end the influence of wealthy contributors, Congress apparently overlooked the incentive for collective action it was creating with PAC limits five times greater than those placed on individuals.

PACs flourished, however, for other reasons. The number of interest groups and the range of their agendas exploded in the 1970s. As citizen loyalties to political parties waned, as the party organizations weakened, and as the parties lost control of campaigns to the media and candidates, interest groups became the political organization of choice for many Americans concerned about specific (and even narrow) interests and issues. PACs were the instruments by which interest groups invaded the home territory of the parties: the politics and campaigns of elections. Their rise marked the end of an informal but historic division of labor in which parties had mobilized support in elections and interest groups brought influence to bear on officials already elected.

Finally, PACs grew in the 1970s because the Federal Election Commission cleared away legal uncertainties about their creation and governance. Sun Oil sought and received an advisory opinion from the FEC that clarified its rights as a corporation vis-à-vis its PAC. By a vote of 4 to 2, the FEC told Sun that it could pay the overhead expenses for a PAC (virtually all expenses except the PAC's direct political contributions) and that it could control its governance and its contribution decisions—so long as the direct political contributions came from a separate fund of money given voluntarily by its stockholders and employees. (See document 5.1.)

Although the specific facts of the SUN PAC advisory opinion applied to a corporation's PAC, the opinion clearly had resonances for other organizations establishing a PAC. The right of the sponsoring organization to spend from its treasury to create and maintain the PAC and to control its operation could scarcely have been more broadly cast. The opinion removed the final impediment to the race of groups to organize PACs and enter electoral politics.

KINDS AND TYPES OF PACS

We talk and write blithely of "PACs," but the term "political action committee" does not appear in federal statutes. PACs are simply a residual category: political committees other than those of political parties. But for one of these committees to qualify for the "$5,000 per candidate per election" limit on contributions, it must be a "multicandidate committee." That is, it must receive contributions from more than fifty people and contribute to at least five candidates for federal office. (If it does not, it is bound by the same $1,000 limit that binds individuals.) Because virtually all nonparty committees registered with the FEC do function as "multicandidate committees," they are the PACs of everyday political discourse.

PACs, moreover, can be divided into two broad types depending on their organizational structure:

the connected and the nonconnected. The connected are the PACs with parent organizations—the PACs of corporations, unions, and membership organizations such as the American Medical Association, the Sierra Club, or the National Association of Securities Dealers. They may solicit only their owners, employees, and members, as the case may be.

In sharp contrast are the nonconnected PACs, the PACs without parent organizations. Their founders are an individual political entrepreneur, or a group of them. Since they have no organizational parent that defines a universe of potential contributors, they are free to solicit any American citizen. Their great burden as "orphans" is that there is no parent to pay their nonpolitical bills—rent, payroll, postage, utilities, phone and fax lines, and solicitation costs. The contributions they raise pay both these expenses and their political expenditures, and it is not uncommon for the former to exceed the latter.

Finally, there are the "leadership PACs," sometimes called personal PACs. They, too, are nonconnected PACs created by a political entrepreneur, but with the distinguishing trait that they serve the personal political interests of the entrepreneur. Most of them have been created by members of Congress or by aspirants for their party's presidential nomination. They may serve the founder's desire to win or hold a leadership position in Congress, to support the leader's authority as a leader, or to increase his or her party's contingent in the House or Senate. They may also be used to pay the travel and networking costs of building support for an incipient bid for the presidency. Whatever the goal, the main means to it is the gratitude and support the "leader" earns by his or her contributions to other candidates. (See document 5.2.)

That special category of PACs aside, for more than twenty years the FEC has divided the connected PACs into five categories by the nature of their parent organizations: PACs of corporations, labor unions, membership organizations, cooperatives, and corporations without stock. Those who write about PACs generally pass by the last two categories because their PACs are so small and so few in number; in 1996, together they accounted only for 3.4 percent of all PAC contributions. To the major categories of connected PACs, of course, one must add the nonconnected PACs, including the leadership PACs.

After the total number of PACs registered with the FEC increased from 608 in 1974 to 4,009 in 1984, that number has remained on a plateau near 4,000. (See document 5.3.) The various kinds of PACs, however, grew at various rates and at different times. Nevertheless, one must resist the temptation to conclude too much about influence from those data. For example, labor PACs had the slowest growth rate for reasons specific to them. As the pioneers among PACs, they were the most advanced PAC sector by 1974. And, given the size of the national unions, labor PACs have always been on average the largest PACs, with the greatest sums to contribute. (See document 5.3.)

As indicators of strength and influence, the data on PAC contributions to congressional campaigns are more reliable. Between 1978 (the first cycle for which data on all types of PACs are available) and 1996, total PAC contributions to congressional candidates rose almost sixfold. The percentage of all the money all candidates raised, however, only increased from 17 to more than 25 percent. (See document 5.4.) The magnitude of the growth of PACs, in other words, very much depends on what is being measured.

By the mid-1990s, moreover, the pattern of PAC contributions (and candidate reliance on them) was well established. PACs gave overwhelmingly to incumbents seeking reelection, both because they were powerful as incumbents and because their chances of winning reelection were so great. As a category of contributors in the 1980s and 1990s PACs were the most risk averse and the most committed to supporting likely winners. Despite the low favor into which incumbent officeholders have

slipped in the 1990s, more than 90 percent of them managed to win reelection. In addition, Democrats raised more money from PACs than did Republicans, both because Democrats found it harder to lure affluent individual contributors and because they were the majority party for most of the life of the FECA (that is, since 1974). In fact, the greater success of Republicans with the access-seeking PACs in 1996 reflects the majority status they won in 1994. (See document 5.5.)

PAC GOALS AND STRATEGIES

The aims of the PAC movement are best discovered indirectly—by studying the choices they make and the destinations of the money they give. From that sifting of evidence emerge some basic categories—for example, the differences between the ideological and the pragmatic PACs. The pragmatic PACs usually view their contributing as partner to the lobbying efforts of their parent organizations. Not surprisingly, they give overwhelmingly to incumbents seeking reelection. The ideological PACs, on the other hand, want to elect like-minded candidates and are therefore more likely to support candidates of a single party and even candidates challenging incumbents. The former look to legislative influence, the latter to influence over elections; a legislative strategy contrasts with an electoral strategy.

In the aggregate, corporate PACs are the classic pragmatic PACs and labor PACs the classic ideological PACs. But there is no unanimity in either camp. In fact, in the 1980s the corporate PAC movement divided openly on whether or not to support the candidates of the Democratic party, which controlled both houses of Congress. The debate notwithstanding, pragmatism carried the day. Labor PACs have been much more closely allied with one party, the Democrats, much more willing to fund challengers, and even more likely to support like-minded Democrats. (See documents 5.6, 5.7, and 5.8.)

However, the dichotomy works out less satisfactorily with the other two main types of PAC: the membership PACs and the nonconnected PACs. The membership PACs are a mixed group that includes, for example, the PACs of the National Rifle Association, the National Organization for Women, and the National Association of Home Builders. Their interests and their organizational forms are enormously diverse, and they include both ideologists and pragmatists in large numbers.

The nonconnected PACs have a diverse set of interests, but some organizational characteristics in common. They have no parent organization to worry about and therefore no worries about a parent group's interests, reputation, and lobbying. Nor do they have members, owners, or employees to placate. Their contributors come from various locales and occupations, united only by the PAC's issue or cause and the art of direct mail solicitation. They are the PAC analogue to communities of single-issue voters in the electorate. They are free to be ideologically pure, and (because they do not often lobby) to take the political risks of ignoring party lines, of spurning incumbents and supporting challengers, and even of making sizable independent expenditures.

For all of these kinds of PACs the ultimate strategic choice is between contributing funds to candidates and spending in other ways: contributions to parties, spending independently to urge the election or defeat of candidates, or spending on "issue advocacy." (For a discussion of the last of these options, see chapter 7.) As for contributions to national party committees, it is a route that PACs have taken in substantial sums, but in sums well below the magnitudes of their contributions to congressional candidates. In 1995–96, they contributed $32.4 million to the party committees, but $200.9 million to candidates for Congress.

Finally, there is the independent spending option. It is spending by any individual or group in an election to urge voters to vote for or against a candidate, which spending is not coordinated or planned with the candidate or the candidate's representatives. The framers of the 1974 legislation expected it and tried to limit it, but the limits on independent spending were struck down in *Buckley* v. *Valeo* (42 U.S. 1 [1976]; document 3.1), leaving only the requirement of disclosure to the FEC. From those reports we know that through the 1994 cycle PACs have made well over 95 percent of independent expenditures—hence their place in this chapter. (For a report on the advent of party committees to independent spending, see chapter 6.)

It took only one PAC—the National Conservative Political Action Committee (NCPAC)—to bring independent spending to the nation's attention. Its well-publicized "hit list" for 1980 had singled out six Democratic liberals running for reelection to the Senate; four lost, and NCPAC ostentatiously took the credit. In that election cycle alone it reported $1.9 million in independent spending, some of it in support of Ronald Reagan's candidacy for the presidency. In 1982, it reported less than $150,000 in independent expenditures and only one victory in its attempt to defeat seventeen incumbents. NCPAC tumbled from sight so quickly for various reasons: the death of its telegenic executive director, divisions within the subsequent leadership, the general overuse of computerized mailing lists, and the increasing ease with which candidates it "targeted" turned independent spending to their advantage. Even the PACs themselves learned that it earned more enmity than gratitude; moreover, they wanted precisely the close political relationship with candidates that independent spending denied them. So, independent spending never really became a major PAC tactic, and by the mid-1990s it averaged only about $5 million in a congressional election cycle.

THE POLITICAL BENEFITS OF PAC ACTIVITY

If PACs have been cast as the "heavy" in devil theories of American campaign finance, it is because large numbers of Americans believe that by their funding of candidates they achieve massive influence over public officials and their decisions. But documenting that conclusion to the satisfaction of scholars has not been so easy. While the flows of money are easily measurable, we have no simple measures for the presence or growth of influence.

Much of the argument hinges on what one makes of simple associations between the contributions of interested money and the subsequent success or failure of the interest's legislative agenda. PAC M gives to Congressman Y who votes M's position after being reelected; PACs of X industry win a major legislative victory with 80 or 90 percent of their beneficiaries voting for X's position on the important roll calls. The contributions may have influenced the votes, but the association may result from another quite simple explanation: the senators and representatives may have gotten the contributions because of their long records of sympathy and support for the positions of the PACs. PACs, like voters, tend to support candidates they agree with. Furthermore, this kind of analysis rarely considers the instances of contributions followed by legislative losses. In almost all major battles in the Congress, there are losing PACs as well as winning PACs.

The debate over PAC influence is also a debate over where one expects to see the effects of influence. The examples above locate it in important roll call votes. Perhaps, however, the influence that PACs achieve can best be found in agenda-setting, in the decisions about which legislation will actually be considered, or in the less formal persuading in the committees and cloakrooms of the Congress. Perhaps, in fact, one ought to expect to see the influence not in great policy debates but in the narrow, special, limited legislative decisions that other interests and constituencies ignore—in, for example, the special clauses written into the tax codes, the exclusions from environmental regulation, the crafting of formulas for aid or reimbursement to the states and localities. Perhaps, indeed, one should look beyond the legislative process and to the success of contributors in electing like-minded men and women in the first place.

Ultimately an assessment of PAC influence must "fit" into a broader, Congress-wide theory of influence. That is, it must be compatible with the simultaneous influence of Congress's home constituencies, its political parties, the values and preferences of the members, the nation's interest groups and their lobbyists, and the president and the leadership of the executive branch. For that reason alone most experts rule out the most sweeping assertions of PAC influence, the ones encapsulated in that old phrase about "the best Congress money can buy." For that reason they also find PAC influence greatest where other structures of influence either nod or withdraw. (See documents 5.9 and 5.10.)

Finally, one does not escape the issue of influence by accepting the assertions, however honestly advanced, that PACs seek only "access." If access brings increased opportunities to make a case or plead an argument, then access is pursued ultimately in order to maximize influence. If access is, as Barry Werth has put it, "the demure cousin of influence," the relationship is within one extended family.[1]

REGULATION: CONSEQUENCES AND CONSTITUTIONALITY

Considering the fears about PACs and their assets and influence, it is not surprising that "doing something" about PACs is a centerpiece of many reform packages. Abolishing their right to contribute to federal candidates was indeed a key provision of the bipartisan plan sponsored by Senators John McCain and Russell D. Feingold in the 104th and 105th Congresses. All of the proposals for "doing something" raise two kinds of questions: those of results and consequences, and those of constitutionality under the First Amendment.

Proposals for curbing PACs are either for crippling them or outlawing them or their contributions. Proposals in the Congress for crippling them usually involve a drastic scaling back of their contribution limit from the present $5,000 to $2,500 or even $1,000. The latter figure would place them in an equal footing with individual contributors, thus removing one of the incentives for PACs. One finds the same weapons in state reform packages, but one more: proposals for aggregate receipt limits that limit candidates to accepting no more than a fixed percent of their receipts or a specified dollar sum from PACs collectively, or from a set of sources that include PACs. Finally, from time to time a proposal surfaces to repeal the right of organizations sponsoring PACs—the parent organizations—to pay the overhead expenses of their PACs.

Obviously, the purpose of these proposals is to reduce the amount of PAC money in the mix of private funding for campaigns. But how likely are the reforms to reduce the flow of PAC money? The history of the reform of campaign finance in the United States suggests that it is difficult to roll back or dry up any source of funds. The prohibited source or channel finds new outlets so long as candidates need money and affluent people want to give it—especially since the giving of it is a right protected by the First Amendment. Candidates and contributors combine their efforts and ingenuities to find new channels for old money. However, their success may, however, be moderated if reform also provides candidates with new or enhanced sources of funds—if, for instance, new restrictions on PACs are accompanied by new public funds or higher contribution limits for individuals or party committees.

From the point of view of PACs, their adaptation to more stringent regulation depends on their alternatives for political action. In the 1980s it appeared that the chief alternative was the newly fashionable independent spending. Given the growing disenchantment with it among both PACs and candidates, it seems not to be as potent a threat in the 1990s. Bundling is now the greater threat. Indeed, it already grows, perhaps in part as a reaction to recent state reforms that have cut back on PAC contributions. Perhaps the growth also reflects the pref-

erence of candidates for funds from sources not identified as PACs.

Bundling is organized individual contributing to candidates. The organizing can be institutionalized; the best-known current exemplar, EMILY's List, a feminist PAC, recruits members who pledge to contribute at least $100 to at least two candidates among the List's endorsed candidates. But that is not the less formal bundling that serves as adaptation to new regulation. EMILY's List, and the few others like it, identifies itself as the bundler, and it makes its political goal clear—in this case, support of Democratic women candidates who favor abortion rights. In most bundling the bundlers are not identified, and the act of bundling and the interests it serves are unknown to the public. Virtually all the important information that PACs must and do disclose to the FEC is lost if organized giving is simply bundled instead.

Alternatively, PACs might simply choose to leave campaign finance. They could turn their resources to more traditional lobbying before legislatures or administrative agencies, or they might mobilize grass-roots lobbying on behalf of their political agendas. Or they might turn to programs of political education and voter mobilization for their members or employees; organized labor has already done that for fifty years. Or they might just abandon politics altogether.

Constitutional challenges will quickly follow any action to seriously limit or to outlaw PAC contributions. The Supreme Court in *Buckley* v. *Valeo* cloaked their contributing with the protections of the First Amendment. Most experts and many members of Congress doubt that an outright ban on PAC activity would stand. Indeed, most such bills in recent Congresses have been written with "backup" clauses providing that, if a total ban were to be struck down, the contribution limits for PACs would be reduced to some specific figure. (See document 5.11.)

The fate of a reduction, say, to $2,000 or $2,500 from the present $5,000 is less certain. One federal court of appeals has already struck down Missouri's attempt to lower the PAC contribution limits to $100 for legislative candidates and $300 for statewide races; *Carver* v. *Nixon,* 72 F.3d 633 (8th Cir. 1995)—document 9.2. Another has held unconstitutional Minnesota's attempt to lower the limits on contributions *to* PACs to $100; *Day* v. *Holahan,* 34 F.3d 1356 (8th Cir. 1994)—document 9.1. These cases involve state regulation, however, and it bears remembering that the magnitudes of contributions and receipts in many state legislative elections are less than one-tenth those for the U.S. House of Representatives.

Finally, one Great Regulator is not subject to the courts or the First Amendment. It is inflation. In purchasing power, the $5,000 limit on PAC contributions, passed in 1974, was in 1996 worth less than one-third what it was in 1974.

CONCLUSION

PACs are not merely organizations of convenience, crafted by the politically inventive to exploit an opportunity or incentive in the 1974 reform legislation. They reflect fundamental social and political change in American society—in the groups people identify with and in how they frame their interests. They reflect the increasing fragmentation of interests in the United States, and at the same time the increasing nationalization and national organization of those fragmented interests. Ultimately PACs reflect the fact that Americans are different political animals than they were fifty or one hundred years ago.

Like political parties, PACs are instruments of representation in a representative democracy. They organize individuals around interests, ideologies, and policy options. By bringing individuals together, they create aggregates of political influence greater than the mere sum of the individuals they bring together. Organized political action has always been more purposeful, better informed, and more resourceful than the actions of scattered individuals. For those reasons, it has also always been more influential.

In a system of private, voluntary funding of campaigns, however, there is no avoiding the hard truth that the people who contribute to campaigns are those with discretionary income. Those who give tend to be those who have. Yet PACs are instruments of political influence as available to (and perhaps more valuable to) the American middle class as to those who are truly affluent. In the building of political power, it is the politically negligible individual who most needs the advantages of organization.

Even the most moderate estimates suggest that at least six million or seven million Americans contribute to PACs registered with the FEC in a given two-year election cycle. By this and all other measures, PACs are a formidable political presence—one rooted in contemporary American life and deeply entrenched in the nation's electoral politics. They are capable of substantial political resistance to any crippling legislation; and if that fails, PACs are now confident and sophisticated enough to plan their adaptations to new regulation and their own concerted defense in the courts.

NOTE

1. Clifford W. Brown Jr., Lynda W. Powell, and Clyde Wilcox, *Serious Money: Fundraising and Contributing in Presidential Nomination Campaigns* (Cambridge University Press, 1995), p. 60.

Federal Election Commission, Advisory Opinion 1975-23 (SUN PAC),
"Establishment of Political Action Committee and Employee Political
Giving Program by Corporation"

In July 1975, not long after the passage of the FECA in 1974, the Sun Oil Company asked the Federal Election Commission for an advisory opinion on its plan to establish a program of political activities. One part of the plan involved the use of corporate funds to establish, administer, and solicit contributions for a political action committee. It asked the FEC to evaluate the legality of the PAC (and other proposed programs) in the light of the new FECA. The FEC's advisory opinion (40 *Federal Register* 45292) was published in December 1975, and it quickly became the most authoritative word on the rights and responsibilities of groups and organizations sponsoring PACs. The final vote to approve the advisory opinion was 4–2; all three Republican commissioners were joined by one Democrat, and the other two Democratic commissioners dissented. This excerpt presents the section of A.O. 1975-23 that dealt with the proposed PAC.

A. INTRODUCTION

Sun Oil proposed to sponsor a bifurcated responsible citizenship program for political activities. One part of this program will involve the expenditure of general corporate treasury funds to establish, administer, and solicit voluntary contributions to a political action committee. This committee (hereinafter SUN PAC) will be maintained as a separate segregated fund and used by Sun Oil for political purposes under the provisions of 16 U.S.C. §610. . . .

The Commission has been asked to evaluate SUN PAC . . . with respect to the requirements of the Federal Election Campaign Act of 1971, as amended (hereinafter the "FECA" or the "Act") [chapter 2] and the proscriptions of 18 U.S.C. § 610. In the following opinion, the Commission will discuss various legal aspects of corporate segregated funds. . . .

B. APPLICABLE LAW

Section 610 of Title 18 of the United States Code provides, in pertinent part, as follows:

Contributions or expenditures by national banks, corporations or labor organizations

It is unlawful for any national bank, or any corporation organized by authority of any law of Congress, to make a contribution or expenditure in connection with any election to any political office, or in connection with any primary election or political convention or caucus held to select candidates for any political office, or for any corporation whatever, or any labor organization to make a contribution or expenditure in connection with any election at which presidential and vice presidential electors or [officials] to Congress are to be voted for, or in connection with any primary election or political convention or caucus held to select candidates for any of the foregoing offices, or for any . . . political committee . . . to accept or receive any contribution prohibited by this section.

As used in this section, the phrase "contribution or expenditure" shall include any direct or indirect payment, distribution, loan, advance, deposit, or gift of money, or any services, or anything of value . . . to any candidate, campaign committee, or political party or organization in connection with any election to any of the offices referred to in this section; but shall not include . . . the establishment, administration, and solicitation of contributions to a separate segregated fund to be utilized for political purposes by a corporation or labor organization. . . : *Provided,* That it shall be unlawful for such a fund to make a contribution or expenditure by utilizing money or anything of value secured by physical force, job discrimination, financial reprisals, or the threat of force, job discrimination, or financial reprisal; or by dues, fees, or other monies required as a condition of membership in a labor organization or as a condition of employment, or by monies obtained in any commercial transaction.

The history of section 610, prior to its amendment by section 205 of the Federal Election Campaign Act of 1971, was set forth in U.S. v. [*United Auto Workers*] , 352 U.S. 567 at 570-90 (1957). Moreover, the history of the 1971 amendment, which permits corporations to establish, administer and solicit contributions to separate segregated funds, was discussed in some detail in *Pipefitters Local 562* v. *United States,* 407 U.S. 385 at 409–13, 421–27, 429–32 (1972). See also, *United States* v. *CIO* [*Congress of Industrial Organizations*], 336 U.S. 106 (1948). There is no need, therefore, to trace that history here in any detail. However, some general conclusions can be made in light of legislative history about the application of section 610 to the corporate political activities proposed by Sun Oil.

C. CONCLUSIONS

(1) First, it is lawful for Sun Oil to expend general treasury funds to defray expenses incurred in establishing, administering, and soliciting contribution to SUN PAC so long as it is maintained as a separate segregated fund. The language of section 610 and the supporting legislative history of the 1971 Amendment to the statute plainly permits such expenditures. See, *Pipefitters, supra,* at 429-33. SUN PAC must register and file reports just as any other political committee is required to do under the FECA.

(2) Secondly, it is lawful for Sun Oil to make any political contributions and expenditures it sees fit in connection with any Federal election so long as the monies used for such purposes are expended from SUN PAC and the fund consists of voluntary contributions.

In situations where SUN PAC makes contributions or expenditures in connection with Federal and non-Federal elections, it may establish and maintain a separate account for use in Federal elections. Thereafter, monies to be expended in non-Federal elections should not be commingled with monies to be expended in Federal Elections. SUN PAC should designate the bank in which it maintains any such account for Federal elections as the campaign depository of the fund. 2. U.S.C. § 437b. All contributions received or expenditures made in connection with Federal elections should be deposited in or drawn from this account. If SUN PAC so decides to maintain a separate account for use in Federal elections, it may file reports pertaining only to the separate Federal account. However, if SUN PAC fails to segregate the accounts and monies to be used in connection with both Federal and non-Federal elections, then SUN PAC will be required to report all contributions and expenditures regardless of whether they are made for non-Federal purposes.

Any political contributions or expenditures made by SUN PAC are subject to the applicable reporting requirements of the FECA and the limitations of 18 U.S.C. §608. Moreover, since individual contributions made to SUN PAC are also contributions within the meaning of 18 U.S.C. §591(e), such contributions are also subject to the limitations of 18 U.S.C. § 608.

(3) Thirdly, it is lawful for Sun Oil to control and direct the disbursement of contributions and expenditures from SUN PAC. When the issue of the control of segregated funds was presented to the Supreme Court in the *Pipefitters* case (which involved a section 610 criminal prosecution against a labor union), the Court held that "such a fund must be separate from the sponsoring union only in the sense that there must be a strict segregation of its monies from union dues and assessments." *Id.* at 414. After an exhaustive review of legislative history, the Court concluded that (*Id.* at 415-417):

Nowhere, however, has Congress required that the political organization (i.e., the fund) be formally or functionally independent of union control or that union officials be . . . precluded from determining how the monies raised will be spent, . . . Senator Taft adamantly maintained that labor organizations were not prohibited from expending those monies [from the fund] in connection with Federal elections. . . . Neither the absence of even a formally separate organization, . . . , nor the method for choosing the candidate to be supported was mentioned as being material. Similarly, the *only* requirements for permissible political organizations were that they be funded through separate contributions [which were voluntary]. (Emphasis added.)

The Court also concluded from the legislative history that (*Id.* at 426):

[T]he term "separate" . . . is synonymous with "segregated." Nothing in the legislative history indicates that the word is to be understood in any other way. . . . It is difficult to conceive how a valid political fund can be meaningfully 'separate' from the sponsoring union in any way other than "segregated."

Since corporations and labor unions are subject to the same restrictions under section 610, it is clear that under the language of the *Pipefitters* case, Sun Oil can exercise control over the operations and activities of SUN PAC.

There is much concern in the business community about the proper class of persons who may be solicited by a corporation with its treasury money for contributions to a political fund. Sun Oil advised in its request for an opinion that "[t]o achieve its purpose, SUN PAC will solicit and accept contributions from individuals and from other political committees." Sun Oil now advises, through counsel, that its solicitation efforts will not be as broad as the language of its request suggested. The Commission is now advised that Sun Oil "will not solicit contributions from members of the general public who are neither Sun employees nor shareholders" but that "Sun does intend to use corporate funds to solicit contributions to SUN PAC from its employees."

(4) It is the opinion of the Commission that Sun Oil may spend general treasury funds for the solicitation of contributions to SUN PAC from stockholders and employees of the corporation. The Federal Election Campaign Act of 1971 [document 2.8] amended section 610 by defining contribution and expenditure and setting forth exemptions to that definition. The first two exceptions permit the use of corporate treasury funds for activities aimed only at stockholders and their families. The third exception places no limitation on the categories of persons who may be solicited for voluntary contributions to a separate segregated fund. However, the legislative history of the 1971 Act clearly states that general treasury money may not be used to solicit the general public. 117 Cong. Rec. 43380-81. The absence of a limitation in the third exception similar to that contained in the first two exceptions, indicates that it was Congress's intent not to limit the use of corporate funds for solicitation of contributions to separate segregated funds only to stockholders. Furthermore, corporations have traditionally solicited their employees for both political and non-political purposes. Absent any express language in the statute or the legislative history prohibiting such solicitations, it would be illogical to conclude that corporations could solicit only their stockholders and not their employees. Finally, section 610 provides that contributions to a separate segregated fund may not be secured by "job discrimination" or "financial reprisals," actions which an employer may take against an employee.

The Commission recognizes, however, that there is in the best-intentioned plans a potential for coercion which is inherent in the employment relationship and which may be triggered by solicitation of employees by or on behalf of an employer. Section 610 forbids coercion or reprisal of any kind in the solicitation of contributions to separate segregated funds. To minimize the appearance or perception of coercion, the Commission recommends the following guidelines on solicitation of political contributions by employees to such funds. First, no superior should solicit a subordinate. Second, the solicitor should inform the solicited employee of the political purpose of the fund for which the contribution is solicited. Third, the solicitor should inform the employee of the employee's right to refuse to contribute without reprisal of any kind.

. . .

(6) Finally, Sun Oil has proposed a detailed organizational plan for SUN PAC. Essentially, SUN PAC will be a voluntary, non-profit, unincorporated, political membership association open to certain employees of Sun Oil and its subsidiaries. Several employees will be appointed by Sun Oil to create SUN PAC. In addition, Sun Oil will appoint the administrative officers of SUN PAC. A contribution committee will manage the overall financial operations of SUN PAC and will designate the donees of contributions. The committee may delegate all of its powers to the Chairman of SUN PAC who is a Sun Oil appointee.

Section 610 does not mandate any formal organizational structure for corporate political committees. However, under 2 U.S.C. § 432, SUN PAC, just as any other political committees, would be required to have a chairman and treasurer in order to accept or make any political contributions. Beyond these requirements, there are no other formal organizational requirements applicable to SUN PAC under Federal law. . . .

Leadership PACs have attracted far more publicity than their limited numbers would seem to warrant. The FEC does not count them as a group, but their number appears to be stable at fifty or so. Perhaps the reason for the attention rests in the kind of influence they hope to muster, or on the fact that leadership PACs explore goals and means that often seem to be only indirectly connected to funding campaigns. Perhaps indeed the issue is the sheer "insidership" of them. In any event, they also exist in substantial number in state legislatures, where recently they have been banned in a number of states.

Today, powerful senior members of Congress and ambitious junior members have a new tool in their struggle for congressional leadership—the so-called leadership PAC. Legislative changes in the 1970s brought about a new development in campaign financing—political action committees (PACs). Leadership PACs, developed toward the end of the decade, are formed by individual members of Congress who use the funds raised by their PACS to support the campaigns of congressional colleagues and candidates for Congress. They do so in order to gain votes from members they have supported to further their own legislative or leadership aspirations. These leadership PACs are not unlike the more usual—and visible—PACs set up by special interest groups, ranging from environmentalists to individual corporations, to raise funds to donate to political candidates in the hope of winning support for their agendas.

Although their numbers are small (since 1978, only fifty such leadership PACs have been formed), their financial impact is significant (they donated $3.5 million in the 1986 elections, an average of $70,000 each). That compares with the $140 million given out in that election by 4,100 outside PACs, which gave out an average of half as much, or $34,000 each. Moreover, funding provided by leadership PACs seems to have been decisive in races for such posts as House majority whip (the number three leadership slot), Budget Committee chair, and chair of the House Democratic Caucus (leadership of the entire Democratic membership of the House).

What is more, leadership PACs are likely to increase in number: For example, David Obey, a member of Congress from Wisconsin and a longtime critic of leadership PACs, formed his own PAC, the Committee for a Progressive Congress, in 1985. Asked about his change of heart, Obey said, "You can't play touch while the other guy's playing tackle [football]."

ORIGINS

The members' PACs have sprung indirectly and primarily from reforms in the early 1970s designed to democratize the way the House of Representatives was run. Although a few reforms occurred in the Senate, the Senate hierarchy was already rather flexible, responding more to the influences of gentle persuasion. The reformers' goals were both to enhance the role of the individual legislator and expand the authority of the party leaders in Congress, to strike a balance.

Since 1910, the seniority system used for determining leadership had enabled aging autocrats from largely conservative, southern districts to hold many key chairmanships. Then, starting in 1971, House members changed the way committee chairs were chosen, allowing approval by the Democratic Caucus by secret ballot instead of a rubber-stamp, open vote. Moreover, in 1973, the Democrats voted to have members *of each committee* vote on the subcommittees' chairs and budgets. Thus, for the first time, House members had greatly increased motives to win colleagues' favor: votes for committee or subcommittee leadership posts.

In another reform, in 1972, the caucus voted to limit the number of chairmanships that any House member could hold; similar restrictions were implemented in the Senate. The number of committees and subcommittees has declined from 385 in the mid-1970s to 299 today, but the percentage of members in chairmanships has remained more or less constant. Roughly half of the 260 House Democrats and 96.3 percent of all Democratic senators hold independent power bases from which to pursue issues—and campaign contributions.

In 1974, some two years after the break-in at the Democratic National Committee headquarters in the Watergate Hotel, and the subsequent cover-up by officials in the Nixon White House, an unusually large freshman class of forty-nine Democrats arrived in Congress eager to open up the House structure. Led by the reformers, the majority-party caucus in 1975 for the first time sacked three committee chairmen, a clear sign that times had changed.

While procedures in Congress were changing, so were the rules about campaign financing. As part of an effort to limit the distorting effect of individual contributions on election campaigns, changes in campaign finance law in 1974 [document 2.9] allowed the formation of corporate political action committees. Congress also allowed any PAC to give more to each political candidate and donate a larger total than individuals could spend. Thus, while individuals now may give $1,000 per candidate in each primary or general election, with a total limit of $25,000, PACs are allowed to give $5,000 per candidate for each primary and election with no cumulative limit.

Although PACs had existed outside of Congress earlier—with 600 of them spending about $20 million on congressional races in 1974—the total number of PACs outside Congress skyrocketed after that year so that 4,268 paid out $148,085,016 in 1988. As a result, much more money is readily available for congressional campaigns.

While members of Congress had previously donated surplus funds to colleagues' campaign chests informally, the funding law changes meant that, from 1974 on, legislators could transfer more money to their colleagues or other candidates by forming their own PACs.

EFFECTS

If the reformers were trying to find a balance between individual initiative and party cohesiveness, the actual changes, including the rise of leadership PACs, have brought a slight shift to a somewhat greater dispersal of party power. The parties' congressional, senatorial, and national committees are no longer the sole disbursers of campaign funds from within the political ranks. Members' gratitude—and commitments to vote a certain way—may thus extend to colleagues who do not necessarily follow the party orthodoxy. And it appears that members who can more easily raise funds on their own feel freer to vote independently.

For lobbyists, the system is more inefficient: there are fifty new PACs to which they may feel obliged to write checks. But from the viewpoint of the party leadership, leadership PACs may actually be an unexpected asset. For whatever reason, the leadership PACs attract donations that the parties' conventional fund-raising arms would not likely draw in. For citizens worried about the power of incumbency, leadership PACs give a larger share of their funds to challengers than do the outside PACs.

Clearly, the rise of leadership PACs over the past decade raises a number of questions that warrant careful examination. It is important that we understand the way they work, the harm and the good they can do, before we decide if they are a part of the American campaign financing system in need of reform.

. . .

DO LEADERSHIP PACs GIVE OUTSIDERS ADDED IMPACT ON THE CHOICE OF CONGRESSIONAL LEADERS?

Another concern is that leadership PACs intensify involvement by those outside Congress in the selection of congressional leaders and give outsiders influence on the choice of party leaders and committee personnel.

The influence exerted by lobbyists on the legislative activities of Congress is long-standing and constitutionally sanctioned. The involvement by lobbyists in the selection of leaders and committee personnel is more recent. It is a practice that has been advanced by the contributions of outsiders to the PACs of their favorite candidates for leadership posts.

Enlisting the services of interest groups is a part of what political scientist Nelson Polsby refers to as the outside strategy for gaining a leadership post. Unlike the inside strategy of treating an election to a leadership post as a "family matter," the outside strategy uses the press and friendly lobbyists.

The leadership contest between Henry Waxman and Richardson Preyer in 1979 saw, in addition to the use of contributions to colleagues, a comprehensive outside strategy that involved activating individuals who could influence a House member to vote for Waxman. One lobbyist who was enlisted in the Waxman campaign believed that Waxman, who was considered an able candidate, used an outside strategy so skillful that he could have won without giving any money to the committee Democrats:

Henry ran a hell of a sophisticated campaign. He found out who were the principal supporters of guys on the committee back in their districts—guys who might prefer Waxman over Preyer. Doug Walgren of Pennsylvania got a call from one of his principal fund-raisers in Pittsburgh and he says, "Doug, we think that Henry Waxman is the kind of guy who should be in leadership and run the subcommittee."

It is interesting that the indignation greeting Waxman's donations to his colleagues did not greet his discreet use of outsiders such as lobbyists and district supporters of colleagues to urge those members to support Waxman. It is also noteworthy that when William Gray appealed openly for lobbyist support in 1988 for his successful bid to head the Democratic Caucus he was roundly criticized in the press. Yet the dismay that greeted Gray's call for lobbyist support likely was a reaction not to the practice but to the public nature of that appeal.

The more extensive involvement of outsiders in what used to be dealt with member to member is now common. And whether contributions to the PACs or personal campaign funds of members are involved, the very nature of interest-group politics makes it virtually certain that the resources of outsiders will be tapped in any important future contest for institutional, party, or committee leadership.

While it is impractical to ban outside involvement in congressional leadership contests, the use of contributions from outsiders to garner support for a leadership post raises questions of propriety and conflict of interest. Just as lobbyists may feel compelled to support any sitting member with influence over legislation they are worried about, they similarly may be pressured to fund the candidate with the inside track for a relevant leadership post.

For example, much of the money raised by Waxman in the 1979 leadership contest came from companies in the health industry with an obvious stake in who chairs the health subcommittee. The existence of member PACs and member-to-member contributions has little influence on the disposition of outsiders to involve themselves in congressional leadership races; they are involved in important ways other than contributing money anyway.

But in their attempts to buy further access and influence, are leadership PACs mimicking outside PACs and thus further reinforcing incumbency and the status quo? Outside PACs generally consider support for an incumbent—however hostile—to be more cost-effective than funding even the most promising challenger, given the high rate of incumbent success: 99 percent in the House and 84 percent in the Senate in 1988.

DO LEADERSHIP PACS PROTECT INCUMBENTS?

Campaign finance reformer Philip M. Stern cites three undesirable results of the pro-incumbent bias of PACs in general.

—They tend to freeze out quality congressional challengers who know that only incumbents can be sure of getting the money needed to campaign.
—This deterrent to challengers limits voters' choice of candidates and of policy alternatives.
—Incumbents' superior access to money protects incompetent or even dishonest officeholders from challenge.

The pattern of contributions by these PACs is biased heavily in favor of incumbents. Congressional data show that more than 84 percent of all—outside and leadership—PAC money goes to incumbents. In 1986, 68.8 percent of all PAC money went to incumbents, but it has been unusual for less than 70 percent of all PAC money in a given cycle to go to them. Political scientist Frank Sorauf identifies this pattern as part of an overall "pragmatic strategy" that "reflects the goal of pursuing and maintaining legislative access, of coordinating PAC contributions with the legislative goals of the parent organization . . . and above all, of not offending powerful incumbents by supporting their opponents."

The pattern of contributions by leadership PACs appears to differ from that of outside PACs in some important respects, and is, in general, less pro-incumbent than are the patterns evident in the contributions of ordinary PACs.

The incumbents most favored by outside PACs are House Democrats. In the 1984 cycle, 82 percent of contributions to House Democrats by outside PACs went to incumbents. In the same year, the share of total contributions to House Democrats that leadership PACs gave to incumbents was smaller, about 64.7 percent. In 1986 and 1988, outside PACs gave 75 percent and 87.5 percent of all House Democratic money to incumbents. In the same two cycles, leadership PACs' shares ran only 48.5 percent and 55.4 percent, respectively (see appendix, table 3).

The incumbents least favored by leadership PACs have been Senate Democratic incumbents. In 1984 and 1986, only about 20 percent of all Senate member–PAC money given to Democrats was given to incumbents. In 1988, when Robert Byrd of West Virginia stepped down as Senate majority leader, the PACs of Senators Daniel K. Inouye of Hawaii and J. Bennett Johnston of Louisiana actively contributed to Senate Democratic incumbents, boosting the percentage of incumbents receiving money to 58 percent. But that is still far short of the 76 percent of Senate Democratic contributions that outside PACs give to incumbents.

The unusually high percentage of contributions to Senate Democratic challengers in 1986 was due to a strenuous—successful—Democratic effort to recapture the Senate, where the Republicans had won control in the 1980 elections. The Republicans mounted a similar effort in 1988, while Democrats, predictably, used contributions in the same year to shore up their incumbents. Republican leadership PACs in 1982 and 1984 favored incumbents in their efforts to preserve the GOP margin in the Senate.

Because leadership PACs give more money to challengers, they actually promote competition. Thus, the evidence suggests that leadership PACs may be disposed to some risk taking by giving to challengers. The pattern in the House and Senate appears to be for the majority party's leadership PACs to use their funds to shore up incumbents and for the minority party to concentrate on funding challengers.

There are several plausible explanations for this tendency on the part of leadership PACs to be more generous to challengers than are outside PACs.

The first explanation is a tactical one associated with campaigns for leadership posts. The votes of incumbent colleagues in a leadership contest are often declared well in advance of the vote. Indeed, one of the devices used by candidates for party or committee posts is to line up impressive numbers of colleagues before even formally announcing. While the firmness of this support is often questionable, there is a tendency for incumbent members to commit themselves early. The number of declared holdouts is usually small. This magnifies the importance of those who *might* be elected—candidates for open seats and challengers—and makes them more inviting targets for contributions that might influence their vote should they win. This has the effect of expanding the leadership electorate.

A second explanation for the greater disposition of leadership PACs to give to nonincumbents is that the objectives of such PACs are only partly legislative. Outside PACs' objectives are virtually exclusively tied to gaining access to specific committees; targeting money on a known incumbent is more prudent than giving money to a nonincumbent whose ultimate committee assignment is unknown. Leadership PACs, in contrast, know that at the very least the new member will have a vote in the party's caucus, which confirms committee chairs and party leadership posts.

Third, a large percentage of this money goes to candidates in special elections because there is pressure to get money to candidates as quickly as possible, and leadership PACs can act quickly.

Finally, the money given out by leadership PACs is probably more discretionary than that of outside PACs. Outside PACs tend to be very conscious of their "batting average," and the claim that the PAC supported winners adds much luster to a PAC director's resume.

For a House member or senator who operates a PAC, supporting winners is only one of many goals. There is less riding on any single contribution, and greater speculation is encouraged. Giving nonessential money to a challenger whose chances are rated about even can pay a handsome dividend in the form of a new colleague who is in your debt even before taking office.

Although the evidence still is skimpy, covering only three election cycles, two categories of incumbent recipients appear to be consistently getting an increasing share of money.

The first is Senate Democratic incumbents, whose share of their chamber's Democratic PAC money rose from roughly 20 percent in 1984 to more than 57 percent in 1988. The status of the senators who are up for reelection affects these figures considerably. A senatorial class with a large number of members under vigorous challenge will produce an outpouring of colleague support. The race to succeed Byrd also influenced this trend and made it difficult to sort out short-run and long-run factors.

The other category of incumbents whose share of leadership PAC money has risen is House Republicans. The percentage of total leadership PAC money going to House Republicans is still a relatively small share of the chamber totals, 43 percent. That figure, however, could be expected to rise dramatically if Robert Michel of Illinois were to announce his retirement as minority leader and there were competition for his post.

It appears that, although PACs may give disproportionately to incumbents and, by this pattern of giving, depress electoral competition, leadership PACs are more evenhanded. . . .

The data on number of PACs come from the official reports of the FEC; in fact, the FEC updates the full historical series of data, starting in 1974, with press releases twice a year. In recent years the number of PACs has been tallied twice a year, on July 1 and on December 31. This table contains only the data for December 31 of the even-numbered years, the election year of the two-year election cycle. A description of the subtypes of PACs may be found in the introduction to this chapter.

Growth of Registered PACs

	Committee type					
	Corporate	Labor	Trade/health/ membership	Nonconnected	Other	Total
1974	89	201	a	a	a	608
1976	433	224	a	a	a	1,146
1978	785	217	453	162	36	1,653
1980	1,206	297	576	374	98	2,551
1982	1,469	380	649	723	150	3,371
1984	1,682	394	698	1,053	182	4,009
1986	1,744	384	745	1,077	207	4,157
1988	1,816	354	786	1,115	197	4,268
1990	1,795	346	774	1,062	195	4,172
1992	1,735	347	770	1,145	198	4,195
1994	1,660	333	792	980	189	3,954
1996	1,642	332	838	1,103	164	4,079

Source: Federal Election Commission.

a. Totals for these categories not available until 1977.

Even though total PAC contributions rose sharply after 1978 and have continued to rise, they began in the 1990s to account for a shrinking percentage of the total money raised by candidates. Candidate receipts from individuals had begun to outpace those from PACs. The data also show a greater stability in the 1990s, not only in total PAC contributions, but also in the contributions of specific types of PACs. The data in the table also document that PAC contributions jump in presidential years. It may be that contributions to PACs themselves are stimulated by the events and issues of the presidential campaign. Since PACs spend very little on the presidential campaigns, however, they then have greater sums of money to spend on congressional races. (The data series here begins in 1978 because breakdowns by type of PAC are not fully available before then.)

Contributions of PACs to All Congressional Candidates
Millions of dollars (unless otherwise noted)

| | Contributions of All PACs | | Contributions by Type of PAC | | | | |
	Total contributions	Percent of candidate receipts	Corporate	Labor	Member.	Non-Conn.	Other
1978	$ 34.1	17.1%	$ 9.5	$ 9.9	$ 11.2	$ 2.5	$ 1.0
1980	55	22.2	19	13.2	15.9	4.9	2
1982	84	23.6	28	20.3	21.9	10.7	3.2
1984	105	26.5	36	24.8	26.7	14.5	3.8
1986	133	28.1	46	29.9	33	18.8	4.9
1988	148	31	50	33.9	38.9	19.2	5.4
1990	150	31.7	53	33.6	42.5	14.3	5.9
1992	179	27.1	64	39.4	51.3	17.4	6.5
1994	179.6	24.2	64.4	40.7	50.3	17.5	6.7
1996	200.9	25.4	69.5	46.6	56.1	22	6.8

Source: Federal Election Commission.

This table is really four tables. The two on the left half show PAC contributions to candidates defined by their status and by their political party affiliations. The two on the right half show the percentage of the receipts of the various categories of candidates coming from PACs. Obviously, the patterns of PAC money for House and Senate candidates, however categorized, are sharply different. Senatorial candidates are less dependent on PAC money because they get more money from large individual contributions. Incumbents in both houses, regardless of party, are the most favored recipients of PAC largesse.

PAC Total Contributions to U.S. House and U.S. Senate General Election Candidates, by Status of Candidate and by Political Party[a]

		Total PAC Contributions (dollars)		Percent of Total Receipts from PACs	
		1994	1996	1994	1996
		Status of Candidate			
House	Incumbents	100,508,413	112,890,870	45.4	40.4
	Challengers	11,706,094	20,402,464	15.5	20.2
	Open Seats	15,786,103	17,838,954	24.6	25.5
Senate	Incumbents	26,349,501	19,185,674	23.2	23.8
	Challengers	5,015,316	6,295,163	4.9	10.9
	Open Seats	13,167,677	15,695,367	20.5	18.8
		Political Party of Candidate			
House	Democrats	85,442,780	75,008,289	44.5	36.3
	Republicans	42,557,830	76,123,999	25.1	31.2
	Total	128,000,610	151,132,288	35.4	33.6
Senate	Democrats	22,190,693	14,946,216	19.1	13.8
	Republicans	22,341,801	27,229,988	13.6	22.9
	Total	44,532,494	42,176,204	15.9	18.6

Source: Data from Federal Election Commission.

a. Major party candidates only.

Theodore J. Eismeier and Philip H. Pollock III, *Business, Money, and the Rise of Corporate PACs in American Elections* (Westport, Conn.: Quorum Books, 1988), pp. 16–24

With very few exceptions, PACs have not embraced popular democracy. The contributors (or "members") have few rights in most PACs other than the right not to give again. But informally, PACs cannot ignore contributor sentiment. Aside from the risk of their stopping their contributions, the contributors are also employees, owners, or members of the PAC's parent organization. Moreover, PACs cannot ignore various influences outside of the PAC either, whether it be the organizational ethos of the parent organization, concern for its customer relations, or the pressure of other PACs. Like all other participants in political processes, PACs are shaped by events and actors around them while they attempt to shape events and actors of importance to them. The following document suggests some of the influences at work on corporate PACs.

Within the real universe of corporate PACs there is a multitude of internal worlds and decision-making methods. For one thing, many corporate committees empower large, multitiered, more vigilant governing boards who may wish to accommodate incumbents representing each of the firm's plant locations. Some, displaying what Edwin M. Epstein calls the "Frawley, Dart, or Ford phenomenon," become personalized vehicles of ideological expression for the company's chief executive. Still many others may have but a single staffer who, when it comes to deciding how to spend the PAC's money, is armed solely with the latest recommendations from the Republican National Committee. Obviously, to say that corporate committees as a class are staff-oriented groups is to say too little about them. What organizational resources—and constraints—help determine the strategies available to PAC decision makers?

SIZE AND CENTRALIZATION

We begin with a variable that, as we shall see, clearly differentiates the basic profiles of corporate PACs—budget size. All else being equal, will the strategic decisions of a PAC staff charged with allocating large sums of money differ from the decisions of those with less to spend? A large contribution budget, of course, signals a condition of abundance, and such "organizational slack" is an important catalyst for

---

Theodore J. Eismeier and Philip H. Pollock III, BUSINESS, MONEY, AND THE RISE OF CORPORATE PACs IN AMERICAN ELECTIONS (Quorum Books, an imprint of Greenwood Publishing Group, Inc., Westport, CT, 1988), pp. 16–24. Reprinted with permission.

organizational change. At a minimum we would expect resource-rich PACs to be more varied in their behavior than smaller operations having only enough funds to meet basic goals. Moreover, if big budgets bring venture capital, there may be a certain pattern to this diversification. To the extent that backing the candidacies of nonincumbents qualifies as innovative behavior, contributions from large committees would be more prone to end up with outsiders.

Even so, a big budget usually carries some organizational baggage that may mitigate the tendency to "develop new purposes and activities chiefly to satisfy staff persons with particular concerns and values." After all, as resources grow so do staffs and, more important, so do staff professionalization and political sophistication. For PACs this may mean the tempering of innovation with a more pragmatic attention to the protection of corporate economic interests. What is more, if increased financial wherewithal heightens the desire to establish a national presence, then a more risk-averse posture almost certainly will be the result. Washington-based staffs, who frequently work closely with the group's lobbying arm, will be more conversant with the arcane aspects of pending legislation, more immersed in the insular world of capital politics, and more attentive to the advantages of dealing with current officeholders. Again, political action committees are not uniquely susceptible to such Potomac-borne afflictions. Michael T. Hayes points out that for most staff groups with stable resource bases, such as organizationally mature public interest lobbies, "[a]ccess has become increasingly important as symbiotic relationships are cultivated with sympathetic legislators, administrators, and reporters." In sum, as we search for patterns in corporate PAC behavior we can be fairly sure of this: Washington committees, for reasons incidental to their size, will be pulled toward strategies of access.

Quite apart from the effects of a Washington location, or perhaps subsuming those effects, are the consequences of the staff group's basic structural form—federated or unitary. Indeed, David B. Truman considers this "the most useful distinction that can be applied to political organizations in the United States," and his rich analysis of its importance is familiar to students of group theory. Federation is, in short, a precarious arrangement: "The fundamental reason for the tendency toward disunity in federated organizations is not obscure, although its ramifications may be highly complex. By acknowledging in formal terms certain spheres of local or constituent autonomy, a federated organization establishes and, as it were, sanctifies subcenters of power." Furthermore, this basic inclination toward disunity is made worse if the subunits antedate the central authority, or if the federation must meet some new threat that transcends local concerns. Truman sees some fascinating subtleties in this distinction. His argument that geographic federations are inherently more stable than those following functional lines is especially interesting:

Though potential cleavages of major importance within a group may exist along geographic lines . . . organization according to function especially tends to encourage interaction growing out of specialized subinterests. Because leadership at the lower levels of the structure is necessarily caught up in these subinterests, the problem of reconciling these potentially conflicting elements is delayed until it reaches the middle or top levels of leadership. . . . On the other hand, the nonfunctional, or geographical, basis of organization tends to settle the task of adjusting conflicting subinterests upon the entire leadership at all levels by emphasizing interaction based on more inclusive shared attitudes.

Perhaps Truman neglects one obvious advantage of federations—they are natural conduits for collecting financial resources—but his analysis does suggest some clear patterns. The staffs of federated

PACs will allocate money in ways that suggest localism and they will be slower to respond to changes in the political environment; unitary PACs will be more mobile and less varied in their spending. And the tendency toward parochialism and immobilism will be more noticeable for PACs whose parents are engaged in a wide range of economic activity.

It would appear that financial strength and its various correlates may add up to something of a mixed blessing for the leaders of large staff groups. In fact, the same forces that typically bring organizational abundance also foster conditions that intrude upon a staff's insularity and inhibit its discretion. In his analysis of the giants within the ranks of trade and membership PACs, John R. Wright finds that, contrary to received wisdom, "allocations are dominated by local inputs—recommendations of active members of the PACs at the state, congressional district, and county levels." Thus the PAC manager who takes full fund-raising advantage of his organizational structure, perhaps in the hope of making the most of a strategy of access, can fall prey to his own success, since "the organizational arrangement *most* conducive to raising money . . . is also the organizational arrangement *least* conducive to influencing congressional voting."

THE IMPORTANCE OF IDEAS

The structural aspect of organizations has enjoyed a prominent position in the study of groups. One reason for this is that the basic way a group is set up often has happy if unintended results. For example, disunity and immobilism may be, in Truman's words, "the diseases of federation," but federated arrangements tend also to foster organizational democracy by providing forums for the expression and channeling of demands by competing factions. Clearly, one can draw links between these traditional notions about organizational structure and the behavior of political action committees. There is another, more difficult parallel we wish to draw between group theory and corporate committees—the importance of ideology.

Indeed, in trying to explain the formation of groups, scholars have come to rely heavily on the role of purposive or expressive rewards. It was Mancur Olson, Jr., of course, who initially questioned the assumption for which Truman is remembered—that like-minded individuals would naturally form groups to protect or promote their shared interests. According to Olson, people must receive more durable and divisible incentives, such as highly valued material inducements, which are not equally available to all potential groups. These selective incentives, of course, need not bear any substantive relation whatever to the collective purposes group elites may wish to pursue. But without them no one will join. Thus for Olson group formalization is at best problematic and in most cases dependent on rewards that are differentially distributed in society.

Paradoxically, Olson's theory achieved widespread acceptance just as a Trumanesque "wave" of group proliferation was apparently taking place. How can we reconcile this phenomenon with Olson's convincing theoretical account? This question has occasioned a variety of theoretical constructions, the best known of which is the notion of the political entrepreneur. A political entrepreneur is a person who is driven by ardent ideological or moralistic convictions and is "willing to forego monetary gratifications entirely or defer them indefinitely" in the interests of establishing an ongoing organization. Armed with considerable charisma or persuasive skills, the entrepreneur becomes the heart of a cadre of leaders who give life to the group. Of course, in order to survive most groups must eventually find more enduring organizational bases. But historically the entrepreneurial impulse has been an essential condition for the mobilization of groups that have had to surmount formidable barriers to collective action.

Yet the evidence suggests as well that entrepreneurialism may be a strategy in the formation of groups facing a variety of initial circumstances, including staff organizations that rely for formation on the benefactions of patrons. Indeed, Walker shows that individual ideological commitment and the willingness to gamble can be a creative admixture: "It requires boldness to provide start-up funds to an untested political entrepreneur or to patronize a cause that might create controversy. My data demonstrate that among all the patrons studied, private individuals are the most likely to provide backing for new organizational ventures, far out-distancing foundations and government agencies in their willingness to take risks." We know that some PAC officials profess rather unexciting reasons for starting their PACs—as a way to gain visibility for their corporation; as a status requirement in keeping up with what other firms are doing; as a convenient "I gave at the office" deflection for the solicitations of candidates. But the more prevalent justifications are either unambiguously ideological or betray ideological awareness tempered by a more pragmatic view of the political world. As one corporate PAC manager put it, "We were set up because management had a strong belief that business has a right and obligation to change the direction of government—and we started when they didn't like the direction of government." Handler and Mulkern, who divide their sample of corporate committees into "pragmatic PACs" and "ideological PACs," find some intense differences of opinion between these two camps. The managers of many ideological PACs take issue both with government's straying from the true way of free enterprise and with the tactics of their pragmatic PAC counterparts:

Some of the criticisms aimed at those who follow the pragmatic path convey strong personal feelings. PACs engaged in split giving [the practice of supporting more than one candidate in the same race] show, according to one respondent, "a complete lack of integrity." The same holds true for those who give indiscriminately to incumbents with antibusiness voting records. These PACs are "locked into a selfish pursuit of access," even though such a policy redounds to the detriment of the business community. "Access," observed an ideological critic, "can mean access to a turkey." PACs that underwrite liberal Democrats, warned another, "are feeding the alligators." A third used stronger language: "The bastards are contributing to the enemies of business."

Now it is unclear just how widespread such sentiments are. But these ideological divisions will almost certainly have noticeable contributory effects, quite apart from other organizational differences between PACs.

And we would add to this specific ideological polarization the general tendency for most organizations, regardless of the circumstances of their creation, to develop ideological interpretations for their behavior. In fact, the use of ideological explanations is pervasive. Even most of Handler and Mulkern's pragmatists—managers who prefer to give priority to corporate legislative interests—bristled at suggestions that they were not worthy defenders of free enterprise, or that they had abandoned the ongoing battle with organized labor. Thus the difference between corporate PACs is not that some develop ideological justifications and others do not. The difference rather is that some behave in ways that suggest ideological direction, while others may use ideological language to promote the PAC to potential donors. Indeed, business associations generally have relied more heavily on ideological appeals than have other economic groups. And although there is conflicting theory and evidence on this point, the frequent reference to collective purpose in PAC solicitation material perhaps reflects a basic organizational reality: Corporate PAC donors are reputedly more conservative—and certainly more Republican—than are the strategies of PAC leaders who pursue a pragmatic, legislative course.

There seems to be ample justification for keeping our analysis open to the importance of ideology in shaping the renewed corporate involvement in politics. To be sure, legal reform is the proximate cause for the numerical growth of political action committees. But the initial decision to take advantage of the laws, and the ongoing decisions about what purposes the PAC is to serve, may be animated by a number of concerns, including corporate ideologies. We regard the ideological response of business to the newer regulatory environment as essential to an understanding of corporate PAC behavior. . . .

OUTSIDE FORCES

Above all else, organizations seek to survive. Less obvious are the reasons why some groups survive and others do not or, to put a finer point on it, why some organizations remain vigorous and unassailable while others, though staying "alive," lurch from one crisis to the next, perpetually on the brink of extinction.

Underlying this gradient are two organizational dimensions. First, according to Wilson, is the group's level of autonomy—"a distinctive area of competence, a clearly demarcated and exclusively served clientele or membership, and undisputed jurisdiction over a function, service, goal or cause." An organization may thus be engaged in a constant struggle, not only with *opponents* (groups with mutually exclusive goals and memberships), but with an army of *competitors* (groups that share stated aims and prospective members). Competition shapes an organization's behavior in various ways. It may use marketlike tactics to lure supporters, touting the extra value of the selective incentives it offers. It may attempt to broaden its base by appealing to individuals who are not directly affected by the goals the group seeks. Or it may resort to extravagant claims of influence or effectiveness in achieving its aims. Among political action committees these stratagems are quite typical of "nonconnected" PACs.

Indeed for all parented committees, autonomy, at least with regard to prospective contributors, is not a serious problem. Of course, to the extent that a corporate PAC competes with others for the sympathies of the same incumbent or for the future loyalty of the same challenger, it may try to distinguish itself, perhaps by tailoring the size and timing of its contributions in an attempt to appear especially pivotal. And some committees may suffer from membership problems that stem from exits by politically disgruntled executives. A few of the larger PACs in fact confer highly visible recognition upon especially generous or faithful donors. By and large, though, Sorauf is right. Since corporate PACs enjoy a monopoly over potential contributors, maintenance considerations do not normally turn on the competitive scramble to provide highly valued incentives.

The interorganizational relations of corporate PACs are shaped less by differences in membership autonomy than by the consequences flowing from a second but related determinant of organizational survival, the sheer level of *resources* in the group's possession:

[A]ssociations [must] be able to lay claim to a more or less stable supply of resources—members, money, issues, causes, and privileged access to governmental or other relevant institutions. In principle, many associations would like to obtain as much of these resources as possible—if not more members, then at least more money and better issues. In practice, the availability of these resources is limited by the number of prospective contributors and their preferences and by the existence of rival organizational claimants.

In fact corporate political action committees vary widely in the resources they control. Budget size, which we have already discussed, is an obvious example, and later in this chapter we will describe the contours of this variable. Still, resources involve other things not so easily measured in dollars. Some committees came into existence early on in the PAC "explosion" and so are thought to possess a certain competence or to enjoy special passage into partisan circles. Others may compensate for their own paltry budgets by acting as middlemen between cash-rich but information-poor PACs and needy or solicitous candidates. For still others inter-PAC communication becomes a goal in itself, and they may want to affect the choices of other committees by shading the information they provide. Indeed, for present purposes it is convenient to divide the PAC world into two strata—an "upper" stratum of the relatively few organizations that command more of the scarce resources of money, information, or access, and a much larger "lower" stratum of committees seeking to survive in a more spartan environment. Of course this is a simplification. But it does have some interesting consequences for the behavior of corporate PACs.

First, it is widely believed that the recommendations of a few prominent committees bear directly on the decisions of PAC managers having compatible partisan or ideological inclinations. These "bellwether PACs" are the huge Washington-based operations with reputations as savvy political insiders or ideological opinion leaders. The committees most frequently anointed by seasoned observers as wielding such influence over corporate PACs are themselves not housed in corporations but rather are established by trade or membership associations. And their resources dwarf all but the very largest corporate PACs. The best known of the breed is the Business Industry Political Action Committee, which boasts an impressive contributions budget, a nationwide organization, and a communications network that supports a wide range of politicizing activities. BIPAC was created by the National Association of Manufacturers, and so its involvements—finding attractive challengers, providing seed money in primaries, and generally reading the partisan tea leaves—reflect the strongly pro-business ideology of its parent. This bellwether's high-profile tactics and recommendations doubtless are familiar to the managers of all corporate PACs, and apparently even are resented by some. The point is that BIPAC, along with perhaps no more than "half dozen major groups"—the PAC established by the Chamber of Commerce is another example—may be influential enough to lend coherence to the individual decisions of the hundreds of corporate PACs whose relative lack of resources makes them open to suggestion.

Such suggestion or direction sometimes comes from a second source—the national party organizations. Of course if money were the only metric for gauging resources, the parties would finish each election cycle a distant second to the aggregate power of PACs. Indeed in much of the literature parties are portrayed as unworthy competitors of political action committees, frequently outmuscled by these well-heeled upstarts. In fact, the parties have become influential contenders among our upper stratum of resource-rich organizations, for they control information and possess political skills that help them to direct the flow of campaign dollars. Of course among corporate PACs it is information supplied by the Republican party that is generally more sedulously sought and provided. However, following their 1980 debacle the Democratic party, specifically Democratic Congressional Campaign Committee Chairman Tony Coelho, apparently decided to exploit the organization's special political resources more fully. Coelho's tactics are legendary: Cajoling, imploring—even thinly veiled threats—have all been brought to bear on those who control the campaign coffers of corporate committees. Again, the success of such overtures is likely to depend not only on a committee's partisan predispositions, but also on the configuration of the other elements that affect its behavior. Yet to the degree that party elites can control vital information about upcoming campaigns, they can have an important impact on the channeling of corporate PAC dollars.

There is a third, less explicit way that the decisions and expectations formed within the upper stratum of organizations can broadly affect the allocations of their more modestly endowed counterparts. As with the appeals of the party committees, this outside force also is partisan in nature. But unlike the specific recommendations about particular races and candidates, this factor is a good deal less concrete, as the term we will use for it—"climate of partisan expectations"—implies. First identified as theoretically important by Gary C. Jacobson and Samuel J. Kernell, the role of partisan prophecy in accounting for the aggregate deployment of political capital is now widely acknowledged. The Jacobson and Kernell model is based on an elegant handful of assumptions, chief of which is the plausible notion that campaign contributors prefer, all else being equal, to put their money into contests expected to be close. Thus in election years proclaimed by pundits to be auspicious for Republicans, campaign dollars will flow to Republican challengers (whose chances for victory are fortuitously enhanced) and to Democratic incumbents (who are perceived to be at risk). If the political grapevine counsels investors to anticipate a pro-Democratic climate, the symmetry changes: Republicans will "circle the wagons" in defense of reputedly endangered incumbents; Democrats will go on the offensive, seeking to install new officeholders in their places.

One can see that the outside influences on PAC behavior are not independent of one another, and clearly they will not always pull in the same direction. For example, bellwether committees or party elites may deliberately try to foster self-serving expectations, or they may rail strenuously and perhaps successfully against the prevailing partisan wind. And there is yet another set of actors that needs to be added to this chorus of outside voices—the candidates themselves, especially incumbents. It is a standard observation, frequently offered in the spirit of an indictment, that an inordinate amount of PAC money goes to incumbents of both parties. To be sure, at least some of this tilt toward incumbents is the product of the simple PAC pragmatism. But there are important demand side effects as well, for incumbents can raise as much money as they think they will need to discourage would-be opponents. Such strategic behavior by incumbents can have palpable effects. There is some evidence, for example, that early and substantial fundraising by Democratic incumbents in the 1983–84 election cycle helped to modulate the generally pro-Republican electoral climate. . . .

DOCUMENT 5.7 Frank J. Sorauf, *Inside Campaign Finance: Myths and Realities*
(Yale University Press, 1992), pp. 106–112

Critics have long berated PACs for their lack of commitment to principle. Their criticism employs words like pragmatic, accommodationist, and opportunistic. Many PACs do in fact regularly support powerful incumbents regardless of party or policy positions. The great exception to these generalizations has for some time been the labor PACs. For the full period of the post-Watergate regime they have supported candidates of the Democratic party more than 90 percent of the time; many of them, in fact, even choose quite systematically among Democrats for those who support labor's agenda. Their ability to sustain their commitment to an ideology and a program in a pragmatic political world says a good deal about the strategic diversity of the 4,000 PACs active in recent years.

THE SPECIAL CASE OF LABOR PACS

Viewing the traditional separation of functions in which parties dominated American electoral politics and groups dominated the politics of representation before government, scholars concluded that the groups were, as political organizations, poorly suited for electoral politics. They were too narrow in scope of interests and issues, too unaccustomed to the risk-taking and hurly-burly of election campaigns, and too unsuccessful in becoming reference symbols for their members or adherents to function successfully in the electoral arena. PACs have attempted to transcend those weaknesses with the one great strength at their command: mountains of cash. Whether or not they have succeeded is precisely the question of the efficacy of PACs as a form of political organization.

Evaluations of PACs usually proceed, however, from the misimpression that a PAC is a PAC and that they are all one kind of political animal. In truth PACs range from those that give a few thousand to those who give a few million, from those promoting a single policy alternative to those with a burning commitment to an all-encompassing ideology, from those led by a single driving force to those encouraging donor democracy. The trick is to find both the great similarities and the main axes of difference beneath all of the diversity.

If one looks at political activity and political choices rather than organizational traits, one set of PACs, those of organized labor, stands out from the rest. Table 1 illustrates with economy the ways in which the labor PACs active in 1988 differed from the corporate, membership, and nonconnected PACs active in the same cycle. In brief, labor PACs have greater average assets than other PACs, they give a signifi-cantly higher percentage of their contributions to nonincumbent candidates, and they make their con-tributions to candidates in much larger sums. Moreover, they are much more "unipartisan" in their contributions; more than 92 percent of their 1988 contributions to House candidates went to Demo-crats. By contrast, the PACs of corporations—the only other group of PACs that compares in issue or ideological homogeneity with the labor PACs—split their 1988 House contributions evenly, 51 percent to Democrats and 49 percent to Republicans.

Table 1. Political Spending of Corporate, Labor, Membership, and Nonconnected PACs, 1988

	Corporate	Labor	Member	Nonconnected
Percent of contributions to Democrats[*]	47.1	92.3	55.2	63.3
Percentage of contributions to incumbents[*]	80.1	64.1	81.2	59.0
Average contribution to candidates[*+]	$1,034	$2,466	$1,454	$1,693
Average total PAC contributions[*+]	$34,750	$138,655	$65,108	$32,269
Percentage of PACs in category active (contributing)	89.0	72.3	80.5	56.5
Total independent expenditures by PACs[*]	$0.1 million	$0.2 million	$3.9 million	$16.2 million

[*]Contributions and independent expenditures are to or for all candidates, both primary- and general-election, for all federal offices (House, Senate, and presidency).

[+]The base includes only those PACs active in the 1987–88 cycle.

Source: Federal Election Commission.

To a far greater extent than other PACs, in other words, labor PACs have escaped the new power of incumbents and retained a viable place for themselves in electoral politics. They give substantially larger sums to challengers and open-seat candidates than do other PACs, and they focus their contributions on the candidates of the party closest to their issue positions (that is, the Democrats). Moreover, their greater support of challengers suggests a greater capacity for taking political risks and for working to-ward longer-term political goals. Better than other PACs, they have been able to achieve a viable mix of legislative and electoral strategies.

Embedded in other categories of PACs there are, to be sure, PACs with labor-like patterns of political activity. A search through the data on the 1988 cycle reveals 275 corporate and membership PACs that met two labor-like criteria: they gave 80 percent or more of their contributions to candidates of one party, and they gave no more than 75 percent of them to incumbents. But they were small PACs with a median receipt total of less than $15,000 and an average of about $58,000; only 11 of them (4 percent) had receipts greater than $250,000. Their average total in contributions to candidates in 1988 was just a shade over $32,000. Apparently an electoral strategy is far easier for the smaller PACs with fewer and more homogeneous pressures on them. The secret, which only labor PACs seem to have found, is to be both large and electorally venturesome.

In explaining the special case of labor PACs, one looks first to the broader labor movement. Labor PACs are clearly national and centralized; major labor unions are, too. On the average labor PACs amass far greater political assets (cash receipts), and they are far fewer in number; in 1987–88, 401 labor PACs had an average of $195,783 in receipts, while 2,008 corporate PACs had an average of $48,265. Further-more, for whatever reasons—greater homogeneity of interests, perhaps—labor has been able to build an influential peak organization, the AFL-CIO and its "peak PAC," the Committee on Political Education (COPE). By 1988 only about 15 percent of all union members in the United States were outside of the AFL-CIO, a reflection of the homogeneity of ideology and goals binding labor unions together politically.

More important, perhaps, is tradition and commitment. Labor PACs substantially predate the period of the FECA [see chapter 2]—one-third of the PACs in existence in 1974 were labor PACs. These PACs developed out of labor commitment to electoral politics, a context typified by labor's endorsements of candidates and its long-standing programs of registering voters and getting them to the polls on election day. Finally, labor has the inestimable advantage of traditions of collective action and militancy, traditions embodied in its anthem, "Solidarity Forever." Collective action is the basic premise of trade unionism, for all depends on solidarity behind shared goals and on collective bargaining and the collective strike. As other PACs were leaving electoral commitment for legislative pragmatism in the 1980s, labor PACs intensified their commitment to electoral politics even in a time of troubles. Millions of union members voted for Ronald Reagan in 1980 and 1984, and union membership declined from 21 million in 1980 to 17 million in 1988. In that span of time, however, labor PACs increased their contributions to federal candidates from $14.2 million in 1980 to $35.5 million in 1988 before sliding to $34.8 million in 1990.

Labor's PAC strategy grows from labor's commitment to the Democratic party, a commitment reflected in its overwhelming support for Democratic candidates (table 1). It is also reflected in the substantial sums that labor PACs give directly to the Democratic campaign committees in the House and Senate; labor support for those committees totaled $1.5 million in 1988, 27 percent of all the PAC funds they received. Moreover, access for labor PACs is access to a majority legislative party, and that fact makes the closeness of their alliance with the Democrats possible. If labor PACs were to face the likelihood or the certainty of Republican majorities in the Congress, the goals of access and of support for an ideologically congenial Democratic party would diverge. Labor PACs would have to make the hard choices corporate PACs now do, the choices inherent in supporting one party while seeking access to the other.

It is in the nonlabor PACs that the weaknesses of PACs as electoral organizations are most apparent. Unlike labor PACs they do not mobilize large numbers of voters, for they have not become reference groups or symbols for their donors (that is, their "members"). The donors' affiliation with the nonlabor PAC is often tenuous and passive, often secondary to other political affiliations or loyalties; political activity via the PAC is for many of them a not very intense or demanding form of political activity. Second, the parents of nonlabor PACs also have limited political goals and commitments. Their political agendas often are very short—a significant contrast to those of the AFL-CIO—and they often act hesitantly, fearing the negative reactions of broader publics such as stockholders, members, or customers. Consequently, in a large number of cases the political action committee becomes a risk-averse organization far more comfortable in achieving focused policy goals through lobbying than through the public contesting of elections.

In that dichotomy among traditional PACs there is a conspicuous in-between case: ideological PACs without parent organizations. They do not have the members and loyalists tied to the broader goals of a parent that labor PACs do, nor do they have labor's wider commitment to voter mobilization. But many of them do recruit political risk-takers around an issue or ideology; and many have long supported challengers. In short, many of them remain committed to electoral politics. Among them, too, are new and evolving organizational forms that go beyond the stereotypical PAC. EMILY's List, for example, is registered as a PAC and makes contributions in the usual ways, but in its pursuit of its feminist agenda it is also a donor network in which membership requires dues of $100 per election and a pledge to contribute at least $100 to at least two candidates endorsed by EMILY's List. It is an organizational form that suits especially the autonomous, politicized contributor, and it may well be a PAC variant with a future. Its future would probably be assured if Congress were to drop the PAC contribution limit to $1,000 or $2,000.

Thus, if one arrays PACs along a continuum from the most party-like to the least party-like, from the most adapted to electoral politics to the least adapted, the labor PACs are much nearer the party pole than other PACs. They are the most inclusive, the most electoral of the PACs; only they are allied with a parent organization's other electoral activities, endorsing candidates and mobilizing voters, and only they approach a party's capacity for organizing large numbers of individuals under comprehensive programs or ideologies. At times they see their loyalists desert to support a candidate of the other party, but so do political parties. With their exception, and the exception of some nonconnected PACs of ideology, PACs generally are overmatched by the incumbents and their legislative parties, the parties in government, in the contesting of elections. It was perhaps inevitable that they should eventually shift to using their participation in campaigns as an adjunct to the legislative politics that had always been the arena of their group success.

The political parties have also been contributors, though relatively insignificant ones, to candidates for the Congress. Although their contributions to all congressional candidates in 1990 ($4.3 million) accounted for only 0.9 percent of candidate receipts, they did spend more than four times that sum, a total of $19.3 million, in coordinated (so-called "on behalf of") expenditures to support their partisans' campaigns. Those totals would appear to entitle the parties to a place with PACs as organized contributors. But appearances are deceiving. It is not the political party spending the money; it is, increasingly, the legislative campaign committee of the party in the House or Senate. The party's incumbents control those committees, and they make sure that they will pursue the individual and collective interests of the incumbents. Moreover, the committees do not necessarily speak for the national party. . . .

. . .

PAC Contributions to House General Election Candidates
by Type of PAC, 1992–96

The data here parallel those on the left side of the table that is document 5.5, except that PAC contributions here are broken down by type of PAC. They document the fund-raising superiority of incumbents and Democrats in the House from the very beginning of the FEC's data. Democratic incumbents enjoyed that edge in substantial measure because they were the majority party in the House and controlled its committees and agenda. Republicans captured control of the House in 1994, however, and the 1996 data indicate that House Republicans did significantly better in raising money from PACs in the 1995–96 cycle.

PAC Contributions to U.S. House General Election Candidates
Millions of dollars[a]

		Contributions by type of PAC					
		Corporate	Labor	Member	Non-connected	Other	Total
		Political party of candidate					
1992	Democrats	$ 21.8	$ 26.8	$ 21.6	$ 6.2	$ 2.8	$ 79.2
	Republicans	18.4	1.3	14.4	3.2	1.4	38.9
	Total	40.3	28.4	36	9.4	4.3	118.4
1994	Democrats	$ 23.1	$ 30.6	$ 21.5	$ 7.1	$ 3.1	$ 85.4
	Republicans	19.4	1.3	16.1	4.2	1.6	42.6
	Total	42.6	32	37.6	11.4	4.7	128.3
1996	Democrats	$ 15.1	$ 35.7	$ 15.8	$ 6.3	$2.2	$ 75.0
	Republicans	35.2	2.5	27.2	8.3	2.9	76.1
	Total	50.4	38.4	43.2	14.8	5.1	151.9
		Status of candidate					
1992	Incumbents	$ 33.8	$ 19.3	$ 28.1	$ 6.0	$ 3.6	$ 90.8
	Challengers	2.3	4	2.5	1.5	0.3	10.7
	Open Seats	4.2	5.1	5.4	1.9	0.4	16.9
1994	Incumbents	$ 36.1	$ 23.4	$ 29.8	$ 7.4	$ 4.0	$ 100.8
	Challengers	2.7	3.7	3.1	1.9	0.3	11.7
	Open Seats	3.7	4.9	4.7	2.1	0.4	15.8
1996	Incumbents	$ 43.9	$21.7	$34.1	$9.2	$4.3	$113.1
	Challengers	1.8	11.5	3.6	3.3	0.3	20.5
	Open Seats	4.8	5.2	5.5	2.3	0.5	18.2

Source: Federal Election Commission.

a. All totals and subtotals include minor party general election candidates.

Center for Responsive Politics, *10 Myths about Money in Politics* (1995), pp. 3–4, 8–9

There is no single case against PACs, but the typical one comes down to an argument centered on the political influence they amass and, moreover, on the uneven distribution of that influence in the American polity. The criticisms of the Center for Responsive Politics, a Washington-based public interest group, are representative. The ones reprinted here are from the booklet published by the Center in 1995. After arguing against myth 1 ("PACs are the problem") that the problem is all interested money, whether it comes from PACs or individuals, the authors go on to demolish myth 2 ("The special interests balance each other out") and myth 5 ("The money only buys access—not votes"). Those latter two "myths" are in any event two of the most prominent defenses of PACs.

Myth 2: The special interests balance each other out.

There is indeed a vast array of "special interests" with lobbyists who attempt to influence public officials at every level of government—federal, state, and local. In Washington, D.C. alone, 7,400 national associations have headquarters—groups ranging from the YMCA and the American Automobile Association to General Motors and the National Rifle Association. In addition, nearly 4,000 PACs are registered with the federal government. The real question, however, is not how many special interests there are, but how much financial clout they have. Here there is very little "balance."

- Between January 1991 and December 1994, business PACs gave three times as much money to members of Congress as did labor PACs—$257 million vs. $85 million.
- Almost all of the money labor gives to members of Congress comes in the form of PAC contributions, as opposed to large individual contributions of $200 or more. (The Federal Election Commission does not require disclosure of information on contributions of less than $200.) If PAC contributions are combined with large individual contributions for both business and labor during the 1991–1992 election cycle, business outgave labor by a factor of 7 to 1.
- During the 1991–1992 election cycle, all environmental groups combined gave members of Congress less than $2 million in campaign contributions, whereas the energy and natural resources industry, which often opposes strict environmental safeguards, gave Congress more than 10 times as much—that is, more than $21 million.

- During the 1991–1992 election cycle, the defense industry outgave peace and disarmament groups by a factor of 20 to 1—$8.3 million to $400,000.
- The National Rifle Association supported gun rights with PAC contributions totaling $1,853,038 in the 1994 elections. On the opposing side, Handgun Control, Inc., the largest gun control PAC, gave $213,691.
- Heavy-hitting campaign contributors who vastly outspend their opponents are as much in evidence at the state level as they are at the federal level. For example:
  —In Washington state, 20 percent of all the money raised for state legislative campaigns during the 1989–1990 election cycle came from construction and development interests.
  —Nevada's gambling industry supplied 39 percent of all traceable campaign funds to candidates for state office in Nevada during the 1989–1990 election cycle.
  —In Connecticut, two hazardous waste firms gave more money to the state's six legislative leadership PACs during 1993 than did organized labor and all single-issue groups combined.
  —In Maine, 25 percent of all the money contributed in amounts of $50 or more to 1994 gubernatorial candidates came from the banking, insurance, and real estate industries, and from lawyers and lobbyists.
  —In North Carolina, banking interests provided one out of every eight dollars given to political committees and candidates for state offices between 1989 and 1992.
  —In recent years, business interests have out-contributed labor interests in Wisconsin, New Mexico, Missouri, North Carolina, and Louisiana by margins of 7.5 to 1; 12 to 1; 13 to 1; 16 to 1; and 25 to 1, respectively.
- Many "special interests" have virtually no financial clout at all. For example, of the 1,197 PACs that gave $20,000 or more to members of Congress during the 1991–1992 election cycle, none represented poor people, parents of public school children, people who are the victims of toxic dumping or agri-chemical contamination, unemployed or underemployed workers, small banking depositors and borrowers, families unable to afford their own homes and those without any homes, or people dependent on public housing, public transportation, public recreational areas, public libraries, and public hospitals.

. . .

Myth 5: The money only buys access—not votes.

- Many former members of Congress, freed from the constraints of raising money and getting reelected, have spoken candidly about what large campaign contributions actually "buy":

"If nobody else cares about it very much, the special interest will get its way. If the public understands the issue at any level, then the special-interest groups are not able to buy an outcome that the public may not want. But the fact is that the public doesn't focus on most of the work of the Congress."

—Former Congressman Vin Weber (R-Minnesota)

"On the tax side, the appropriations side, the subsidy side, and the expenditure side, decisions are clearly weighted and influenced . . . by who has contributed to candidates."

—Former Congressman Mel Levine (D-California)

"Senators and representatives, faced incessantly with the need to raise even more funds to fuel their campaigns, can scarcely avoid weighing every decision against the question, 'How will this affect my fundraising prospects?' rather than 'How will this affect the national interest?'"

—Former U.S. Senator Barry Goldwater (R-Arizona)

"The payoff may be as obvious and overt as a floor vote in favor of the contributor's desired tax loophole or appropriation. Or it may be subtle . . . a floor speech not delivered . . . a bill pigeonholed in subcommittee . . . an amendment not offered. . . . Or the payoff can come in a private conversation with four or five key colleagues in the privacy of the cloakroom."

—Former U.S. Senator William Proxmire (D-Wisconsin)

"One question . . . had to do with whether my financial support in any way influenced several political figures to take up my cause. I want to say in the most forceful way I can: I certainly hope so."

—Charles Keating, Former operator of the failed Lincoln Savings & Loan,
who raised over $1.3 million for the campaigns and causes of five U.S. senators
in an effort to thwart investigations of his S&L by federal bank officials, 1988

- Money influences votes at the state level as well:

"I don't know whether you want to call it corrupt or not, because we have a very gray line in this state. . . . What is corrupt? It's legal in Alabama, for instance, if there is a bill on the floor to address an envelope [to me], and I'm walking out of the Senate floor, and one of these people can walk up to me and hand me a check for $10,000 and say to me: 'Senator, now this is for your next campaign. This is not anything to do with swaying your vote on the bill.' That's legal in Alabama and it's rotten."

—Alabama state senator Charles D. Bishop, 1994

"What goes on . . . every day . . . in Sacramento [California] is that the same lobbyist comes in and on Monday he talks to you about how he's arranging for a campaign contribution to come from his client, and on Tuesday he comes back and asks you to vote on a piece of legislation for that same client. It doesn't take very long before the least-bright legislator figures out that if he keeps ignoring the Tuesday request then the lobby-ist is going to stop coming to his fundraisers. And especially when you talk about a lobbyist who controls over $1 million a year of campaign money, who can make or break one's career, it's very easy for legislators to come to the conclusion that his arguments are persuasive.

—Alan Robbins, former California state senator who served
two years in state prison after pleading guilty to corruption charges, 1993

- While it is almost impossible to document *quid pro quos* where money has bought a particular vote, instances in which money *correlates* with votes are commonplace:

—In a 1992 congressional vote on whether to transfer $16.8 billion from the military budget to domestic programs, those who voted to keep the money in the military budget had received an average of $27,000 from military-related PACs and the PACs of the top 100 military contractors during that election cycle. Those who voted to transfer the money to domestic programs had received an average of $10,000 from those same sources.
—The 26 Democrats in the U.S. House of Representatives who joined most Republicans in calling for a repeal of the ban on assault-style weapons in January of 1995 had received, on average, four times more financial support from pro-gun groups than the average Democrat during the previous six years: $22,059 vs. $5,549.
—Between 1991 and 1994, the 166 congressional cosponsors of the 1995 Safe Drinking Water Act (which would gut existing federal standards) had received campaign contributions totaling almost $10 million (an average of $60,000 each) from industries favoring passage of the Act—energy and natural resources, agricul-tural chemicals, chemical manufacturing, real estate, and home building. During the same period, the same members of Congress had received less than $200,000 (an average of $1,200 each) from pro-environment groups that opposed the Act.
—Between 1991 and 1994, the 201 congressional cosponsors of the 1995 Private Property Owners Bill of Rights (or the "takings" bill, which would make government protection of environmentally sensitive areas financially prohibitive in many instances) received campaign contributions totaling nearly $9 million (an average of $44,000 each) from industries favoring this bill—energy and natural resources, agricultural chemi-cals, chemical manufacturing, real estate, and home building. During the same period, the same members of Congress had received less than $30,000 (an average of $149 each) from pro-environment groups that op-posed the bill.

- Even without special access to elected officials, as long as campaign contributions from monied interests determine who runs for and who wins elected office, government policy will be driven by those interests, rather than by the public interest.

. . .

The defenses of PACs, apart from those that rest on their First Amendment rights, usually highlight the PACs' expression of American pluralism and their ability to mobilize citizen action and participation. In those respects, the following defense is representative. Except for two introductory paragraphs, it is the entire statement of Steven F. Stockmeyer, executive vice president of the National Association of Business Political Action Committees, given to the Committee on House Oversight. NABPAC is an organization of some 120 PACs of corporations and trade associations; it is not itself a PAC.

. . .

Authorized fully in the 1976 amendments to the Federal Election Campaign Act [document 2.10], PACs today are the virtual embodiment of American pluralism and among the finest examples of Americans exercising their rights to participate in the nation's political process. Currently over 4,000 PACs represent many different interests covering the total spectrum of citizen, economic, issue and philosophical affinities. PACs have educated, motivated and stimulated an estimated 12 million Americans to involve themselves voluntarily in politics and government—many for the first time.

In the last 20 years, PACs have become the premiere way for Americans of average means to band together and support the election of candidates that they believe have their best interests at heart. Through PACs, like-minded citizens can have more impact and be involved in more campaigns than they could acting alone. Far more than mere fund raising and dispensing operations, PACs promote greater citizen involvement in all elements of government through publications, seminars, vote drives and the like.

What's more, PACs are one of the few reforms of the 70's, if not the only one, which has worked as intended. The PAC mechanism took what was under the table and without limit and brought it into the sunshine under tight limits and regulation. Since their creation, there have been no significant abuses attributable to PACs. The sanctioning of PACs thus helped clean up a major part of the old discredited system of campaign finance and continues to do so to this day.

Because of all these positive achievements, we submit that PACs are a very healthy part of the current system and should be considered a model reform. As long as we have private funding of campaigns— something which is certainly more desirable than taxpayer funding and will always be guaranteed by the Constitution—there will never be a cleaner or better form of involvement than PACs.

Unfortunately, however, PACs have become the whipping boy of the campaign finance debate. For 20 years, professional reform groups have engaged in a McCarthy-like attack on PACs and this narrow view has been repeated by an unquestioning media. A recent study showed that 98.4% of media coverage of

PACs since 1990 is negative—a higher negative percentage than those for Oklahoma City bomber Timothy McVeigh or retired Los Angeles Detective Mark Fuhrman. These unprovoked attacks have created a false impression of corruption through innuendo, guilt-by-association and constant repetition.

As the most fully disclosed form of political giving, PACs are obvious and easy targets. But these attempts to smear PACs and the recipients of their support, I believe, are a part of a larger strategy to discredit all forms of private financing in order to build a case for forcing taxpayers to foot the bill.

We are concerned that these tactics have been so successful in creating a political imperative, albeit phony, that members of the House have felt it necessary to introduce a record number of anti-PAC bills this year. We would urge that this committee, before being caught up in the growing hysteria, pause to consider the positive role of PACs and the very negative consequences of these proposals.

Campaign finance law has always been uniquely plagued by unintended consequences and here are some of the more obvious that would develop if PACs were banned:

1. Broad citizen participation in funding campaigns would be reduced and the vital role that PACs have played to encourage involvement beyond funding would be lost.
2. Candidates would have to spend even more time raising funds, just the reverse of the stated goal of many reform measures.
3. An even greater advantage for and reliance on wealthy individuals would develop; and small minority groups would be shut down leading to domination by large, well-heeled interests.
4. Campaign money will be less accountable as interests are forced to channel support in largely undisclosed and unlimited ways.
5. Voter communication and education will suffer as one third of campaign funding disappears without being replaced.

Beyond avoiding these consequences, the committee should reject the PAC ban proposals on constitutional grounds alone. Even the authors recognize the dubious constitutionality of the ban by including a fall back contribution reduction provision if it is found unconstitutional which it surely will be. The ban is an example of the type of gross overreach prompted by the demagoguery of the professional reform community and the media. It's proposals like these that obfuscate real, achievable and constitutional reform.

If it's the appearance of influence peddling that the Congress seeks to correct, there are any number of remedial approaches the committee should consider shy of trampling on the rights of average Americans to associate for political expression. Among these are restricting the fund-raising period, prohibiting fund raising while Congress is in session, removing lobbyists from the contribution decisionmaking and delivery process, and prohibiting candidates from carrying over large treasuries from one election to the next.

Finally, we submit that there is almost nothing about the appearance problems of the current system that could not be solved by the conduct of members of Congress themselves. There is nothing that forces our representatives to raise more than they need for their campaigns, to raise funds all year round or to solicit or accept funds from sources with business before their committees. If voluntary restraint is not sufficient then the House should pass mandatory restraints as a part of its ethics rules. If the appearance problems are indeed as severe as some suggest, then each member of Congress needs to be part of the solution by examining and restricting demand.

NABPAC believes that there is a historic opportunity for constructive reforms whether it's through the immediate work of this committee and/or the broader agenda suggested for a blue-ribbon commission by the Speaker. NABPAC supports both efforts. We urge you to focus on restoring public confidence and increasing participation in the system while protecting precious constitutional guarantees.

"Prepared Statement of Joel M. Gora, Professor of Law, Brooklyn Law School,
On Behalf of the American Civil Liberties Union,"
Senate Committee on Rules and Administration, February 1, 1996
(reprinted in Senate Hearing 104-542), pp. 47, 51–54

Scholarly opinion has been overwhelmingly on one side of the constitutional debate over prohibiting PACs from contributing to congressional candidates. It has been negative. In the excerpt below Joel M. Gora, a law professor appearing on behalf of the American Civil Liberties Union, estimates the likely judicial reaction to all of the PAC restrictions in the John McCain–Russell Feingold bill of 1995–96. It is taken from his statement given to the Senate Committee on Rules and Administration. There may be a published defense of the constitutionality of these proposals, but it does not surface in the usual indexes and abstracts.

. . .

II. The complete ban on, as well as the "fallback" restrictions of, Political Action Committees are invalid under clear Supreme Court precedent.

Subtitle A of Title II, the Draconian provision which proudly proclaims that it enacts "Elimination of Political Action Committees from Federal Election Activities" and which bans PAC political activity, is flatly unconstitutional. In outlawing all political expenditures and contributions "made for the purpose of influencing an election for Federal office"—except those made by political parties and their candidates,—Section 201 of the bill cuts to the heart of the First Amendment's protection of freedom of political speech and association. It gives a permanent political monopoly to political parties and political candidates, and would silence all those groups that want to support or oppose those parties and candidates.

"PAC's" of course have become a political dirty word. We tend to think of the real estate PAC's or the Trial Lawyers' PAC or the insurance and medical PAC's or the tobacco-related PAC's. But the ACLU's first encounter with a "PAC" was when we had to defend a handful of old-time dissenters whom the government claimed were an illegal "political committee." The small group had run a 2-page advertisement in the *New York Times,* urging the impeachment of President (and reelection candidate) Richard Nixon for bombing Cambodia and praising those few hardy Members of Congress who had voted against the bombing. In the summer of 1972, before the ink was dry on the brand new Campaign Act of 1971 [document 2.8], the Justice Department used that "campaign reform" law to haul the little group into court, label them a "political committee" and threaten them with injunctions and fines unless they complied with the law—all for publicly speaking their minds on a key political issue of the day. The Court of Appeals quickly held that the group was an *ad hoc* issue organization, not a covered "political committee." But we got an early wake-up call on what "campaign reform" really meant.

Of course "real" PAC's, i.e., those that give or spend money to or on behalf of federal candidates, come in all sizes and shapes. They can be purely ideological or primarily self-interested, or both simultaneously. And they span the political spectrum. Labor PAC's were organized first, in the 1940s, usually to provide funds, resources and personnel to assist political candidates, usually Democrats. Corporate PAC's came on line in the early 1970's, usually on the Republican side. And both corporate and labor PAC's were legitimized and liberated by the "reforms" of the FECA, which allowed those and all other PAC's to contribute *five* times as much money to federal candidates as individuals could. All this turned the Federal Election Campaign Act into the PAC Magna Carta Act.

We think all that PAC activity is simply a reflection of the myriad groups and associations that make up so much of our political life. And so many of them are an effective way for individuals to maximize their political voice by giving to the PAC of their choice. While many PAC contributors and supporters probably do fit the stereotype of the glad-handling, Washington-based influence peddler, millions of PAC supporters contribute less than $50 and expect nothing from the candidates in return. Indeed, for millions of Americans, writing a check to the candidate, committee or cause of their choice is a fundamental political act, second in importance and meaning only to voting.

Proposals to restrict, restrain or even repeal PAC's would suppress the great variety of political activity those PAC's embody. Most of those proposals are doomed to defeat as unconstitutional. All of them are doomed to defeat as futile.

Banning PAC Contributions. There is not a word in *Buckley* v. *Valeo* [document 3.1] or any of the other relevant cases on regulation of PAC's which suggests that the Court would uphold a total ban on PAC contributions to federal candidates. Political contributions are fundamentally protected by the First Amendment, as embodiments of both speech and association. PAC's do amplify the political voices of their contributors and supporters across the entire spectrum of Amerian politics, and the Court is not likely to let you still all those voices.

Moreover, banning PAC contributions is futile as a reform. All the PAC money that cannot be contributed directly to candidates will go instead into an upsurge of independent expenditure campaigns for favored or against disfavored candidates.

Banning PAC Expenditures. The Supreme Court made it clear that independent PAC expenditures are at the *core* of the First Amendment and totally off limits to restriction. *Federal Election Commission v. National Conservative Political Action Committee,* 470 U.S. 480 (1985). It may be a little less tidy to run an independent campaign, than to write a check to your favored candidate, but PAC's will adapt. They're good at that. And little will have been gained—except making it harder for candidates to raise money since you will have deprived them of a major source of resources, without providing any alternatives. Candidates of moderate means will be particularly vulnerable to campaigns by personally wealthy opponents.

Reducing PAC Contributions. The "fallback" provision, which goes into effect when the flat ban is ruled unconstitutional, as it surely will be, would lower PAC contributions from $5,000 to $1,000 per candidate per election. This might be a closer constitutional question. But the Court threw out a $250 limit on contributions to a referendum campaign committee. See *Citizens Against Rent Control* v. *Berkeley,* 454 U.S. 290 (1981). Indeed, just recently the Eighth Circuit likewise invalidated a $300 contribution limitation for donations to statewide candidates. *Carver* v. *Nixon*, — F.2d —, 64 Law Week 2407 (8th Cir. 1995) [document 9.2]. And *Meyer* v. *Grant*, 486 U.S. 414 (1988) held that people had a right to spend money to hire others to gather election petition signatures, strongly reaffirming the right of a person to use his or her resources to enlist others to advance their causes. In any event, this provision is fatally overbroad because it treats all PAC's alike, even those made up only of small contributions.

Finally, apart from the First Amendment issues, what purpose is served by reducing the ability of candidates to raise money without providing alternatives?

Bundling. The same objections pertain to the ban on "bundling" of individual PAC contributions. This fallback proposal would abridge freedom of association which the Supreme Court has recognized as a "basic consitutional freedom." *Kusper* v. *Ponlikes*, 414 U.S. 51, 57 (1973). And the Court has pointedly observed that "the practice of persons sharing common views banding together to achieve a comon end is deeply embedded in the American political process." *Citizens Against Rent Control* v. *Berkeley*, 454 U.S. 290, 294 (1981). The practice of bundling reflects broad issue support to a candidate, indicating that continued support is dependent on continued adherence to the views represented by the group. The proposed bill would severely restrict ideological groups like EMILY's List, which have made a critical contribution to expanding political opportunity and opening up political doors to candidates and groups so long excluded.

Receiving PAC Contributions. The fallback provision would also prohibit any PAC from making a contribution which raises a candidate's PAC receipts above 20% of the campaign expenditure ceilings applicable to that election. But this restraint also seems overbroad. The corruption concern becomes very attenuated in this setting, and the rationale for the overall 20 percent limit seems weak against First Amendment standards. Once the limit is reached, candidates and PAC's, in effect, would be banned totally from political interaction with one another, which would seem as constitutionally vulnerable as a total ban and have the effect of a limitation on campaign expenditures. And what of new groups that wanted to support a candidate after the candidate's PAC quota had been reached, especially if the campaign turns on an issue—abortion for example—of great moment to that group?

Finally, all of this begins to resemble yet another backdoor effort to limit overall campaign *expenditures*, in violation of *Buckley*'s core principles.

Limiting Out-of-State Political Contributions. Somehow, I have always found particularly troublesome those proposals to limit the amount of out-of-district or out-of-state contributions to candidates. Section 241 does not seem to operate as a direct ban on out-of-state contributions. Rather it provides that a candidate must receive not less than 60 percent of their overall contributions from in-State individuals in order to remain in compliance with the spending limits and receive the statutory benefits. Obviously, this is a back-door effort to limit PAC contributions to candidates, since so many PAC contributors come from states different from the candidates their PAC's contribute to, as do the PAC's themselves. It also seems to be an effort to insulate incumbents from well-funded challenges supported from another state.

Any potential justification for this ban seems highly unlikely to pass constitutional muster. Analogizing this restriction to a voter's residency requirement falls short after *McIntyre* v. *Ohio Board of Elections*, —U.S.— (1995) which held that restrictions on political speech about candidates or referenda cannot be upheld on the grounds that they are merely ballot or electoral regulations, because, in reality, they are free speech limitations. Indeed, a federal court in Oregon recently so held in overturning a requirement that State and local candidates had to raise all their campaign funds from individuals who resided within their election districts. *Vannatta* v. *Keisling,* —F.Supp.— (D. Ore. 1995) [document 9.5].

Moreover, in-State limitations could deprive particular kinds of underfinanced, insurgent candidates of the kind of out-of-State support they need. Just as much of the civil rights movement was funded by contributors and supporters from other parts of the nation, so, too, are many new and struggling candidates supported by interests beyond their home states. This proposal would severely harm such candidacies. Perhaps, that is its purpose.

Finally, Congress is our national legislature, and although its representatives come and are elected from separate districts and States, the issues you deal with are, by definition, national issues that transcend district and state lines and may be of concern to citizens all over the nation. When such issues become central in certain campaigns, people and groups from all over the country should be entitled to have their views and voices heard on those issues. Any other approach takes a disturbingly insular and isolated view of political accountability and the obligations of a Member of Congress.

. . .

CONTENTS

INTRODUCTION BY ANTHONY CORRADO

The financing of political parties has been a source of controversy for the better part of the last two decades. As major party revenues have grown from $60 million in 1976 to more than $881 million twenty years later, advocates of reform have issued increasingly sharp critiques of party fund-raising practices. Most of this criticism has been directed toward a specific form of funding (known as "soft money" in campaign finance parlance) that emerged in the 1980s. In recent years, soft money contributions have become a staple of national party fund-raising, reaching a total of more than $262.1 million in 1996, or ten times more than the amount received a decade ago. This type of fund-raising occurs outside of the scope of federal laws, so it provides national party organizations with a means of soliciting unlimited contributions from individuals, or gifts from sources such as corporations and labor unions that have long been banned from giving money in federal elections (see chapter 2).

Reformers charge that these soft money contributions have rendered the limits established by federal law meaningless and have resurrected the problems of corruption and undue influence that made the campaign finance reforms of the 1970s necessary. They further argue that party organizations spend these funds in ways that help federal candidates, thus circumventing the Federal Election Campaign Act's restrictions on party assistance to candidates. Party advocates, however, counter that the national parties' recent financial success heralds a resurgence of the role of parties in national

elections. They note that changes in party financing have strengthened these organizations by encouraging a wide range of party-building activities, a trend they support as an essential means of promoting citizen participation in the political process. The efficacy of the regulations governing party funding have thus become a central topic in the current debate over campaign finance reform.

In 1996, this controversy reached a peak. Revelations concerning the role of President Bill Clinton and Vice President Al Gore in party fund-raising efforts, the use of the White House as a venue for party fund-raising activities, and the solicitation of possibly illegal foreign contributions by the Democratic National Committee (DNC), dominated the headlines and became major issues in the final weeks of the presidential campaign. The DNC ultimately admitted receiving more than $3 million from possibly illegal or improper sources and was forced to return the gifts. Subsequent investigations revealed that many donors who had given the Democrats gifts of $100,000 or more had been invited to private White House coffees with President Clinton, attended special receptions with administration officials, and even spent the night in the Lincoln Bedroom. A significant share of this money was used for party advertisements designed to benefit the president's reelection, raising questions about the Clinton campaign's compliance with federal spending limits. The Democrats thus found themselves in the midst of the most highly publicized fund-raising scandal since Watergate. Within months of the election, the Federal Election Commission (FEC), the Justice Department, and both houses of Congress had begun investigations into Democratic activities.

The scope of the Democrats' suspect fund-raising activity in 1996 was certainly unprecedented, but the issues raised by the party's activities were commonplace. Although the president and the DNC were the focal points of public attention, the Republicans were not without problems of their own. They too were widely criticized for providing major donors with special access to elected officials and for accepting large contributions of $100,000 and more. They also spent tens of millions of dollars on issue advocacy advertisements designed to benefit their federal candidates. So, while the primary focus in 1996 was on the Democrats, both parties were cited by critics as examples of the need for fundamental reform.

The flow of money in the 1996 election demonstrates how dramatically the world of party fund-raising has changed since the amendment of the Federal Election Campaign Act (FECA) in 1974 (document 2.9). Regulatory changes have created a new legal environment in which parties once again have access to the types of unlimited contributions that were supposed to be eliminated after Watergate. Innovations in party campaign strategies have created new approaches to spending that have encouraged national party organizations to spend unlimited amounts on election-related activities. Parties have thus adapted to the act's regulatory approach in unanticipated ways. To understand these innovations and the success party committees have had in avoiding financial restraint, it is necessary to review both the evolution of the law and the ways national party committees have reacted to the new regulatory regime.

STRETCHING THE LIMITS

As with other forms of campaign funding, the act sets stringent limits on the contributions and expenditures of political party committees. Under the law, national party organizations can receive annual contributions of no more than $20,000 from an individual and $15,000 from a political action committee (PAC). Any contribution from an individual, however, is subject to the annual limit of $25,000 that is imposed on an individual's aggregate donations to federal candidates and national party organizations, which include the national party committees and senatorial and congressional campaign committees. In accordance with long-standing provisions of federal law, the 1974 act also strictly prohibits contributions from corporations or labor union treasury funds in connection with federal elections. The only exception to this prohibition in the original legislation applied to contributions received for a special exempt category of funding known as a "building fund," which was an account established to receive contributions to pay for the construction of a party headquarters or office building. Outside of bricks and mortar, parties are required to pay for all federal election–related activities with monies raised from limited contributions from individuals and PACs.

In addition to restricting contributions *to* party organizations, the law also restricts contributions or other forms of direct assistance *from* party organizations. With respect to direct contributions, each national, congressional, and state party campaign committee can give $5,000 to a House candidate at each stage of the election process, including a primary, runoff, and general election. So the maximum amount that may be contributed, assuming a runoff election in addition to a primary and general election, is $15,000 per committee. The parties' national and senatorial campaign committees can give slightly more, a combined total of $17,500, in an election cycle to a Senate candidate. State party committees can contribute an additional $5,000 to a Senate candidate.

Parties are also allowed to spend money *on behalf of* individual candidates. These outlays are usually referred to as "coordinated expenditures" because they can be made in direct coordination with a candidate's campaign. (They are also known as 441a(d) monies, since this is the section of Title 2 of the *United States Code* (U.S.C.) that authorizes this form of spending.) These expenditures differ from campaign contributions in that both the party and the candidate share control of them, giving the party some influence over how these monies are spent. Unlike contributions, which are usually monetary donations to a candidate, coordinated expenditures generally take the form of some kind of campaign service paid for by the party, such as polls, television commercials, direct mailings, or issue research. Coordinated spending also differs from direct party contributions in that such expenditures can only be made in connection with a general election campaign, whereas other party contributions can be made at each stage of a federal contest.

The FECA's limits on coordinated spending are based on formulas established for each type of election at the federal level. Under the original terms set in 1974, national party committees could spend up to $10,000 per candidate in a House general election campaign, except in those states with only one congressional district, where the limit was $20,000. In Senate general elections, the limit was $20,000 or two cents times the state's voting-age population (whichever was greater), while the presidential election ceiling was simply two cents times the voting age population, or approximately $2.9 million in 1974. Each of these limits was indexed for inflation, so they have increased with each new election cycle. By 1996, they were roughly three times their original amounts: National party committees could spend $12 million on behalf of a presidential candidate, or $30,910 for a House candidate ($61,820 in a single-district state), and from $61,820 in the smallest states, to $1.4 million in California on behalf of a Senate candidate.

State party committees are allowed to spend the same coordinated amounts as the national party organizations in House and Senate races. State party committees, however, often lack the funds to fulfill their coordinated spending limit. But this problem can be overcome through a practice known as "agency agreements." In those states or districts where a state party lacks adequate funding to meet the coordinated spending limit and a national party committee, usually a congressional or senatorial campaign committee, considers a race strategically important, the state and national party committees form an "agency agreement" that transfers the state party's spending quota to the national committee. In these instances, the national committee acts as the agent of the state committee; the national committee is thus allowed to double its coordinated spending in that district or state, since it is essentially acting as both the national and state committees. Such agreements have become increasingly common in recent election cycles, thereby allowing national party organizations to maximize their state spending in crucial contests.

These complex limits on party spending were first put into effect in the 1976 elections, and questions about the legal status of different types of party funding immediately arose. Traditionally, party organizations had spent significant sums on activities such as voter identification efforts, get-out-the-vote programs, generic party advertising (messages like "Vote Democratic" or "Support Republican Candidates"), and the production of bumper stickers, buttons, and slate cards, that might *indirectly benefit* federal candidates but did not constitute direct assistance to a particular candidate. Were these expenditures governed by the new spending ceilings?

Under the act's original guidelines, the costs of many of these activities, especially grass-roots campaign materials such as bumper stickers, lawn signs, and slate cards that mentioned particular federal candidates, could be considered in-kind campaign contributions subject to the law. This became a particular concern in the 1976 presidential race, because the public funding program established by the FECA prevented the party nominees from accepting campaign contributions in the general election period. As a result, party leaders had to rely on presidential campaign funds for election-related paraphernalia. Yet both presidential campaigns chose to concentrate their limited resources on media advertising rather than grass-roots political activities. As a result, party leaders complained after the election that the FECA had indirectly limited traditional grass-roots and party-building activities, thus reducing the role of party organizations in national elections.

Congress responded to these concerns by accepting a recommendation made by the Federal Election Commission to ease the restrictions placed on party contributions and expenditures. The new rules, which were included in the 1979 FECA amendments (document 2.12), changed the legal definition of "contribution" and "expenditure" to exclude the amounts spent on certain "grass-roots" political activities, provided that the funds for those activities were raised in compliance with FECA limits (see documents 6.1 and 6.2). This change was designed to allow state and local party organizations to pay for certain specified activities that might indirectly benefit a federal candidate without having to count this spending as a contribution or expenditure under the act. Its purpose was to encourage state and local parties to engage in supplemental campaign activity in hopes of promoting civic participation in the elections process.

It is worth noting that the 1979 amendments did not allow national party organizations to receive unlimited contributions or to accept corporate or labor funds. Any gifts received by a national party committee were still subject to the limits established in 1974. The 1979 revision thus did not create "soft money"; it simply exempted any federal monies ("hard dollars") a party committee might *spend* on certain political activities from being considered a contribution to a candidate under the law. Furthermore, the activities that were to be considered exempt under this provision were narrowly defined. Basically, the 1979 law specified three types of state and local party activity that committees may un-

dertake and noted certain restrictions that govern the conduct of these activities.

State and local party committees may pay for grass-roots campaign materials, such as pins, bumper stickers, brochures, posters, yard signs, and party newspapers. These may be used only in connection with volunteer activities and may not be distributed by direct mail or through any other general public advertising. These materials may not be purchased by national party committees and delivered to the local committees or paid for by funds donated by national committees for this purpose. Nor may a donor designate funds for this purpose to be used to purchase materials for a particular federal candidate.

State and local party committees may prepare and distribute slate cards, sample ballots, palm cards or other printed listings of three or more candidates for any public office for which an election is held in the state. However, one of the candidate listings may be displayed by such means of general public political advertising as broadcast, newspaper, magazine, or billboard advertising.

State and local party committees may conduct voter registration and turnout drives on behalf of their parties' presidential and vice-presidential nominees, including the use of telephone banks operated by volunteers, even if they are developed and trained by paid professionals. However, if a party's House or Senate candidates are mentioned in such drives in a more than incidental way, the costs of the drives allocable to those candidates must be counted as contributions to them. As with campaign materials, these voter drives may not involve the use of general public political advertising and may not be paid for with funds donated by a national party committee or from funds designated by donors for particular candidates.

Congress thus gave party organizations broader leeway to spend federal funds with respect to election-related activities. In addition to direct contributions and coordinated expenditures, party organizations could spend unlimited amounts on voter registration and identification, certain types of campaign material, and voter turnout programs. Congress supported this revision because these tasks were considered important "party-building" activities that would help develop organizational support for party candidates and promote citizen participation in electoral politics. Moreover, such spending, while it might indirectly benefit federal candidates, was not considered to be a form of direct assistance to a particular candidate. It therefore did not significantly undermine the integrity of the limits on direct candidate assistance.

So in 1979 Congress authorized a circumscribed realm of unlimited party expenditures. But it did not sanction unlimited spending on activities designed to assist a particular candidate for federal office. Nor did it open the door to unrestricted fund-raising or party committee receipt of corporate or labor donations. Instead, it was the Federal Election Commission, the agency empowered to enforce the law, that changed the rules governing party fund-raising and gave birth to a new form of funding: soft money.

THE RISE OF SOFT MONEY

The provisions of the act had raised another major issue with respect to party financing: how to accommodate the federal and nonfederal roles of party organizations. The act imposed limits on party financing for all activities conducted in connection with federal elections. But party organizations also play a significant role in nonfederal elections—gubernatorial races, state contests, legislative elections, and campaigns for major local offices. Their financial efforts in these races are governed by state campaign finance laws, which are generally much more permissive than federal law. For example, most states allow parties to accept corporate and labor union contributions, and, as of 1992, sixteen states had placed no limit on individual gifts, while nineteen had no limits for PAC

giving. National party organizations could thus receive contributions for nonfederal purposes that are not allowed in federal elections.

The issue of nonfederal party funding first arose in 1976. The Illinois Republican State Central Committee asked the FEC for guidance on how to allocate nonfederal and federally regulated funds in paying some of their general overhead and operating expenses, as well as the expenses of voter registration and get-out-the-vote drives that would benefit both federal and nonfederal candidates. The party sought the FEC's opinion in part because Illinois allowed corporate and labor contributions that were not permissible under federal law.

In its Advisory Opinion 1976-72, the FEC clearly stated that corporate or labor union money could not be used to finance such federal election–related activities as a voter registration drive: "Even though the Illinois law apparently permits corporate contributions for State elections, corporate/union treasury funds may not be used to fund any portion of a registration or get-out-the-vote drive conducted by a political party" (see document 6.3). However, the Commission did approve the use of nonfederal funds to finance a portion of the party's overhead and administrative costs, since these costs—for example, rent, utilities, office supplies, salaries—supported the administration of activities related to both federal and nonfederal politics. The agency approved an allocation formula based on the proportion of federal to state elections being held that year, with greater weight given to federal races. To pay these costs, the Illinois party had to establish separate federal and nonfederal accounts; the federal account could be used only to accept contributions permissible under the act, and the nonfederal account solely for monies allowed under state laws. The proportionate share of administrative costs would be paid from the relevant account; that is, the federal election–related share of the costs would be paid from the federal account, and vice versa.

The FEC's attempt to hold the line on corporate

contributions was short-lived. Less than two years after their 1976 advisory opinion, the Commission again faced the issue of corporate and labor funding of party voter mobilization efforts. This time the Republican State Committee of Kansas sought the Commission's approval to use corporate and union funds, which were legal under Kansas law, in a voter drive that would benefit both federal and state candidates. Specifically, the Kansans asked the Commission how they should allocate funds between federal and nonfederal funds for their voter registration and get-out-the-vote efforts. In a surprising ruling, two Republican commissioners switched their earlier positions and joined two Democrats in approving Advisory Opinion 1978-10, which reversed the 1976 decision (see document 6.4). Instead of prohibiting use of corporate and union money, the agency declared that the Kansas party could use these funds to finance a share of their voter drives, so long as they allocated their costs to reflect the federal and nonfederal shares of any costs incurred. The decision thus opened the door to the use of nonfederal money on election-related activity conducted in connection with a federal election.

Commissioner Thomas E. Harris, a Democrat, believed so strongly that the ruling violated both the letter of the law and Congress's intent in framing the act that he took the unusual step of filing a written dissent (see document 6.4). In it, he noted that there would normally be more state and local races than federal races taking place in a state, so most of the costs of voter drives could be financed from monies not permissible under federal law. His point was not lost on party leaders, who quickly began to adapt their financial strategies to take advantage of the new opportunities inherent in the FEC's decision.

Although the FEC's 1978 ruling was issued in response to a state party request, it applied equally to national parties. Like state party committees, national party committees are involved in both federal and nonfederal politics. National parties serve as umbrella organizations that work with party leaders and elected officials at all levels of government. They make contributions and provide campaign assistance to federal, state, and local candidates. They work with state and local party organizations on a variety of party-building and election-related activities. National party leaders therefore argued that they too could allocate administrative costs and other expenses between federal and nonfederal funds, so long as they maintained federal and nonfederal accounts to handle the different types of money.

So just at the time that Congress was allowing party organizations to spend unlimited amounts of money raised under federal rules on voter programs and other activities, the FEC was allowing them to pay a share of such costs with funds not subject to federal limits. These two streams of regulatory change converged in the 1980 election, leading to widespread use of nonfederal money at the federal level.

During the 1980 election cycle, national party organizations began to raise millions of dollars in nonfederal money from corporations, labor unions, and individuals who had already given the maximum amount allowed under federal law. A share of these funds were used to defray a portion of the national party committees' administrative costs, as well as the expenses incurred in raising nonfederal monies. They were also used to pay a proportionate share of the costs of voter targeting and turnout programs designed to assist the presidential ticket or party candidates engaged in strategically important state contests. In many instances, the national party organizations raised the funds needed to pay for these programs and transferred the amounts to state party committees that actually conducted the voter drives, sometimes with assistance from organizers recruited by the national party committees.

This nonfederal funding quickly became known as "soft money," because it was not subject to the "hard" limits of federal law. National committees could solicit unlimited amounts from donors throughout the country, and then use the money to pay their own costs or redistribute these funds to those states where they were considered most necessary. As long as the contributions were legal under state law, the gifts were permissible. So a national party fundraiser could solicit $1 million from a donor and use the monies for a variety of purposes, or even transfer the entire amount to a state that had no limits on political contributions. In essence, the new rules gave party organizations a green light to engage in unrestricted fund-raising.

The use of soft money by national party organizations also had the added benefit of freeing up hard monies that could be contributed directly to candidates or used for coordinated expenditures. In other words, in 1976 if a party had overhead costs of $10 million, that entire sum would have been paid with hard money; in 1980, a party could pay a share of their overhead (perhaps as much as one-third) with soft money, thus "freeing up" $3 million in hard money that could be used for direct candidate assistance. Soft money also constituted a means of indirectly assisting federal candidates, since the effect of successful party voter drives would be to increase the identification and turnout of partisan voters who were likely to support the party's presidential and congressional candidates. The monies spent on these voter drives were exempt from the hard limits imposed on direct assistance to federal candidates, so long as the parties adhered to the conditions set forth by the FEC.

Given these advantages, it is no surprise that parties quickly took advantage of the relaxed regulatory environment. The only question remaining for party officials was how to allocate soft money with respect to different activities. The FEC took the position that party committees could allocate funds on any reasonable basis. By 1982, when the DNC requested the FEC's guidance on how to pay for a party midterm conference, the agency had approved at least five methods of allocation and afforded party committees notable leeway in selecting their approach (see document 6.5). Party committees could thus increase their use of soft money by selecting the allocation method that permitted the greatest nonfederal share.

As a result, soft money became a substantial component of national party finance in the 1980s. How substantial a component is difficult to determine. Because these contributions were used for nonfederal activity, they were not subject to federal disclosure laws. National party committees were therefore only required to report their soft money receipts and expenditures in the states where the money was spent, where disclosure requirements were often either nonexistent or wholly ineffective. It is therefore impossible to determine the exact amounts raised and spent by the national party organizations. The best available estimates suggest that the two major parties spent $19.1 million in soft money during the 1980 election cycle, with the Republicans spending $15.1 million and the Democrats $4 million. In 1984, they received an estimated $21.6 million, with the Republicans once again outpacing the Democrats by a margin of $15.6 million to $6 million.

REGULATION AND RESPONSE

This expansion of soft money in the early 1980s did not go unnoticed or unchallenged. Opponents, especially Common Cause and other groups interested in campaign reform, were outspoken in their criticism of the practice, arguing that soft money violated the contribution and spending limits of the FECA, and significantly undermined the intentions and purposes of the act. In November 1984, Common Cause filed a rulemaking petition with the FEC in an effort to get the Commission to review its decisions and put an end to nonfederal funding. The group's petition argued that nonfederal funds were being raised "in connection with" federal elections and therefore violated federal law (see document 6.6A). In April 1986 the FEC finally ruled on the petition, after conducting public hearings, soliciting public comment, and listening to oral testimony by Common Cause, the Center for Responsive Politics, and the Republican National Committee (see document 6.6B). The Commission rejected the petition, claiming that the need for further regulations had not been established.

Unsatisfied with the FEC's conclusion, Common Cause took the agency to court. A 1987 decision by the U.S. District Court for the District of Columbia rejected many of Common Cause's arguments; *Common Cause* v. *Federal Election Commission*, 692 F.Supp. 1391 (D.D.C. 1987). However, it maintained that the Commission's regulations provided no guidance whatsoever on which allocation methods a state or local party may use and thus found that a revision of the regulations was warranted (see document 6.6C). A year later, new regulations had not yet been developed, and Common Cause pressed the issue, petitioning the District Court for enforcement of its order. In *Common Cause* v. *Federal Election Commission*, 692 F.Supp. 1397 (D.D.C. 1988), Common Cause reviewed its arguments against soft money and asked the court to impose a timetable on the FEC and require the agency to propose allocation rules for party money within thirty days (see document 6.7). The Court noted that it would "not countenance further delay simply because regulations cannot be readied in time for November" and ruled that the FEC should report every ninety days on its progress in promulgating new allocation rules.

In 1990, after an arduous rulemaking process that included considerable consultation with political party lawyers and accountants, the FEC finally issued new soft money regulations that took effect on January 1, 1991 (see document 6.8). The regulations changed the disclosure requirements for soft money and the methods by which party organizations could allocate their expenditures. Under these rules, all party committees raising and spending soft money in conjunction with federal elections must file regular disclosure reports of their contributions and disbursements with the FEC. These reports must identify any contributors who give more than $200 to soft money accounts or party building-fund accounts. Monies raised and spent by state and local committees that are unrelated to federal election activity, however, do not have to be reported to the FEC. These funds remain subject to the reporting requirements of applicable state disclosure laws.

The rules also replaced the FEC's "any reasonable method" approach to allocation with a complicated system of formulas that account for different types of party committees and different types of soft money activities. In an effort to establish some consistency in the formulas, the regulations require that during a presidential election year, national party committees must charge at least 65 percent of the costs of voter drives and administrative expenses to their federal (hard money) accounts. In nonpresidential election years, at least 60 percent of these costs must be paid for with federal funds. For state and local party organizations, these costs must be allocated on the basis of the composition of the particular state's general election ballot—the percentages must reflect the proportion of federal offices to total offices on the general election ballot. In the 1992 election cycle, the allocation ratios produced by this ballot composition method ranged from a low of 25 percent federal (hard money) funds in Rhode Island and four other states, to a high of 75 percent federal in Maryland.

Flexible allocation methods were retained for other types of activity. The shares for fund-raising costs, for example, are based on the relative amounts of federal and nonfederal money raised as a result of a particular fund-raising solicitation or event. So if 60 percent of the money raised at an event is soft money, 60 percent of the costs can be paid for with soft money. The shares for telephone banks or other types of party communications are based on the relative benefit that each candidate receives from the telephoning conducted by the bank, or from the space in a publication or time on the air in a party communication.

Yet while the new rules placed some restraints on soft money spending by fixing the allocation rates on certain expenses, they placed no restrictions on soft money fund-raising, or on the amounts that could be spent. The general effect of the guidelines was thus to give party organizations a clearer sense of how to spend soft money legally, and in at least some instances, to permit them by regulation to pay a greater share of their costs with soft money than they had been before. As a result, the use of soft money increased substantially. In 1992, the major party organizations raised more than $83 million in soft money, about four times the amount spent in 1984. The Republican party committees received a combined $49.8 million in soft money in 1991 and 1992, while their Democratic counterparts raised more than $36.3 million.

Yet the substantial amounts raised in 1992 paled in comparison to the extraordinary sums of soft money generated in 1996. The Republican national party committees solicited more than $138.2 million, an increase of 178 percent over 1992; the Democratic committees raised $123.9 million, an increase of 242 percent over their efforts four years earlier. Not surprisingly, in both parties, soft money disbursements were up by more than 200 percent over 1992.

Soft money financing soared in 1996 for primarily two reasons. Both parties sought soft money contributions more aggressively than ever before, and both were successful at raising hundreds of contributions of six figures or more from corporations, labor unions, and wealthy individuals. In addition, soft money was spent in ingenious new ways, which greatly increased the demand for soft dollars. Most importantly, both parties used soft money to finance the broadcast of "issue advocacy" ads (see chapter 7). These ads, which featured themes and issues that were designed to benefit the parties' respective presidential and congressional candidates, were not considered to be federal election expenditures because they did not "expressly advocate" the election or defeat of a particular can-

didate. Indeed, even when the Commission did find that these ads could influence federal elections, they still allowed the parties to spend as much as they wanted, so long as they used the mix of hard and soft money required by the allocation regulations (see document 6.9). The parties were therefore free to spend as much money as they wished—and they did. By Election Day, each of the major parties had spent tens of millions of dollars on "issues ads," with much of the money coming from their soft money accounts.

Party committees also took advantage of an additional opportunity to spend hard money. Since the act was adopted, parties had been prohibited from engaging in independent expenditures. The basic assumption behind the law was that party organizations were uniquely associated with their candidates—an association that was tacitly acknowledged in the law's coordinated spending provisions. The Supreme Court's decision in *Colorado Republican Federal Campaign Committee* v. *Federal Election Commission*, 116 S. Ct. 2309 (1996) (document 3.4), questioned this assumption. Several justices suggested that parties should have an unlimited right to spend in coordination with or contribute directly to their federal candidates, although a majority of the court did not address this issue (see chapters 3 and 7). The ruling thus opened the door to yet another form of party spending.

The Republicans wasted little time in responding to the court's ruling. By August 1996, they had established a political operation separate from the National Republican Senatorial Committee to make independent expenditures on behalf of Republican Senate candidates. By early October, this committee had already spent more than $2 million in open Senate races.

The Democrats sought a clarification of the law before engaging in independent spending. The Democratic Senatorial Campaign Committee and Democratic Congressional Campaign Committee went to court, seeking a ruling that the parties (which had already begun making coordinated expenditures in connection with the 1996 elections) could not be considered capable of making "independent" expenditures in the 1996 cycle. The court dismissed their claim. The Democrats next turned to the FEC, seeking a ruling on the matter as well as regulations that would govern party independent expenditure efforts if they were to be allowed by the courts. But the FEC was unwilling to issue a quick ruling on so important a matter only weeks before an election, agreeing only to examine the issue and promulgate additional regulations if needed. However, any regulatory action would have to come well after the election.

Having failed to thwart this form of spending, the Democrats began to engage in independent expenditures of their own, patterning their activity after the Republicans. As with the Republicans, only the Senatorial campaign committee and selected state and local party committees spent money independently. Yet overall, these committees combined to spend $11.5 million on independent expenditures, though the committees did not begin until the general election campaign was well under way. The Republicans were responsible for most of these expenditures, outspending the Democrats by a margin of $10 million to $1.5 million.

THE REFORM DEBATE

The scope of party fundraising activities in recent years has revived many of the issues that inspired the creation of the FECA more than twenty years ago (see document 6.10). The revival of unlimited donations from sources that have been prohibited from participating in federal elections for much of this century once again raises questions about the role of large contributors in the political process. These contributions also raise concerns that these donors may be getting special privileges or other quid pro quos in exchange for their largesse. The experience of the 1996 election, especially the controversy surrounding President Clinton's fundraising activities and the likelihood that illegal gifts from foreign sources found their way into Democratic coffers, has served to reinforce these concerns and give rise to increasingly vocal demands for fundamental reform of the rules governing party finance.

Many observers have also noted that soft money and independent spending by political parties constitute direct challenges to the ability of the act to effectively limit fund-raising and spending by political parties. These developments severely undermine the ceilings on coordinated expenditures, since party committees that reach this limit can simply shift their spending to issue advocacy ads or independent expenditures that can benefit a candidate without counting against any party spending ceilings. Indeed, given the advantages of these forms of spending, it is likely that parties will devote more money to these types of expenditures in the future.

For these reasons, many advocates of reform have argued that it is essential to reform party spending, especially soft money, if meaningful campaign finance reform is to be achieved. Others argue that the scandals associated with soft money in the 1996 election cycle do not indicate the need for systematic reform. For example, Brent Thompson, director of the Fair Government Foundation, a group that opposes further regulation of campaign finance, notes that soft money has allowed party organizations to play a greater role in election campaigns and thus strengthened the "federalism" of the American party structure (see document 6.11). He also contends that these party contributions help to reduce the potential for corruption in the system by severing the links between donors and candidates, which reduces the possibilities of quid pro quos for campaign dollars. Others respond by noting that candidates, such as President Clinton, are directly involved in soliciting soft money contributions that pay for party activity that benefits their campaigns.

The controversy surrounding party funding has generated a variety of reform proposals. The FEC has responded to the events of 1996 by continuing its investigations into party funding. It has also proposed revised regulations to tighten the legal definition of "coordination" between party committees and candidates, and new regulations to account for the *Colorado Republican* decision and govern any independent expenditures conducted by party organizations ("Proposed Rules," *Federal Register,* vol. 62, no. 86 [May 5, 1997], p. 24372). The FEC is also examining ways to modify its rules regarding soft money. Members of Congress and President Clinton have petitioned the FEC to use its administrative rulemaking procedures to eliminate this form of funding, but others question whether the FEC has this authority.

Most of the proposals submitted in recent Congresses seek to eliminate soft money. The major exception are proposals like that submitted by Congressman John Doolittle (R-Calif.) that retain nonfederal party funding but strengthen the disclosure requirements imposed on this type of funding. But the general approach reflected in recent reform proposals is to adopt strict prohibitions against soft money and other new forms of party spending. The broadest approach seeks to eliminate all soft money by preventing federal officials and party organizations from participating in soft money financing in any way. The John McCain-Russell Feingold bill, for example, would prohibit national party organizations from accepting soft money funds, and further prohibit federal officeholders, party officials, and federal candidates from participating in the solicitation of soft money funds. The bill would even require that state party organizations engaged in voter drives or other activities use hard money funds to pay the total costs of these activities, thus eliminating the use of nonfederal funds by state and local parties. Other suggested reforms include the elimination of the building funds provision of current law and tighter definitions of "coordination" to reduce the ability of party organizations to spend money independently of their candidates.

Other advocates of reform support approaches that change party financing without weakening the role of party organizations in national and state elections. For example, the proposal presented in document 9.9 by Ornstein, Mann, Taylor, Malbin, and Corrado seeks to eliminate soft money fundraising by national party organizations and public officials. However, it increases the limits on hard money contributions to party committees in order to compensate these organizations for the anticipated loss of revenue from the elimination of corporate and labor money, and frees the parties to spend their hard money as they see fit. Other proposals retain soft money for specific purposes, such as voter drives and campaign materials, but place limits on soft money donations received by national party committees.

What follows is the statutory language from the Federal Election Campaign Act (FECA) that legally defines "contributions" and "expenditures" in federal elections. The 1979 amendments to this act excluded from these definitions funds spent by local and state parties to promote grass-roots political participation in federal elections, but they did not permit parties to receive unlimited and unregulated "soft money" contributions. Contributions that did not meet the narrow requisites of these definitions were still subject to the limits established by the 1974 amendments (document 2.9).

. . .

(8) (A) The term "contribution" includes—

(i)   any gift, subscription, loan, advance, or deposit of money or anything of value made by any person for the purpose of influencing any election for Federal office; or

(ii) the payment by any person of compensation for the personal services of another person which are rendered to a political committee without charge for any purpose.

(B) The term "contribution" does not include—

(i)   the value of services provided without compensation by any individual who volunteers on behalf of a candidate or political committee;

(ii) the use of real or personal property, including a church or community room used on a regular basis by members of a community for noncommercial purposes, and the cost of invitations, food, and beverages, voluntarily provided by an individual to any candidate or any political committee of a political party in rendering voluntary personal services on the individual's residential premises or in the church or community room for candidate-related or political party-related activities, to the extent that the cumulative value of such invitations, food, and beverages provided by such individual on behalf of any single candidate does not exceed $1,000 with respect to any single election, and on behalf of all political committees of a political party does not exceed $2,000 in any calendar year;

(iii) the sale of any food or beverage by a vendor for use in any candidate's campaign or for use by or on behalf of any political committee of a political party at a charge less than the normal comparable charge, if such charge is at least equal to the cost of such food or beverage to the vendor, to the extent that the cumulative value of such activity by such vendor on behalf of any single candidate does not exceed $1,000 with respect to any single election, and on behalf of all political committees of a political party does not exceed $2,000 in any calendar year;

(iv) any unreimbursed payment for travel expenses made by any individual on behalf of any candidate or any political committee of a political party, to the extent that the cumulative value of such activity by such individual on behalf of any single candidate does not exceed $1,000 with respect to any single election, and on behalf of all political committees of a political party does not exceed $2,000 in any calendar year;

(v) the payment by a State or local committee of a political party of the costs of preparation, display, or mailing or other distribution incurred by such committee with respect to a printed slate card or sample ballot, or other printed listing, of 3 or more candidates for any public office for which an election is held in the State in which such committee is organized, except that this clause shall not apply to any cost incurred by such committee with respect to a display of any such listing made on broadcasting stations, or in newspapers, magazines, or similar types of general public political advertising;

(vi) any payment made or obligation incurred by a corporation or a labor organization which, under section 441b(b) of this title, would not constitute an expenditure by such corporation or labor organization;

. . .

(viii) any gift, subscription, loan, advance, or deposit of money or anything of value to a national or a State committee of a political party specifically designated to defray any cost for construction or purchase of any office facility not acquired for the purpose of influencing the election of any candidate in any particular election for Federal office;

. . .

(x) the payment by a State or local committee of a political party of the costs of campaign materials (such as pins, bumper stickers, handbills, brochures, posters, party tabloids, and yard signs) used by such committee in connection with volunteer activities on behalf of nominees of such party: *Provided*, That—
   (1) such payments are not for the costs of campaign materials or activities used in connection with any broadcasting, newspaper, magazine, billboard, direct mail, or similar type of general public communication or political advertising;
   (2) such payments are made from contributions subject to the limitations and prohibitions of this Act; and
   (3) such payments are not made from contributions designated to be spent on behalf of a particular candidate or particular candidates;

(xi) the payment by a candidate, for nomination or election to any public office (including State or local office), or authorized committee of a candidate, of the costs of campaign materials which include information on or reference to any other candidate and which are used in connection with volunteer activities (including pins, bumper stickers, handbills, brochures, posters, and yard signs, but not including the use of broadcasting, newspapers, magazines, billboards, direct mail, or similar types of general public communication or political advertising): *Provided*, That such payments are made from contributions subject to the limitations and prohibitions of this Act;

(xii) the payment by a State or local committee of a political party of the costs of voter registration and get-out-the-vote activities conducted by such committee on behalf of nominees of such party for President and Vice President: *Provided*, That—

(1) such payments are not for the costs of campaign materials or activities used in connection with any broadcasting, newspaper, magazine, billboard, direct mail, or similar type of general public communication or political advertising;

(2) such payments are made from contributions subject to the limitations and prohibitions of this Act; and

(3) such payments are not made from contributions designated to be spent on behalf of a particular candidate or candidates;

. . .

(9)(A)The term "expenditure" includes—

(i) any purchase, payment, distribution, loan, advance, deposit, or gift of money or anything of value, made by any person for the purpose of influencing any election for Federal office; and

(ii) a written contract, promise, or agreement to make an expenditure.

(B)The term "expenditure" does not include—

(i) any news story, commentary, or editorial distributed through the facilities of any broadcasting station, newspaper, magazine, or other periodical publication, unless such facilities are owned or controlled by any political party, political committee, or candidate;

(ii) nonpartisan activity designed to encourage individuals to vote or to register to vote;

(iii) any communication by any membership organization or corporation to its members, stockholders, or executive or administrative personnel, if such membership organization or corporation is not organized primarily for the purpose of influencing the nomination for election, or election, of any individual to Federal office, except that the costs incurred by a membership organization (including a labor organization) or by a corporation directly attributable to a communication expressly advocating the election or defeat of a clearly identified candidate (other than a communication primarily devoted to subjects other than the express advocacy of the election or defeat of a clearly identified candidate), shall, if such costs exceed $2,000 for any election, be reported to the Commission in accordance with section 434(a)(4)(A)(i) of this title, and in accordance with section 434(a)(4)(ii) of this title with respect to any general election;

(iv) the payment by a State or local committee of a political party of the costs of preparation, display, or mailing or other distribution incurred by such committee with respect to a printed slate card or sample ballot, or other printed listing, of 3 or more candidates for any public office for which an election is held in the State in which such committee is organized, except that this clause shall not apply to costs incurred by such committee with respect to a display of any such listing made on broadcasting stations, or in newspapers, magazines, or similar types of general public political advertising;

(v) any payment made or obligation incurred by a corporation or a labor organization which, under section 441b(b) of this title, would not constitute an expenditure by such corporation or labor organization;

. . .

(viii) the payment by a State or local committee of a political party of the costs of campaign materials (such as pins, bumper stickers, handbills, brochures, posters, party tabloids, and yard signs) used by such committee in connection with volunteer activities on behalf of nominees of such party: *Provided*, That—

(1) such payments are not for the costs of campaign materials or activities used in connection with any broadcasting, newspaper, magazine, billboard, direct mail, or similar type of general public communication or political advertising;

(2) such payments are made from contributions subject to the limitations and prohibitions of this Act; and

(3) such payments are not made from contributions designated to be spent on behalf of a particular candidate or particular candidates;

(ix) the payment by a State or local committee of a political party of the costs of voter registration and get-out-the-vote activities conducted by such committee on behalf of nominees of such party for President and Vice President: *Provided*, That—

(1) such payments are not for the costs of campaign materials or activities used in connection with any broadcasting, newspaper, magazine, billboard, direct mail, or similar type of general public communication or political advertising;

(2) such payments are made from contributions subject to the limitations and prohibitions of this Act; and

(3) such payments are not made from contributions designated to be spent on behalf of a particular candidate or candidates; and

(x) payments received by a political party committee as a condition of ballot access which are transferred to another political party committee or the appropriate State official.

The Federal Election Commission issued regulations to conform with the provisions of the Federal Election Campaign Act of 1971, as amended in 1974, 1976, and 1979 (see document 6.1). The following are excerpts of the FEC's regulations from the *Code of Federal Regulations:* section 100.7 defines contributions, section 100.8 defines expenditures, and section 110.7 provides party committee expenditure limitations.

A. 11 C.F.R. § 100.7

. . .

(b) The term "contribution" does not include the following payments, services or other things of value:

    (1) (i) Funds received solely for the purpose of determining whether an individual should become a candidate are not contributions. Examples of activities permissible under this exemption if they are conducted to determine whether an individual should become a candidate include, but are not limited to, conducting a poll, telephone calls, and travel. Only funds permissible under the Act may be used for such activities. The individual shall keep records of all such funds received. See 11 CFR 101.3. If the individual subsequently becomes a candidate, the funds received are contributions subject to the reporting requirements of the Act. Such contributions must be reported with the first report filed by the principal campaign committee of the candidate, regardless of the date the funds were received.

       (ii) This exemption does not apply to funds received for activities indicating that an individual has decided to become a candidate for a particular office or for activities relevant to conducting a campaign. Examples of activities that indicate that an individual has decided to become a candidate include, but are not limited to:

         (A) The individual uses general public political advertising to publicize his or her intention to campaign for Federal office.

         (B) The individual raises funds in excess of what could reasonably be expected to be used for exploratory activities or undertakes activities designed to amass campaign funds that would be spent after he or she becomes a candidate.

         (C) The individual makes or authorizes written or oral statements that refer to him or her as a candidate for a particular office.

(D) The individual conducts activities in close proximity to the election or over a protracted period of time.

(E) The individual has taken action to qualify for the ballot under State law.

(2) Any cost incurred in covering or carrying a news story, commentary, or editorial by any broadcasting station, newspaper, magazine, or other periodical publication is not a contribution unless the facility is owned or controlled by any political party, political committee, or candidate, in which case the cost for a news story (i) which represents a bona fide news account communicated in a publication of general circulation or on a licensed broadcasting facility, and (ii) which is part of a general pattern of campaign-related news accounts which give reasonably equal coverage to all opposing candidates in the circulation or listening area, is not a contribution.

(3) The value of services provided without compensation by any individual who volunteers on behalf of a candidate or political committee is not a contribution.

. . .

(8) Any unreimbursed payment for transportation expenses incurred by any individual on behalf of any candidate or any political committee of a political party is not a contribution to the extent that: the aggregate value of the payments made by such individual on behalf of a candidate does not exceed $1,000 with respect to a single election; and on behalf of all political committees of each political party does not exceed $2,000 in a calendar year. Additionally, any unreimbursed payment from a volunteer's personal funds for usual and normal subsistence expenses incidental to volunteer activity is not a contribution.

(9) The payment by a State or local committee of a political party of the costs of preparation, display, or mailing or other distribution incurred by such committee with respect to a printed slate card, sample ballot, palm card, or other printed listing(s) of three or more candidates for any public office for which an election is held in the State in which the committee is organized is not a contribution. The payment of the portion of such costs allocable to Federal candidates must be made from funds subject to the limitations and prohibitions of the Act. If made by a political committee, such payments shall be reported by that committee as disbursements, but need not be allocated in committee reports to specific candidates. This exemption shall not apply to costs incurred by such a committee with respect to the preparation and display of listings made on broadcasting stations, or in newspapers, magazines, and similar types of general public political advertising such as billboards.

. . .

B. 11 C.F.R. § 100.8

. . .

(b) The term "expenditure" does not include the following payments, gifts, or other things of value:

(1) (i) Payments made solely for the purpose of determining whether an individual should become a candidate are not expenditures. Examples of activities permissible under this exemption if they are conducted to determine whether an individual should become a

candidate include, but are not limited to, conducting a poll, telephone calls, and travel. Only funds permissible under the Act may be used for such activities. The individual shall keep records of all such payments. See 11 CFR 101.3. If the individual subsequently becomes a candidate, the payments made are subject to the reporting requirements of the Act. Such expenditures must be reported with the first report filed by the principal campaign committee of the candidate, regardless of the date the payments were made.

    (ii) This exemption does not apply to payments made for activities indicating that an individual has decided to become a candidate for a particular office or for activities relevant to conducting a campaign. Examples of activities that indicate that an individual has decided to become a candidate include, but are not limited to:

        (A) The individual uses general public political advertising to publicize his or her intention to campaign for Federal office.

        (B) The individual raises funds in excess of what could reasonably be expected to be used for exploratory activities or undertakes activities designed to amass campaign funds that would be spent after he or she becomes a candidate.

        (C) The individual makes or authorizes written or oral statements that refer to him or her as a candidate for a particular office.

        (D) The individual conducts activities in close proximity to the election or over a protracted period of time.

        (E) The individual has taken action to qualify for the ballot under State law.

(2) Any cost incurred in covering or carrying a news story, commentary, or editorial by any broadcasting station, newspaper, magazine, or other periodical publication is not an expenditure, unless the facility is owned or controlled by any political party, political committee or candidate, in which case the cost for a news story (i) which represents a bona fide news account communicated in a publication of general circulation or on a licensed broadcasting facility, and (ii) which is part of a general pattern of campaign-related news accounts which give reasonably equal coverage to all opposing candidates in the circulation or listening area, is not an expenditure.

(3) Any cost incurred for nonpartisan activity designed to encourage individuals to register to vote or to vote is not an expenditure, except that corporations and labor organizations shall engage in such activity in accordance with 11 CFR 114.4 (c) and (d). For purposes of 11 CFR 100.8(b)(3), "nonpartisan activity" means that no effort is or has been made to determine the party or candidate preference of individuals before encouraging them to register to vote or to vote.

(4) Any cost incurred for any communication by a membership organization to its members, or by a corporation to its stockholders or executive or administrative personnel, is not an expenditure, so long as the membership organization or corporation is not organized primarily for the purpose of influencing the nomination for election, or election, of any individual to Federal office, except that the costs incurred by a membership organization, including a labor organization, or by a corporation, directly attributable to a communication expressly advocating the election or defeat of a clearly identified candidate (other than a communication primarily devoted to subjects other than the express advocacy of the election or defeat

of a clearly identified candidate) shall, if those costs exceed $2,000 per election, be reported to the Commission on FEC Form 7 in accordance with 11 CFR 104.6

. . .

C. 11 CFR § 110.7

§110.7 Party committee expenditure limitations (2 U.S.C. 441a(d)).

(a) (1) The national committee of a political party may make expenditures in connection with the general election campaign of any candidate for President of the United States affiliated with the party.

(2) The expenditures shall not exceed an amount equal to 2 cents multiplied by the voting age population of the United States.

(3) Any expenditure under this paragraph (a) shall be in addition to—

(i) Any expenditure by a national committee of a political party serving as the principal campaign committee of a candidate for President of the United States; and

(ii) Any contribution by the national committee to the candidate permissible under § 110.1 or § 110.2.

(4) The national committee of a political party may make expenditures authorized by this section through any designated agent, including State and subordinate party committees.

(5) The national committee of a political party may not make independent expenditures (see Part 109) in connection with the general election campaign of a candidate for President of the United States.

(6) Any expenditures made by the national, state and subordinate committees of a political party pursuant to 11 CFR 110.7(a) on behalf of that party's Presidential candidate shall not count against the candidate's expenditure limitations under 11 CFR 110.8.

(b) (1) The national committee of a political party, and a State committee of a political party, including any subordinate committee of a State committee, may each make expenditures in connection with the general election campaign of a candidate for Federal office in that State who is affiliated with the party.

(2) The expenditures shall not exceed—

(i) In the case of a candidate for election to the office of Senator, or of Representative from a State which is entitled to only one Representative, the greater of—

(A) Two cents multiplied by the voting age population of the State; or

(B) Twenty thousand dollars; and

(ii) In the case of a candidate for election to the office of Representative, Delegate, or Resident Commissioner in any other State, $10,000.

(3) Any expenditure under paragraph (b) shall be in addition to any contribution by a committee to the candidate permissible under § 110.1 or § 110.2.

(4) The party committees identified in (b)(1) shall not make independent expenditures in connection with the general election campaign of candidates for Federal office.

(c) For limitation purposes, State committee includes subordinate State committees. State committees and subordinate State committees combined shall not exceed the limits in paragraph (b)(2) of this section. To ensure compliance with the limitations, the State committee shall administer the limitation in one of the following ways:

(1) The State central committee shall be responsible for insuring that the expenditures of the entire party organization are within the limitations, including receiving reports from any subordinate committee making expenditures under paragraph (b) of this section, and filing consolidated reports showing all expenditures in the State with the Commission; or

(2) Any other method, submitted in advance and approved by the Commission which permits control over expenditures.

The following is a Federal Election Commission Advisory Opinion written by then-Chairman Vernon W. Thomson to David E. Brown of the Illinois Republican State Central Committee. The FEC ruled that the party could finance its general overhead and administrative costs with both federally regulated and nonfederal funds according to a federally-weighted formula, as long as the state party maintained separate accounts. However, the Commission found that these nonfederal accounts could not be used to finance voter registration drives that benefit both state and federal candidates, because nonfederal accounts may contain corporate and union funds that are illegal federal contributions.

This is in response to your letter of August 13, 1976, in which you request an advisory opinion on behalf of the Illinois Republican State Central Committee as to the method of allocating general party overhead and operating expenditures between Federal and non-Federal activities. The types of expenses you refer to are for "rent, utilities, office supplies, salaries, etc., and for general campaign activities like registration drives and precinct training courses."

You state that there are 188 separate races in Illinois this year, 25 (not including Vice President) of which are for Federal office, five for statewide office, and 158 for State legislative offices. You ask whether a ratio of 25/188, or 15%/85%, would be a proper allocation between Federal and non-Federal candidates.

It is the opinion of the Commission that in the specific situation you describe, a reasonable allocation of Federal to non-Federal expenditures would be 1/3 to 2/3. This reflects the view that the Federal offices should be given proportionately more weight, and not be equated on a one-to-one basis with, for example, State legislative offices. This formula may be applied in every year.

Among the general party expenses you describe, however, are registration drives. Section 441b of Title 2, United States Code, permits the use of corporate and union treasury funds only for "non-partisan registration and get-out-the-vote campaigns by a corporation aimed at its stockholders and executive or administrative personnel and their families, or by a labor organization aimed at its members and their families;" (see § 114.1(a)(2)(ii) of the Commission's proposed regulations). The only exceptions to this general rule are contained in § 114.4 (d) which allows corporations and labor organizations to support a nonpartisan voter registration drive if:

(i) the corporation or labor organization jointly sponsors the drives with a civic or other non-profit organization which does not support or endorse candidates or political parties and if the activities are conducted by the other organization; and

(ii) These services are made available without regard to the voter's political preference.

2) A corporation or labor organization may donate funds to be used for non-partisan registration and get-out-the-vote drives to civic and other nonprofit organizations which do not endorse candidates or political parties.

Thus, even though the Illinois law apparently permits corporate contributions for State elections, corporate/union treasury funds may not be used to fund any portion of a registration or get-out-the-vote drive conducted by a political party.

You state that you have two accounts; one is "restricted" and contains, among others, corporate contributions; the other is "unrestricted" and contains personal and partnership checks, presumably not in excess of the contribution limitations of 2 U.S.C. § 441a. You state that "[a]lmost all expenses to date have been paid from unrestricted funds," and you ask how funds from the restricted account can be transferred to the unrestricted account to reimburse it for disbursements made for non-Federal candidates and general overhead expenses.

Section 102.6(b) of the proposed regulations provides in relevant part that committees supporting Federal candidates "may not receive transfers from an account or committee established by a State committee . . . except from a committee or account" receiving only contributions permissible under the Federal Election Campaign Act of 1971, as amended ("the Act") [see chapter 2].

Therefore, you may not transfer funds from your "restricted" account to your "unrestricted" account, since the "restricted" account contains funds which may not be properly contributed under the Act, see 2 U.S.C. § 441b. There is no limitation, however, on funds being transferred from the "unrestricted" to the "restricted" account. You may, therefore, draw a check on each account reflecting the allocation for a particular overhead expense, or you may transfer funds from the "unrestricted" to the "restricted" account, and draw one check on the "restricted" account for the total expenditure.

Notwithstanding the foregoing conclusion, and in view of the transition that will be necessary to conform your committee organization to the requirements of § 102.6, the Commission will allow a one-time adjustment of the described expenses allocable to your Federal activities based on the foregoing formula. In other words, at the time (before the close of the next reporting period) you determine the allocable Federal share of the described overhead and general campaign expenses incurred since January 1, 1976, that amount may be reimbursed to the Federal committee from the "restricted" account if the past practice of the State committee would have been to pay only the allocable Federal share from the "unrestricted" account. In the future the "restricted" account must [be kept separately from the "unrestricted" account by] the State committee, assuming you select the alternative set forth in § 102.6 (a)(2)(i) which is the only lawful structure by which the State committee may continue to receive corporate funds if the State party desires to continue to benefit Federal candidates through its general party activity.

It should be further noted that § 102.6 establishes two permissible organizational structures for political committees: a committee receiving contributions designated for, and contributing to, Federal candidates; or a committee receiving contributions designated for, and making contributions to, both Federal and State candidates. In both cases, the committee may not receive any funds unlawful under the Act, such as funds from a corporate or labor organization treasury, or contributions in excess of the limits in 2 U.S.C. § 441a. Unless it establishes a separate committee for State and local candidates, the Illinois Republican State Central Committee may not receive corporate contributions as described in your letter.

This response relates to your opinion request but may be regarded as informational only and not as an advisory opinion since it is based in part on proposed regulations of the Commission which must be submitted to Congress. The proposed regulations may be prescribed in final form by the Commission only if not disapproved either by the House or the Senate within 30 legislative days from the data received by them. 2 U.S.C. § 438(c). The proposed regulations were submitted to Congress on August 3, 1976.

This case presented a fact pattern to the Federal Election Commission that was similar to the one it reviewed in Advisory Opinion 1976-72 (document 6.3). Corporate and union contributions were legal in Kansas, and the Republican State Committee sought instruction on how to allocate federally regulated and nonfederal dollars to finance a voter drive that would benefit both federal and state candidates. When two Republican Commissioners switched their positions, the FEC reversed its ruling in A.O. 1976-72 and allowed parties to finance portions of voter drives with nonfederal dollars as long as they allocated their costs to respective federal and nonfederal shares. Democratic Commissioner Thomas E. Harris took the unusual step and issued a written dissent to lament this opening of the door to nonfederal dollars in federal election-related activity.

This responds to your letters ... requesting an advisory opinion concerning application of the Federal Election Campaign Act of 1971, as amended ("the Act") and Commission regulations to various expenditures of the Republican State Committee of Kansas ("State Committee").

. . .

Your letter of March 29, 1978, poses three questions concerning the allocation of expenses incurred by the Kansas Republican party for voter registration and get-out-the-vote drives, presumably to be conducted this election year when 6 Federal offices (5 House and 1 Senate) will be on the November ballot as well as 6 State executive offices (elected on statewide basis including Governor, Lieutenant Governor, Secretary of State, Attorney General), 5 seats on the State school board (elected on district basis) and 125 seats in the State legislature (elected on district basis). You ask:

(1) Is a voter registration drive allocable as a contribution to a candidate?
(2) If a get-out-the-vote effort contacts voters on behalf of non-federal candidates only, do the expenses of this effort have to be paid for from a federal account?
(3) If a part of such an effort is in behalf of federal candidates, does the entire cost have to be paid from a federal committee?

It is the Commission's opinion that the costs of registration and get-out-the-vote drives by the Kansas Republican Party should be allocated between Federal and non-Federal elections in the same manner as other general party expenditures. That portion of the costs allocable to Federal elections under the above allocation must come from funds contributed in accord with the Act—that is, funds contributed in accordance with the limitations and prohibitions contained in 2 U.S.C. § 441. The costs allocable to non-Federal elections may be paid out of Party funds raised and expended pursuant to applicable Kansas law. This conclusion modifies and supersedes the Commission's responses to Advisory Opinion Requests 1976-72 and 1976-83, issued respectively on October 6 and 12, 1976.

It is also the Commission's view that with respect to an election in which there are candidates for Federal office, expenditures for registration and get-out-the-vote drives need not be attributed as contributions to such candidates unless the drives are made specifically on their behalf. For example, if the purpose of the drive advocates the election of a candidate or candidates for Federal office, then the cost must be attributed to that candidate or candidates for limitation and reporting purposes. However, the Party may use printed material in a voter registration (or get-out-the-vote) drive which identifies candidates for Federal office without allocating any costs to particular candidates, if those materials are within the slate card or sample ballot exemption.

. . .

Dated: August 29, 1978.

Dissenting Opinion of Commissioner Thomas E. Harris to Advisory Opinion 1978-10

The Commission has decided today that the Kansas State Republican Party may allocate or apportion its expenditures in connection with a state-wide registration and get-out-the-vote drive between state and federal candidates, and may pay those expenditures allocated to state candidates out of any contributions not violative of Kansas State law. This means that Kansas corporations and unions may now finance a major part of the costs associated with a partisan registration and get-out-the-vote drive out of general treasury funds.

This decision not only reverses the Commission's earlier position in answer to Advisory Opinion Requests 1976-72 and 1976-83 but is clearly impermissible under the Act. Subject to enumerated exceptions, section 441b bars any contribution or expenditure of general corporate or union funds in connection with a federal election. The only possibly applicable exception is § 441b(b)(2)(B), which permits:

(B) non-partisan registration and get-out-the-vote campaigns by a corporation aimed at its stockholders and executive or administrative personnel and their families, or by a labor organization aimed at its members and their families. . . .

Obviously the contributions now sanctioned by the Commission do not fall within this language: the party committee drives will be conducted by a party committee and not the corporation or union, and will not be restricted to stockholders, members, etc.

The definitions section of the statute does exclude from "expenditure," "non-partisan activity designed to encourage individuals to register to vote, or to vote"; § 431(f)(4)(B). This definition, unlike the language quoted above, applies to all registration and get-out-the-vote activities, not just those of corporations and labor unions, and hence is not restricted as to the classes at which such drives may be aimed. However, as respects "expenditures" by corporations and labor unions, this definition must be read in conjunction with the ban on expenditures "in connection with a federal election" language of section 441b.

It has been argued that there is tension between these two statutory provisions quoted above, and that it is unclear whether corporations and unions may contribute to non-partisan drives aimed not at their restricted classes (stockholders, members, etc.), but at the general public.

To the degree that any tension may have existed, the Conference Report on the 1976 Act undertook to resolve the ambiguity. The report states:

... these provisions [§ 431(f)(4)(B) and 441b(2)(B)] should be read together to permit corporations both to take part in non-partisan registration and get-out-the-vote activities that are not restricted to stockholders and executive or administrative personnel, if such activities are jointly sponsored by the corporations and an organization that does not endorse candidates and are conducted by that organization; and to permit corporations, on their own, to engage in such activities restricted to executive or administrative personnel and stockholders and their families. The same rule, of course, applies to labor organizations. (p. 63)

Thus the report concludes that corporate and union general treasury funds may not be contributed for registration drives by party committees, but only for nonpartisan drives conducted by a civic or other organization that itself does not endorse political candidates.

Neither statutory provision treating registration and get-out-the-vote activities permits the contributions which the Commission is now sanctioning. Furthermore, parties may choose among three methods by which expenditures for both a federal and a nonfederal purpose may be allocated, all of which are virtually certain to result in the allocation of more costs to the party's state account than to its federal account. The first method, set forth in the Commission's regulations entails the calculation of the ratio between party funds spent for or contributed directly to federal candidates and those expenditures for and contributions to non-federal candidates. That ratio is then applied to the category of administrative or overhead expenses in question, in this case the costs of the registration and get-out-the-vote drive, to determine what portion must be paid out of federal funds and what out of state funds. For example, if the party makes contributions and expenditures totaling $10,000 in connection with federal candidates but makes contributions and expenditures totaling $100,000 in connection with its state candidates, then the costs of a voter-registration drive benefiting both state and federal candidates could be apportioned one-tenth payable out of the federal committee or account and nine-tenths payable out of the non-federal account. In short, under the majority's decision, nine-tenths of the cost of the drive could be financed with corporate and union treasury money.

A second method which the Commission has approved for allocation of expenditures for federal and non-federal purposes uses the ratio of statewide offices on the ballot to federal offices on the ballot as the allocation formula. This method was approved in Advisory Opinion 1976-72 for application to general overhead and administrative expenses of the Illinois Republican State Party and resulted in the allocation of one-third of these expenses to the federal account/committee and two-thirds to the state account. Since most states have more state offices on the ballot than federal in an election year, most state parties using this formula will be able to allocate a majority of the costs expended on registration and get-out-the-vote to their non-federal account and thus fund such drives, where permissible under state law, largely through the use of corporate and union treasury money.

The third method which the Commission has approved for the allocation of expenditures for federal and nonfederal purposes constructs the allocation formula from a ratio of (i) the total funds received by the party's federal campaign to (ii) the total of all receipts (with certain exclusions) by the party organization for both federal and state candidates. This formula too is weighted so that it will inevitably result in the allocation of more expenditures to the party's state account than to its federal account with the same result as described above.

Among those voting with the majority today was Commissioner Vernon Thomson. This is significant but puzzling since Commissioner Thomson authored that portion of the Commission's response to Advisory Opinion Request 1976-72 which forbids state party committees from making expenditures for registration and get-out-the-vote drives from state party accounts containing corporate and union treasury funds [see document 6.3]. Then, Commission Thomson argued, in language which was adopted as part of the opinion, that " . . . even though the Illinois law apparently permits corporate contributions for state elections, corporate/union treasury funds may not be used to fund any portion of a registration or get-out-the-vote drive conducted by a political party." See the Commission's response to Advisory Opinion request 1976-72. Today, Commissioner Thomson, without explanation, voted for the majority opinion which reaches a conclusion directly opposite to his statement above.

This sort of unexplained and inexplicable change of position on an important issue, which was carefully examined and decided two years ago, confuses those covered by the Act and discredits the Commission.

Dated: August 25, 1978.

Following the FEC's reversal in Advisory Opinion 1978-10 (document 6.4), national party organizations began raising millions of dollars in nonfederal money to support portions of overhead costs and proportionate shares of voter drives that benefitted state and federal candidates. In this opinion, the FEC offered several acceptable allocation methods for this "soft money," or contributions that escaped federal hard limits. The Commission allowed great leeway to these party committees by deciding that they could allocate their soft dollars to different activities on "any reasonable basis." As he did four years earlier, Commissioner Thomas E. Harris issued a written dissent.

This responds to your letter dated February 8, 1982, and supplementary materials submitted on March 15, 1982, requesting an advisory opinion on behalf of the Democratic National Committee ("DNC"), and the 1982 Democratic Conference Arrangements Committee, Inc. ("the Conference Committee"), concerning application of the Federal Election Campaign Act of 1971, as amended, ("the Act"), and Commission regulations to certain aspects of a national party conference to be held in June, 1982.

You state that the DNC, in conjunction with the Conference Committee, will hold a three day "National Party Conference" in June, 1982, in Philadelphia, Pennsylvania. The National Chairman's letter to State Party Chairs contained in your supplementary materials states that the Conference will provide a "forum for discussion on public policy issues . . . and a mechanism for party-building and training of candidates and political workers. . . ." You state that the first day of the conference will be devoted to "workshops and skills training programs in campaign and Democratic party organizing with emphasis on 1982 Democratic campaigns." These campaign workshops will focus on fundraising, polling, research, targeting, and media for party workers, and Federal, state and local candidates. The second day of the conference will include workshops for the purpose of discussing issues of public policy. . . . Each workshop will include a presentation by a panel of elected Democrats and experts followed by a dialogue between panelists and workshop participants.

The participants in the Conference will include members of the DNC, individuals selected by the Central Committees of the State Democratic Parties and other Democratic organizations, as well as one hundred participants selected "at large." The party resolution calling for the conference provides for the selection of "replacement" participants in the event any originally selected participants are unable to attend the conference. You indicate that replacement participants may attend any of the campaign training and issue workshops held during the conference. You indicate further that persons other than participants and replacement participants may observe the issue workshops held during the conference.

You indicate further that persons other than participants and replacement participants may observe the issue workshops held on the second conference day.

You ask first, whether the Conference Committee may accept and use corporate and labor organization treasury funds and funds donated by persons in excess of the contribution limits of 2 U.S.C. § 441a to defray that portion of the expenses of the described 1982 party conference which may be allocated to non-federal conference activity. Second, you ask for Commission guidance with respect to the manner of determining the portion of conference expenses that may be allocated to non-federal election activity. In this regard, you describe several methods of allocation of expenses that you wish the Commission to approve for use by the DNC and the Conference Committee in allocating the expenses of the conference between Federal and non-federal election activity.

Your questions with respect to financing the planned DNC conference raise the threshold issue of whether conference expenses are required to be allocated at all since it does not appear that the conference is being held for the purpose of influencing, or in connection with, the specific election of any clearly identified candidate for Federal office. The Commission considered this issue but could not agree by the requisite four affirmative votes that conference expenses were required or were not required to be allocated to Federal and non-federal elections.

Since your request indicates the DNC's intention to allocate conference expenses pursuant to 11 CFR 102.5 and 106.1 and since you have sought the Commission's guidance as to the reasonableness of several allocation formulas, the Commission will address each proposed method.

Ballot Position Method. Allocation of expenses to reflect Federal and non-federal activity would be based on a ratio of Federal ballot positions to non-federal ballot positions in the November 1982 election on a nationwide basis. The Commission recognizes that the number of non-federal ballot positions is substantially greater than the number of Federal ballot positions, and that many state and local offices are not comparable to Federal offices. The Commission concludes that the use of this allocation method with respect to allocating conference expenses would be reasonable under the Act and regulations.

Funds Expended Method. Under this method, the DNC's allocation of conference expenses would be based on a ratio of funds expended in direct support of Federal candidates to funds expended in direct support of non-federal candidates over a certain period of time. "Direct support" of Federal candidates would include only those contributions by the DNC (including the Democratic congressional and senatorial campaign committees) to candidates for Federal office which were subject to the contribution limits of 2 U.S.C. § 441a, and coordinated party expenditures made pursuant to 2 U.S.C. § 441a(d) on behalf of Federal candidates. "Direct support" of non-federal candidates would include contributions to and expenditures directly on behalf of such candidates by the DNC including any of its auxiliary units. General administrative costs not directly attributed to a particular candidate would not be included in this formula. The Commission concludes that use of this allocation method would be reasonable under the Act and regulations in determining the allocation of expenses of the planned DNC conference. The time period on which a ratio would be based using this allocation method would be the election cycle directly preceding or subsequent to this conference. Thus, the Conference Committee would have the option of basing a ratio on the 1980 election cycle or on the 1982 election cycle. . . .

Funds Received Method. Use of this method would not be permissible to allocate the expenses of the planned conference, because allocation of expenses is determined by the nature of the activity engaged in, rather than the amount of contributions received by a party committee during a given period of time. This method is designed for use by organizations that engage in direct support of candidates and must allocate their indirect support expenses.

Ratio of time in the conference agenda devoted to activities pertaining to federal elections in relation to total time for conference activities. Under this formula, the Federal portion of the conference would be calculated by dividing the time devoted to Federal candidates or elections by the total conference time and multiplying the conference costs by the resulting percentage. The Commission concludes that the use of this allocation method to allocate the conference expenses between Federal and non-federal activity would be reasonable under the Act and regulations.

Ratio of participating Federal candidates and their workers to participating non-federal candidates and their workers. The Commission concludes that use of this formula would be reasonable under the Act and regulations provided that participants who are identified as belonging to both Federal and non-federal categories or to neither category, are factored into the ratio in the same proportion as the number of Federal candidates and workers bears to the number of state and local candidates and workers.

The foregoing methods are not exhaustive of those that may be reasonable, but they are the methods you have asked the Commission to consider at this time. Regardless of the allocation method that the Conference Committee chooses to use in allocating conference expenses, actual allocation may not be possible until some time after the close of the conference. Thus, a preliminary estimate may be used with adjustments made when actual proportions are determined. The Conference Committee should maintain detailed records supporting the allocations that are performed and the percentage derived should be applied to all conference expenses.

. . .

Dated: April 21, 1982.

Dissenting Opinion of Commissioner Thomas E. Harris to Advisory Opinion 1982-5

I dissent from the majority opinion in this matter for reasons previously stated in Advisory Opinions 1978-10 and 1978-46.

Congress has forbidden corporations and unions to make contributions or expenditures in connection with Federal elections, with certain exceptions not here applicable. Congress has not, however, barred corporation or union money from state elections, again with certain exceptions. The tension between these two policies stems from the fact that almost any corporate or union contributions in connection with state elections will have beneficial side effects in Federal elections.

Certainly corporations and unions may give directly to state candidates or their committees (state law permitting), but even there there may be some effect on Federal elections. The impact is clearer when corporations and unions are allowed to contribute to political parties, since contributions to political parties for state candidates will free individual contributions for use in the Federal campaigns. Perhaps the clearest example is contributions to party committees for get-out-the-vote drives. Not only do such contributions free individual contributions for Federal campaigns, but get-out-the-vote drives directly impact on Federal elections in those states which have simultaneous Federal and state elections, as nearly all do. In [Advisory Opinion] 1976-72, involving the Illinois Republican State Committee, the Commission adopted a reasonable compromise which allowed use of corporate or union money for an allocable portion of general party overhead and operating expenditures between Federal and non-Federal activity, but barred any use for get-out-the-vote drives [document 6.3]. Unfortunately, the Commission subsequently abandoned this compromise in favor of allowing an allocable portion of corporate money even in get-out-the-vote drives. As is too frequently the case, the Commission proffered no explanation for this about-face.

Corporate contributions for get-out-the-vote drives are not sanctioned either by the statute or by Commission regulations. The only relevant regulation is 11 CFR Section 106.1(e), which allows administrative expenses by party committees to be allocated on a reasonable basis between their Federal and non-Federal accounts.

Quite clearly, these administrative expenses are meant to encompass rent, utilities, office supplies, salaries, etc. and not campaign expenses. The use of corporate or union money even for administrative expenses is in my view not legally justifiable in the case of a national party whose primary concern is the election of Federal candidates.

The Commission's unwarranted, but customary, permissiveness has now brought it to the point where a national party, which is holding a national conference to rev up for the 1982 congressional and 1984 presidential elections, is asking sanction to use corporate and union subsidies under the pretense that the conference will primarily benefit state and local election campaigns.

The majority opinion opens a loophole in Section 441b which invites corporations and unions to buy influence with the national parties. Worse, three of the Commissioners would go far beyond the advisory opinion request and allow the complete underwriting of the national conference by corporations and unions. It is hard to conceive a more blatant disregard of the letter and intent of § 441b.

Dated: April 16, 1982.

In 1984, Common Cause asked the Federal Election Commission to review its rulings on the issue of nonfederal dollars and federal election activities. This advocacy group wanted the FEC to end the use of nonfederal dollars by party committees, and thereby stem the use of the so-called "soft-money loop-hole." This request for a rulemaking action on soft money was transmitted to the Federal Election Commission in the form of a letter dated November 5, 1984 to Lee Ann Elliott, Federal Election Commission chair, from Fred Wertheimer, president of Common Cause (document 6.6A). More than one year later, the FEC rejected the petition (document 6.6B). **In 1987, the U.S. District Court for the District of Columbia** issued an Order, instructing the FEC to reconsider the Petition for Rulemaking on the single issue of allocating federal and nonfederal accounts of state party committees, but it did not impose a timetable for this reconsideration (document 6.6C).

A. Common Cause, "Petition for Rulemaking on Soft Money (1984)," *Federal Register*, vol. 50 (January 4, 1985), p. 477

I am writing on behalf of Common Cause to express our deep concern about the improper role that "soft money" has been playing in federal campaigns and about the Federal Election Commission's inattention to this very serious problem.

It appears that "soft money" is being used in federal elections in a manner that violates and severely undermines the contribution limits and prohibitions contained in the federal campaign finance laws. While these practices and abuses have received considerable public attention, the Federal Election Commission to our knowledge has failed to take any formal action in this area.

In using the term "soft money" we are referring to funds that are raised by Presidential campaigns and national and congressional political party organizations purportedly for use by state and local party organizations in nonfederal elections, from sources who would be barred from making such contributions in connection with a federal election, e.g., from corporations and labor unions and from individuals who have reached their federal contribution limits.

According to various press reports and public statements, including statements by campaign and party officials, it appears clear that "soft money" in fact is not being raised or spent solely for nonfederal election purposes. Such funds are being channeled to state parties with the clear goal of influencing the outcome of federal elections.

Under the federal campaign finance laws "soft money" is prohibited from being spent "in connection with" federal elections. There is no question that "soft money" currently is being spent "in connection with" federal elections, if that term as used in the federal campaign laws is to be given any realistic meaning. If the Commission leaves such "soft money" practices unchecked it will be implicitly sanctioning potentially widespread violation of the current federal campaign finance laws.

Soft money practices are facilitating the reemergence in national political fundraising of campaign contributions from sources such as corporations and unions that have been prohibited for decades from providing such funds for federal elections. They are similarly facilitating the reemergence of large individual campaign contributions that have been prohibited since 1975.

These contributions are highly visible to national campaign and party officials notwithstanding their purported use by state party organizations for nonfederal election purposes. When national campaign and party officials who work with federal candidates raise and coordinate or channel the distribution of "soft money" to state organizations, the potential for corruption is exactly the same as it was when those national campaign and party officials directly received that kind of money. If the Commission leaves soft money practices unchecked, it will directly undermine a core protection against corruption in the federal campaign finance laws.

Soft money practices are also undermining the disclosure provisions of federal campaign finance laws. Very substantial sums of money are being channeled to and through state parties in order to influence federal elections without these sums being disclosed as contributions or expenditures under the federal law. A primary purpose of the federal campaign finance laws is to open the political financing process to public scrutiny. If the Commission leaves soft money practices unchecked, it will allow the national campaigns and political parties to potentially hide millions of dollars in federally related campaign funds from public view, thereby creating widespread opportunities for actual and apparent corruption.

Furthermore, in presidential campaigns, "soft money" returns private funds to a potentially prominent role and thereby subverts the purpose of the presidential public financing system. In 1979, Congress amended the federal campaign finance laws to permit state parties to spend money in connection with presidential campaigns, but only for certain limited purposes and only with funds subject to the limitations and prohibitions of the federal law [document 2.12]. Congress did not intend to authorize centralized national fundraising of private funds from proscribed sources to supplement the presidential public financing system. If the Commission leaves soft money practices unchecked, just that will continue to occur.

Common Cause believes that it is essential for the Commission to make the "soft money" problem a top priority in carrying out its statutory responsibility to enforce the federal campaign finance laws. The Commission's current approach, which appears to be limited to sporadic policing of political committee account allocation rules, is totally inadequate.

We therefore strongly urge that the Commission promptly take the following steps:

(1) initiate on a priority basis its own broad-ranging factual investigation into soft money practices, with a view toward prosecuting actual past violations;

(2) initiate a rulemaking proceeding to establish what broader administrative tools, such as additional disclosure requirements, are needed to facilitate the Commission's effective enforcement of the current laws; and

(3) undertake a review of the current laws to determine what additional statutory remedies may be required to assure that soft money abuses are most effectively curtailed.

"Soft money" is a very serious problem. The Commission must address it aggressively. It is not sufficient for the Commission, in this or other key areas, to sit back and wait for private parties to bring these matters of enforcement responsibility to its attention. The Commission must be out in front of, not forced into, these issues.

B. Federal Election Commission, "Rulemaking Petition; Notice of Disposition," *Federal Register*, vol. 51, no. 82 (April 29, 1986), p. 15915

Summary: The Federal Election Commission announces its denial of a Petition for Rulemaking filed on November 6, 1984 by Common Cause. 50 FR 477 (January 4, 1985). The petition requested that the Commission revise several regulatory provisions to address the alleged improper use of "soft money," particularly funds ostensibly raised for use in state and local elections, to influence federal elections. . . .

Supplementary Information: On November 4, 1984, Common Cause filed a petition for rulemaking with the Commission. The petition requested that the Commission initiate a rulemaking to address the alleged improper use of "soft money," purportedly raised for use in nonfederal elections, to influence federal elections. The Commission has made several efforts to solicit comments on the petition. . . .

After reviewing the comments on the petition and evaluating the implications of the proposed revisions, the Commission has decided to deny Common Cause's petition for rulemaking. Common Cause has not presented evidence of instances in which "soft money" has been used to influence federal elections sufficient to justify the stringent rules proposed in its petition. Most of the examples it cites to support its allegations consist of anecdotal and boastful comments of party committee officials and campaign staff that have been quoted in the press. These statements do not constitute concrete evidence demonstrating that the Commission's regulations have been abused so that funds purportedly raised for use in nonfederal elections have in fact been transferred to the state and local level with the intent that they be used to influence federal elections. Indeed, other evidence presented during this proceeding indicates that many transfers to the state and local levels were made from federal funds and were reported to the Commission.

Therefore, at its open meeting of April 17, 1986, the Commission voted to deny the petition for rulemaking filed by Common Cause. . . .

Dated: April 17, 1986

Joan D. Aikens, *Chairman, Federal Election Commission*

C. *Common Cause* v. *Federal Election Commission*, 692 F. Supp. 1391 (D.D.C. 1987)

Opinion: Memorandum
Thomas A. Flannery, United States District Judge

. . . In this action, plaintiffs Common Cause and certain named members (hereinafter "Common Cause") challenge a Federal Election Commission ("FEC" or "Commission") decision denying a Petition for Rulemaking that Common Cause filed on November 7, 1984 [document 6.6A].

I. BACKGROUND

In its Petition, plaintiff Common Cause alleged that there were violations of the Federal Election Campaign Act ("FECA"), 2 U.S.C. § 431, et seq., associated with the use of "soft money" in connection with federal elections. In its Petition, Common Cause defined "soft money" as:

. . . funds that are raised by Presidential campaigns and national and congressional political party organizations purportedly for use by state and local party organizations in nonfederal elections, from sources who would be barred from making such contributions in connection with a federal election, e.g., from corporations and labor unions and from individuals who have reached their federal contribution limits.

Common Cause further alleged that this "soft money" was not being raised or spent solely for nonfederal election purposes, but was instead "being channeled to state parties with the clear goal of influencing the outcome of federal elections."

. . .

On December 5, 1985, the General Counsel recommended to the Commission that it "seek information and comment on the factual and legal issues raised in the 'soft money' discussion and hold hearings to determine whether problems do in fact exist of the nature alleged by Common Cause." Based on this recommendation, the Commission scheduled two days of public hearings, and approved a Notice of Inquiry for publication in the *Federal Register*. The Notice of Inquiry set forth in six pages of detail the allegations of Common Cause. . . . The Commission received 15 responses. The Commission also received testimony from Common Cause, the Center for Responsive Politics, and the Republican National Committee.

On April 17, 1986, the Commission acted on plaintiffs' Petition, denying it as to each of 7 proposed revisions, and failing, by a 3-3 vote, to act as to an 8th proposed revision [document 6.6B]. . . . It is this agency action which plaintiffs challenge in the present action.

. . .

III. PLAINTIFF'S MOTION FOR SUMMARY JUDGMENT

In its motion for summary judgment, plaintiff Common Cause sets forth two theories under which it urges the court to set aside the Commission's actions. First, Common Cause contends that, as a matter of statutory construction, the FEC's interpretations of portions of the FECA pertaining to the "soft money" issue are contrary to law and must therefore be set aside. Second, Common Cause contends that, given the material before the Commission in the form of comments and testimony, the denial of plaintiffs' rulemaking petition based on a supposed insufficiency of supporting evidence constituted arbitrary and capricious agency action that must also be set aside by the court on review.

A. Statutory Construction:

With respect to statutory construction, Common Cause focuses on two aspects of the FEC's decision and argues that they are inconsistent with the Commission's enabling statute. First, Common Cause argues that the FECA's ban on the use of contributions from certain sources in federal elections is absolute, and that any use of nonfederal funds in connection with federal elections is a violation of the FECA—regardless of intent. Common Cause argues that the FEC improperly considered intent as a factor in its determination that non-federal funds have not "been transferred to the state and local level with the intent that they be used to influence federal elections." Common Cause suggests that the FEC has overlooked violations simply because there was no evidence of intent to influence federal elections, a statutorily irrelevant consideration.

Common Cause is correct in its interpretation of the FECA as an absolute ban on the use of certain funds in connection with federal elections. Common Cause errs, however, in reading so much into the FEC's use of the word "intent" in its Notice of Disposition. The Commission's brief statement cannot fairly be read as making intent a critical or even relevant factor in the denial of rulemaking now at issue. Instead, the Commission's Notice of Disposition states clearly that "Common Cause has not presented evidence of instances in which 'soft money' has been used to influence elections sufficient to justify the stringent rules proposed in its petition." The Commission determined not that there was an inadequate showing of intent to influence federal elections, but, more basically, that there was inadequate evidence of any use of "soft money" in the ways plaintiffs alleged in their Petition. Indeed, the Commission's word choice closely parallels Common Cause's language in its definition of "soft money," and should not be given any greater significance than that.

Thus, plaintiffs' strained reading of the Commission's statement, as well as plaintiffs' extensive discussion of the history and meaning of the FECA, are largely irrelevant to the present inquiry. A misreading of the controlling statute by plaintiffs cannot itself form the basis for a challenge to the Commission's actions as "otherwise not in accordance with law." The court need not even reach the issue of the degree of deference appropriately paid to the FEC's interpretation, since the court may instead conclude that the parties are in agreement that intent is not a factor in enforcement of the FECA.

Common Cause's second challenge to the FEC's interpretation of the FECA has greater merit. Congress amended the FECA in 1979 to permit state and local party committees to spend money for campaign materials used for volunteer activities, voter registration, and "get-out-the-vote" activities. The amendment provides that, with respect to these activities, state and local committees must only spend monies that are "subject to the limitations and prohibitions of this Act." However, under the Commission's 1976 regulations, 11 C.F.R. §§ 102.5, 106.1, state and local political committees are permitted to spend money from both their federal and non-federal accounts to finance these activities, allocating "on a reasonable basis." 11 C.F.R. § 106.1(e). If, for example, a state committee spends monies to register voters in an election year in which both federal and state/local offices are up for election, the state committee may determine what portion of its efforts affects the federal as opposed to the state/local elections, and may allocate monies from its separate accounts accordingly—with no guidance from the FEC.

In its Petition, Common Cause pointed to this allocation system (or lack thereof) as a source of "soft money" abuse. Common Cause alleged that, with no regulations on how to go about allocating monies from federal and nonfederal accounts, state party committees could use "soft money" for volunteer materials, voter registration, and "get-out-the-vote" efforts that would have a significant impact on federal as well as state/local elections. Indeed, the General Counsel noted this potential for abuse in its Draft Notice of Inquiry, which the Commission adopted, published, and distributed. In the Draft Notice, the General Counsel stated that:

These statutory exemptions should not be used as a shield to spend nonfederal funds for the benefit of federal candidates, particularly through the use of allocation methods which permit a committee to expend funds raised for use in nonfederal elections and therefore free federal funds for contributions and expenditures.

Common Cause goes well beyond the General Counsel, and contends that the 1979 exemptions for certain state and local party committee activities, discussed above, represent a congressional determination that those activities necessarily have an impact on federal elections. Common Cause reasons from this premise that no allocation method is permissible under that Act, and that even exempt activities undertaken solely with respect to state elections must be paid for with "hard money."

This reading of the amendments goes too far. It is clear from the statute as a whole that the FECA regulates federal elections only. This limit on the FECA's reach underlies the entire act. Congress would have had to have spoken much more clearly in the amendments at issue to contradict this. Moreover, as the Commission points out in its pleadings, the House Report on the amendments expressly contemplated allocation of funds with respect to the activities at issue, stating:

If a State or local party organization prepares a slate card which includes both Federal and State candidates, the party organization may allocate or apportion the costs attributable to all the Federal candidates and all the State candidates. The portion of costs attributable to Federal candidates must be paid with funds subject to the prohibitions and limitations of the Act.

H. Rep. No. 422, 96th Cong., 1st Sess., 8 (1979) (permitting similar allocation for campaign materials used for volunteer activities). With respect to voter registration and get-out-the-vote activities, the House Report speaks only of such activities "on behalf of the Presidential and Vice-Presidential nominees." Nothing in the language of these amendments suggests that they reach beyond federal elections and into the realm of state elections. Given this, it cannot be argued that allocation is as a whole barred by the amendments.

Common Cause is nonetheless correct that the FEC's failure to regulate improper or inaccurate allocation between federal and nonfederal funds with respect to these activities was contrary to law, since Congress stated clearly in the FECA that all monies spent by state committees on these activities vis-a-vis federal elections must be paid for "from contributions subject to the limitations and prohibitions of this Act." 2 U.S.C. §§ 431(8)(B)(x)(2), 431(8)(B)(xii)(2), 431(9)(B)(viii), 431(9)(B)(ix)(2). That is, with respect to federal elections, "soft money" cannot properly be used for these activities under the FECA.

In his recommendations to the Commission at the close of the comment period, and after public hearings on plaintiffs' Petition, the General Counsel recommended denying Common Cause's Petition. Yet, he also urged the Commission to revise its rules on allocation, "to resolve several questions that have arisen concerning their application." The General Counsel noted that:

The current regulations leave a great deal of discretion to the [state or local political] committee in choosing a method to allocate its expenses and provide little guidance on what methods the Commission considers to be appropriate. . . . Moreover, committees are not currently required to report the method used to allocate their expenses. There is therefore no way to routinely determine whether committees are allocating their expenses in a manner that accurately reflects the effort that an activity has on federal elections.

These conclusions by the General Counsel echo Common Cause's allegations in the Petition before the Commission. It was these recommendations on which the Commission failed to act on by a vote of 3–3.

The plain meaning of the FECA is that any improper allocation of nonfederal funds by a state committee would be a violation of the FECA. Yet, the Commission provides no guidance whatsoever on what allocation methods a state or local committee may use; the potential for abuse, intended or not, is obvious. Thus, a revision of the Commission's regulations to ensure that any method of allocation used by state or local party committees is in compliance with the FECA is warranted. This is especially so given the General Counsel's strongly worded recommendations. Indeed, it is possible that the Commission may conclude that no method of allocation will effectuate the Congressional goal that all monies spent by state political committees on those activities permitted in the 1979 amendments be "hard money" under the FECA. That is an issue for the Commission to resolve on remand. . . . The FECA unambiguously requires that state party committee money spent for the limited purposes set forth in the 1979 amendments—volunteer materials, voter registration, and "get-out-the-vote" activities—must be paid for solely from funds subject to the limitations and prohibitions of the FECA. It is not for the Commission to evade that mandate by permitting a variety of allocation methods and providing no guidance or supervision to those in whose interest it is to use as much "soft money" in federal elections as they can. Such agency interpretation of the statute it is designated to enforce is entitled to no deference, and must be set aside.

However, the court need not go so far as to order the Commission to adopt the proposals of Common Cause, which appear to go beyond what the FECA requires in this area. Instead, the court need only require the Commission to review Common Cause's Petition for Rulemaking in light of this opinion, with an eye to revising 11 C.F.R. §§ 102.5 and 106.1, as they relate to the portions of the 1979 FECA amendments discussed above.

B. The Commission's Alleged Arbitrary and Capricious Conduct:

Finally, Common Cause contends that as to all the issues raised in its Petition, there was ample evidence to justify a rulemaking, and that failure to so find was arbitrary and capricious on the part of the Commission. Here, the court must disagree. The Commission opened its doors to comments from each of the fifty state election finance agencies, as well as both major parties and various other groups interested in the issue of campaign financing. Only fifteen responses were received, some of which adamantly stated that there were no abuses of the type alleged by Common Cause. Indeed, there was testimony that some of the anecdotes submitted by Common Cause were factually erroneous. Agency action will be held to be arbitrary and capricious only in exceptional situations of egregious error, and a review of the record makes clear that it was not arbitrary and capricious for the Commission to decline to initiate a rulemaking based on the evidence before it, except with respect to the allocation issue discussed above.

IV. THE COMMISSION'S MOTION FOR SUMMARY JUDGMENT

The FEC moves for summary judgment affirming its decision to deny plaintiffs' Petition. For the reasons set forth above with respect to Common Cause's motion, such relief is proper as to all issues except that of allocation between federal and nonfederal accounts of state party committees of expenses of voter registration and other limitedly exempt activities, as discussed above.

An appropriate Order accompanies this Memorandum.

Order—August 3, 1987, Filed. . .

ORDERED that Plaintiffs' Motion for Summary Judgment is granted in part and denied in part; and it is further

ORDERED that Defendant's Motion for Summary Judgment is granted in part and denied in part; and it is further

ORDERED that this matter be and hereby is remanded to defendant Federal Election Commission, which is instructed to reconsider the Petition for Rulemaking of plaintiffs Common Cause, et al., in light of this court's Memorandum and Order of this date.

Following the FEC's denial of Common Cause's petition for rulemaking on soft money (see document 6.6B), Common Cause sought relief in the courts. The United States District Court for the District of Columbia decided in 1987 that the allocation requirements for nonfederal dollars merited revision (document 6.6C). When the FEC failed to issue revised regulations one year later, Common Cause pressed the court for enforcement. This is an excerpt from the court's decision that ordered the FEC to report every ninety days on its progress towards revising its soft money allocation rules.

Opinion: Memorandum
Thomas A. Flannery, United States District Judge

Common Cause and the other plaintiffs in this case have filed a motion seeking to enforce this court's order that the Federal Election Commission (FEC) reconsider its refusal to promulgate rules, under the Federal Election Campaign Act (FECA) [see chapter 2], regulating so-called "soft money" in federal elections. The plaintiffs have asked the court to order the FEC to propose rules within 30 days, to compel the FEC to make the proposed regulations final as soon as is practicable thereafter, and to retain jurisdiction to ensure that the FEC complies with the mandate. For the reasons set forth herein, the court will not, at this time, impose a timetable on the FEC in the manner sought by Common Cause, but will instead retain jurisdiction and hold this motion in abeyance. While the motion is in abeyance, the FEC will report to the court on its progress toward compliance.

I.

"Soft money" denotes contributions to federally regulated campaign committees in excess of the aggregate amounts permitted for federal elections by the FECA; these contributions, even if directed to national campaign entities, are permissible if the money is not to be used in connection with federal elections. But Common Cause has contended that these excess contributions, purportedly devoted to state and local purposes, are pervasively and unlawfully dedicated to activities that influence federal elections, such as voter registration drives and other party-building activities that redound to the benefit of federal candidates.

Although the campaign committees are required to count a portion of such expenditures toward their federal limits on a "reasonable basis," Common Cause alleged in a petition to the FEC for rulemaking that there has been widespread abuse of this allocation requirement, and that the FEC's failure to regulate this allocation process more closely is contrary to law [document 6.6A]. The FEC denied the petition [document 6.6B], and Common Cause sought review of that denial in this court. In a Memorandum and Order filed on August 3, 1987, the court granted partial summary judgment to Common Cause and ordered the FEC to reconsider the petition for rulemaking [document 6.6C].

After rejecting a contention by Common Cause that no allocation process is permissible at all under the FECA as amended, the court held that

Common Cause is nonetheless correct that the FEC's failure to regulate improper or inaccurate allocation between federal and nonfederal funds with respect to these activities was contrary to law, since Congress clearly stated in the FECA that all monies spent by state committees on these activities vis-a-vis federal elections must be paid for "from contributions subject to the limitations and prohibitions of this Act." . . . That is, with respect to federal elections, "soft money" cannot properly be used for these activities under the FECA.

Chiding the Commission for "permitting a variety of allocation methods and no clear guidance to those in whose interest it is to use as much 'soft money' in federal elections as they can," the court held that the FEC had interpreted the FECA "in a way that flatly contradicts Congress's express purpose." The FEC was ordered to reconsider the petition "with an eye to revising" the pertinent regulations. None of the parties sought review of the court's decision.

More than seven months after the decision, the FEC published a Notice of Inquiry, assertedly to generate "comment on the utility of allocation methods considered in the past as well as suggestions for alternative approaches." Three comments were submitted, and four months have passed since the close of the comment period without further consideration by the Commission. At a hearing on this motion, counsel for the FEC would project no timetable for further action on the soft money issue, other than to represent that the comments already submitted will be before the Commission sometime in September, 1988. FEC counsel attributed this uncertainty to the many demands on Commission resources during an election year.

During the pendency of this issue, public attention to allegations of "soft money" abuses by the major political parties has increased, and these allegations find some confirmation in pronouncements by party leaders, who reportedly are set on exploiting the absence of regulation in fundraising for the 1988 presidential race. While it is not for the court to pass on the accuracy of these reports or to assess the magnitude of the problem at this juncture, it is undisputed that there is a public perception of widespread abuse, suggesting that the consequences of the regulatory failure identified a year ago are at least as unsettling now as then.

II.

Common Cause correctly has identified two jurisdictional bases for its current motion: first, the court has inherent jurisdiction to interpret and enforce its prior orders, jurisdiction recognized in the federal courts' statutory authority to issue all writs "necessary or appropriate in aid of their respective jurisdiction"; second, the court has federal question jurisdiction to "compel agency action unlawfully withheld or unreasonably delayed" under the Administrative Procedure Act.

. . .

The Commission's arguments . . . counsel against court imposition of a strict timetable for the promulgation of new rules governing the use of soft money, but there are several circumstances that undermine the FEC's conclusion that court supervision is altogether unwarranted. First, the Commission's response to the mandate has been laggard: more than seven months passed before the Notice of Inquiry, and in four months since the close of the comment period the FEC has not yet completed its evaluation of the three comments received. A year is a relatively short period on any agency's rulemaking schedule, but this particular rulemaking was preceded by years of inaction that "flatly contradicted Congress's express purpose." The cumulative delay is made more troubling by the fact that, in this round, the Commission was not starting from scratch, but already had considerable record evidence on the issue before it; although deference ordinarily is accorded to an agency's decision to supplement the record, the plaintiffs' petition does not involve complex scientific or factual issues, and this court's decision "did not contemplate going back to square one."

The court also must reject the FEC's characterization of the harm resulting from its languid pace. Although lives do not hang in the balance, the climate of concern surrounding soft money threatens the very "corruption and appearance of corruption" by which "the integrity of our system of representative democracy is undermined," and which the FECA was intended to remedy. Soft money does not present discrete and isolated FECA violations, but allegedly comprises system-wide abuse. The asserted availability of the administrative complaint procedure, moreover, gives little solace to the plaintiffs, who understandably assume that the complaint and the petition would be the procedural equivalent of "a race between the tortoise and the tortoise."

In light of the importance of the issue and the Commission's lack of expedition in meeting the court's mandate, a modicum of supervision appears to be appropriate even though the showing that would support imposition of a strict timetable has not been met. The court therefore will hold the Motion to Enforce in abeyance, and will order the FEC to report on its progress on the soft money issue every ninety days. This may entail a small intrusion into the Commission's election-year agenda, but the Commission could have addressed this problem long before the elections neared. The court will not countenance further delay simply because regulations cannot be readied in time for November; to do so would reward inaction with further immunity from judicial review.

The burden of reporting will not be great, and this approach will preserve the agency's autonomy while ensuring that the issue is not permitted to languish altogether. Such an order avoids "direct judicial meddling," while hastening "a clear end point to the regulatory snarl" that has brought the plaintiffs back before the court.

Conclusion

Common Cause has not shown that the Commission's delay, thus far, warrants the intrusive relief sought by the plaintiffs. Nonetheless, the FEC's delay in responding to the court's mandate is sufficiently troubling that the court will retain jurisdiction and hold the Motion to Enforce in abeyance, and each ninety days from this date the Federal Election Commission will submit a concise report on its progress toward rules regulating soft money expenditures that influence federal elections. . . .

This document summarizes the new regulations for soft money reporting and allocations that were adopted by the Federal Election Commission in 1990 in response to the Court order in *Common Cause* v. *Federal Election Commission* (see document 6.7).

REVISED ALLOCATION RULES: SUMMARY

Who Must Allocate

New Sections 106.5(a)(1) and 106.6(a) explain that the allocation rules apply both to:

—Political committees that maintain separate accounts for federal and nonfederal activity (as opposed to political committees that conduct mixed activity from one federal account); and
—Committees that are not "political committees" as defined under the Federal Election Campaign Act but that make disbursements for both federal and nonfederal activity.

The rules specify that the following types of committees must allocate federal/nonfederal expenses, whether or not they are "political committees" under the Act:

—National party committees;
—The House and Senate campaign committees of national parties;
—State and local party committees;
—Separate segregated funds; and
—Nonconnected committees.

What Costs Must Be Allocated

The revisions provide committees with significantly more guidance than current rules on how to allocate expenses. The revised rules at 11 CFR 106.1(a), 106.5(a)(2) and 106.6(b) describe several categories of joint federal/nonfederal activity subject to allocation:

—Administrative expenses (e.g., rent, utilities, office supplies, salaries);

—Generic voter drive activities (e.g., voter-identification, voter-registration and get-out-the-vote drives that do not mention specific candidates);

—Fundraising programs or events through which one committee collects both federal and nonfederal funds;

—"Exempt party activities" conducted by state and local party committees in conjunction with nonfederal election activity;[1] and

—Direct support of specific federal and nonfederal candidates, and fundraising on behalf of specific federal and nonfederal candidates. (Direct support and fundraising on behalf of specific federal candidates result in in-kind contributions, independent expenditures or coordinated party expenditures (2 U.S.C. §441a(d); 11 CFR 106.1(a)(1).)

Allocation Methods

The revised rules contain several allocation methods:

—Fixed or minimum percentage;
—Funds expended ratio;
—Funds received ratio;
—Time or space (communication) ratio; and
—Ballot composition ratio.

As explained in the paragraphs below, the specific method used to allocate an expense depends on the category of activity and the type of committee conducting the activity.

Administrative Expenses/Generic Voter Drives

National Party Committees. The revised rules provide that, in Presidential election years, national party committees must allocate to their federal accounts at least 65 percent of administrative expenses and costs for generic voter drives. In other years, they must allocate at least 60 percent of such costs to their federal accounts. These are *fixed percentages.* 11 CFR 106.5(b)(2).

House and Senate Campaign Committees of National Parties. Under the revised rules, these committees allocate administrative expenses and costs for generic voter drives according to the *funds expended* method, but at least 65 percent of such costs must be allocated to the federal account. (This is a *minimum percentage.*) Under the funds expended method, expenses are allocated based on the ratio of federal expenditures to total federal and nonfederal disbursements made during a two-year federal

---

1. Exempt party activities are certain election-related activities conducted by state and local party committees that are not considered contributions or expenditures on behalf of the federal candidates benefiting from the activity. The three types of exempt activities are: slate cards, campaign materials and Presidential voter drives. 11 CFR 100.7(b)(9), (15) and (17) and 100.8(b)(10), (16) and (18).

election cycle. In calculating the ratio, the committee uses only amounts spent on behalf of specific federal and nonfederal candidates, excluding overhead and other generic costs.

State and Local Party Committees. The revised rules provide that state and local party committees must allocate their administrative and generic voter drive expenses using the *ballot composition* method: the ratio of federal offices to total federal and nonfederal offices expected to be on the ballot in the next general election to be held in the committee's state or geographic area. The ratio is determined by the number of categories of offices on the ballot. The revised rules specify the categories to be included and the number of offices that may be counted in each category.

In states that do not hold federal and nonfederal elections in the same year, state and local party committees allocate the costs of generic voter drives using the ballot composition method (described above) calculated for the current calendar year. These committees allocate their administrative expenses using the ballot composition method calculated for the two-year federal election cycle. 11 CFR 106.5(d).

Separate Segregated Funds and Nonconnected Committees. Under the revised rules, these committees allocate their administrative and generic voter drive expenses using the *funds expended* method. (A separate segregated fund must allocate administrative expenses only if they are not paid by the connected organization.) Under this method, expenses are allocated based on the ratio of federal expenditures to total federal and nonfederal disbursements made during the two-year federal election cycle. In calculating the ratio, the committee uses only amounts spent on behalf of specific federal and nonfederal candidates, excluding overhead and other generic costs. (This is the same method used by party House and Senate campaign committees; however, separate segregated funds and nonconnected committees are not required to allocate a minimum federal percentage.) 11 CFR 106.6(c).

Exempt Activities: State and Local Party Committees. The revised rules provide that expenses for exempt party activities must be allocated according to *the proportion of a communication's time or space* that is devoted to federal elections as compared with the entire communication. In the case of a publication, committees apply the ratio to the space. In the case of a phone bank, committees apply the ratio to the number of questions or statements. 11 CFR 106.5(e).

Fundraising Expenses: All Committees. A committee must allocate the direct costs of each fundraising program or event in which the committee collects federal and nonfederal funds. (In the case of a separate segregated fund, fundraising costs must be allocated only if they are not paid by the connected organization.) Fundraising costs must be allocated according to the *funds received* method: the ratio of federal funds received to total receipts for the program or event. 11 CFR 106.5(f) and 106.6(d).

Expenses for Direct Support of Specific Candidates: All Committees

Under the revised rules, committees must allocate payments involving both expenditures on behalf of one or more specific federal candidates and disbursements on behalf of one or more specific nonfederal candidates according to the benefit reasonably expected to be derived. For example, in the case of a communication, the costs must be allocated in proportion to the *time or space devoted* to federal candidates compared with the total time or space devoted to all candidates. In the case of a fundraising program in which funds are collected by the committee for specific federal and nonfederal candidates, the allocation is based on the proportion of *funds received* by federal candidates compared with the total receipts of all candidates.[2] 11 CFR 106.1(a).

Note that expenditures on behalf of federal candidates result in in-kind contributions, independent expenditures or coordinated party expenditures (2 U.S.C. §441a(d)). 11 CFR 106.1(a)(1).

Payment of Allocated Expenses

Payment Options. Under the revised rules, committees that have established separate federal and nonfederal accounts (whether or not they are "political committees" under federal law) may choose one of two methods to pay for joint federal and nonfederal activities. Under the first method, a committee pays the entire amount from its federal account, transferring funds from the nonfederal account to cover the nonfederal share of an allocable expense. The second method allows a committee to establish a separate allocation account solely for the purpose of paying allocable expenses. In this case, the committee transfers funds from the federal and nonfederal accounts to the allocation account in amounts proportionate to the federal and nonfederal share of each allocable expense. The allocation account is considered a federal account, subject to federal reporting requirements. 11 CFR 106.5(g)(1) and 106.6(e)(1).

The revised rules amend 11 CFR 102.5(a)(1)(I), which currently prohibits committees from transferring funds from a nonfederal account to a federal account. The revision permits committees to make such transfers for the limited purpose of paying the nonfederal share of allocated expenses.

Timing of Transfers. As a general rule, transfers to pay for allocable expenses (either from a nonfederal account to a federal account or from both the federal and nonfederal accounts to the allocation account) must be made after the final cost of the activity is determined. Transfers may be made in advance of this determination only if advance payment is required by the vendor and if the payment is a reasonable estimate of the activity's final cost, as determined by the committee and the vendor.

In any event, transfers must be made within a 40-day time period: no more than 10 days before or 30 days after the payment for which the funds are designated is made. 11 CFR 106.5(g)(2) and 106.6(e)(2).

Reporting Federal and Nonfederal Activity. The new reporting requirements for allocable expenses apply only to committees that qualify as federal "political committees" and that have established separate federal and nonfederal accounts. The revised rules at section 104.10 set out procedures for reporting allocation ratios and for reporting transfers and disbursements made to pay for allocable expenses.

. . .

Additional Reporting Rules for National Party Committees. Under the revised rules, national party committees must disclose information on their nonfederal accounts and building fund accounts, as well

---

2. These allocation methods (used to allocate disbursements between federal and nonfederal candidates) are also used to allocate expenditures made on behalf of federal candidates only.

as their federal accounts, applying the same itemization thresholds to all three types of accounts. Transfers from a national party committee's nonfederal account to the nonfederal accounts of state and local party committees are also reportable. The revised reporting rules for national party committees are located at 11 CFR 104.8(e) and (f) and 104.9(c)-(d).

. . .

Party Committee Solicitations. Revised section 102.5(a)(3) creates the presumption that funds resulting from party committee solicitations that refer to a federal candidate or a federal election are raised for the purpose of influencing a federal election and are thus subject to the limits and prohibitions of the Federal Election Campaign Act. This presumption may be rebutted by demonstrating that the funds were solicited with express notice that they would not be used for federal election purposes.

The Republican National Committee requested an advisory opinion in 1995 concerning its plans to sponsor media advertisements to influence congressional legislative proposals. The FEC ruled that these activities could be allocated between nonfederal and federal accounts, and thus permitted the allocation of soft money for issue advocacy.

This responds to [letters from David A. Norcross, general counsel] dated August 9 and June 27, 1995, requesting an advisory opinion on behalf of the Republican National Committee ("RNC"), concerning the application of the Federal Election Campaign Act of 1971, as amended ("the Act") [see chapter 2], to costs incurred by the RNC in connection with certain activities to be undertaken in 1995.

You state that the RNC plans to produce and air media advertisements on a series of legislative proposals being considered by the U.S. Congress, such as the balanced budget debate and welfare reform. The purpose of the ads will be to inform the American people on the Republican and Democratic positions on these issues, as well as to attempt to influence public opinion on particular legislative proposals. The ads are intended to gain popular support for the Republican position on given legislative measures, and thereby influence the public's positive view of Republicans and their agenda.

You further state that your request is predicated on the following assumptions: (1) There may or may not be a reference to a Federal officeholder who has also qualified as a candidate for Federal office. (2) If there is reference to a Federal officeholder who is also a Federal candidate, there will not be any express advocacy of that officeholder's election or defeat, nor will there be any "electioneering message" or reference to Federal elections. (3) If there is a "call to action," it will be to urge the viewer or listener to contact that Federal officeholder urging support for, or defeat of, a particular piece of legislation. (4) The appropriate Federal Communications Commission disclaimer identifying the RNC as sponsor will be included within each advertisement. (5) The RNC will allocate the salaries of employees associated with this media effort based upon 11 CFR 106.5. (6) The RNC will report this media activity and its associated expenses, as appropriate, on financial disclosure reports filed with the Commission.

In response to the Commission's request for the text of one or more advertisements that have been or may be disseminated as part of this series, you have provided the texts for three such ads—one urging support for the Balanced Budget Amendment and the other two urging that the Medicare program be saved and restructured. Two ads do not mention a Federal candidate, and all three urge support for the Republican position on the issues discussed. The third advertisement (titled "Too Young To Die") mentions President Clinton's name six times, although only in the context of Medicare policy; there is no reference to any election. You state that none of these ads served as the basis for this advisory opinion request, and that this material may or may not be comparable to other such advertisements which the RNC may air in the future.

You further state that it is impossible to determine what effect these types of advertisements have on the electability of candidates at the Federal, state and local level. You believe the costs incurred in connection with these ads should be considered "administrative expenditures" under the Commission's rules on allocation of certain expenditures between Federal and non-federal accounts. If so considered, the regulations provide that the costs should be allocated at least 60% to the RNC's Federal campaign account and 40% to its non-federal account. See 11 CFR 106.5 (a) and (b)(2)(ii).

The Act requires that contributions accepted and spent to influence any Federal election be received subject to certain limitations and prohibitions. See 2 U.S.C. § § 441a, 441b, 441c, 441e, 441f, and 441g. Most of these restrictions do not apply to funds raised and spent to influence only state and local elections.

Commission regulations set forth the procedures to be followed by party committees that make disbursements in connection with both Federal and non-federal elections. 11 CFR 106.5. Under section 106.5(a), party committees may make such disbursements in one of two ways: They may make them entirely from funds raised subject to the prohibitions and limitations of the Act; or, if they have established separate Federal and non-federal accounts pursuant to 11 CFR 102.5, they may allocate them between these accounts according to various formulas set forth in section 106.5.

The allocation formulas for national party committees to allocate their administrative expenses and generic voter drive costs are found at 11 CFR 106.5(b)(2). The Explanation and Justification to these rules notes that these formulas reflect the national party committees' primary focus on presidential and other Federal candidates and elections, while still recognizing that such committees also participate in party-building activities at state and local levels of the party organizations. 55 *Fed. Reg.* 26058, 26063 (June 26, 1990).

After reviewing the additional material provided by the requester, the Commission concludes that legislative advocacy media advertisements that focus on national legislative activity and promote the Republican Party should be considered as made in connection with both Federal and non-federal elections, unless the ads would qualify as coordinated expenditures on behalf of any general election candidates of the Party under 2 U.S.C. § 441a(d). See Advisory Opinions 1991-33, 1985-14, and 1984-15. Thus, such costs should be allocated in accordance with 11 CFR 106.5. The Supreme Court in *Buckley* v. *Valeo*, 424 U.S. 1, 79 (1976) [document 3.1], noted that the major purpose of political committees is the nomination or election of candidates, so their expenditures are, by definition, campaign related. Similarly, the Internal Revenue Code defines the "(tax) exempt function" of a political organization, including a political party or committee, as "the function of influencing or attempting to influence the selection, nomination, election or appointment of any individual to any Federal, State, or local public office . . . or the election of Presidential or Vice Presidential electors." 26 U.S.C. § 527(e).

Section 106.5(a)(2) establishes four categories of costs to be allocated under these rules: administrative expenses; the direct costs of a fundraising program or event; the cost of activities that are exempt from the definitions of contribution and expenditure because they relate to specific state and local party activity; and generic voter drive costs.

You state that you believe the costs of the advertisements should be characterized as administrative expenses, which are defined in a non-inclusive listing at 11 CFR 106.5(a)(2)(i) to include such expenses as rent, utilities, office supplies, and salaries. The Commission notes that, depending on content, the costs of some advertisements may also be characterized as generic voter drive costs, which are defined at 11 CFR 106.5(a)(2)(iv) to include, *inter alia*, costs of "activities that urge the general public to register, vote or support candidates of a particular party or associated with a particular issue, without mentioning a specific candidate." Although you state that the advertisements in question will not reference Federal elections or contain an electioneering message, their stated purpose—to gain popular support for the Republican position on given legislative measures and to influence the public's positive view of Republicans and their agenda—encompasses the related goal of electing Republican candidates to Federal office. This result is also contemplated by the Commission's regulations at 11 CFR 110.8(e), which recognize that certain party-building activities under specific conditions can feature the appearance of the party's candidates at a "bona fide party event or appearance." Advocacy of the party's legislative agenda is one aspect of building or promoting support for the party that will carry forward to its future election campaigns.

For purposes of the allocation rules, however, it is immaterial whether these costs are characterized as administrative costs or as generic voter drive costs. Under 11 CFR 106.5(b)(2), the costs of both types of activities are allocated 60% to the Federal account and 40% to the non-federal account in non-presidential election years, and 65% to the Federal account and 35% to the non-federal account in presidential election years. FEC Schedules H3 and H4, on which joint activity is reported, similarly do not distinguish between administrative and voter drive costs. Rather, they classify them jointly as "administrative/voter drive" costs.

Since 1995 is a non-presidential election year, the Commission concludes that the proper allocation for these expenditures is at least 60% to the Federal account, with a corresponding allocation to the non-federal account. Should the RNC continue these activities into 1996, a presidential election year, the Federal share will rise to at least 65% of these costs.

This response constitutes an advisory opinion concerning application of the Act, or regulations prescribed by the Commission, to the specific transaction or activity set forth in your request. See 2 U.S.C. § 437f.

Dated: August 24, 1995.

In this piece that appeared just after the 1996 election, Peter H. Stone chronicles the many and varied soft money excesses that characterized the campaign, and draws a parallel with the atmosphere of scandal that preceded the post-Watergate campaign finance reforms of 1974 (document 2.9).

Wooing big donors has long been a staple of presidential campaign machines. But in its aggressive quest for corporate cash, the Democratic National Committee (DNC) in 1996 developed a Financial Advisory Board, a new and pricier fund-raising engine to prod donors and fund raisers to kick in $350,000 or more. The 170-member board includes such major moneymen as Hollywood mogul Lew Wasserman, investment banker Steven Rattner and Washington lobbyist Daniel A. Dutko.

On the Republican side, some of the biggest corporate donors to the GOP who usually pony up $100,000 in "soft" money during presidential election years groused that requests for more money never stop. In response, the Republican National Committee (RNC) offered its fattest cats a sweet deal: If they upped their giving to $250,000 this year, they'd get "season tickets" to attend all of the party's glitziest galas and receive such perks as photo ops for their top executives with party leaders. About two dozen large corporate donors, including Amway Corp., Eli Lilly and Co., Philip Morris Cos. Inc., Union Pacific Corp. and U.S. Tobacco Co. (UST) agreed to the offer.

These fund-raising stratagems symbolize the unprecedented efforts that Democrats and Republicans alike mounted this election cycle to raise record volumes of soft money. Campaign finance analysts estimate that the two national party committees each raised about $100 million in soft money, with a large chunk of the money going to pay for issues advertisements to help their presidential candidates.

Both parties have placed a premium on soft money because it is largely unregulated. Individuals, corporations and unions can give unlimited amounts of money for such party-building activities as get-out-the-vote drives and generic issues ads. By exploiting campaign financing loopholes, the parties turned the race for the White House into the political money equivalent of an arms race.

Indeed, the parties have become increasingly sophisticated and aggressive in their efforts to snare big donors with elaborate party functions, dinners and receptions that offer ample access to high-level Administration and congressional leaders. For the Democrats, who have long trailed the Republicans in capitalizing on soft money, this year has witnessed a full-court press to catch up.

Democratic moneymen credited the Clinton White House with taking fund raising to a new level. "The level of vigor and enthusiasm on the part of the President and the Vice President are second to none," said Charles T. Manatt, a former DNC chairman and major fund raiser, who is a name partner in the Washington office of Manatt Phelps & Phillips, a Los Angeles-based law firm. "I've never seen anything like it on the Democratic side."

But late in the campaign, the Democratic soft-money drive sparked a political firestorm because at least a few of its largest contributions came from questionable, possibly illegal, foreign sources, including wealthy individuals and companies with links to India, Indonesia and South Korea.

John Huang, a leading DNC fund raiser and a former Commerce Department official whom President Clinton has praised for his "aggressive" money-raising efforts, was relieved of his fund-raising duties at the DNC last month after he was linked to a few highly dubious fund-raising projects.

"This is the year of the loophole," said Larry Makinson, the deputy director of the Center for Responsive Politics, a Washington-based nonprofit group that tracks the influence of money in politics. "There are no limits. There are no rules."

Many party insiders see no problem with soft money. "It's taken people 20-some years to figure out that there's nothing wrong with giving a large soft-money check," RNC finance director Albert E. Mitchler said. "There was a lot of shyness about big checks after Watergate, but now it doesn't seem to matter anymore. The world doesn't end with disclosure."

Other concerns about soft money have been spurred because it is not supposed to be used to directly influence federal elections. But some analysts maintain that this year, both parties went too far in their ad efforts on behalf of presidential candidates. . . .

[Observers point] out that the soft money spent on these ads was crucial for both Clinton's and GOP presidential candidate Robert Dole's prospects earlier this year as each sought to gain advantage before the conventions. In Clinton's case, the party's spending allowed him to "save" key campaign funds for later, and in Dole's case, the party ads helped "prop up" his campaign when he had hit spending limits.

Moreover, in October, Common Cause charged that both parties used soft money illegally in ad campaigns to help their candidates in the presidential primaries and asked the Justice Department to appoint an independent counsel to investigate the matter.

The furor over the gargantuan sums and new uses of soft money this election season has prompted demands for reform by campaign finance experts and leading Members of Congress. Late in the campaign, Clinton and Dole called for a ban on soft-money contributions.

. . .

BIG BUCKS

The explosion of soft money to buttress the presidential campaigns is particularly ironic given that the campaign financing system set up after Watergate was supposed to be paid for largely by public monies. Clinton and Dole each received $62 million in federal funds for the general election. In exchange for the money, they pledged to limit spending to that amount. Also, each of the party committees is permitted to spend $12 million in hard money from its presidential trust to support its nominee.

Under the current campaign finance system, individual contributions are restricted to $1,000 per election cycle and political action committees can give up to $5,000 for each election. Corporate and labor union contributions are barred in federal elections. But through the soft-money loophole, there's no limit on what companies, unions and individuals can give to finance what are loosely defined as party-building activities.

. . .

Both parties have pursued soft money zealously. As of mid-October, the RNC had already raised about $87 million and the DNC approximately $84 million. By contrast, in the last election cycle, the Republicans raised $36 million and the Democrats $32 million in soft money.

Some lobbyists and fund raisers say that soft money has become a juggernaut that's out of control. "When you get caught up in this spiral for more money, the need to have it almost seems to overpower the need to know where it's coming from," said Robert Healy, the chief Washington lobbyist for Atlantic Richfield Co., a major giver to both parties. "It may be a casualty of big-time politics, or big-time politics may be a casualty of it."

Still, campaign finance analysts say that the current presidential financing system—which started when the Federal Election Commission (FEC) opened the soft-money loophole with a ruling in 1979—worked relatively well until eight years ago.

"The breakdown started in the 1988 election, when the Dukakis campaign and the Bush campaign started taking these huge contributions and claiming they were for the parties rather than the presidential campaign," said Fred Wertheimer, the former Common Cause president and longtime advocate of campaign finance reform. "The FEC bought it," he added.

Wertheimer blames the boom in soft money partly on the FEC's long track record of weak and slow enforcement and the apparent decisions by both parties to push the envelope this year. "People basically decided to walk right through the laws on the basis that there wouldn't be any consequences to pay and the stakes were so high," he said. "It's happened in part because everyone reached the collective judgment that the FEC wasn't enforcing the law" and that whatever actions the agency took would be imposed far in the future.

. . .

GOING FOR THE GREEN

For the Democrats, soft money proved invaluable in helping Clinton gain an early edge against Dole and sustain his campaign by supplementing what he could legally spend with millions of dollars more in issues ads.

According to *The Choice*, Bob Woodward's book about the early stages of this year's presidential race, the White House last year worked with the DNC to launch an ad campaign around medicare that was paid for largely by soft-money contributions. That advertising effort, which started in mid-1995 and lasted almost a year, cost an estimated $34 million, including $22 million in soft money, according to Common Cause.

The success of the Democratic fund-raising machine is attributable in part to the President's willingness to participate in all sorts of events to wine and dine fat cats. Clinton made two critical decisions this election season: not to concede issues and not to concede big money, which, in effect, meant to "out-Republican" the GOP at the money game, a Democratic fund raiser in Washington said.

Clinton promised early on that "he'd be available for small gatherings of 20–50 people" in Washington and elsewhere, another Democratic fund raiser said. These events, of which there were dozens this year, often took place in Washington at the Hay-Adams Hotel and started around 7:30 P.M. with receptions that included picture-taking with officials such as Sen. Christopher J. Dodd, D-Conn., the DNC general chairman. Clinton would come in a little later and "thank folks for their support and talk about issues of the day," the fund raiser said.

. . .

Vice President Albert Gore Jr. and a few Cabinet officials have also done a lot of heavy lifting on the fund-raising front. Gore has been heavily involved with the Democratic Business Council, a group of big donors whose membership has soared to 1,700 from about 240 members a few years ago. More than a fourth of the members are corporations that kick in $15,000 annually so that their executives can talk to and mingle with top Administration officials at the meetings. The other members are individuals who pay $10,000 a year to participate in the council.

. . .

The DNC's ardent pursuit of soft money started to cause embarrassment last year, when stories appeared in the *Chicago Sun-Times* about how some of the party's biggest donors were being lured with invitations to attend two dinners with Clinton and two with Gore. After those reports came out, the party quietly deep-sixed its official titles of trustee for $50,000 donors and managing trustee for $100,000 donors. But the DNC says that during this cycle it has 400 donors of $100,000 or more.

In any event, they've hardly been forgotten or allowed to feel unappreciated. In fact, the DNC and the White House showered these and other big donors with oodles of special attention at this year's national convention in Chicago. Several stellar parties and outings were held at the August convention to make sure that big donors reaped the access to top Democratic officials they wanted. There was a DNC-sponsored luncheon cruise, for instance, for about 400 of its biggest donors.

The Administration's willingness to market its top officials and in some cases to go the extra mile for special contributors paid off not only for the party but also for some donors. Among the big soft-money donors that have gotten a lot more than photos and meals from the Administration are trial lawyers, who have been among the DNC's most generous soft-money patrons. In the 1992 elections, trial lawyers were leading soft-money givers to the Clinton campaign. And in 1996, several have once again come through. Lawyers with Nix & Associates, a Texas law firm, have given $360,000 to the DNC, and the firm ranks eighth among its soft-money donors, according to the Center for Responsive Politics.

Clinton showed his gratitude to the trial lawyers—and won their fealty—late last year, when after a White House meeting with some prominent trial lawyers, he vetoed a bipartisan bill that would have curbed suits against the securities industry.

GOP MONEY

For the Dole campaign, the RNC's ability to use the soft-money loophole also helped. After Dole's long and expensive primary battles, his presidential campaign faced a financial quandary a few months before the convention because it had already approached the $37 million limit on spending permitted before the August convention.

But the RNC's soft-money machine came to his aid. Before the convention, according to Common Cause estimates, the party spent at least $14 million ($9 million in soft money) on ads that touted Dole's themes and in some ways were tantamount to Dole for President ads.

Meanwhile, Dole appeared at party fund-raisers held for other candidates and raised more soft money for the RNC. The RNC picked up the tab for Dole's travel costs, which, in effect, allowed Dole to continue campaigning even though he was running out of money. During this time period, Dole raised about $25 million, three-fourths of it in soft money.

. . .

Over all, the RNC estimates that it will raise $90 million–$100 million in soft money this election cycle, about 40 percent of its expected total take of $250 million.

To raise the bigger chunks of soft money, Dole and other party leaders have attended a host of functions around the country. "In the past, events have been more Washington-oriented, with big regional events," an RNC insider said. But this year, there was a veritable road show by party leaders, including late fund-raising trips by RNC chairman Haley Barbour and House Speaker Newt Gingrich of Georgia to Colorado, Oklahoma and Texas, which pulled in more than $2 million and featured high-dollar receptions with "grip and grins" for donors of $5,000 and $10,000. "There's not a state that we haven't had an event in," the RNC fund raiser boasted.

The soft money for the party this year started flowing early and fast, when the RNC hosted its January gala in Washington, an event that grossed a record-setting $16 million, of which about half was soft money, according to party officials. "It was a reflection of the goodwill of the donors," said Robert Odell, the chairman of Odell, Roper and Sims, a Falls Church (Va.)-based consulting and direct-mail firm and the coordinator of the event's fund-raising efforts. "The giving community is involved and got a big lift out of the 1994 elections."

Other RNC special-donor programs brought in soft money, too. The Team 100 program, set up for donors who contribute $100,000, doubled from about 200 in 1992 to 400 in [1996]. The Republican Eagles, a group of individuals who contribute $15,000 and corporate donors who give $20,000, has almost 400 members.

But perhaps the most glaring example of the party's commitment to raising big dollars was the season ticket program for contributors who give at least $250,000. Why do companies lavish this kind of largesse on the parties? Some of these super contributors say that by making bigger donations they can participate more in the political process and have their voices heard on vital issues.

"We looked at the season ticket as a substitute for buying tables at a number of events that we would have done anyhow," said Ronald Stowe, the chief Washington lobbyist for Indianapolis-based Eli Lilly, one of the new givers. "We've tried to tie our contributions very much to publicizing and raising issues that we think are important."

. . .

Other big soft-money donors such as Philip Morris, UST and other tobacco companies have pumped greater percentages of their donations into Republican coffers because of Dole's and the party's strong opposition to Clinton Administration plans to regulate tobacco as a drug. Philip Morris leads all soft-money donors to either party this election cycle and has poured $1.1 million into the RNC's coffers.

FIXING THE SYSTEM

Given the influx of soft money in 1996 and the controversies that it spawned, the period right after the election may offer a rare window of opportunity for eliminating what campaign finance reform advocates, many fund raisers and a growing number of politicians regard as a political embarrassment.

. . .

[C]ampaign finance reform advocates have charged that both Clinton and Dole have flouted campaign finance laws and been hypocritical in their calls for reform.

"President Clinton and Dole signed commitments to limit spending as a condition for getting taxpayer money," former Common Cause president Wertheimer said. "They've clearly broken faith with the American people. They ignored not just the spirit, but the letter of the law. It's been blatant, brazen and an insult to the American people and a rip-off to the taxpayer. There are apparently no ends that the presidential campaigns won't go to, to get their hands on money."

DOCUMENT 6.11

In this piece, Brent Thompson, executive director of the Fair Government Foundation, defends soft money against attacks of "hyperbole and misinformation." He argues that soft money empowers parties and severs the links between donors and candidates, and thus there is no systemic problem to remedy.

Soft money is the latest target of the self-appointed "good government" lobby. Like so many aspects of campaign finance, soft money is a victim of a deliberate campaign of hyperbole and misinformation. So rather than a natural consequence of healthy political association and functioning federalism, soft money is painted as a legal loophole nothing short of legalized bribery.

Contrary to the caricature, non-federal (soft) money is not some sort of renegade system of unregulated, undisclosed political activity. Disclosure of soft money is fully regulated by the FEC, which requires detailed reporting of all activity. How soft money is raised and spent, in turn, is regulated by state law, as befits a federal system.

Accordingly, the national party committees serve the interests of the political parties broadly defined. That means in addition to Congressional and presidential elections, the parties play a significant role in state and local elections.

Soft money funds democracy, from dog catcher to top dog.

A substantial portion of the funds help support the many state and local party organizations that make the two-party system a reality. During the most recent election cycle, of the $124 million the Democratic National Committee raised, $69 million went to state and local parties. The Republicans, likewise, sent $55 million of the $138 million raised to state and local parties. Soft money is also used for generic party building activities ("vote Democratic"), voter registration drives, and issue advocacy—all worthy activities that would not occur if soft money were banned.

Despite the good works accomplished with non-federal funds, soft money has suffered grave reputational harm. The "appearance of impropriety," as the familiar lament goes, requires redress. Concededly, the Clinton Administration has done more than any past administration in giving credence to the critics.

. . .

The Clinton Administration reached a new low in crassness with its brazen peddling of White House perks and presidential "face-time." And while many would like it otherwise (and despite the consider-

---

able efforts of the Democrats and the press), the scandal is firmly confined to the practices of one political party.

There is thus no systemic problem in need of remedy. It's not the fault of the "system." There is no "soft money scandal" separate and apart from the Clinton/DNC affair. But bad taste, bad judgment, illegal activities, and limited self-respect cannot be allowed to undermine an otherwise legitimate and desirable practice. In short, one bad apple shouldn't be permitted to spoil the whole bunch.

Clinton's brazenness notwithstanding, and in defense of non-federal activities, there is a key difference between contributions to parties and contributions to candidates. By definition, contributions to party organizations greatly diminish the possibility of *quid pro quo* arrangements for the simple and amply sufficient reason that parties don't make policy.

Indeed, political parties provide a useful and salutary buffer between candidates and donors, a fact that characteristically goes unmentioned in the campaign finance debate.

The Supreme Court in the recent *Colorado* [*Republican Federal Campaign Committee* v. *Federal Election Commission,* 116 S. Ct. 2309 (1996) (document 3.4)]decision . . . casts doubt on the opinion holding that Congress may ban non-federal contributions to the parties without violating the Constitution. To the extent such contributions are used to fund issue advocacy, for example, a ban would arguably be at odds with the Court's precedents protecting issue advocacy from any governmental regulation whatsoever—including disclosure requirements.

It is unlikely that a court that just recently identified the right of political parties to make unlimited independent expenditures would turn around and deny parties the right to raise and expend funds for issue advocacy.

Even if no constitutional questions exist, outlawing soft money would deal a grievous blow to the American political party system. If political parties are to be anything more than big federal PACs, they must be free of regulatory entanglements that deprive them of the ability to marshal and distribute adequate resources.

A political party renaissance, of sorts, has been quietly under way and is due in no small measure to the willingness of the parties to be less inhibited in exercising political freedoms. It is therefore no accident that the infusion of soft money has coincided with the return of the parties to their rightful place in the democratic process.

CONTENTS

INTRODUCTION BY TREVOR POTTER

Political issue advocacy exploded into the public consciousness during the 1996 congressional and presidential elections. Organizations and interest groups saturated the local radio and television airwaves across the country with issue-oriented advertisements, with the stated purpose of shaping public opinion on selected policy matters. The Democratic National Committee initiated the air wars as early as 1995 with advertisements designed to bolster President Clinton's support by portraying him as saving the nation from the Republican Congress. The AFL-CIO followed up with an announcement of a $35 million advertising campaign attacking the legislative records of potentially vulnerable Republican House incumbents (especially freshmen members). In the summer of 1996, a business coalition responded with advertising praising the congressional voting records of the incumbent Republicans in those districts.

Moreover, the Democratic and Republican national committees ran "issue ads" featuring their presidential nominees before the party conventions (see document 7.1). This was important for the Republicans, as the Dole campaign had nearly reached its primary spending limit in March 1996, five months before the party's August convention. After the conventions, many other issue groups— usually tax-exempt 501(c)(4) organizations (the Sierra Club, Americans for Tax Reform, and others)—took to the airwaves with significant expenditures for "issue ads" in targeted districts and states.

Because these "issue advocacy" advertisements were designed to avoid the narrow legal definition of federal election spending, the sponsors were free to underwrite the campaigns with money that is prohibited or severely restricted when used in connection with federal elections—including corporate and labor treasury funds and unlimited individual contributions. Moreover, because the advertisements were not deemed to be "in connection with a federal election," the sponsoring organizations were not required to disclose the sources of their funding, or where and how it was spent.

To many observers, these issue advertisements were clearly designed to influence the outcome of selected congressional races and the presidential contest. Indeed, on occasion the sponsors proudly claimed that the advertisements had achieved this goal. In some congressional districts, unlimited and undisclosed funds spent on "issue" broadcasts and mailers exceeded that spent by the candidates themselves. There are now calls for disclosure of "issue advocacy," and regulation of its funding. But what exactly is issue advocacy, and where did it come from?

Simply stated, issue advocacy has come to mean political speech that may mention specific candidates or political parties *but* does not "expressly advocate" the election or defeat of a clearly identified federal candidate through the use of words such as "vote for," "oppose," "support," and the like. As a legal construct, issue advocacy was created by the U.S. Supreme Court when it narrowed the reach of the federal election laws in the *Buckley* v. *Valeo* decision, 424 U.S. 1 (1976); see document 7.3). Although the definition is relatively simple to state, distinguishing between issue advocacy (exempt from federal campaign finance regulation) and express advocacy (subject to reporting requirements and limits on sources of payment) has proven exceedingly contentious in practice over the past twenty years.

This introduction traces the evolution of issue advocacy from the Supreme Court's seminal *Buckley* decision through the ensuing decisions of the lower federal courts. It also discusses the Federal Election Commission's (FEC) response to these major court rulings.

ISSUE ADVOCACY: WHAT IS IT, AND WHERE DID IT COME FROM?

As noted previously, issue advocacy is best understood by what it does *not* do—it is a communication that does not "expressly advocate" the election or defeat of a clearly identified federal candidate. Whether it must affirmatively do something else— such as present a clear view about a political, social, or economic issue—is less clear.

The Genesis: *Buckley* v. *Valeo*

Buckley was, on its face, a constitutional challenge to the Federal Election Campaign Act of 1971 (FECA) as amended in 1974. (For a discussion of the FECA, see chapter 2; for a complete account of the *Buckley* decision, see document 3.1.) This meant that the courts had no specific political spending before it but were judging the constitutional validity of the FECA as drafted by Congress. As a result, the courts were declaring general principles of constitutional law disconnected from any practical application in specific election contests.

The first decision in *Buckley* came from the Court of Appeals for the D.C. Circuit, which largely upheld the law as passed by Congress. However, the D.C. Circuit did strike down a broad "issue advocacy" provision that would have required disclo-

sure of all contributions of more than $10 received by any organization that publicly referred to any candidate or the candidate's voting record or positions, or official acts of candidates who were federal officeholders; *Buckley* v. *Valeo,* 519 F.2d 821, 869—878 (D.C. Cir. 1975)—document 7.2.

The D.C. Circuit held that this language—which regulated even nonpartisan communications by groups that were not political committees, using a broad phrase, "for the purpose of influencing the outcome of an election"—was both unconstitutionally vague (providing no real guidance as to regulated or unregulated speech) and too inclusive (requiring disclosure by groups not overtly involved in political activity). This provision, intended by Congress to provide disclosure of all donors to Common Cause, the ACLU, and "many groups, including liberal, labor, environmental, business and conservative organizations," was declared unconstitutional in its entirety by the D.C. Circuit, and that holding was the only part of the D.C. Circuit's decision not appealed to the Supreme Court.[1]

In *Buckley,* the Supreme Court confronted a wide array of congressionally enacted prohibitions and restrictions on contributions and expenditures in connection with federal elections. Congress had written the FECA broadly, regulating all spending "in connection with," or "for the purpose of influencing" a federal election, or "relative to" a federal candidate. One of the questions the Court faced was whether these statutory phrases were so vague and overly broad that they provided an unconstitutional lack of notice to persons potentially affected by the FECA. The Court stressed that vagueness concerns are especially acute where, as here, "the legislation imposes criminal penalties in an area permeated by First Amendment interests. . . . The test is whether the language . . . affords the '[p]recision of regulation [that] must be the touchstone in an area so closely touching our most precious freedoms.'" The Court noted that Congress had failed to define "in connection with" an election or "relative to a candidate."

The D.C. Circuit Court of Appeals had sought

to avoid vagueness problems by narrowing "relative to a candidate" to communications "advocating the election or defeat of such candidate." However, the Supreme Court held that greater precision and clarity were required to avoid unconstitutional vagueness. The Court held that *explicit words of advocacy of election or defeat* are required. The Court indicated that the following explicit advocacy terms satisfied the strict "express advocacy" test: "'vote for,' 'elect,' 'support,' 'cast your ballot for,' 'Smith for Congress,' 'vote against,' 'defeat,' 'reject.'"[2] Such a strict line was required because "the distinction between discussion of issues and candidates and advocacy of election or defeat of candidates may often dissolve in practical application. Candidates, especially incumbents, are intimately tied to public issues involving legislative proposals and governmental actions. Not only do candidates campaign on the basis of their positions on various public issues, but campaigns themselves generate issues of public interest."

Buckley cautioned that a standard which turned on the speaker's purpose or the listener's understanding would have a chilling effect on political speech.

Similarly, the Court in *Buckley* narrowed a provision in the FECA requiring every person who makes contributions or expenditures over $100 in connection with a federal election to file a disclosure statement with the FEC. The FECA defined "contributions" and "expenditures" as providing money or other valuable assets "'for the purpose of . . . influencing' . . . [an] election." Again, to avoid vagueness, the Court narrowed the definition of "expenditure" to "reach only funds used for communications that expressly advocate the election or defeat of a clearly identified candidate. This reading is directed precisely to that spending that is unambiguously related to the campaign of a particular federal candidate."

In narrowing the reach of the FECA to avoid declaring it unconstitutionally vague, the Court in *Buckley* significantly restricted the reach of the federal election laws. Instead of Congress's intended broad coverage of "all spending" to "influence" federal elections (phrases presumably to be defined with greater specificity over time by the courts and the Federal Election Commission), the law as interpreted by the Supreme Court now regulated only speech that constituted "express advocacy." Though that new term was not yet defined in practice, it clearly meant that much political speech Congress had intended to be regulated and disclosed would instead be beyond the reach of the campaign finance laws.

The First Supreme Court Application of the Express Advocacy Test: *Federal Election Commission* v. *Massachusetts Citizens for Life, Inc.*

Although the Supreme Court enunciated the express advocacy test in *Buckley* in 1976, it was not until ten years later, in *Federal Election Commission* v. *Massachusetts Citizens for Life, Inc.,* 479 U.S. 238 (1986) (*MCFL*), that the Supreme Court had occasion to apply the test to an actual communication (see document 7.4). MCFL was a nonprofit, nonstock corporation organized to advance anti-abortion goals. In 1973, MCFL began publishing a newsletter that typically contained information on the organization's activities, including the status of various proposed bills and constitutional amendments. In September 1978—just weeks before the primary elections—MCFL published a special edition of the newsletter. Though earlier newsletters has been sent to 2,000 to 3,000 people, MCFL published more than 100,000 copies of the special edition. The front page of the publication was headlined "EVERYTHING YOU NEED TO KNOW TO VOTE PRO-LIFE," and readers were reminded that "[n]o pro-life candidate can win in November without your vote in September." "VOTE PRO-LIFE" appeared in large black letters on the back page, and a coupon was available to clip and take to the polls to remind voters of the names of the "pro-life" candidates. Next to this statement was the following disclaimer: "This special election edition does not represent an endorsement of any particular candidate." An accompanying flyer placed a "y" next to the names of candidates who supported the MCFL view on a particular issue; an "n" indicated that a candidate opposed MCFL's position.

Section 441b of the FECA prohibits any corporation from using treasury funds "in connection with" a federal election and requires that any expenditure for such purpose be financed by voluntary contributions into separate segregated funds, commonly known as political action committees (PACs). The FEC alleged that MCFL's expenditures in financing the special election newsletter constituted an illegal corporate contribution to the candidates named in the newsletter. As in *Buckley*, the Court ruled "that an expenditure must constitute 'express advocacy' in order to be subject to the prohibition of § 441b."

However, the Court went on to hold that the MCFL newsletter was express advocacy because it urged readers "to vote for 'pro-life' candidates" and provided the names and photographs of candidates meeting that descriptions. Said the Court: "The Edition cannot be regarded as a mere discussion of public issues that by their nature raise the names of certain politicians. Rather, it provides in effect an explicit directive: vote for these (named) candidates. The fact that this message is marginally less direct than 'Vote for Smith' does not change its essential nature. The Edition goes beyond issue discussion to express electoral advocacy. The disclaimer of endorsement cannot negate this fact."[3]

The Court's application of the express advocacy test in *MCFL* is noteworthy in two respects. In determining whether the MCFL newsletter was express advocacy, the Court did not appear to consider any factual circumstances outside of the communication itself. These external circumstances could have included, for example, the proximity of the publication to the election, the number of copies published (which was well in excess of the normal newsletter distribution), and the intent of the speakers. In this regard, *MCFL* is fully consistent with *Buckley*—the express advocacy test turns on the communication itself with no consideration of external events. In addition, the Court broadened (even if only slightly) the *Buckley* definition of express advocacy to include words that are "in effect" an explicit directive "marginally less direct" than the *Buckley* language.[4] As a result, *MCFL* has been used by the FEC in court pleadings to justify a definition of express advocacy based, at least in part, on implied electoral meanings.

Competing Approaches: *Federal Election Commission* v. *Furgatch* and *Faucher* v. *Federal Election Commission*

After *Buckley* and *MCFL*, the federal courts struggled to apply the express advocacy test, often with what appeared to be inconsistent results. Perhaps the most pro-regulatory decision is the Ninth Circuit's ruling in *Federal Election Commission* v. *Furgatch*, 807 F.2d 857 (1987), *cert. denied*, 484 U.S. 850 (1987) (see document 7.5). In *Furgatch*, an individual published a full-page advertisement in the *New York Times* one week before the 1980 presidential election. The advertisement read:

DON'T LET HIM DO IT.

The President of the United States continues degrading the electoral process and lessening the prestige of the office.

It was evident months ago when his running mate outrageously suggested Ted Kennedy was unpatriotic. The President remained silent.

And we let him.

It continued when the President himself accused Ronald Reagan of being unpatriotic.

And we let him do it again.

In recent weeks [Jimmy] Carter has tried to buy entire cities, the steel industry, the auto industry, and others with public funds.

We are letting him do it.

He continues to cultivate the fears, not the hopes, of the voting public by suggesting the choice is between "peace and war," "black or white," "north or south," and "Jew vs. Christian." His meanness of spirit is divisive and reckless McCarthyism at its worst. And from a man who once asked, "Why not the best?"

It is an attempt to hide his own record, or lack of it. If he succeeds the country will be burdened with four more years of incoherences, ineptness and illusion, as he leaves a legacy of low-level campaigning.

DON'T LET HIM DO IT. [*Furgatch*, 807 F.2d at 858 (emphasis in original)]

The Ninth Circuit ruled that the advertisement was "express advocacy" and therefore could be regulated under the FECA. The court began its analysis by contending that the *Buckley* express advocacy test "does not draw a bright and unambiguous line. . . . [W]here First Amendment concerns are present, we must construe the words of the regulatory statute precisely and narrowly, *only as far as is necessary to further the purposes of the [FECA] . . .*" (*Furgatch*, 807 F.2d at 861 [emphasis added]). Because of these important regulatory concerns, the court concluded in *Furgatch* that it must "prevent speech that is clearly intended to affect the outcome of a federal election from escaping, either fortuitously or by design, the coverage of the Act. This concern leads us to fashion a more comprehensive approach to the delimitation of 'express advocacy,' and to reject . . . overly constrictive rules of interpretation."

The Ninth Circuit in *Furgatch* rejected the notion that express advocacy is limited to the list of specific terms identified by the Supreme Court in *Buckley*. The court stated presciently that "[a] test requiring the magic words 'elect,' 'support,' etc., or their nearly perfect synonyms for a finding of express advocacy would preserve the First Amendment right of unfettered expression only at the expense of eviscerating the Federal Election Campaign Act. 'Independent' campaign spenders working on behalf of candidates could remain just beyond the reach of the Act by avoiding certain key words while conveying a message that is unmistak-

ably directed to the election or defeat of a named candidate" (*Furgatch*, 807 F.2d at 863). The Ninth Circuit ruled that when evaluating whether a communication constitutes express advocacy, a reviewing court must take into account the context in which the communication is made. The court established a standard that, to be express advocacy, speech "must, when read as a whole, and with limited reference to external events, be susceptible of no other reasonable interpretation but as an exhortation to vote for or against a specific candidate." The Ninth Circuit made it clear that implied meanings can form the basis for a finding of express advocacy: "A consideration of the context in which speech is uttered *may clarify ideas that are not perfectly articulated, or supply necessary premises that are unexpressed but widely understood by readers or viewers.* We should not ignore external factors that contribute to a complete understanding of speech, especially when they are factors that the audience must consider in evaluating the words before it. However, context cannot supply a meaning that is incompatible with, or simply unrelated to, the clear import of the words" (emphasis added).

However, the Ninth Circuit was not willing to allow the government to use only subjective standards to identify express advocacy. Instead, it enunciated a murky standard requiring that speech *not* be susceptible to interpretation as "issue advocacy" and that it clearly advocate a specific electoral outcome. The *Furgatch* standard has three specific components. "First, even if it is not presented in the clearest, most explicit language, speech is 'express' for present purposes if its message is unmistakable and unambiguous, *suggestive of only one plausible meaning.* Second, speech may only be termed 'advocacy' if it presents a clear plea for action, and thus speech that is merely informative is not covered by the Act. Finally, it must be clear what action is advocated. Speech cannot be 'express advocacy of the election or defeat of a clearly identified candidate' when reasonable minds could differ as to whether it encourages a vote for or against a candidate or encourages the reader to take some other kind of action" (emphasis added). The third *Furgatch* component would appear to require advocacy of *electoral* action for or against a particular candidate, without more, as opposed to a communication that included a plea for some other kind of action, such as writing an officeholder or making a political contribution.

Applying the foregoing standard, the Ninth Circuit ruled that the Furgatch advertisement expressly advocated the defeat of President Jimmy Carter. In making this determination, the court focused on the words "'don't let him.' They are simple and direct. 'Don't let him' is a command. The words 'expressly advocate' action of some kind." The court acknowledged that there was no express indication in the advertisement of what kind of action the reader should take. However, it ruled "that this failure to state with specificity the action required does not remove political speech from [the Act].... *Reasonable minds* could not dispute that Furgatch's advertisement urged readers to vote against Jimmy Carter" (emphasis added).

Opening an important debate which has engaged the FEC and commentators ever since, the Ninth Circuit stressed that its conclusion was reinforced by the timing of the advertisement, which was less than a week before the election. The court also sought to distinguish the advertisement from issue-oriented speech: "The ad directly attacks a candidate, not because of any stand on the issues of the election, but for his personal qualities and alleged improprieties in the handling of his campaign. It is the type of advertising that the Act was enacted to cover."

The *Furgatch* decision is notable in many respects. The court was willing to find express advocacy based on implied electoral meanings. In addition, the Ninth Circuit held that in determining whether express advocacy exists, reviewing courts may go beyond the text of the communication itself and consider external, contextual factors—including the proximity of the communication to the election. And although *Furgatch* purportedly requires the communication to clearly advocate *electoral* action as opposed to some other kind of action, the court found express advocacy even without an explicit electoral plea in Furgatch's advertisement, apparently because no nonelectoral issue message could plausibly be found in the ad. Finally, contrary to language in the Supreme Court's *Buckley* ruling, the court in *Furgatch* suggested that it was possible to distinguish between attacks on candidates and incumbents involving personal issues but no "vote for, support/oppose" explicit language (which it said could be regulated) and what it termed "issue-oriented speech" (which it said could not be). *Furgatch* remains the most pro-regulatory, and increasingly isolated, decision in the issue advocacy area. The Supreme Court denied a petition to review the Ninth Circuit's decision; *cert. denied,* 484 U.S. 850 (1987).

At the other end of the spectrum is the First Circuit's ruling in *Faucher* v. *Federal Election Commission,* 928 F.2d 468 (1991), *cert. denied sub nom.,* 502 U.S. 820 (1991); see document 7.6. In that case, the Maine Right to Life Committee (MRLC) published a voting guide surveying the positions of federal and state candidates on pro-life issues, and distributed it widely immediately before election day. The MRLC financed the voting guide out of its general corporate monies. MRLC's 1988 guide was entitled "November Election Issue 1988!" was subheaded "Federal & State Candidate Surveys Enclosed—Take-along Issue for Election Day!," included candidate and party positions on pro-life issues, and contained the following statement: "PLEASE NOTE: A 'yes' response indicates agreement with the National Right to Life position on each question." The guide carried the following disclaimer: "The publication of the MRLC November Election Candidate Survey does not represent an endorsement of any candidate(s) by MRLC."

The First Circuit, relying on *Buckley* and *MCFL,* hewed to a strict definition of express advocacy requiring explicit "vote for, support/oppose" type language in the communication. The court stressed that "'[d]iscussion of public issues and debate on the qualifications of candidates are integral to the operation of the system of government established by our Constitution.' The FEC nevertheless has sought to restrain that very same activity which the [Supreme] Court in *Buckley* sought to protect. This we cannot allow."

The First Circuit ruled that the MRLC voting guide was not express advocacy, concluding that "trying to discern when issue advocacy in a voter guide crosses the threshold and becomes express advocacy invites just the sort of constitutional questions the [Supreme] Court sought to avoid in adopting the bright-line express advocacy test in *Buckley*." The effect of the court's ruling is that a voting guide that contains a discussion of public policy issues and does not include "elect" or "defeat" or any of the other "magic words" identified in *Buckley* is *per se* issue advocacy and cannot be regulated—even if candidates are also discussed in the guide and the manner in which the issues are discussed is favorable or unfavorable to particular candidates. At the very least, *Faucher* can be read as rejecting any consideration of implied meanings in determining whether a communication contains express advocacy.

Other Major Court Rulings

Several other circuit courts have adopted the strict approach to express advocacy exemplified by *Faucher*. For example, in *Federal Election Commission v. Central Long Island Tax Reform Immediately Committee*, 616 F.2d 45 (2d Cir. 1980) (*CLITRIM*), the Second Circuit considered whether an issues bulletin published by a nonprofit association prior to a general election was express advocacy.

The bulletin detailed and attacked the voting record of a local congressional representative but did not refer to any federal election, did not mention the representative's party affiliation, and did not identify the representative's electoral opponent.

The FEC contended that the bulletin was express advocacy. The Second Circuit rejected the Commission's contention, reaffirming that the federal election laws do not "'reach all partisan discussion . . . [but only] those expenditures that expressly advocate a particular election result.' This is consistent with the firmly established principle that the right to speak out at election time is one of the most zealously protected under the Constitution." The court stressed that "contrary to the position of the FEC, the words 'expressly advocating' mean exactly what they say. . . . [T]he FEC would apparently have us read 'expressly advocating the election or defeat' to mean for the purpose, express or *implied*, of encouraging election or defeat. This would, by statutory interpretation, nullify the change in the statute ordered in *Buckley* v. *Valeo* and adopted by Congress in the 1976 amendments [document 2.10]. The position is totally meritless (emphasis in original).

Similarly, in *Federal Election Commission v. Christian Action Network*, 894 F. Supp. 946 (W.D. Va. 1995), the district court adopted a strict view of express advocacy, and the Fourth Circuit summarily affirmed; 92 F.3d 1178 (4th Cir. 1996)—see document 7.7A. The Christian Action Network is a grassroots organization that seeks to inform the public about "traditional Christian family values." During the weeks immediately before the 1992 presidential election, the network aired television advertisements criticizing the alleged "militant homosexual agenda" of the Clinton/Gore ticket. As described by the court, the advertisement opened

with a full-color picture of candidate Bill Clinton's face superimposed upon an American flag, which is blowing in the wind. Clinton is shown smiling and the ad appears to be complimentary. However, as the narrator begins to describe Clinton's alleged support for 'radical' homosexual causes, Clinton's image dissolves into a black and white photographic negative. The negative darkens Clinton's eyes and mouth, giving the candidate a sinister and threatening appearance.

Simultaneously, the music accompanying the commercial changes from a single high pitched tone to a lower octave.

The commercial then presents a series of pictures depicting advocates of homosexual rights, apparently gay men and lesbians, demonstrating at a political march.

. . .

As the scenes from the march continue, the narrator asks in rhetorical fashion, "Is this your vision for a better America?" Thereafter, the image of the American flag reappears on the screen, but without the superimposed image of candidate Clinton. At the same time, the music changes back to the single high pitched tone. The narrator then states, "for more information on traditional family values, contact the Christian Action Network." (*Christian Action Network*, 894 F. Supp. at 948–49)

The FEC argued that any viewer would understand the advertisement to advocate Clinton's defeat. The Commission argued that the way the American flag was used in the commercial sent an explicit anti-Clinton message: "By graphically removing Clinton's superimposed image from the presidential setting of the American flag, the advertisement visually conveys the message that Clinton should not become president. [It] is a powerful visual image telling voters to defeat Clinton." The FEC also pointed to the following aspects of the commercial: "(1) the visual degrading of candidate Clinton's picture into a black and white negative; (2) the use of visual text and audio voice-overs; (3) ominous music; (4) unfavorable coloring; (5) codewords such as 'vision' and 'quota'; (6) issues raised that are relevant only if candidate Clinton became president; (7) the airing of the commercial in close proximity to the national election; and (8) abrupt editing linking Clinton to the images of the gay rights marchers."

The court ruled that the Christian Action Network's advertisement was constitutionally protected issue advocacy that could not be regulated:

Concededly, the advertisements "clearly identified" the 1992 Democratic presidential and vice presidential candidates. . . . Similarly, it is beyond dispute that the advertisements were openly hostile to the proposals believed to have been endorsed by the two candidates. Nevertheless, the advertisements were devoid of any language that directly exhorted the public to vote. Without a frank admonition to take electoral action, even admittedly negative advertisements such as these, do not constitute "express advocacy" as that term is defined in *Buckley* and its progeny ("It is clear from the cases that expressions of hostility to the positions of an official, implying that [the] official should not be reelected—even when that implication is quite clear— do not constitute . . . express advocacy").

After summarily affirming the district court's ruling, the Fourth Circuit later awarded the Christian Action Network attorneys fees and costs under the Equal Access to Justice Act, 28 U.S.C. § 2412(d)(1)(A). *Federal Election Commission v. Christian Action Network*, 110 F.3d 1049 (4th Cir. 1997); see document 7.7B. In a blistering opinion highly critical of the FEC's legal arguments, the Fourth Circuit found that the Commission's legal position "if not assumed in bad faith, was at least not 'substantially justified.'" The court held that there was no legal basis for the FEC's contention that the Christian Action Network's advertisement was express advocacy:

In the face of the unequivocal Supreme Court and other authority discussed, an argument such as that made by the FEC in this case, that "*no* words of advocacy are necessary to expressly advocate the election of a candidate," simply cannot be advanced in good faith much less with "substantial justification." It may be that "images and symbols without words can also convey unequivocal meaning synonymous with literal text." It may well be that "metaphorical and figurative speech can be more pointed and compelling, and can thus more successfully express advocacy, than a plain, literal recommendation to vote for a particular person" and that "it would indeed be perverse to require FECA regulation to turn on the degree to which speech is literal or figurative, rather than on the clarity of its message," "given that banal, literal language often carries less force." It may even be, as the FEC contends in this particular case, that "the combined message of words and dramatic moving images, sounds, and other non-verbal cues such as film editing, photographic techniques, and music, involving highly charged rhetoric and provocative images . . . taken as a whole, sent an unmistakable message to oppose [Governor Clinton]. But the Supreme Court has unambiguously held that the First Amendment forbids the regulation of our political speech under such indeterminate standards. "Explicit words of advocacy of election or defeat of a candidate," "express words of advocacy," the Court has held, are the constitutional minima. To allow the government's power to be brought to bear on less, would effectively be to dispossess corporate citizens of their fundamental right to engage in the very kind of political issue advocacy the First Amendment was intended to protect—as this case well confirms.

Consensus of the Circuit Courts

A clear pattern emerges from the foregoing rulings on issue and express advocacy. Other than the Ninth Circuit in *Furgatch,* every other federal appeals court that has considered the issue—including the First, Second, and Fourth Circuits—has ruled that the express advocacy test set out in *Buckley* can only be met by communications that contain *explicit* and unambiguous words that urge readers (or viewers) to elect or defeat a clearly identified candidate. These circuits have rejected the FEC's repeated attempts to find express advocacy based on implied electoral meanings, even if the implicit electoral message is clear and arguably unmistakable. In several cases, they have done so while acknowledging that this standard will effectively exempt much candidate-related political speech intended to affect the outcome of federal elections from the law's disclo-

sure requirements and restrictions on corporate and labor funding.

The FEC Responds

In the wake of these Supreme Court and lower federal court rulings, in 1995 the FEC promulgated new regulations on what kinds of communications constitute express advocacy (11 C.F.R. § 100.22; see document 7.8).

Two aspects of the FEC's new express advocacy regulation bear comment. Part (a) of the regulation includes all of the express advocacy terms that the Supreme Court identified in *Buckley* and thereby incorporates the Court's decision into the Commission's regulations. More importantly, part (b) of the regulation is a clear attempt to incorporate the broader *Furgatch* express advocacy standard into the FEC's regulations, which are in effect throughout the country. As a result, it is not surprising that the FEC's new "express advocacy" regulations have already been successfully challenged in the First Circuit, which has taken a stricter view than the Ninth Circuit of the permissible scope of the FEC's regulatory authority. In *Maine Right to Life Committee, Inc.* v. *Federal Election Commission,* 914 F. Supp. 8 (D. Me. 1996), the court held that subpart (b) of the Commission's new regulations are unconstitutional on their face, regardless of how they might be applied. The First Circuit summarily affirmed the district court's decision on appeal; 98 F.3d 1 (1st Cir. 1996) *petition for cert. filed,* 65 U.S.L.W. 3783 (May 14, 1997) (No. 96.1818) (document 7.9).

In *Maine Right to Life,* the district court judge stressed that he believed his decision was compelled by binding Supreme Court precedent, even if the ruling served to restrict the scope of the federal election laws and leave much election-related speech unregulated:

If the Supreme Court had not decided *Buckley* and [*MCFL*] and if the First Circuit had not decided *Faucher,* I might well uphold the FEC's subpart (b) definition of what should be covered. After all, the Federal Election Campaign Act is designed to avoid excessive corporate financial interference in elections and the FEC presumably has some expertise on the question [of] what form that interference may take based on its history of complaints, investigations and enforcement actions.

. . .

But there is another policy at issue here and it is one that I believe the Supreme Court and the First Circuit have used to trump all the arguments suggested above. Specifically, the Supreme Court has been most concerned not to permit intrusion upon "issue" advocacy—discussion of the issues on the public's mind from time to time or of the candidate's positions on such issues—that the Supreme Court has considered a special concern of the First Amendment. . . . *FEC restriction of election activities was not to be permitted to intrude in any way upon the public discussion of issues. What the Supreme Court did was draw a bright line that may err on the side of permitting things that affect the election process, but at all costs avoids restricting, in any way, discussion of public issues.* The Court seems to have been quite serious in limiting FEC enforcement to *express* advocacy. (*Maine Right to Life,* 914 F. Supp. at 11—12 [emphasis added]).

The court also highlighted the tensions between the purposes of the election laws (as upheld by the Supreme Court) and the Supreme Court's strict express advocacy test: "The advantage of this [strict] approach, from [a] First Amendment point of view, is that it permits a speaker or writer to know from the outset exactly what is permitted and what is prohibited. In the stressful context of public discussions with deadlines, bright lights and cameras, the speaker need not pause to debate the shades of meaning in language. The result is not very satisfying from a realistic communications point of view and does not give much recognition to the policy of the election statute to keep corporate money from influencing elections in this way, but it does recognize the First Amendment interest as the Court has defined it."

An Unresolved Issue: What Happens When Issue Advocacy Sponsors Coordinate Spending with Candidates?

The Supreme Court in *Buckley* distinguished between "independent" advocacy and advocacy coordinated with a candidate when it declared restrictions on independent spending by individuals unconstitutional:

Independent advocacy . . . does not presently appear to pose dangers of real or apparent corruption comparable to those identified with large campaign contributions. The parties defending [the law] contend that it is necessary to prevent would-be contributors from avoiding the contribution limitations by the simple expedient of paying directly for media advertisements or for other portions of the candidate's campaign activities. They argue that expenditures controlled by or coordinated with the candidate and his campaign might well have virtually the same value to the candidate as a contribution and would pose similar dangers of abuse. Yet such controlled or coordinated expenditures are treated as contributions, rather than expenditures under the Act. Section 608(b)'s contribution ceilings . . . prevent attempts to circumvent the Act through prearranged or coordinated expenditures amounting to disguised contributions . . . The absence of prearrangement and coordination of an expenditure with the candidate or his agent not only undermines the value of the expenditure to the candidate, but also alleviates the danger that expenditures will be given as a *quid pro quo* for improper commitments from the candidate. (*Buckley,* 424 U.S. at 46–47)

Thus, as previously noted, after *Buckley, National Conservative Political Action Committee,* and the *Colorado Republican* decisions, individuals, PACs, and political parties are permitted to make unlimited "independent expenditures" in connection with a federal election, including communications containing express advocacy, provided that the expenditures are made independently of candidates and their agents.[5] If, however, an entity's expenditures are "coordinated" with candidates, the expenditures are treated as in-kind contributions that are applicable to the entity's contribution limits.[6]

The FEC's regulations currently define coordination as any activity "made with the cooperation or with the prior consent of, or in consultation with, or at the request or suggestion of, a candidate or any agent or authorized committee of the candidate"; 11 C.F.R. § 109.1(b)(4) (1997).

The FEC General Counsel's Office recently proposed that the Commission adopt a significantly broader definition of coordination, which would be met by any involvement in the spending by the candidate or any person who had been an agent of the candidate at another point in the election cycle.[7]

The question then becomes whether individuals and organizations who fund issue advocacy must also act independently of candidates to avoid regulation. A lower federal court recently shed some light on this issue. In *Clifton* v. *Federal Election Commission*, 927 F. Supp. 493 (D. Me. 1996), the court struck down the FEC's latest voting guide regulations and held that a nonprofit corporate advocacy group could contact candidates orally to obtain information to be published in an issue-oriented voter guide without making an illegal in-kind contribution to the candidates. The Commission's latest voter guide regulations prohibited *any* contact between voting guide corporate sponsors and candidates, with the sole exception that sponsors were allowed to direct questions to be included in the guide to the candidates in writing, and the candidates were allowed to respond in writing; 11 C.F.R. § 114.4(c)(4) & (5).

In *Clifton,* a nonprofit corporate sponsor contended that it had the constitutional right to engage in issue advocacy even while communicating with candidates beyond the minor exception permitted by the FEC's regulation—such as by contacting candidates directly and orally discussing their positions on various issues. In striking down the Commission's regulations, the court distinguished between mere "contact" between an issue-advocacy sponsor and a candidate, which the court

ruled cannot be regulated, and issue advocacy that is "coordinated" with or authorized by a candidate, which the court suggested could be. The court pointed out that "*Buckley* talked only about prohibiting expenditures 'authorized or requested by the candidate,' interpreted at its broadest as 'all expenditures placed in cooperation with or with the consent of a candidate'. The FEC has gone far beyond 'cooperation' or 'consent' in these prohibitions of all contact and consultation in the preparation of voter guides . . ."; *Clifton,* 927 F. Supp. at 499. In so ruling, the court emphasized that "as long as the Supreme Court holds that expenditures for issue advocacy have broad First Amendment protection, the FEC cannot use the mere act of communication between a corporation and a candidate to turn a protected expenditure for issue advocacy into an unprotected contribution to the candidate."

The court in *Clifton* did not indicate what kind of communications (if any) between issue advocacy sponsors and candidates will result in spending "authorized or requested" or "in cooperation with or with the consent of" a candidate, and thus might be considered "coordinated" expenditures, with potential federal election law disclosure and limit implications. However, it did state in dictum that any issue advocacy "made 'on behalf of' a candidate'" can be regulated consistent with the Constitution (quoting *MCFL,* 479 U.S. at 248).

Clearly, one of the next contentious areas of federal election law is whether the FEC can regulate issue advocacy which has been "coordinated" with a candidate. That is, what definition of "coordination" will prevail, and will the presence of coordination serve to convert some otherwise protected independent issue advocacy into spending authorized or requested by a federal candidate, and thus subject to regulation? For instance, Common Cause has filed a complaint with both the Justice Department and the FEC alleging that Democratic and Republican National Committee issue advertisements in 1996 should be considered contributions by those committees to their party's presidential candidates (and thus subject to limits and restrictions on the use of soft money), because these ads were planned with the candidates or their agents. In the case of President Clinton, a wide range of published accounts by former White House officials have detailed the president's personal role in authorizing the issue advertising campaign, editing and approving the ads, selecting the locations for their broadcast, and raising the funds needed to pay for the advertisements.

THE LAW GOVERNING ISSUE ADVOCACY AND EXPRESS ADVOCACY: A SHORT SUMMATION

If a communication contains "*express advocacy*" of the election or defeat of a clearly identified candidate, the communication may be regulated under federal law.

In addition, if a communication does not contain "express advocacy" and is instead "*issue advocacy*" (an issue-oriented discussion of public policy matters), it is not deemed to be "in connection with" a federal election (unless it raises coordination issues noted here). The sponsor may therefore run an unlimited number of such "issue advocacy" communications and may pay for the communication however it chooses, including from sources and in amounts prohibited by the federal election laws. Corporations, unions, and political parties are permitted to engage in issue advocacy.

If a communication containing issue advocacy has been made in consultation with a candidate, it may be considered "*coordinated.*" This *may* result in an in-kind contribution by the speaker to the candidate, depending upon the outcome of current and future legal battles over the definition of "coordination" and whether courts will allow coordinated issue advocacy to be regulated.

Finally, none of this involves "*independent expenditures,*" which are communications "expressly advocating" the election or defeat of a clearly identified

federal candidate, are financed with federal "hard" dollars and are publicly disclosed. Independent expenditures may not be coordinated with any candidate or campaign committee.

CONCLUSION

The year 1996 was a watershed in American politics. Special interest groups, individuals, and political parties inundated the air waves with unregulated issue-oriented advertisements that undoubtedly had an impact on federal elections. In some U.S. House races, more money was spent on issue advocacy than was spent by the two major-party candidates combined. Election law reformers are concerned that the success of these issue spots will embolden political activists to use them even more aggressively in future campaigns. Clearer legal standards may emerge from litigation arising out of the 1996 issue advocacy campaigns. In the meantime, the law in this high-stakes area remains uncertain.

A variety of proposals to regulate issue advocacy now exist. They range from attempts to require disclosure of the sources of funding for public communications that mention a clearly identified candidate within ninety days of an election, to proposals to define such communications as "express advocacy," thereby limiting the funding sources to "hard money," and closing off labor and corporate funding. (See document 7.10 and the reform proposals formulated by Ornstein, Mann, Taylor, Malbin, and Corrado [document 9.9].) One of the strategies of reformers is to pass new legislation restricting issue advocacy (with a lengthy congressional factual record demonstrating the corrupting potential of such spending) and then challenge the Supreme Court to allow Congress to expand the definition of express advocacy, or otherwise allow regulation of issue advocacy if it can be shown to be a form of campaign spending.

NOTES

1. The D.C. Circuit cited with approval another issue advocacy case decided in 1972 by the Second Circuit, *United States* v. *National Committee for Impeachment*, 469 F.2d 1135, 1142 (2d Cir. 1972). The Department of Justice had prosecuted a group that took out newspaper advertisements urging the impeachment of President Nixon for failure to register as a political committee under the disclosure provisions of the 1971 act (document 2.8). The Second Circuit held that communications primarily directed toward advocacy of a position on a public issue, rather than urging a vote for or against a candidate, did not qualify as an election expenditure, and thus did not trigger political committee status.

2. The Court did not state whether the foregoing list was exhaustive. Most commentators, however, do not regard the list as being so, and this reading is consistent with language in the Court's opinion. *Buckley,* 424 U.S. at 44 n.52 (describing the list of terms as "express words of advocacy of election or defeat, *such as* 'vote for,' 'elect' . . .") (emphasis added).

3. Because the Court found the MCFL newsletter to be express advocacy, it ruled that MCFL's expenditures violated the FECA. The Court then ruled that the ban on federal election expenditures by incorporated entities was unconstitutional as applied to issue-oriented organizations such as MCFL, and other 501(c)(4)-type organizations that are not themselves funded by for-profit corporations. In reaching this conclusion, the Court first noted that the expenditures were made independently of any candidate ("independent expenditures 'produce speech at the core of the First Amendment'") (quoting *Federal Election*

Commission v. *National Conservative Political Action Committee,* 470 U.S. 480, 493 (1985) ("*NCPAC*") (invalidating a $1,000 cap on independent PAC expenditures); *Buckley,* 424 U.S. at 39 (invalidating $1,000 limit on independent individual expenditures). Second, the Court relied on several institutional aspects of MCFL that differentiated the organization from most corporations. These aspects included that MCFL "was formed for the express purpose of promoting political ideas, and cannot engage in business activities," "has no shareholders or other persons affiliated so as to have a claim on its assets or earnings," and "was not established by a business corporation or a labor union, and [has a] policy not to accept contributions from such entities"; *MCFL,* 479 U.S. at 264. For a fuller discussion of *MCFL,* see chapter 3.

4. *MCFL,* 479 U.S. at 249 (concluding that the MCFL publication provides "*in effect* an explicit directive: vote for these (named) candidates") (emphasis added); (acknowledging that the electoral message in MCFL is "marginally less direct than 'Vote for Smith' [and the other terms identified in *Buckley*]").

5. See *Colorado Republican Federal Campaign Committee* v. *Federal Election Commission,* 116 S. Ct. 2309 (1996) (holding that political parties have a constitutional right to make unlimited independent expenditures) (document 3.4).

6. In *Colorado Republican,* the Supreme Court remanded to the lower courts the issue of whether political parties have a constitutional right to make unlimited coordinated expenditures.

7. "Proposed Rules," *Federal Register,* vol. 62, no. 86 (May 5, 1997), p. 24372.

Issue advocacy was a hot topic during the 1996 congressional elections. The AFL-CIO launched a widely publicized $35 million advertising effort to highlight issues unfavorable to House Republicans. The U.S. Chamber of Commerce and other organizations friendly to Republicans sponsored an advertising blitz in response. This is a newspaper article describing how these issue advocacy air wars played out in several key congressional districts.

———————

PHILADELPHIA—The message in the TV ads is unmistakable: Don't re-elect this guy. He's tight with Newt Gingrich. He'll hurt you.

On television and radio last week, in 32 congressional districts across 26 states, the AFL-CIO has been hammering away at Republican incumbents. The ads in first-term Rep. Phil English's Erie, PA., district show a mother worrying aloud. "My husband and I both work," she says. "And next year, we'll have two kids in college."

To which the announcer adds: "Working families are struggling. But Congressman Phil English voted with Newt Gingrich to cut college loans, while giving tax breaks to the wealthy."

About the only thing the ad doesn't tell viewers is to throw English out of office.

And there's a good reason for that.

By avoiding such explicit advocacy, the union steers around campaign law and the 1943 ban on unions spending money to influence a federal election [see chapter 2].

The AFL-CIO is in good company. Unaccounted millions are being spent this year on a new kind of political pitch: "issue ads." Ask Jon D. Fox in Montgomery County, PA., one of labor's targets. Or Robert G. Torricelli in New Jersey, under fire from the GOP. Or Bob Dole. Or Bill Clinton.

Such spending was supposed to be regulated by the post-Watergate campaign laws that limit giving and spending and require public disclosure of those activities.

But a series of federal court decisions has allowed unlimited sums from any source to be spent on so-called issue advocacy ads like the one aimed at English. These ads ostensibly promote or criticize public policy positions—without using explicit words like "vote for" or "defeat." That places them beyond the reach of election laws, courts have ruled.

———

Pushing Rules to the Edge

This year, issue ads have emerged as the weapon of choice on the political battlefield from groups ranging from the AFL-CIO to the U.S. Chamber of Commerce, the Sierra Club and the major parties.

The upshot, says Trevor Potter, former chairman of the Federal Election Commission, is that "this election is going to tell everyone that there really isn't any barrier anymore to spending funds to influence an election."

Donald Simon, executive vice president and counsel to Common Cause, the self-styled citizens' lobby, describes issue ads more bluntly: "It provides an easy way to cheat."

"It's a scam," said Simon. "What we're seeing as issue ads are candidate campaign ads dressed up and called issue ads for the purpose of evading the law."

Bruce Josten, an executive vice president of the U.S. Chamber of Commerce, which is spearheading its own issue ad campaign to counter the AFL-CIO barrage and to keep Congress Republican, said: "Modern political history is being made, because the magnitude of these ads is greater than any previous election. You're seeing a gigantic leap in the number of these ads."

The escalation has been fueled largely by two events.

Last fall, the AFL-CIO announced plans for a $35 million political mobilization, including radio and TV ads aimed at Republicans in Congress, and paid for with $1.80 out of each union member's annual dues.

And in February, a federal judge in Maine tossed out an FEC proposal to regulate such ads. [*Maine Right to Life Committee, Inc.* v. *Federal Election Commission,* 914 F. Supp. 8 (D. Me.), *aff'd* 98 F.3d 1 (1st Cir. 1996), excerpted in the introduction to chapter 7.]

"What you're seeing is a lot more of these organizations pushing against the line, seeing how far they can go," said Lawrence Noble, the FEC's general counsel.

Earlier this year, Noble warned the House oversight Committee that the latest court rulings meant "labor unions and corporations can spend unlimited amounts of 'soft' money to mail the letters, publish the ads or broadcast the commercials day and night right up to the election. . . . And not only is there no limit on the source or amount of the money, but there is no requirement that either the expenditures or the source of the money be disclosed."

Events have proven him right.

One campaign finance expert, Darrell West, a Brown University political scientist, calls the election rules "so loose now you can drive a Mack truck through them."

Even the judge who threw out the FEC's bid to regulate the ads acknowledged in his ruling that it did not "give much recognition to the policy of the election statute to keep corporate money from influencing elections."

But judges worry that reining in such ads would trample on the First Amendment. Thus, the latest rulings have become a road map for getting around federal election laws.

Now, almost anything goes.

Last year, for example, a federal judge in Virginia ruled that a 30-second Christian Action Network TV spot attacking Bill Clinton just before the 1992 election wasn't "express advocacy." [*Federal Election Commission* v. *Christian Action Network,* 894 F. Supp. 946 (W.D. Va.), *aff'd mem.* 92 F.3d 1178 (4th Cir. 1996), document 7.7A.]

This despite the fact that the ad told of Clinton's support for "radical" homosexual causes, and depicted his face dissolving into a black-and-white negative that gave him, in the judge's view, "a sinister and threatening appearance."

But the judge noted: "Nowhere in the commercial were viewers asked to vote against" anyone.

Corporations have been banned since 1907 from direct spending to influence a federal election; unions, since 1943. But issue ads have effectively reopened the doors to union and company money. So, too, individuals, other special interests and the political parties.

Hitting Vulnerable Races

Fox, the first-term Republican from Montgomery County, knows this only too well.

Two years ago, he won with less than 50 percent of the vote—a sign of vulnerability that the AFL-CIO is working hard to exploit. The union has run seven radio ad campaigns against Fox since July 1995—ads that Fox's people estimate have cost $550,000. (Union officials say this year's anti-Fox ads have cost $400,000.)

In one of the ads, the anti-Fox message—much like the ad aimed at English in Erie last week—was clear: "Last year," the announcer said, "Jon Fox voted with Newt Gingrich to cut Medicare, and give new tax breaks to the wealthy."

The U.S. Chamber of Commerce has responded to the labor blitz by bringing 29 industry groups under one umbrella known as The Coalition to mount its own issue ads. "What we're trying to do is create an informed dialogue," said the chamber's Josten.

The Clinton-Dole race is another case in point.

The law limits each party to spending no more than $12 million on its presidential candidate.

But by offering ads that ostensibly discuss policy, the parties can use what critics claim is the biggest loophole of all: "soft money."

Each party can bankroll its ads with some of the tens of millions raised this year for so-called party-building.

There's no limit on raising such funds.

"Both parties are really pushing the envelope," said Lisa Rosenberg, who monitors issue ads for the nonpartisan Center for Responsive Politics, which tracks campaign money.

"The presidential campaigns are publicly funded, and when you start allowing private money to filter in, you defeat the purpose of public funding, which is to prevent the candidates from being beholden to large contributors."

Buckley v. *Valeo,* 519 F. 2d 821 (D.C. Cir. 1975), *aff'd* in part, *rev'd* in part, 424 U.S. 1 (1976)

DOCUMENT 7.2

The D.C. Circuit upheld almost all of the provisions of the 1974 Federal Election Campaign Act (document 2.9) in the face of a challenge from a broad coalition of conservatives (Senator James Buckley) and liberals (Senator Eugene McCarthy and the American Civil Liberties Union). However, the D.C. Circuit did strike down as unconstitutional a requirement to disclose the names of all donors who gave more than $10 to groups engaging in issue advocacy. The court found the provision unconstitutionally overbroad. Below are excerpts from that decision.

[In *Buckley,* the court of appeals invalidated then sec. 437a of FECA (2 U.S.C. §437a), which provided in part:

Any person (other than an individual) who expends any funds or commits any act directed to the public for the purpose of influencing the outcome of an election, or who publishes or broadcasts to the public any material referring to a candidate (by name, description, or other reference) advocating the election or defeat of such candidate, setting forth the candidate's position on any public issue, his voting record, or other official acts (in the case of a candidate who holds or has held Federal office), or otherwise designed to influence individuals to cast their votes for or against such candidate or to withhold their votes from such candidate shall file reports with the Commission as if such person were a political committee.]

. . .

Section 437a is susceptible to a reading necessitating reporting by groups whose only connection with the elective process arises from completely nonpartisan public discussion of issues of public importance. For while the reporting requirement plainly obtains when a group publishes or broadcasts to the public material "set[ting] forth a candidate's position on any public issue, his voting record, or other official acts" with a "design . . . to influence" voting at an election, it is not at all certain that the requirement is inoperative where those activities are unaccompanied by any such design.

Thus section 437a calls for disclosure, for example, by plaintiff Human Events, Inc., the publisher of a weekly newspaper devoted primarily to events of political importance and interest, and to discussion of public issues, public officials, political leaders and candidates.

. . .

[S]ection 437a may also demand disclosure by plaintiff New York Civil Liberties Union. The District Court found that this organization is forbidden by the constitution and policies of its parent body from endorsing or opposing any candidate for public office, but that it does engage publicly in nonpartisan activities which "frequently and necessarily refer to, praise, criticize, set forth, describe or rate the conduct or actions of clearly identified public officials who may also happen to be candidates for federal office." The organization also publicizes in newsletters and other publications the civil liberties voting records, positions and actions of elected public officials, some of whom are candidates for federal office. Since the published material regularly gives "candidates' positions on . . . public issues, [their] voting records, or other official acts," the organization may be subject to section 437a.

. . .

As we have said, [Section 437a] may undertake to compel disclosure by groups that do no more than discuss issues of public interest on a wholly nonpartisan basis. To be sure, any discussion of important public questions can possibly exert some influence on the outcome of an election preceding which they were campaign issues. But unlike contributions and expenditures made solely with a view to influencing the nomination or election of a candidate, see 2 U.S.C. §§ 431(e), 431(f), issue discussions unwedded to the cause of a particular candidate hardly threaten the purity of elections. Moreover, and very importantly, such discussions are vital and indispensable to a free society and an informed electorate. Thus the interest of a group engaging in nonpartisan discussion ascends to a high plane, while the governmental interest in disclosure correspondingly diminishes.

The Supreme Court has indicated quite plainly that groups seeking only to advance discussion of public issues or to influence public opinion cannot be equated to groups whose relation to political processes is direct and intimate.

. . .

Public discussion of public issues which also are campaign issues readily and often unavoidably draws in candidates and their positions, their voting records and other official conduct. Discussions of those issues, and as well more positive efforts to influence public opinion on them, tend naturally and inexorably to exert some influence on voting at elections. In this milieu, where do "purpose" and "design . . . to influence" draw the line? Do they connote subjectively a state of mind, or objectively only a propensity to influence? Do they require, irrespective of state of mind, a capability of influencing, and if so how substantial a capability? What do they demand with respect to materials which "advocate the election or defeat of [a] candidate," or which "set . . . forth the candidate's position on [a] public issue" or "his voting record," beyond the inherent tendency of those materials to influence? What references to "other official acts" of the candidate, with what mental element, bring the section into play? To these questions, among a multitude of others, neither the text nor the legislative history of section 437a supplies any clear answer. And while we have continued our struggle for an interpretation of section 437a which might bypass its vagueness and overbreadth difficulties, we have been unable to do so.

. . .

Below are excerpts from the Supreme Court's landmark ruling in *Buckley* v. *Valeo*. *Buckley* (document 3.1) was a facial constitutional challenge to the Federal Election Campaign Act of 1971 as amended in 1974 (document 2.9). The plaintiffs included a presidential candidate and a sitting United States Senator. *Buckley* was the high Court's first pronouncement on the constitutional protections that exist for issue advocacy. The Court established the "express advocacy" test for distinguishing between those communications that contain explicit words of election or defeat of a candidate, and those communications, like issue advocacy, that do not. As these excerpts show, the Court ruled in *Buckley* that express advocacy can be regulated consistent with the Constitution, but that issue advocacy cannot be restricted.

. . .

Discussion of public issues and debate on the qualifications of candidates are integral to the operation of the system of government established by our Constitution. The First Amendment affords the broadest protection to such political expression in order "to assure [the] unfettered interchanges of ideas for the bringing about of political and social changes desired by the people." *Roth* v. *United States,* 354 U.S. 476, 484 (1957). Although First Amendment protections are not confined to "the exposition of ideas," *Winters* v. *New York,* 333 U.S. 507, 510 (1948),

there is practically universal agreement that a major purpose of that Amendment was to protect the free discussion of governmental affairs, . . . of course includ[ing] discussions of candidates . . . .

Mills v. *Alabama.* 384 U.S. 214, 218 (1966). This no more than reflects our "profound national commitment to the principle that debate on public issues should be uninhibited, robust, and wide-open," *New York Times Co.* v. *Sullivan,* 376 U.S. 254, 270 (1964).

. . .

A restriction on the amount of money a person or group can spend on political communication during a campaign necessarily reduces the quantity of expression by restricting the number of issues discussed, the depth of their exploration, and the size of the audience reached.[1] This is because virtually

---

1. Being free to engage in unlimited political expression subject to a ceiling on expenditures is like being free to drive an automobile as far and as often as one desires on a single tank of gasoline.

every means of communicating ideas in today's mass society requires the expenditure of money. The distribution of the humblest handbill or leaflet entails printing, paper, and circulation costs. Speeches and rallies generally necessitate hiring a hall and publicizing the event. The electorate's increasing dependence on television, radio, and other mass media for news and information has made these expensive modes of communication indispensable instruments of effective political speech.

. . .

Section 608(e)(1) provides that

[n]o person may make any expenditure . . . relative to a clearly identified candidate during a calendar year which, when added to all other expenditures made by such person during the year advocating the election or defeat of such candidate, exceeds $1,000.

The plain effect of § 608(e)(1) is to prohibit all individuals, who are neither candidates nor owners of institutional press facilities, and all groups, except political parties and campaign organizations, from voicing their views "relative to a clearly identified candidate" through means that entail aggregate expenditures of more than $1,000 during a calendar year. The provision, for example, would make it a federal criminal offense for a person or association to place a single one-quarter page advertisement "relative to a clearly identified candidate" in a major metropolitan newspaper.[2]

Before examining the interests advanced in support of § 608(e)(1)'s expenditure ceiling, consideration must be given to appellants' contention that the provision is unconstitutionally vague. Close examination of the specificity of the statutory limitation is required where, as here, the legislation imposes criminal penalties in an area permeated by First Amendment interests. See *Smith* v. *Goguen*, 415 U.S. 566, 573 (1974); *Cramp* v. *Board of Public Instruction*, 368 U.S. 278, 287–288 (1961); *Smith* v. *California*, 361 U.S. 147, 151 (1959).[3] The test is whether the language of § 608(e)(1) affords the "[p]recision of regulation [that] must be the touchstone in an area so closely touching our most precious freedoms." *NAACP* v. *Button*, 371 U.S., at 438.

The key operative language of the provision limits "any expenditure . . . relative to a clearly identified candidate." Although "expenditure," "clearly identified," and "candidate" are defined in the Act, there is no definition clarifying what expenditures are "relative to" a candidate. The use of so indefinite a phrase as "relative to" a candidate fails to clearly mark the boundary between permissible and impermissible speech, unless other portions of § 608(e)(1) make sufficiently explicit the range of expenditures covered by the limitation. The section prohibits "any expenditure . . . relative to a clearly identified candidate

2. [Ed. note: The record indicates that, as of January 1, 1975, one full-page advertisement in a daily edition of a certain metropolitan newspaper cost $6,971.04—almost seven times the annual limit on expenditures "relative to" a particular candidate imposed on the vast majority of individual citizens and associations by § 608(e)(1).]

3. In such circumstances, vague laws may not only "trap the innocent by not providing fair warning" or foster "arbitrary and discriminatory application" but also operate to inhibit protected expression by inducing "citizens to 'steer far wider of the unlawful zone' . . . than if the boundaries of the forbidden areas were clearly marked." *Grayned* v. *City of Rockford*, 408 U.S. 104, 108–109 (1972), quoting *Baggett* v. *Bullitt*, 377 U.S. 360, 372 (1964), quoting *Speiser* v. *Randall*, 357 U.S. 513, 526 (1958). "Because First Amendment freedoms need breathing space to survive, government may regulate in the area only with narrow specificity." *NAACP* v. *Button*, 371 U.S. 415, 433 (1963).

during a calendar year which, *when added to all other expenditures . . . advocating the election or defeat of such candidate,* exceeds $1,000." (Emphasis added.) This context clearly permits, if indeed it does not require, the phrase "relative to" a candidate to be read to mean "advocat[ing] the election or defeat of" a candidate.

But while such a construction of 608(e)(1) refocuses the vagueness question, the Court of Appeals was mistaken in thinking that this construction eliminates the problem of unconstitutional vagueness altogether. For the distinction between discussion of issues and candidates and advocacy of election or defeat of candidates may often dissolve in practical application. Candidates, especially incumbents, are intimately tied to public issues involving legislative proposals and governmental actions. Not only do candidates campaign on the basis of their positions on various public issues, but campaigns themselves generate issues of public interest. In an analogous context, this Court in *Thomas* v. *Collins,* 323 U.S. 516 (1945), observed:

Whether words intended and designed to fall short of invitation would miss that mark is a question both of intent and of effect. No speaker, in such circumstances, safely could assume that anything he might say upon the general subject would not be understood by some as an invitation. In short, the supposedly clear-cut distinction between discussion, laudation, general advocacy, and solicitation puts the speaker in these circumstances wholly at the mercy of the varied understanding of his hearers and consequently of whatever inference may be drawn as to his intent and meaning.

Such a distinction offers no security for free discussion. In these conditions it blankets with uncertainty whatever may be said. It compels the speaker to hedge and trim.

Id., at 535.

. . .

The constitutional deficiencies described in *Thomas* v. *Collins* can be avoided only by reading § 608(3)(1) as limited to communications that include explicit words of advocacy of election or defeat of a candidate, much as the definition of "clearly identified" in § 608(e)(2) requires that an explicit and unambiguous reference to the candidate appear as part of the communication. This is the reading of the provision suggested by the non-governmental appellees in arguing that "[f]unds spent to propagate one's views on issues without expressly calling for a candidate's election or defeat are thus not covered." We agree that in order to preserve the provision against invalidation on vagueness grounds, § 608(e)(1) must be construed to apply only to expenditures for communications that, in express terms advocate the election or defeat of a clearly identified candidate for federal office.[4]

. . .

C. SECTION 434(3)
Section 434(e) requires "[e]very person (other than a political committee or candidate) who makes contributions or expenditures" aggregating over $100 in a calendar year "other than by contribution to a political committee or candidate" to file a statement with the Commission.

---

4. This construction would restrict the application of § 608(e)(1) to communications containing express words of advocacy of election or defeat, such as "vote for," "elect," "support," "cast your ballot for," "Smith for Congress," "vote against," "defeat," "reject."

2. Vagueness Problems

In its effort to be all-inclusive, however, [Section 434(e)] raises serious problems of vagueness, particularly treacherous where, as here, the violation of its terms carries criminal penalties and fear of incurring these sanctions may deter those who seek to exercise protected First Amendment rights.

Section 434(e) applies to "[e]very person . . . who makes contributions or expenditures." "Contributions" and "expenditures" are defined in parallel provisions in terms of the use of money or other valuable assets "for the purpose of . . . influencing" the nomination or election of candidates for federal office. It is the ambiguity of this phrase that poses constitutional problems.

Due process requires that a criminal statute provide adequate notice to a person of ordinary intelligence that his contemplated conduct is illegal, for "no man shall be held criminally responsible for conduct which he could not reasonably understand to be proscribed." *United States* v. *Harriss,* 347 U.S. 612, 617 (1954). *See also Papachristou* v. *City of Jacksonville,* 405 U.S. 156 (1972). Where First Amendment rights are involved, an even "greater degree of specificity" is required. *Smith* v. *Goguen,* 415 U.S. at 573. See *Grayned* v. *City of Rockford,* 408 U.S. 104, 109 (1972); *Kunz* v. *New York,* 340 U.S. 290 (1951).

There is no legislative history to guide us in determining the scope of the critical phrase "for the purpose of . . . influencing." It appears to have been adopted without comment from earlier disclosure Acts.

. . .

When we attempt to define "expenditure" . . . we encounter line-drawing problems of the sort we faced in 18 U.S.C. § 608(e)(1). Although the phrase, "for the purpose of . . . influencing" an election or nomination, differs from the language used in § 608(e)(1), it shares the same potential for encompassing both issue discussion and advocacy of a political result. The general requirement that "political committees" and candidates disclose their expenditures could raise similar vagueness problems, for "political committee" is defined only in terms of amount of annual "contributions" and "expenditures," and could be interpreted to reach groups engaged purely in issue discussion. The lower courts have construed the words "political committee" more narrowly. To fulfill the purposes of the Act, they need only encompass organizations that are under the control of a candidate or the major purpose of which is the nomination or election of a candidate. Expenditures of candidates and of "political committees," so construed, can be assumed to fall within the core area sought to be addressed by Congress. They are, by definition, campaign related.

But when the maker of the expenditure is not within these categories—when it is an individual other than a candidate or a group other than a "political committee"—the relation of the information sought to the purposes of the Act may be too remote. To insure that the reach of § 434(e) is not impermissibly broad, we construe "expenditure" for purposes of that section in the same way we construed the terms of § 608(e)—to reach only funds used for communications that expressly advocate the election or defeat of a clearly identified candidate. This reading is directed precisely to that spending that is unambiguously related to the campaign of a particular federal candidate. . . .

FEC v. *Massachusetts Citizens for Life* (*MCFL*) was the Supreme Court's first occasion to apply the "express advocacy" test announced in *Buckley*. *MCFL* concerned whether the Federal Election Commission could regulate a purportedly nonpartisan voting guide published by a nonprofit, issue-oriented group. Many commentators contend that the "express advocacy" test leaves little room for regulation of election-related communications. However, the Court found the test to be satisfied in *MCFL* and ruled that the FEC could regulate the communication.

. . .

B.

In September 1978, MCFL prepared and distributed a "Special Edition" prior to the September 1978 primary elections. While the May 1978 newsletter had been mailed to 2,109 people and the October 1978 newsletter to 3,119 people, more than 100,000 copies of the "Special Edition" were printed for distribution. The front page of the publication was headlined "EVERYTHING YOU NEED TO KNOW TO VOTE PRO-LIFE," and readers were admonished that "[n]o pro-life candidate can win in November without your vote in September." "VOTE PRO-LIFE" was printed in large bold-faced letters on the back page, and a coupon was provided to be clipped and taken to the polls to remind voters of the names of the "pro-life" candidates. Next to the exhortation to vote "pro-life" was a disclaimer: "This special election edition does not represent an endorsement of any particular candidate."

To aid the reader in selecting candidates, the flyer listed the candidates for each state and federal office in every voting district in Massachusetts, and identified each one as either supporting or opposing what MCFL regarded as the correct position on three issues. A "y" indicated that a candidate supported the MCFL view on a particular issue and an "n" indicated that the candidate opposed it. An asterisk was placed next to the names of those incumbents who had made a "special contribution to the unborn in maintaining a 100% pro-life voting record in the state house by actively supporting MCFL legislation." While some 400 candidates were running for office in the primary, the "Special Edition" featured the photographs of only 13. These 13 had received a triple "y" rating, or were identified either as having a 100% favorable voting record or as having stated a position consistent with that of MCFL. No candidate whose photograph was featured had received even one "n" rating.

. . .

[MCFL] argues that the definition of an expenditure under § 441b necessarily incorporates the requirement that a communication "expressly advocate" the election of candidates, and that its "Special Edition" does not constitute express advocacy. The argument relies on the portion of *Buckley* v. *Valeo*, 424 U.S. 1(1976) [documents 3.1 and 7.4], that upheld the disclosure requirement for expenditures by individuals other than candidates and by groups other than political committees. See 2 U.S.C. § 434(c). There, in order to avoid problems of overbreadth, the Court held that the term "expenditure" encompassed "only funds used for communications that expressly advocate the election or defeat of a clearly identified candidate." 424 U.S., at 80 (footnote omitted). The rationale for this holding was:

"The distinction between discussion of issues and candidates and advocacy of election or defeat of candidates may often dissolve in practical application. Candidates, especially incumbents, are intimately tied to public issues involving legislative proposals and governmental actions. Not only do candidates campaign on the basis of their positions on various issues, but campaigns themselves generate issues of public interest." *Id.*, at 42 (footnote omitted).

We agree with [MCFL] that this rationale requires a similar construction of the more intrusive provision that directly regulates independent spending. We therefore hold that an expenditure must constitute "express advocacy" in order to be subject to the prohibition of § 441b. We also hold, however, that the publication of the "Special Edition" constitutes "express advocacy."

Buckley adopted the "express advocacy" requirement to distinguish discussion of issues and candidates from more pointed exhortations to vote for particular persons. We therefore concluded in that case that a finding of "express advocacy" depended upon the use of language such as "vote for," "elect," "support," etc., *Buckley, supra*, at 44, n. 52. Just such an exhortation appears in the "Special Edition." The publication not only urges voters to vote for "pro-life" candidates, but also identifies and provides photographs of specific candidates fitting that description. The Edition cannot be regarded as a mere discussion of public issues that by their nature raise the names of certain politicians. Rather, it provides in effect an explicit directive: vote for these (named) candidates. The fact that this message is marginally less direct than "Vote for Smith" does not change its essential nature. The Edition goes beyond issue discussion to express electoral advocacy. The disclaimer of endorsement cannot negate this fact. The "Special Edition" thus falls squarely within § 441b, for it represents express advocacy of the election of particular candidates distributed to members of the general public.

. . .

Federal Election Commission v. Furgatch, 807 F.2d 857 (9th Cir. 1987), cert. denied, 484 U.S. 850 (1987)

During the last ten years, the lower federal courts have struggled to apply the "express advocacy" test, often with what appears to be radically different results. One of the most pro-regulatory decisions was issued by the United States Court of Appeals for the Ninth Circuit in *Federal Election Commission* v. *Furgatch. Furgatch* is commonly cited by commentators who seek to aggressively regulate campaign-related communications. On the other end of the spectrum is the First Circuit's ruling in *Faucher* v. *Federal Election Commission,* 928 F.2d 468 (1st Cir. 1991), *cert. denied,* 502 U.S. 820 (1991), in which court strictly applied the "express advocacy" test. The First Circuit has been a difficult forum for the FEC ever since. Excerpts from both *Furgatch* and *Faucher* (document 7.6) follow.

. . .

I.

On October 28, 1980, one week prior to the 1980 presidential election, the *New York Times* published a full page advertisement captioned "Don't let him do it," placed and paid for by Harvey Furgatch. The advertisement read:

DON'T LET HIM DO IT.

The President of the United States continues degrading the electoral process and lessening the prestige of the office.

It was evident months ago when his running mate outrageously suggested Ted Kennedy was unpatriotic. The President remained silent.

And we let him.

It continued when the President himself accused Ronald Reagan of being unpatriotic.

And we let him do it again.

In recent weeks, [Jimmy] Carter has tried to buy entire cities, the steel industry, the auto industry, and others with public funds.

We are letting him do it.

He continues to cultivate the fears, not the hopes, of the voting public by suggesting the choice is between "peace and war," "black or white," "north or south," and "Jew vs. Christian." His meanness of spirit is divisive and reckless McCarthyism at its worst. And from a man who once asked, "Why Not the Best?"

It is an attempt to hide his own record, or lack of it. If he succeeds the country will be burdened with four more years of incoherences, ineptness and illusion, as he leaves a legacy of low-level campaigning. DON'T LET HIM DO IT.

. . .

III.

The FEC argues that Furgatch's advertisement expressly advocates the defeat of Jimmy Carter and therefore is an independent expenditure which must be reported to the FEC. The examples of express advocacy contained in the *Buckley* [documents 3.1 and 7.3] opinion (i.e., "vote for," "support," etc.), the FEC argues, merely provide guidelines for determining what constitutes "express advocacy." Whether those words are contained in the advertisement is not determinative. The test is whether or not the advertisement contains a message advocating the defeat of a political candidate. Furgatch's advertisement, the FEC contends, contains an unequivocal message that Carter must not "succeed" in "burden[ing]" the country with "four more years" of his allegedly harmful leadership.

The FEC further argues that the advertisement is, in the words of the Supreme Court, "unambiguously related to the campaign of a particular federal candidate." *Buckley*, 424 U.S. at 80. Nothing more, it contends, is required to place this advertisement under coverage of the Act. The FEC grounds this argument on the Court's effort in *Buckley* to distinguish between speech that pertains only to candidates and their campaigns and speech revolving around political issues in general. The FEC argues that because the advertisement discusses Carter, the candidate, rather than the political issues, Furgatch must report the expenditure.

Furgatch responds that the mere raising of any question on this issue demonstrates that it is not express advocacy. We would not be debating the meaning of the advertisement, he contends, if it were express. He argues that the words "don't let him do it" do not expressly call for Carter's defeat at the polls but an end to his "attempt to hide his own record, or lack of it." The advertisement, according to Furgatch, is merely a warning that Carter will be reelected if the public allows him to continue to use "low-level campaign tactics."

. . .

IV.

As this litigation demonstrates, the "express advocacy" language of *Buckley* and section 431(17) does not draw a bright and unambiguous line. We are called upon to interpret and refine that standard here. Mindful of the Supreme Court's directive that, where First Amendment concerns are present, we must construe the words of the regulatory statute precisely and narrowly, only as far as is necessary to further the purposes of the Act, we first examine those purposes in some detail for guidance.

In *Buckley*, the Court described the function of section 434(e) as follows:

Section 434(e) is part of Congress' effort to achieve "total disclosure" by reaching "every kind of political activity" in order to insure that the voters are fully informed and to achieve through publicity the maximum deterrence to corruption and undue influence possible. The provision is responsive to the legitimate fear that efforts would be made, as they had been in the past, to avoid the disclosure requirements by routing financial support of candidates through avenues not explicitly covered by the general provisions of the Act.

424 U.S. at 76.

Thus there are two important goals behind these disclosure provisions. The first, that of keeping the electorate fully informed of the sources of campaign-directed speech and the possible connections between the speaker and individual candidates, derives directly from the primary concern of the First Amendment. The vision of a free and open marketplace of ideas is based on the assumption that the people should be exposed to speech on all sides, so that they may freely evaluate and choose from among competing points of view. One goal of the First Amendment, then, is to ensure that the individual citizen has available all the information necessary to allow him to properly evaluate speech.

Information about the composition of a candidate's constituency, the sources of a candidate's support, and the impact that such financial support may have on the candidate's stand on the issues or future performance may be crucial to the individual's choice from among the several competitors for his vote. . . . Therefore, disclosure requirements which may at times inhibit the free speech that is so dearly protected by the First Amendment, are indispensable to the proper and effective exercise of First Amendment rights. The allowance of free expression loses considerable value if expression is only partial.

The other major purpose of the disclosure provision is to deter or expose corruption, and therefore to minimize the influence that unaccountable interest groups and individuals can have on elected federal officials. The disclosure requirement is particularly directed at attempts by candidates to circumvent the statutory limits on their own expenditures through close and secretive relationships with apparently "independent" campaign spenders. The Supreme Court noted that efforts had been made in the past to avoid disclosure requirements by the routing of campaign contributions through unregulated independent advertising. Since *Buckley* was decided, such practices have apparently become more widespread in federal elections, and the need for controls more urgent. *See, e.g.,* "The $676,000 Cleanup," *The New Republic,* Vol. 195, No. 22 (December 1, 1986) at 7.

We conclude that the Act's disclosure provisions serve an important Congressional policy and a very strong First Amendment interest. Properly applied, they will have only a "reasonable and minimally restrictive" effect on the exercise of First Amendment rights. *Buckley,* 424 U.S. at 82. Although we may not place burdens on the freedom of speech beyond what is strictly necessary to further the purposes of the Act, we must be just as careful to ensure that those purposes are fully carried out, that they are not cleverly circumvented, or thwarted by a rigid construction of the terms of the Act. We must read section 434(c) so as to prevent speech that is clearly intended to affect the outcome of a federal election from escaping, either fortuitously or by design, the coverage of the Act. This concern leads us to fashion a more comprehensive approach to the delimitation of "express advocacy," and to reject some of the overly constrictive rules of interpretation that the parties urge for our adoption.

V.

A.

We begin with the proposition that "express advocacy" is not strictly limited to communications using certain key phrases. The short list of words included in the Supreme Court's opinion in *Buckley* does not exhaust the capacity of the English language to expressly advocate the election or defeat of a candidate. A test requiring the magic words "elect," "support," etc., or their nearly perfect synonyms for a finding of express advocacy would preserve the First Amendment right of unfettered expression only at the expense of eviscerating the Federal Election Campaign Act. "Independent" campaign spenders working on behalf of candidates could remain just beyond the reach of the Act by avoiding certain key words while conveying a message that is unmistakably directed to the election or defeat of a named candidate.

B.

A proper understanding of the speaker's message can best be obtained by considering speech as a whole. Comprehension often requires inferences from the relation of one part of speech to another. The entirety may give a clear impression that is never succinctly stated in a single phrase or sentence. Similarly, a stray comment viewed in isolation may suggest an idea that is only peripheral to the primary purpose of speech as a whole. Furgatch would have us reject intra-textual interpretation and construe each part of speech independently, requiring express advocacy from specific phrases rather than from speech in its entirety.

We reject the suggestion that we isolate each sentence and act as if it bears no relation to its neighbors. This is not to say that we will not examine each sentence in an effort to understand the whole. We only recognize that the whole consists of its parts in relation to each other.

. . .

D.

More problematic than use of "magic words" or inquiry into subjective intent are questions of context. The FEC argues, for example, that this advertisement cannot be construed outside its temporal context, the 1980 presidential election. Furgatch, on the other hand, maintains that the court must find express advocacy in the speech itself, without reference to external circumstances.

The problem of the context of speech goes to the heart of some of the most difficult First Amendment questions. The doctrines of subversive speech, "fighting words," libel, and speech in the workplace and in public fora illustrate that when and where speech takes place can determine its legal significance. In these instances, context is one of the crucial factors making these kinds of speech regulable. First Amendment doctrine has long recognized that words take part of their meaning and effect from the environment in which they are spoken. When the constitutional and statutory standard is "express advocacy," however, the weight that we give to the context of speech declines considerably. Our concern here is with the clarity of the communication rather than its harmful effects. Context remains a consideration, but an ancillary one, peripheral to the words themselves.

. . .

VI.

With these principles in mind, we propose a standard for "express advocacy" that will preserve the efficacy of the Act without treading upon the freedom of political expression. We conclude that speech need not include any of the words listed in *Buckley* to be express advocacy under the Act, but it must, when read as a whole, and with limited reference to external events, be susceptible of no other reasonable interpretation but as an exhortation to vote for or against a specific candidate. This standard can be broken into three main components. First, even if it is not presented in the clearest, most explicit language, speech is "express" for present purposes if its message is unmistakable and unambiguous, suggestive of only one plausible meaning. Second, speech may only be termed "advocacy" if it presents a clear plea for action, and thus speech that is merely informative is not covered by the Act. Finally, it must be clear what action is advocated. Speech cannot be "express advocacy of the election or defeat of a clearly identified candidate" when reasonable minds could differ as to whether it encourages a vote for or against a candidate or encourages the reader to take some other kind of action.

We emphasize that if any reasonable alternative reading of speech can be suggested, it cannot be express advocacy subject to the Act's disclosure requirements. This is necessary and sufficient to prevent a chill on forms of speech other than the campaign advertising regulated by the Act. At the same time, however, the court is not forced under this standard to ignore the plain meaning of campaign-related speech in a search for certain fixed indicators of "express advocacy."

VII.

Applying this standard to Furgatch's advertisement, we reject the district court's ruling that it does not expressly advocate the defeat of Jimmy Carter. We have no doubt that the ad asks the public to vote against Carter. It cannot be read in the way that Furgatch suggests.

. . .

In Furgatch's advertisement we are presented with an express call to action, but no express indication of what action is appropriate. We hold, however, that this failure to state with specificity the action required does not remove political speech from the coverage of the Campaign Act when it is clearly the kind of advocacy of the defeat of an identified candidate that Congress intended to regulate.

Reasonable minds could not dispute that Furgatch's advertisement urged readers to vote against Jimmy Carter. This was the only action open to those who would not "let him do it." The reader could not sue President Carter for his indelicate remarks, or arrest him for his transgressions. If Furgatch had been seeking impeachment, or some form of judicial or administrative action against Carter, his plea would have been to a different audience, in a different forum. If Jimmy Carter was degrading his office, as Furgatch claimed, the audience to whom the ad was directed must vote him out of that office. If Jimmy Carter was attempting to buy the election, or to win it by "hid[ing] his own record, or lack of it," as Furgatch suggested, the only way to not let him do it was to give the election to someone else. Although the ad may be evasively written, its meaning is clear.

Our conclusion is reinforced by consideration of the timing of the ad. The ad is bold in calling for action, but fails to state expressly the precise action called for, leaving an obvious blank that the reader is compelled to fill in. It refers repeatedly to the election campaign and Carter's campaign tactics. Timing the appearance of the advertisement less than a week before the election left no doubt of the action proposed.

. . .

Faucher v. *Federal Election Commission,* 928 F.2d 468 (1st Cir. 1991),
cert. denied, 502 U.S. 820 (1991)

OPINION: TORRUELLA, Circuit Judge

. . .

[The Maine Right to Life Committee] publishes a bimonthly newsletter, containing educational articles and news of local chapter activities, which is mailed directly to all dues-paying members and is also made available to the general public through schools, churches, etc. Before elections, MRLC conducts candidate surveys to ascertain federal and state candidates' positions on pro-life issues. The survey responses are published in the newsletter. Publication costs for the newsletter are drawn from the corporation's general and educational funds rather than the separate segregated funds of its political action committee.

. . . The 1988 guide was entitled "November Election Issue 1988!," was subheaded "Federal & State Candidate Surveys Enclosed—Take-along Issue for Election Day!," featured candidate and party positions on pro-life issues, and contained the following statement: "PLEASE NOTE: A 'yes' response indicates agreement with the National Right to Life position on each question." The guide did, however, also carry a disclaimer which read: "The publication of the MRLC November Election Candidate Survey does not represent an endorsement of any candidate(s) by MRLC."

. . .

Section 441b(a) of the FECA [Federal Election Campaign Act] prohibits corporations from using general treasury funds to make "contribution[s] or expenditure[s] in connection with any [federal] election." The FEC, entrusted with regulatory power under the FECA, has interpreted this provision very broadly to include a ban on corporate financed activities involving express advocacy as well as issue advocacy. The regulation in question, 11 C.F.R. § 114.4(b)(5), states:

(5) *Voter guides.* (i) A corporation . . . may prepare and distribute to the general public nonpartisan voter guides consisting of questions posed to candidates concerning their positions on campaign issues and the candidates' responses to those questions. The following are factors that the Commission may consider in determining whether a voter guide is nonpartisan:

(C) The wording of the questions presented does not suggest or favor any position on the *issues* covered;

(D) The voter guide expresses no editorial opinion concerning the *issues* presented nor does it indicate any support for or opposition to any candidate or political party. (Emphasis added).

A.

First, we face the question of whether the FEC has the authority, under section 441b(a), to restrict issue advocacy or whether the FEC may only restrict express advocacy.

. . .

We begin by defining the scope of the statute. On its face, the statute appears to allow for a very broad application. Our inquiry, however, does not end there.

The Supreme Court, recognizing that such broad language as found in section 441b(a) creates the potential for first amendment violations, sought to avoid future conflict by explicitly limiting the statute's prohibition to "express advocacy." *Buckley* v. *Valeo*, 424 U.S. 1, 42–43 (1976) [documents 3.1 and 7.3]. Express advocacy is language which "in express terms advocate[s] the election or defeat of a clearly identified candidate" through the use of such phrases as "vote for," "elect," "support," "cast your ballot for," "Smith for Congress," "vote against," "defeat," and "reject." *Buckley*, 424 U.S. at 44 and n. 52. This express advocacy test was again embraced by the Supreme Court in the more recent case of *Massachusetts Citizens for Life*. *See Massachusetts Citizens for Life*, 479 U.S. at 249 [document 7.4]. The FEC, however, maintains that the language relied upon in *Massachusetts Citizens for Life* was mere dictum and therefore not binding on this court. We do not agree. All nine Justices assented to that portion of the opinion which states: "We therefore *hold* that an expenditure must constitute 'express advocacy' in order to subject to the prohibition of § 441b." *Id.* at 249. (emphasis added). We cannot accept that in resolving constitutional issues such as the one presented in *Massachusetts Citizens for Life*, the Supreme Court proclaims the law lightly. The Court's "basis for deciding [should] not [later be treated as] dictum [simply] because a critic would have decided on another basis." Friendly, *In Praise of Erie—And of the New Federal Common Law*, 39 N.Y.U.L.Rev. 383, 385–86 (1964).

. . .

In limiting section 441b(a) to express advocacy, the Court in *Buckley* clearly had the protection of issue advocacy in mind. *Buckley* reads: "In a republic where the people are sovereign, the ability of the citizenry to make informed choices among candidates for office is essential." *Buckley*, 424 U.S. at 14–15. "Discussion of public issues and debate on the qualifications of candidates are integral to the operation of the system of government established by our Constitution." *Id.* at 14. The FEC nevertheless has sought to restrain that very same activity which the Court in *Buckley* sought to protect. This we cannot allow.

B.

In the alternative, the FEC argues that even if section 441b(a) is restricted to express advocacy, the speech sought to be regulated in this case was express advocacy and therefore falls within the scope of the FECA. To the extent that this argument asks us to treat the regulation, despite its multiple references to "issue advocacy," as reaching only "express advocacy," the Supreme Court has barred such word games. *See, e.g., Buckley*, 424 U.S. at 42–44 (expressing concern that the "distinction between discussion of issues and candidates may often dissolve in practical application" and adopting a bright-line test that expenditures must "in express terms advocate the election or defeat of a candidate" in order to be subject to limitation); *see also Massachusetts Citizens for Life*, 479 U.S. at 249. In *Buckley*, the Court quoted *Thomas* v. *Collins*, 323 U.S. 516 (1945), approvingly, on the difficulty of interpreting the meaning and effects of words:

Whether words intended and designed to fall short of invitation would miss that mark is a question both of intent and of effect. No speaker, in such circumstances, safely could assume that anything he might say upon the general subject would not be understood by some as an invitation. In short, the supposedly clear-cut distinction between discussion, laudation, general advocacy, and solicitation puts the speaker in these circumstances wholly at the mercy of the varied understanding of his hearers and consequently of whatever inferences may be drawn to his intent and meaning.

Such a distinction offers no security for free discussion. In these conditions it blankets with uncertainty whatever may be said. It compels the speaker to hedge and trim.

Buckley, 424 U.S. at 43 (quoting *Collins*, 323 U.S. at 535).

In our view, trying to discern when issue advocacy in a voter guide crosses the threshold and becomes express advocacy invites just the sort of constitutional questions the Court sought to avoid in adopting the bright-line express advocacy test in *Buckley*.

. . .

One of the most extended discussions of issue advocacy is in the *Federal Election Commission* v. *Christian Action Network* case, which originated in the Western District of Virginia (document 7.7A). Judge James C. Turk's scholarly opinion highlights many of the practical, fact-intensive difficulties in applying the "express advocacy" test to different kinds of communications. The Fourth Circuit recently affirmed Judge Turk's ruling and took the extraordinary step of awarding the Christian Action Network its attorneys' fees and costs in litigating against the FEC (document 7.7B). Excerpts from both opinions follow.

A.

Federal Election Commission v. Christian Action Network,
894 F. Supp. 946 (W.D.Va. 1995), *aff'd mem.*, 92 F.3d 1178 (4th Cir. 1996)

. . .

The Christian Action Network is a nonprofit corporation created in 1990 under the laws of the Commonwealth of Virginia. CAN is a grass-roots organization that seeks to inform the public about issues which it believes affect "traditional Christian family values." During the weeks leading up to the November 3, 1992 presidential election, CAN spent approximately sixty-three thousand dollars, ($63,000.00), from its general treasury fund to produce television and print advertisements. These advertisements assailed what the Defendants believed to be the militant homosexual agenda of the Democratic candidates for president and vice-president, William Jefferson Clinton and Albert Gore, Jr. (hereinafter "Bill Clinton" and "Al Gore").

The television advertisement consisted of a thirty second spot entitled "Clinton's Vision for a Better America".[1] It opens with a full-color picture of candidate Bill Clinton's face superimposed upon an American flag, which is blowing in the wind. Clinton is shown smiling and the ad appears to be complimentary. However, as the narrator begins to describe Clinton's alleged support for "radical" homosexual causes, Clinton's image dissolves into a black and white photographic negative. The negative darkens

---

1. Between September 26 and November 2, 1992, the television commercial was broadcast at least 250 times in twenty-four cities throughout the country. The commercial was broadcast up until November 2, 1992, the day before the presidential election took place. In addition to the regular broadcasting of the commercial, copies of the ad were also sent by CAN to group contributors.

Clinton's eyes and mouth, giving the candidate a sinister and threatening appearance. Simultaneously, the music accompanying the commercial changes from a single high pitched tone to a lower octave.

The commercial then presents a series of pictures depicting advocates of homosexual rights, apparently gay men and lesbians, demonstrating at a political march. While the narrator discusses the candidates' alleged agenda for homosexuals, short captions paraphrasing their positions are superimposed on the screen in front of the marchers. These images include: marchers carrying a banner saying "Libertarians for Gay and Lesbian Concerns" accompanied by the superimposed text "Job Quotas for Homosexuals"; the same banner accompanied by the superimposed text "Special Rights for Homosexuals"; two individuals with their arms around each other's shoulders and text saying "Homosexuals in the Armed Forces"; and a man wearing a shirt which reads "Gay Fathers" with the text "Homosexuals Adopting Children."

As the scenes from the march continue, the narrator asks in rhetorical fashion, "Is this your vision for a better America?" Thereafter, the image of the American flag reappears on the screen, but without the superimposed image of candidate Clinton. At the same time, the music changes back to the single high pitched tone. The narrator then states, "for more information on traditional family values, contact the Christian Action Network."

. . .

FECA Section 441b(a) and the Express Advocacy Standard

A literal reading of FECA section 441b(a) suggests that corporate entities are strictly prohibited from using general treasury funds to make independent expenditures in connection with federal elections. The provision states: "It is unlawful for . . . any corporation whatever . . . to make a contribution or expenditure in connection with [Federal elections] . . . or any officer or director of any corporation . . . to consent to any contribution or expenditure by the corporation prohibited by this section. 2 U.S.C. § 441b(a); *see also* 11 C.F.R. § 114.3(a)(1)(1995)."

However, a significant judicial gloss has been read into section 441b making the provision's ban less severe than it initially appears. Specifically, before an expenditure is subject to the prohibition of § 441b, it must be found to "expressly advocate" the election or defeat of a "clearly identified" federal candidate. *Federal Election [Commission]* v. *Massachusetts Citizens for Life, Inc.* 479 U.S. 238, 249 (1986) [document 7.4].

. . .

Acknowledging that political expression, including discussion of public issues and debate on the qualifications of candidates, enjoys extensive First Amendment protection, the vast majority of these courts have adopted a strict interpretation of the "express advocacy" standard. *See Central Long Island Tax Reform*, 616 F.2d at 53 ("Contrary to the position of the FEC, the words 'expressly advocating' means exactly what they say. . . . The FEC would apparently have us read 'expressly advocating the election or defeat' to mean for the purpose, express or *implied*, of encouraging election or defeat. This would, by statutory interpretation, nullify the change in the statute ordered by *Buckley* . . . "). Thus, courts generally have been disinclined to entertain arguments made by the Commission that focus on anything other than the actual language used in an advertisement. *Faucher*, 928 F.2d at 472 [document 7.6] ("In our view, trying to discern when issue advocacy in a voter guide crosses the threshold and becomes express advocacy invites just the sort of constitutional question the [Supreme] Court sought to avoid in adopting the bright-line express advocacy test in *Buckley*"); [*Colorado Republican Federal Campaign Committee*], 839 F.Supp. at 1456 ("Trying to determine whether the surrounding circumstances, coupled with the implications of the advertisement, constitute 'express advocacy' leads to the type of semantic dilemma which the [Supreme] Court sought to avoid by adopting a bright-line rule").

The one notable exception, on which the FEC relies heavily in the instant case, is the Ninth Circuit's decision in *FEC v. Furgatch* [document 7.5].

. . .

THE DEFENDANTS' ADVERTISEMENTS DID NOT EXPRESSLY ADVOCATE THE DEFEAT OF CANDIDATES CLINTON AND GORE

Having thoroughly reviewed the case law addressing the "express advocacy" standard, the court finds that the Defendants' advertisements are not subject to regulation under FECA. This is true whether CAN's television commercial is viewed individually or in conjunction with the two print advertisements. Concededly, the advertisements "clearly identified" the 1992 Democratic presidential and vice presidential candidates. Bill Clinton's face was prominently displayed in the television commercial and both Clinton and Gore were mentioned by name in all three advertisements. Similarly, it is beyond dispute that the advertisements were openly hostile to the proposals believed to have been endorsed by the two candidates. Nevertheless, the advertisements were devoid of any language that directly exhorted the public to vote. Without a frank admonition to take electoral action, even admittedly negative advertisements such as these, do not constitute "express advocacy" as that term is defined in *Buckley* and its progeny. *See Colorado [Republican]*, 839 F.Supp. at 1455 ("Even assuming the advertisement indirectly discourages voters from supporting [the candidate], it does not contain a direct plea for specific action required from *Buckley* and *Furgatch*"); *SEFI*, 1994 U.S. Dist. LEXIS 210, at *6, 1994 WL 9658 at *3 ("It is clear from the cases that expressions of hostility to the positions of an official, implying that [the] official should not be reelected—even when that implication is quite clear—do not constitute the express advocacy which runs afoul of [FECA]"), *American Federation*, 471 F.Supp. at 317 ("Although the poster includes a clearly identified candidate and may have tended to influence voting, it contains communication on a public issue widely debated during the campaign. . . . As such, it is the type of political speech which is protected from regulation").

CAN's television commercial addressed political issues. It informed the public on what the organization believed to be the "gay agenda" of the Democratic candidates. Specifically, the commercial questioned whether homosexuals should be afforded protection under federal civil rights laws. It also questioned the propriety of integrating homosexuals into the armed services and permitting their adoption of children. Moreover, through the use of the narrator's rhetorical question at the end of the commercial—"Is this your vision of a better America?"—the Defendants made it clear that they were adamantly opposed to such action.

At the same time, despite the *implication* that the Democratic candidates favored such changes, no-where in the commercial were viewers asked to vote against them. As the Defendants correctly note, the November general election, the political party of the candidates, and their potential opponents were never even mentioned during the commercial. Instead, viewers were presented with the candidates' views on homosexual rights and told that they sharply contrasted with those held by the Defendants. The only immediate action called for by the commercial was for viewers to contact CAN if they agree with the Defendants' opposition to a "gay rights agenda." As the final statement in the commercial in-structed, "for more information on traditional family values contact the Christian Action Network." *See NOW*, 713 F. Supp. at 435 (defendant did not go beyond issue discussion to express advocacy; it merely attempted to make its views known and gain new members). . . .[2]

. . .

THE FEC'S PROPOSED APPROACH TO THE EXPRESS ADVOCACY STANDARD IS LEGALLY AND LOGISTICALLY UNTENABLE

The FEC seeks to avoid the weight of authority calling for a strict interpretation of the "express advo-cacy" test by arguing that the instant case is unique. Unlike previous decisions which dealt exclusively with print and radio advertisements, the FEC argues that a different analysis is appropriate when, as here, a television commercial is at issue. According to the FEC, a different standard is justified because imagery and other more subtle forms of non-verbal communication used in the television medium are sufficient to meet the *Buckley* express advocacy standard. The FEC finds support for this contention from the *Buckley* decision itself, and from several First Amendment decisions in which non-verbal communication has been recognized as protected political speech.

Especially significant, the FEC argues, is the strong message conveyed by the use of the American flag in the CAN television commercial. According to the FEC, the television advertisement "makes its anti-Clinton message explicit by concluding with the same full-color image of the rippling flag as opened the commercial—but without the superimposed image of Clinton." "By graphically removing Clinton's superimposed image from the presidential setting of the American flag, the advertisement visually con-veys the message that Clinton should not become president." "[It] is a powerful visual image telling voters to defeat Clinton."

In addition to the symbolic use of the American flag, the FEC notes several other aspects of CAN's television commercial which it believes are relevant to the court's express advocacy analysis. These in-clude: (1) the visual degrading of candidate Clinton's picture into a black and white negative; (2) the use of visual text and audio voice-overs; (3) ominous music; (4) unfavorable coloring; (5) codewords such

---

2. The FEC also points to contemporaneous press statements made by spokesmen for CAN, including Defendant Mawyer as president of the organization, in which they stated that the purpose of the television commercial was to educate the "voting" public about the Clinton/Gore position on homosexual rights. Even if the court were to consider these random statements in conjunction with the advertisements, they do not suggest that the Defendants did anything other than inform the public about their views on an election issue. *See Furgatch*, 807 F.2d at 863 (stating that a speaker's intent is less important than the message conveyed by the speech itself because the speaker may expressly advocate regardless of his intention); *[Federal Election Commission v. Colorado Republican Federal Campaign Committee]*, 839 F. Supp. 1448, 1456 (D.Colo. 1993) (rejecting the FEC's argument that contemporaneous press statements made by officers for the Defendant's organization were relevant to the court's analysis.)

as "vision" and "quota;" (6) issues raised that are relevant only if candidate Clinton became president; (7) the airing of the commercial in close proximity to the national election; and (8) abrupt editing linking Clinton to the images of the gay rights marchers.

. . .

While the approach to the "express advocacy" standard proposed by the Commission is resourceful, the court cannot accept it. Under the Commission's approach, courts would be asked to consider not only the words used in a television advertisement, but also more nebulous characteristics such as the ad's use of color, music, tone, and editing. The Supreme Court's decision in *Buckley* simply does not permit this type of judicial inquiry. In *Buckley*, the Court recognized that, depending on the audience, the language used in a political communication can be interpreted to have a variety of meanings. What one person sees as an exhortation to vote, the Court reasoned, another might view as a frank discussion of political issues.

. . .

Therefore, in order to avoid the possibility that a speaker's intent or meaning would be misinterpreted, the Court in *Buckley* limited FECA's restrictions to communications containing express words of advocacy. By creating a bright-line rule, the Court ensured, to the degree possible, that individuals would know at what point their political speech would become subject to governmental regulation.

It takes little reflection to realize that messages conveyed by imagery are susceptible to even greater misinterpretation than those that are conveyed by the written or spoken word.[3] Consequently, if courts were to begin considering the images created by a communication to determine if a call to electoral action was present, the likelihood that protected speech would be chilled would be far greater. Given this inevitable result, the court cannot accept the FEC's invitation to delve into the meaning behind an image. To expand the express advocacy standard enunciated in *Buckley* in this manner would be to render the standard meaningless. Such an expansion of the judicial inquiry would open the very Pandora's Box which the Supreme Court consciously sought to keep closed.

. . .

The FEC . . . distorts the holding in *Furgatch* by attaching undue significance to the timing of the Defendants' advertisements. Repeatedly, the Commission insists that because the Defendants' advertisements appeared just prior to the general election they conveyed a singular message—vote against candidates Clinton and Gore. Such a "magic timing" approach is no better than one which insists upon the presence of the "magic words" found in *Buckley* and it would lead to anomalous results.[4] As the court explained to the parties during oral argument, the First Amendment does not include a proviso stating

---

3. If the adage "a picture is worth a thousand words" is accurate, then the difficulty in interpreting a message conveyed by a picture is undoubtedly far greater than one conveyed by mere words.

4. For example, under such analysis, the same political communication could be regulated by FECA if it appeared on November 2 of an election year, and yet be fully protected under the First Amendment if it were aired a week later.

"except in elections" and the court refuses to accept an approach to the express advocacy standard that would effectuate such a result.

. . .

[*Following this decision, the Fourth Circuit not only upheld the District Court's decision, but awarded attorney's fees to the Christian Action Network, a very rare outcome in an enforcement case brought by a government agency. The Fourth Circuit found that the FEC's claim that the speech was "express advocacy" was "foreclosed by clear well-established Supreme Court case law."*]

B.
Federal Election Commission v. *Christian Action Network,* 110 F.3d. 1049 (4th Cir. 1997)

LUTTIG, Circuit Judge

. . .

B.

Against [the] overwhelming weight of (and, in the case of the Supreme Court decisions, dispositive) authority, the FEC argued before the district court [document 7.7a] and before us the concededly "novel" position, that, even though the Christian Action Network's advertisements did not include any explicit words or language advocating Governor Clinton's defeat, the expenditure of corporate funds for these advertisements nonetheless violated section 441b because, considered as a whole with the imagery, music, film footage, and voice intonations, the advertisements' nonprescriptive language unmistakably conveyed a message expressly advocating the defeat of Governor Clinton. That is, the FEC argued the position that "*no* words of advocacy are necessary to expressly advocate the election of a candidate," that an advertisement which does not include *any* "express words of advocacy" may nevertheless constitute "express words of advocacy" may nevertheless constitute "express advocacy" as defined by the Supreme Court in *Buckley* [documents 3.1 and 7.3] and *MCFL* [document 7.4], provided it unmistakably conveys a message urging action with respect to a particular candidate for public office.

. . .

Stripped of its circumlocution, the FEC's argument was (and is) that the determination of whether a given communication constitutes "express advocacy" depends upon all of the circumstances, internal and external to the communication, that could reasonably be considered to bear upon the recipient's interpretation of the message.

. . .

The FEC thus argues that "when included as part of the message, the speaker's identity becomes part of the communication itself, and what matters is not what the viewer or the courts will infer about the speaker's intent, but what a reasonable person, informed about the speaker's identity (and thus potential biases and passions), understands the communication to mean."

. . .

To quote the following passage, in which the FEC articulates some of the multitude of factors that would be considered under its interpretation in determining whether a given communication was prohibited, is to appreciate the breadth of power that the FEC would appropriate to itself under its definition of "express advocacy".

Express electoral advocacy [can] consist . . . not of words alone, but of the combined message of words and dramatic moving images, sounds, and other non-verbal cues such as film editing, photographic techniques, and music, involving highly charged rhetoric and provocative images which, taken as a whole, send an unmistakable message to oppose [a specific candidate].

This is little more than an argument that the FEC will know "express advocacy" when it sees it.

. . .

Indeed, the commercial and advertisements that the FEC here contend fall squarely within its regulatory purview are precisely the kinds of issue advocacy that the Supreme Court sought to protect in *Buckley* and *MCFL*; and the FEC's interpretation of these advertisements is exactly that contemplated by the Court when it warned of the constitutional pitfalls in subjecting a speaker's message to the unpredictability of audience interpretation, see *Buckley*, 424 U.S. at 43.

In sum, unlike even the advertisment in *Furgatch*, which was "bold in calling for action, but fail[ed] to state expressly the precise action called for," *Furgatch*, 807 F.2d. at 865; *see also FEC Opposition to Certiorari in Furgatch* at 8 (noting that Furgatch's advertisement included "explicit exhortation"), in neither the video nor in the print advertisements at issue in this case is there any action urged with respect to any candidate. There are no words expressly advocating the defeat of Governor Clinton in the 1992 presidential election, or, for that matter, any words urging voters to take any action whatsoever as to the Governor. As the district court found, these advertisements are simply "devoid of any language that directly exhorted the public to vote" for or against any particular candidate.

. . .

Even absent binding Supreme Court precedent, we would bridle at the power over political speech that would reside in the FEC under such an interpretation. The American Civil Liberties Union observes in its amicus brief in support of the Christian Action Network that if the FEC's interpretation were to prevail, "ads attacking an identified candidate's political positions during a campaign would virtually always, if not *per se*, amount to 'express advocacy' of that candidate's defeat at the polls." And, from the Commission's argument that advertisements which "make it absolutely clear that [the group sponsoring the ads] considers homosexual behavior and the support of additional rights for gay men and lesbians to be abhorrent" can "only reasonably" be interpreted as "asking others to join its fight to defeat Clinton and thereby foreclose his asserted homosexual rights agenda," this would appear to be precisely the consequence of the agency's interpretation.

D.

Whether we would agree with the FEC's interpretation of its authority under the Federal Election Campaign Act, or find its interpretation reasonable, were this a matter of first impression, however, is not ultimately the question. The question for us is only whether the FEC was "substantially justified" in taking the position it did, in light of the Supreme Court's unambiguous pronouncements in *Buckley* and *MCFL* that explicit words of advocacy are required if the Commission is to have standing to pursue an enforcement action. The simple answer to this question must be that it was not so justified. As we stated in adopting the district court's opinion, the FEC's position was based not only "on a misreading of the Ninth Circuit's decision in Furgatch," but also on a "profound misreading" of the Supreme Court's decisions in both *Buckley* and *MCFL. Christian Action Network,* 894 F. Supp. at 958–59.

. . .

The FEC is fully aware that the Supreme Court has required explicit words of advocacy as a condition to the Commission's exercise of power, as evidenced by its own dissembling before this court.

. . .

II.

In the face of the unequivocal Supreme Court and other authority discussed, an argument such as that made by the FEC in this case, that "*no* words of advocacy are necessary to expressly advocate the election of a candidate," simply cannot be advanced in good faith (as the disingenuousness in the FEC's submissions attests), much less with "substantial justification." It may even be, as the FEC contends in this particular case, that "the combined message of words and dramatic moving images, sounds, and other non-verbal cues such as film editing, photographic techniques, and music, involving highly charged rhetoric and provocative images . . . taken as a whole . . . sent an unmistakable message to oppose [Governor Clinton]." But the Supreme Court has unambiguously held that the First Amendment forbids the regulation of our political speech under such indeterminate standards. "Explicit words of advocacy of election or defeat of a candidate," "express words of advocacy," the Court has held, are the constitutional minima. To allow the government's power to be brought to bear on less, would effectively be to dispossess corporate citizens of their fundamental right to engage in the very kind of political issue advocacy the First Amendment was intended to protect—as this case well confirms.

For the reasons stated, the case is remanded to the district court for a determination of the amount of fees and costs properly awardable to the Christian Action Network under the authority of the Equal Access to Justice Act, 28 U.S.C. § 2412(d)(1)(A). . . .

11 C.F.R. § 100.22 "Expressly Advocating (2 U.S.C. § 431[17])";
Federal Register, vol. 60, no. 129 (July 6, 1995), pp. 35304–305

DOCUMENT 7.8

After the Supreme Court's ruling in *Federal Election Commission* v. *Massachusetts Citizens for Life, Inc.* (document 7.4), the FEC promulgated new regulations on what kinds of communications constitute express advocacy. Below are the new regulations, which remain in effect today (except in the First Circuit, where part (b) has been held to be unconstitutional).

Expressly advocating means any communication that—(a) Uses phrases such as "vote for the President," "re-elect your Congressman," "support the Democratic nominee," "cast your ballot for the Republican challenger for U.S. Senate in Georgia," "Smith for Congress," "Bill McKay in '94," "vote Pro-Life" or "vote Pro-Choice" accompanied by a listing of clearly identified candidates described as Pro-Life or Pro-Choice, "vote against Old Hickory," "defeat" accompanied by a picture of one or more candidate(s), "reject the incumbent," or communications of campaign slogan(s) or individual word(s), which in context can have no other reasonable meaning than to urge the election or defeat of one or more clearly identified candidate(s), such as posters, bumper stickers, advertisements, etc. which say "Nixon's the One," "Carter '76," "Reagan/Bush" or "Mondale!"; or

(b) When taken as a whole and with limited reference to external events, such as the proximity to the election, could only be interpreted by a reasonable person as containing advocacy of the election or defeat of one or more clearly identified candidate(s) because—

(1) The electoral portion of the communication is unmistakable, unambiguous, and suggestive of only one meaning; and

(2) Reasonable minds could not differ as to whether it encourages actions to elect or defeat one or more clearly identified candidate(s) or encourages some other kind of action.

In *Maine Right to Life* v. *FEC,* the United States District Court for the District of Maine ruled that the FEC's new express advocacy regulations are unconstitutional. After the First Circuit summarily affirmed, the FEC sought rehearing en banc. The FEC's request is currently pending. Regardless of what happens in the First Circuit, the losing party is likely to seek Supreme Court review. Below are excerpts from the FEC's petition for rehearing. They are perhaps the agency's most forceful articulation of its argument that it has the authority and needs the power to regulate issue advocacy.

. . .

The Supreme Court has consistently recognized that § 434c and § 441b of the Act serve compelling governmental interests in protecting the integrity of federal elections from the specter of corruption and in ensuring an informed electorate. The district court gave these compelling interests no weight in its evaluation of the validity of the Commission's regulation, but the Supreme Court has cautioned that "in construing [a statute] narrowly to avoid constitutional doubts, we must . . . avoid a construction that would seriously impair the effectiveness of the [statute] in coping with the problem it was designed to alleviate." *United States* v. *Harriss,* 347 U.S. 612, 623 (1954). *See also Austin* [v. *Michigan State Chamber of Commerce*], 494 U.S. at 658, 660 (statute burdening expressive activity is constitutional if it is "justified by a compelling state interest" and "sufficiently narrowly tailored to achieve its goal") [document 3.3]; *Buckley,* 424 U.S. at 25 [documents 3.1 and 7.3] (statute burdening First Amendment activity "may be sustained if the State demonstrates a sufficiently important interest and employs means closely drawn to avoid unnecessary abridgment of associational freedoms"). Thus, the proper approach to such a question, which contrasts starkly with that of the district court here, was stated in *Furgatch* [document 7.5]:

Although we may not place burdens on the freedom of speech beyond what is strictly necessary to further the purposes of the Act, we must be just as careful to ensure that those purposes are fully carried out, that they are not cleverly circumvented, or thwarted by a rigid construction of the terms of the Act.

807 F.2d at 862.

As noted above, the district court agreed that its conclusion gave short shrift to the implementation of the compelling purposes of the statute, but felt that it was bound by precedent to ensure that the Act's "restriction of election activities . . . not be permitted to intrude in any way upon the public discussion of issues." 914 F. Supp. at 12. We have already shown . . . that this Court's decision in *Faucher* did not reach this question. The Supreme Court's discussion of "express advocacy" in *Buckley* and *MCFL* [document 7.4] also do not mandate the rigidly narrow construction adopted by the district court. Although the Supreme Court held in *MCFL* that "an expenditure must constitute 'express advocacy' in order to be subject to the prohibition of § 441b," 479 U.S. at 249, the Court demonstrated in that case that this did not mean protecting issue advocacy at all costs, as the district court believed. The newsletter in that case contained both issue advocacy and electoral advocacy, but the Court did not find that the inclusion of issue advocacy immunized the newsletter from regulation. Rather, the court concluded that, even though its language was not as direct as the examples of express advocacy listed in *Buckley*, the newsletter was not a "mere discussion of public issues" because its "essential nature" went "beyond issue discussion to express electoral advocacy," and therefore fell within the prohibition of § 441b even though it also addressed issues. 479 U.S. at 249. The Court thus made clear in *MCFL*—the only case in which it has applied the "express advocacy" standard to specific facts—that when these two types of advocacy are combined in a single communication, the Act can still be applied even though it also affects the issue advocacy.[1]

Subpart (b) of the Commission's regulation is, as the district court acknowledged, an extremely narrow regulation that is highly protective of First Amendment interests. It precludes application of the Act unless a communication has an "electoral portion" in which advocacy of election or defeat of a candidate is "unmistakable, unambiguous, *and* suggestive of only one meaning" (emphasis added). On its face, this requirement by itself rules out the possibility that the regulation would be applicable to communications containing only issue advocacy: if a communication has "only one meaning" and that meaning is unmistakably and unambiguously about election advocacy, its message cannot be a mere discussion of issues. The regulation also requires that reasonable people "could not differ" on whether the electoral message encourages action "to elect or defeat" a candidate rather than some other kind of action. The regulation explicitly implements the Court's requirement in *Buckley* that regulation of independent expenditures be "directed precisely to that spending that is unambiguously related to the campaign of a particular federal candidate," 424 U.S. at 80, and incorporates the distinction at the heart of *Buckley* "between discussion of issues and candidates and advocacy of election or defeat of candidates." 424 U.S. at 42. This is enough to warrant upholding the Commission's regulation under the established standard of review on a facial challenge, which will "not foreclose challenges to its actual operation" in particular factual situations. *Kines* v. *Day*, 754 F.2d 28, 30 (1st Cir. 1985). *Accord, Massachusetts v. United States*, 856 F.2d 378, 384 (1st Cir. 1988).

The panel's rejection of this narrow regulation, explicitly limited to "unambiguous" communications, can only mean that the Act cannot be applied even to expenditures for communications that are "unambiguously related to the campaign of a particular federal candidate," 424 U.S. at 80, if the communication does not use the terms, or their synonyms, from the short list of examples set out in *Buckley*, 424 U.S. at 44 n.52.[2] As the Ninth Circuit has explained, such a ruling opens the door to just the sort of

---

1. The *MCFL* Court also demonstrated that form should not be elevated over substance. The newsletter's call for action regarding particular candidates was merely implied, since its literal exhortation was only to "Vote Pro-Life." Moreover, the newsletter contained a disclaimer that it did not endorse any candidates, yet the Court refused to allow the disclaimer to negate the express advocacy. 479 U.S. at 249.

2. Unambiguous figurative speech such as "Smith is running for re-election—send him to the unemployment line!" is an example of a communication that avoids magic words but still sends an unambiguous electoral message under subpart (b), as is the exhortation found to be express advocacy in *Furgatch*.

unreported spending by corporations and unions that the Supreme Court has found to be a threat to the integrity of federal elections.

The short list of words included in the Supreme Court's opinion in *Buckley* does not exhaust the capacity of the English language to expressly advocate the election or defeat of a candidate. A test requiring the magic words "elect," "support," etc., or their nearly perfect synonyms for a finding of express advocacy would preserve the First Amendment right of unfettered expression only at the expense of eviscerating the Federal Election Campaign Act. "Independent" campaign spenders working on behalf of candidates could remain just beyond the reach of the Act by avoiding certain key words while conveying a message that is unmistakably directed to the election or defeat of a named candidate.

Furgatch, 807 F.2d at 863.

The *Furgatch* court noted that since *Buckley* the practices at which the statute was aimed had "apparently become more widespread in federal elections, and the need for controls more urgent." 807 F.2d at 862. As the *amicus curiae* in the instant case has shown, evasively written but unambiguously clear election advocacy has since then become even more pervasive. *See* Brief of *Amicus Curiae* Common Cause at 15–24. Indeed the 1996 election campaign was rife with allegations about millions of dollars being spent by corporations, unions and others to influence federal elections by unambiguously attacking clearly identified candidates, while carefully avoiding the terms listed in *Buckley*. The panel's decision would not only open the floodgates for such election spending in this Circuit, but would also permit independent spending of this type to go entirely undisclosed to the electorate, since "express advocacy" is also the touchstone for requiring disclosure of independent expenditures. Nothing in *Buckley*, *MCFL*, or *Faucher* requires this perverse result, and the district court candidly acknowledged that its "rigid" interpretation "does not give much recognition to the policy of the election statute to keep corporate money from influencing elections," 914 F. Supp. at 12—13.

In sum, if the express advocacy requirement is read too narrowly, the prohibitions of § 441b will require little more than careful diction and will do almost nothing to prevent millions of dollars from the general treasuries of unions and corporations from directly influencing federal elections. To hold that unlimited corporate and union spending on unambiguous election advocacy cannot be restricted so long as it manages to shy away from a finite set of proscribed words, ignores the long-standing judgment of Congress, the teachings of the Supreme Court, and common sense. Because this Court's summary decision provides little guidance and creates a split in the circuits on an issue of exceptional national importance, the Commission respectfully requests rehearing and suggests that rehearing in banc is appropriate.

. . .

Representative Bill Thomas, "Ads Could Be Regulated in Last 90 Days of Election," *Roll Call* (Campaign Reform Policy Briefing), January 9, 1997, p. 32

DOCUMENT 7.10

A number of proposals to regulate issue advocacy have been advanced in the aftermath of the 1996 elections. The constitutionality of many of the proposals is questionable. One of the more interesting proposals was offered by Representative Bill Thomas (R-Calif.). Mr. Thomas is chairman of the House Oversight Committee, which has exclusive jurisdiction in the House over campaign finance issues. He proposes regulating issue advocacy based on the proximity of the advocacy to election day. This is a recent article by Mr. Thomas outlining his proposal.

The 1996 election represents a fundamental shift in the way campaigns for federal office are conducted in America, and the way in which we approach campaign reform. In no election since the passage of the Federal Election Campaign Act [document 2.7] more than 20 years ago has a new campaign strategy had a more dramatic impact.

The 1996 elections will be remembered for the explosion of undisclosed, unregulated campaign spending by special interests from all parts of the political spectrum, and perhaps even from foreign sources. Among the most far-reaching reforms Congress could consider would be to require disclosure and perhaps regulate the sources of funds for this campaign-related spending.

I am referring, particularly, to the money spent on so-called "issue attack ads" and various other "educational" campaigns that identified specific candidates and were clearly intended to influence voters' opinions and their Election Day choices. These communications were exempt from regulation or even disclosure under current federal election law as long as they did not expressly advocate the election or defeat of a candidate.

An example of such an ad paid for by the AFL-CIO includes this: "Our Congressman voted to block a minimum wage increase, after he voted to cut Medicare and cut college loans—all to give a big tax break to the rich. Let's tell Congressman [Jon] Christensen [R-Neb]—raise the minimum wage. And start voting for America's working families."

The amount spent on advertisements like these is nearly impossible to calculate and is not disclosed. The AFL-CIO indicated that it would spend at least $35 million in non-campaign funds to influence the election, but the total may have been far higher. The Republican National Committee estimates that unions spent at least $53 million for such ads. And other groups from across the political spectrum made similar expenditures in the tens of millions of dollars that were also exempt from the requirements of the law. For example, The Coalition, an alliance of business groups, announced its intention to raise as much as $10 million in funds for such advertising in 1996.

While the exact sources of these funds is unknown, in the case of unions, a large portion came from mandatory dues money. These dues were paid by union members as a condition of their right to vote in union elections. Union elections select the representatives who bargain for pay and working conditions of all union workers.

Surveys show that more than one-third of union members voted for Republican Congressional candidates, yet unions made virtually all of their political expenditures, which came from the dues of these members, against Republicans.

These campaign practices and others emphasize the need for reform of our election laws. The overall goal of campaign reform in the 105th Congress, as in previous Congresses, should be to ensure that information is available to voters to encourage informed decision making. We should ensure that elections are fair and honest so that voters have a real choice. And we should ensure that ordinary citizens remain at the center of the campaign finance process.

At the same time, remember that at the core of our democracy is the freedom of political speech guaranteed by the First Amendment. In the long run, no government is immune from a temptation to use the law and its accompanying police power to silence critics. We must be extremely skeptical about giving those in power the ability to punish or put at a disadvantage those they decry who spend too much campaigning against incumbents. When an individual or group can be fined or even go to jail for spending too much to challenge someone in power, we are all at risk.

The Supreme Court, while fiercely protective of the First Amendment, does not, however, take the position that First Amendment rights are absolute. As Oliver Wendell Holmes said a century ago, the right to free speech does not include the right to cry "fire" in a crowded theater.

In the case of *Buckley* v. *Valeo* [424 U.S. 1 (1976)] the Court upheld limits on the amount that could be contributed from a single source to federal candidates or committees to prevent "corruption or the appearance of corruption" [documents 3.1 and 7.3]. However, the Court refused to allow limits on the total amount that could be spent by a candidate, or by an independent expenditure in support or opposition to a candidate. Contribution limits could be justified, but not mandatory spending limits that strike at the heart of free speech.

As the Court opinion declared, "By contrast with a limitation upon expenditures for political expression, a limitation upon the amount that any one person or group may contribute to a candidate or political committee entails only a marginal restriction upon the contributor's ability to engage in free communication."

The Court reasoned, "The overall effect of the Act's contribution ceilings is merely to require candidates and political committees to raise funds from a greater number of persons and to compel people who would otherwise contribute amounts greater than the statutory limits to expend such funds on direct political expression, rather than to reduce the total amount of money potentially available to promote political expression."

The Court struck down a $1,000 limit on independent expenditures, which it concluded were essential to the right of free expression.

In *Buckley*, the Court also affirmed the constitutionality of a requirement that federal committees and candidates disclose their spending and major contributors. The value of this information to the public and its value in deterring and detecting corruption outweighed any burden on candidates, committees, or contributors.

This year, in the Supreme Court's most recent major election law case, *Colorado Republican Federal Campaign Committee* v. *FEC* [116 S. Ct. 2309 (1996)] [document 3.4], the Court again emphasized the central role of free speech in the interpretation of campaign finance law. The Court affirmed the right of a political party to make unlimited "independent" expenditures as long as the expenditures are truly independent. Such expenditures could certainly be considered independent at a time when the party making the expenditures had not yet selected a candidate, and might be considered independent under other circumstances as well.

It is important to note, however, that the independent expenditures in Colorado met three vital criteria. First, they were fully disclosed and reported in a timely fashion to the public. Second, the sources of these funds were reported according to law, and federal committees that contributed to the Colorado GOP account also were required to report their contributors. Third, the expenditures were made with funds legally permitted to influence federal elections.

No corporate or union funds were allowed, so only funds voluntarily contributed by individuals directly or through federal committees were used. No individual contributions greater than the annual limit of $20,000 to a national party or $5,000 to a state party were used. And no foreign nationals could contribute to this federal committee.

The funds spent by the Colorado Republican party for independent expenditures, as permitted by the Supreme Court, are in sharp contrast to the funds spent by unions and other groups on "attack ads" and "voter education" in close proximity to the 1996 election.

The law requires no disclosure of the funds used by the unions and other groups for non-express advocacy communications. Such expenditures could come, not just from voluntary contributions, but from treasuries of union corporations, from individuals in excess of federal limits, or from foreign nationals.

There is nothing in today's law that prohibits a foreign source, or any source, from secretly contributing an unlimited amount of money to influence the outcome of a U.S. election. Such cash flow is unlimited with funds spent in the "gray zone" of unreported, unregulated attack advertising, or biased "voter education" that praises or condemns federal candidates without using express words of support or opposition.

Without reform in this area, remaining campaign laws are virtually meaningless. What use is disclosure for PACs, parties, and candidates when secret, unlimited funds are available that special interests fear to disclose?

And why prohibit contributions from foreign nationals at all, if these same sources are free to secretly contribute unlimited amounts for campaign spending that is unaccountable?

It is precisely the threat of corruption, and the clear appearance of corruption, that may constitutionally justify, not a limit on the total amount of election-related spending by any one group, but disclosure and perhaps limits on the size and source of election-related contributions to such a group.

For any such regulations to be constitutional under the Supreme Court's *Buckley* reasoning, the definition of funds spent for an "election-related purpose" must be clear and unambiguous, but not so broad that it unduly restricts the rights of individuals and groups to free expression and uninhibited discussion of issues.

The House of Representatives rules offer a way to make a "bright-line" distinction. House Rules now prohibit mass mailings of taxpayer-financed material by incumbents within 90 days of a primary or general election. These rules were adopted because during the time period, the taxpayer-funded material's potential election-related impact is judged to outweigh its purely informative value.

In the same fashion, contributions and expenditures for all mass communications that refer to a clearly identified federal candidate within 90 days of an election in which that candidate is on the ballot or qualified to be a write-in candidate, could be subject to regulation under federal law.

Seeking to create a vague and imprecise distinction between voter-education programs that favor one candidate over another and those programs that are purely "educational" is precisely the sort of doomed enterprise that the Supreme Court warned against in *Buckley*. Because no such rule or distinction could be clear in every case, no speaker could know in advance when they were engaging in regulated speech, and every speaker's right of speech could be chilled. The alternative of limiting regulation to the 90-day period immediately prior to an election makes the definition clear to everyone.

The term "mass communications" should cover all paid communications, including radio and broadcast advertising, mailings, and other forms of information dissemination. Exempted from coverage would be news programming, public candidate debates, and direct access to media, or other forms of communication provided on an equal basis to all candidates in a particular race.

The regulation, under federal campaign law, of mass communications that mention a federal candidate within 90 days of an election offers a rule that the Court could sustain to serve a compelling government interest. The Court has clearly recognized that interest: fighting corruption or the appearance of corruption.

Perhaps such covered contributions and expenditures should be subject to the same limits as all federal contributions and expenditures for the purpose of influencing a federal election. In other words, they could be paid for only with reported contributions as allowed under federal law.

Under these rules, candidates, parties, and PACs would continue to have exactly the same rights to make contributions and independent expenditures that they do today. Membership organizations would retain the same rights to freely communicate with their members as they do under current law. Candidates, parties, and other political committees, funded ultimately by voluntary contributions from individuals, would remain at the center of our electoral system.

Some will argue that any restrictions, however narrowly tailored and for whatever compelling justifications, are too great. But at the very least, contributions and expenditures for such mass communications mentioning a clearly identified candidate or candidates could be subject to all of the disclosure requirements. Disclosure would ensure that the public knows how much groups and individuals are spending, and the sources of the money.

The public's right to this information on who is seeking to influence the outcome of an election is a key part of the ability of an electorate to make informed choices that lead to a healthy democracy.

Many who expressed reservations about other campaign reform proposals in the past have declared their support for full disclosure as the most desirable method of campaign reform. Perhaps a first step in reforming our campaign laws could be a consensus, bipartisan measure to apply disclosure to this most critical area of our election process.

THE FEDERAL ELECTION COMMISSION

CHAPTER 8

Implementing and Enforcing Federal Campaign Finance Law

CONTENTS

Implementing and Enforcing Federal Campaign Finance Law

INTRODUCTION BY THOMAS E. MANN

The absence of effective enforcement machinery has plagued campaign finance law from the outset. Compliance with the Federal Corrupt Practices Act of 1925 (document 2.4) was notoriously weak, at least in part because no public agency was given the authority, resources, and incentives to administer it. In line with this practice, the Federal Election Campaign Act (FECA) of 1971 (document 2.8) dispersed authority for compliance and enforcement among the Clerk of the House, the Secretary of the Senate, the General Accounting Office, and the Secretary of State for the state where campaign activities took place. As related by Brooks Jackson in *Broken Promise: Why the Federal Election Commission Failed* (document 8.1), after the Watergate hearings uncovered serious campaign abuses in both parties, Congress passed amendments to the FECA that for the first time created an agency, the Federal Election Commission (FEC), mandated to enforce the law. But Congress had no interest in an independent, powerful FEC. It designed the agency carefully to ensure that it would operate on a tight leash held firmly by its master.

Although ostensibly modeled on traditional regulatory agencies such as the Federal Trade Commission (FTC), the Federal Communications Commission (FCC), and the Securities and Exchange Commission (SEC), the Federal Election Commission was distinct in at least one crucial respect: only two of its six voting members were to be appointed by the president, the others by leaders of the House and Senate. (The Commission also was to include

two nonvoting, ex officio members, the Secretary of the Senate and the Clerk of the House.) The six voting members were to be equally divided between Democrats and Republicans, making it difficult if not impossible for the Commission to move against a campaign in a way that would be seen as injurious to one of the parties. The FEC was given no authority to sanction violators. For criminal prosecutions, it had to refer cases to the Justice Department; for civil penalties, its only recourse was to ask a federal court to impose penalties. Congress also gave itself veto power over FEC rules and regulations, although it lost that power when the Supreme Court declared all legislative vetoes unconstitutional in 1983 (*Immigration and Naturalization Service* v. *Chadha*, 462 U.S. 919 [1983]).

The Supreme Court in its *Buckley* v. *Valeo* decision (424 U.S. 1 [1976]; document 3.1) upset these arrangements by ruling unconstitutional the role Congress played in appointing four of the six members of the FEC. The Court stated that the statute violated the Constitution's appointments clause by encroaching on the president's authority to appoint the "Officers of the United States" with the advice and consent of the Senate. (Seventeen years later the D.C. appeals court in *Federal Election Commission* v. *NRA Political Victory Fund* [6 F.3d 821 (1993)] took the additional step of declaring that the presence of the two ex officio members violated the Constitution's separation of powers. Excerpts from the decision are included in this chapter as document 8.2.) In the middle of the 1976 presidential nominating season, with responsibility for administering the new public financing system, the FEC was out of business.

Congress resurrected the FEC by giving the president the power to appoint the six voting members of the Commission, but it moved in other ways to tighten its hold on the agency. A new provision was added to the statute requiring that four of the six commissioners vote affirmatively for any action to be taken. Another forbade the Commission from investigating anonymous complaints, however well founded they might appear. Yet another required the FEC to seek negotiated agreements with violators before taking them to court for civil action. Perhaps most importantly, as Jackson points out, Congress retained enormous influence over the selection of commissioners despite its loss of legal authority. Presidents were "persuaded" to select appointees from lists prepared by congressional leaders. Over time that often took the form of reappointing long-term commissioners who were considered safe by the politicians whose campaign finance practices these appointees were charged with overseeing.

In the early years of the FEC, Congress took other actions to ensure that delay and timidity would become the watchwords of the agency. It denied the Commission the multiyear budgeting authority that other independent agencies enjoyed and skeptically viewed requests for real budget increases to help the FEC cope with a rapidly expanding workload. Congress banned random audits of candidates. It insisted on procedural requirements that were incredibly time consuming and often made it impossible for the Commission to take timely action against abuses. And it kept up a barrage of criticism that weakened the FEC's legitimacy and reinforced the contempt with which political operatives came to view the Commission.

The basic responsibilities, activities, and workload of the Commission are summarized in its *Twenty Year Report,* a part of which is reprinted here as document 8.3. Although its responsibilities are broad (including, for example, "administering the public funding of Presidential elections" and "serving as a clearinghouse for information on election administration"), its most important duty involves disclosing the sources and amounts of funds used to finance federal elections. Within forty-eight hours of receipt, every committee's report of receipts and disbursements is made available for public inspection by the Public Records Office. As the number of pages of information has grown (topping 12 million at the end of 1994), on-line access to the Commission's computer database has been relied on more and more. An electronic filing system was developed in recent years that, if it becomes mandatory, could dramatically improve the timely disclosure of campaign finance information.

The Commission also has a broad responsibility for "ensuring that candidates" and political committees "comply with the limitations, prohibitions and disclosure requirements of" federal election law. This responsibility is discharged initially through information and advice (in the form of a toll-free hotline, publications, workshops, and conferences) provided to candidates, committees, and parties to encourage voluntary compliance. More formal, legally binding guidance is available in the form of Advisory Opinions, which are issued by the Commission within sixty days of a request (or twenty days if submitted by a candidate's committee just before an election). These Advisory Opinions, which now number in excess of 1,000, serve both as guidance to a particular committee and as precedent for others in similar situations. Beyond these measures to encourage voluntary compliance, the Commission also reviews all reports, requests additional information where appropriate, conducts formal audits when warranted, and, if violations are suspected, proceeds as necessary with confidential investigations, conciliation, and litigation.

However robust this set of responsibilities and activities, the FEC's resources have not kept pace with its expanding workload. The budgetary strain on the agency is evident in the recent FEC requests for higher appropriations. For example, in her testimony before the Senate Committee on Rules and Administration on January 30, 1997, FEC Vice Chairman Joan D. Aikens walked a tightrope. She struggled to convey the increasing mismatch between the Commission's exploding workload and its stagnant budget without offending its fiscally constrained overseers at the Office of Management and Budget (OMB) and in Congress. Aikens noted the unparalleled scale of alleged violations in the 1996 campaign—involving fundraising from foreign nationals, the use of soft money to circumvent spending limits of publicly funded presidential candidates, coordination of assertedly independent expenditures, and massive, undisclosed expenditures on issue advertisements with an election message—and requested supplementary funds to investigate potential violations of current law.

Though the case Aikens made for additional resources was strong, it implicitly and perhaps inadvertently confirmed that the Commission's shortcomings go well beyond its inadequate budget. Only months after the election, with the FBI well into its own criminal investigation and Congress debating the scope of its hearings, did the FEC propose to investigate the apparent collapse of federal election law in the 1996 campaign.

How can the administration and enforcement of campaign finance law be improved? The remaining documents in this chapter offer a variety of answers. The Commission offers its own recommendations to Congress as part of its annual reporting requirement; a sampling of its most recent suggestions is included as document 8.4. The fifty-seven legislative recommendations the Commission made in 1997 range from minor technical adjustments to substantial changes in law and procedure. The latter include the following:

—Providing the Commission with authority to mandate electronic filing;

—Restoring the Commission's authority to conduct random audits;

—Ensuring that it has independent authority to conduct its own litigation;

—Giving the Commission explicit authority to refer appropriate matters to the Justice Department for criminal prosecution at any stage of its proceedings;

—Providing a statutory definition of express advocacy;

—Stipulating that issue advocacy communications may not be coordinated with a candidate or campaign;

—Effectively eliminating leadership political action committees (PACs); and

—Dropping state expenditure limits for publicly financed presidential candidates.

The substantive weight of these recommendations might surprise those critics who assume the Commission's present structure and limited authority render it fully housebroken. Of course, many of the Commission's proposals are perennials—dutifully served up each year by the FEC and ignored by Congress, which has had little appetite for strengthening the Commission or imposing new limits on candidates.

No criticism of the FEC is more telling than its failure to provide expeditious and effective enforcement of campaign finance law. That failure primarily results not from staff deficiencies or deadlocked, party line votes of the commissioners but from shortcomings in the law. In document 8.5, former FEC Associate General Counsel Kenneth A. Gross reviews the procedures in place for civil and criminal enforcement and finds them both wanting. Individuals accused of violations are denied due process protections. The statutory enforcement scheme under FECA constrains the Commission's ability to deter violations. And criminal law plays too limited a role in enforcing campaign finance law. Gross proposes a number of reforms to deal with these shortcomings, ranging from the use of adjudicatory proceedings conducted by Administrative Law Judges to the addition of a civil penalty provision to the conflict-of-interest statute.

However constructive such changes in the enforcement process might be, many critics argue that more radical surgery is required to invigorate the agency. Brooks Jackson provides one such blueprint (document 8.6), which calls for replacing the current commissioners with a five-member panel, including one public commissioner not aligned strongly with either major party, headed by a strong chair and empowered with new rules and procedures and adequate budgetary resources. Former FEC Chairman Trevor Potter reminds us that plans to strengthen the FEC face an uphill battle in Congress, whose members fear it will use any new powers to intervene directly in campaigns, harass candidates and parties, and threaten political freedom (see document 8.7). It may be possible to identify a middle range of reform proposals that balance the desire of reformers for a genuinely independent enforcement with Congress's interest in maintaining some degree of control over the agency. Promising ideas include a nonvoting permanent chairman, a private right of legal action, independent litigating authority for the Commission, and a multiyear budget cycle. A similar list of midrange proposals is contained in the reform package offered by Ornstein, Mann, Taylor, Malbin, and Corrado (see document 9.9).

Lest anyone think these or other proposals to strengthen the FEC are noncontroversial, we include as document 8.8 an article by Brent Thompson, who argues forcefully that the Commission has been too independent and too aggressive in regulating political speech. Thompson is particularly upset by the Commission's efforts to enforce its own definition of express advocacy that, in his view, brings much ordinary political activity under FEC regulation. He fears any moves to give the Commission enhanced authority, such as those included in the John McCain–Russell Feingold bill, will inevitably lead to an abridgement of political speech.

Concern about the administrative and enforcement implications of McCain-Feingold is not limited to those with a distinctly libertarian perspective on the regulation of money in politics. In document 8.9, Trevor Potter explores whether the FEC has the capacity, authority, and resources to administer a significantly more complicated and more expansive law, one that includes voluntary spending limits. Potter concludes that as presently structured and financed, the Commission could not come close to enforcing the provisions of McCain-Feingold. He also questions whether having an agency sufficiently large, powerful, and aggressive to do the job would be good for American democracy.

Brooks Jackson, "The Case of the Kidnapped Agency: Wayne Hays and 'Scared Rats': Designed to Fail," in *Broken Promise: Why the Federal Election Commission Failed,* a Twentieth Century Fund Paper (New York: Priority Press, 1990), pp. 23–37

DOCUMENT 8.1

In this excerpt from his Twentieth Century Fund paper, veteran journalist Brooks Jackson shows how the establishment of the Federal Election Commission in 1974 (document 2.9), and its reconstitution after the Supreme Court in its *Buckley* decision found its method of appointment unconstitutional, was orchestrated carefully by Congress to ensure little independence and relatively weak enforcement of the new law. Over the years Congress placed additional statutory, budgetary and informal restrictions on the Commission, rendering it even less able to meet the expectations of reformers.

Federal regulatory agencies are often born in a spasm of reform and then slowly become captives of the industries they are supposed to regulate. But the Federal Election Commission [FEC] was not so much captured as it was kidnapped and held hostage.

The FEC presents a special case. Those it regulates include the members of Congress who wrote its charter, control its budget, and influence selection of its membership. From the start, Congress repeatedly used its power to weaken the commission and to club it into submission whenever it showed signs of independence. After all, many lawmakers hadn't wanted an election commission of any sort. They were shamed into setting up the FEC by the widespread and bipartisan embarrassment that resulted from public reaction to the Watergate scandal of 1972, and as soon as public outrage began to fade, they started backtracking.

1971: WAYNE HAYS KILLS AN "UNNECESSARY COMMISSION"

Early hostility flowed from House Democrats led by Representative Wayne Hays of Ohio, the party's point man on campaign finance issues. He is remembered now chiefly for having retired in disgrace after his mistress Elizabeth Ray revealed that he had put her on the House payroll despite her inability to type. But during the early 1970s he was both the House Democrats' chief fund-raiser, as chairman of the Democratic Congressional Campaign Committee, and its chief campaign finance policymaker, as chairman of the House Administration Committee, which shaped legislation on the subject. Indeed, if it hadn't been for Hays there might have been an independent enforcement agency in place even before Watergate.

In those days Republicans and a few liberal Democrats were the main advocates of an independent election commission. Hays fought them tooth and claw. In 1971, Senate Majority Leader Hugh Scott of Pennsylvania and several of his GOP colleagues advocated an independent federal election commission. Congress was about to enact the first effective requirement that federal candidates reveal their political income and expenditures, and Scott wanted a credible overseer of those disclosure requirements. It was to be a small, lean agency that would investigate disclosure violations and send them to the Justice Department for disposition. It would get by with five part-time commissioners, a full-time executive director, and staff borrowed "to the fullest extent practicable" from the Justice Department and the congressional General Accounting Office (GAO). "I do not really envision this to be a large, unyielding body," said one of the sponsors, Republican senator James Pearson of Kansas.

For nearly half a century, an earlier disclosure law, the 1925 Federal Corrupt Practices Act [document 2.4], had proved to be a failure. Candidates got around it with ease, using such gimmicks as unregulated campaign committees in the District of Columbia. One of the most criticized features of the old act was its nearly total lack of enforcement machinery; Senate candidates filed their reports—such as they were—with the Secretary of the Senate, and House members filed theirs with the clerk of the House. Any optimists who expected tough enforcement were disappointed; congressional employees weren't in a position to quarrel with their bosses. In practice, many lawmakers simply ignored the law. Campaigns were financed in part with unreported cash that lobbyists handed over in white envelopes and brown paper bags. Blatantly illegal donations from corporations and labor unions were commonplace.

Groups outside Congress had been urging an independent enforcement agency for decades, and a bill to create one had actually been introduced in 1928. President John F. Kennedy's 1962 Commission on Campaign Costs recommended one. So did a 1970 task force sponsored by the Twentieth Century Fund. Accordingly, the 1971 GOP plan seemed overdue to many. "An independent elections commission would stand on its own, bearing the full consequences of its decisions and rendering objective judgments on the facts of each case," wrote John Gardner, chairman and founder of a year-old reform group called Common Cause. "It would be free from even the appearance of Congressional influence." And the *New York Times* editorialized, "The GOP members are emphatically right in preferring an electoral commission with its own staff over the growing Democratic predisposition to leave enforcement to the Clerk of the House and the Secretary of the Senate." The Senate approved the idea 89–2, after it was modified to provide for a six-member panel evenly divided between Democrats and Republicans.

But House members, led by Hays, killed the idea, fearful of giving President Nixon power to appoint their overseers and afraid that even such a weak commission might haul them into court. "I have a fixation, you might call it, against unnecessary commissions, and I think this is another unnecessary commission," Hays told his colleagues during debate. "It affects every one of you perhaps more than any other piece of legislation you will have. Under the Senate bill you are transferring to the executive branch a part of the control over your election and to the courts the rest of it. . . . I would suspect if this becomes law, we would have practically every election in the country tied up in the courts before and during and after the elections. I believe that is very dangerous."

. . .

House Republicans argued vainly against Hays's alternative, which kept the status quo for congressional campaigns. "This is tantamount to putting the fox in charge of the chicken coop," said Representative Bill Frenzel, a moderate Republican from Minnesota. Some liberal Democrats also wanted an independent agency, or at least a special office within the GAO. Jonathan B. Bingham, a liberal Democrat from New York, said that if enforcement were left to the House and Senate employees, "The American public are going to say, 'There they go again, no matter what is in the bill it is not going to do any good, they will take care of themselves, and this whole thing is a farce.'" But the House sided with Hays 79–52.

Hays also prevailed later in a House-Senate conference, making it clear he was willing to scuttle the entire new disclosure bill unless the senators dropped the commission and accepted his method of enforcement. Thus did Congress avoid creating an election commission on the very eve of Watergate. In the 1972 elections, candidates of both parties would engage in new extremes of corrupt financing.

1972–79: BORN HANDICAPPED, THEN KIDNAPPED

The Watergate affair shamed Democrats as well as Republicans. It didn't stop with the wiretapping burglars who had been paid with laundered $100 bills from Richard Nixon's reelection committee, or their invasion of the Democratic party's headquarters in Washington's Watergate Hotel. Nor did it end with the uncovering of illegal corporate campaign donations to Nixon's campaign, the ambassadorships bartered by his aides for donations, or the unreported campaign cash stored in a White House safe and used as hush money to finance an unsuccessful cover-up. The Watergate investigations also brought to light illegal donations to the campaigns of Democrats, including the 1972 presidential primary campaigns of Hubert Humphrey and Wilbur Mills.

Humphrey's 1972 presidential campaign manager went to jail, and Mill's presidential campaign manager invoked his Fifth Amendment privilege against self-incrimination when asked to testify before the Senate Watergate Committee. The two top leaders of the nation's largest dairy-farmer cooperative, Associated Milk Producers Inc., went to prison for making illegal donations to candidates of both parties, including a $63,500 payment to the Democratic National Committee for the 1968 Humphrey presidential campaign and contributions to several Democratic senate races.

As this spectacle was unfolding, the Senate once again cleared a measure to set up a federal election commission, this time approving important powers to write regulations and issue subpoenas. The Senate Watergate Committee said creation of such an agency would be "the most significant reform that could emerge from the Watergate scandal."

But again, Wayne Hays balked. If there was to be an agency, as now seemed inevitable, he wanted one with as little independence and power as possible. The House approved a commission consisting not of presidentially appointed members but of the House clerk, the Senate secretary, the comptroller general (appointed by the president but responsible to Congress), and four additional members appointed by congressional leaders. The House plan also gave either house of Congress the power to veto any commission regulations by a simple majority vote.

The compromise that became law in 1974 was a commission with six voting members; only two were appointed by the president and the other four were appointed by the leaders of the House and Senate. The House clerk and the Senate secretary were nonvoting, "ex officio" members. The idea of commissioners appointed by Congress was unique; no other federal agency was so harnessed to the legislative branch.

The design of the agency ensured it would be weak. It would have no strong chair, as other agencies did. Instead, the chair would rotate among the six commissioners, each serving in turn for only a year, and without much power at that. The chair would preside at meetings, sign correspondence, and exert perhaps a small influence over internal procedures and the agenda. But otherwise it was a commission of equals.

Even that didn't put the agency firmly enough under the congressional thumb to suit Hays. When the FEC was barely a month old, he shouted down to its chairman, former Republican representative Thomas Curtis, informing him that the new agency wouldn't get the multiyear budgeting authority that other independent agencies enjoyed. "You're not going to set the ground rules," Hays roared. "As chairman, I'll tell you. You're coming back every year for an authorization."

Democratic commissioner Neil Staebler later recalled: "There was a serious problem . . . when Wayne Hays was chairman. . . . He was against the act to begin with, and then after it was passed he tried to influence us to the extent of actually trying to change specific regulations. We strenuously resisted."

But Hays had his way. Once the commission proposed a requirement that Senate and House candidates file their reports directly with the commission, rather than relaying them through the House clerk and Senate secretary. It was a petty point, but one that the commissioners should have known would infuriate Hays and his colleagues. The House voted it down. The commission also proposed to treat as campaign funds the unregulated private accounts—"slush funds," critics called them—that many senators used to finance some of their expenses. The Senate vetoed that. Congress was already having serious second thoughts. "We created a monster," said Senator John O. Pastore, a Rhode Island Democrat, during that debate. "It is our own fault. We were running like scared rats. . . . We thought the stronger we make it, the tougher we make it, the more people would believe us."

The stormy life of the fledgling FEC was interrupted after barely a year by the Supreme Court's landmark *Buckley v. Valeo* decision [document 3.1]. Although best know[n] for overturning the new law's limits on campaign spending, *Buckley* also forced Congress to loosen its grip on the FEC. The high court struck down unanimously the congressional appointments as an unconstitutional encroachment on the executive branch's power. Only the president could make such appointments, the Court ruled. The commissioners were suddenly out of a job, and the FEC was out of business.

But, despite its growing doubts, Congress was under strong practical pressure to revive the commission. The 1976 presidential primary campaigns were already under way, and the FEC was the agency that controlled the dispensing of subsidies to candidates under a new public financing arrangement. No commission, no money.

In resuscitating the FEC, however, Congress took the opportunity to limit the commission's power even more. To get rid of chairman Curtis, Hays insisted on prohibiting commissioners from outside business interests; Curtis had made it clear that he wanted to maintain his St. Louis law practice and be a part-time regulator. He subsequently asked President Ford not to appoint him to the reconstituted panel. The new law also required four of the six commissioners to vote affirmatively for any commission action to be taken, thus giving either party's commissioners the power to paralyze the agency. It also retained the secretary of the Senate and the clerk of the House as *ex officio,* nonvoting members of the commission, making them privy to the FEC's most secret discussions about enforcement matters concerning the reelection campaigns of lawmakers. And it retained the provision allowing either house of Congress to veto any FEC regulation, a power the lawmakers exerted over several agencies until the Supreme Court ruled in another case that such legislative vetoes were unconstitutional.

Another new restriction, prompted by the FEC's investigation of the unsigned letter about Representative Charles Rose, denied the commission the power to investigate anonymous complaints, no matter how detailed or well founded they might appear on their face. The new law also required the FEC to rely on conciliation, a negotiated settlement akin to plea bargaining, before taking any alleged violator to court for civil action.

Perhaps most importantly, Congress as a practical political matter retained enormous influence over the selection of the commissioners, even though it had lost the legal authority to appoint four members directly. President Ford set the precedent by reappointing all the original commissioners except Curtis, who refused to accept the working conditions Hays had arranged.

In 1977, President Jimmy Carter wanted to appoint Susan King, who had the backing of Common Cause and the United Auto Workers union, but was forced to back down when House Speaker Thomas P. "Tip" O'Neill objected, reportedly calling her a "do-good, Common Cause type." Instead, Carter appointed one of O'Neill's faithful cronies, John McGarry, who had also worked for Hays as an employee of the Administration Committee. McGarry was eventually confirmed, despite opposition from Common Cause and some difficulties about the accuracy of his tax returns. "I think the conclusion is inescapable that McGarry's appointment was in some way an attempt by O'Neill to keep a thumb on the FEC," said the commissioner he replaced, Neil Staebler. McGarry was subsequently reappointed for second and third terms by Presidents Ronald Reagan and George Bush.

Carter was also stymied when he refused to choose from a list of three names sent to him by Senate Republicans to fill a GOP seat on the commission. Carter's first choice, moderate Republican Sam Zagoria, was forced to withdraw after Republicans delayed his confirmation for more than eight months. Beaten, Carter chose conservative Max L. Friedersdorf from a list supplied by Senate Republicans. Friedersdorf was hardly a zealot; he said he had spent six years opposing creation of the commission on which he was about to serve. As soon as Ronald Reagan was elected, Friedersdorf resigned to become a White House lobbyist.

Hays soon departed from Congress because of his payroll-sex scandal, but the FEC had acquired new enemies. It had inflicted some wounds on itself, earning a reputation as a fusspot by among other things bringing lawsuits against dozens of fringe candidates who failed to file disclosure reports after losing with only a handful of votes. "In effect, it is prosecuting the widows and orphans of the political process," complained Washington attorney John Bolton in 1978.

. . .

[T]he FEC was also damaged by trying to do its job: ensuring that voters received honest disclosure by candidates for Congress. After the 1976 elections it selected 10 percent of candidates for random audits, something like the examinations the Internal Revenue Service uses to keep taxpayers honest. The examinations turned up problems in the reports of more than half the candidates checked, and surprisingly showed that nearly a third of incumbents had accepted small corporate or union contributions despite the longstanding laws against such funds. But most of the problems were minor. Lawmakers, far from being pleased that the audits had demonstrated a tolerable level of compliance, were outraged.

In 1978, the House Administration Committee voted 19–2 to deny any funding for more random audits. The House upheld the anti-audit provision by voice vote, but dropped it in conference with the Senate. Reacting to the mounting criticism, the Democratic members of the FEC, in a 3–3 party-line vote, defeated a GOP proposal to continue random audits of congressional candidates. Instead, the commission decided to concentrate on auditing political parties and policial action committees, which hadn't yet received attention. But it was too late; in 1979, Congress approved an outright ban on random audits of candidates.

In effect, Congress put itself on the honor system. The FEC may now audit candidates only when gross discrepancies show up on the face of their reports, but even that requires a four-vote majority decision by the commissioners. In practice, candidates are now audited hardly at all. Candidates who wish to conceal from the voters any embarrassing or improper donations or expenditures may do so without much fear of oversight by the FEC, so long as they take care to square up the numbers on their reports.

THE 1980s: REPUBLICAN DEREGULATION

During the 1980s, Republicans turned against the commission they had helped to create. Reagan Republicans had a philosophical objection to government intrusions of any sort. Indeed, as early as 1976 Reagan, as a presidential prospect, had urged President Ford to veto the legislation reveiving the FEC after it had been disbanded by the *Buckley* decision. The GOP also had a practical aversion to regulation of its vast supplies of political money, which the post-Watergate limits kept it from deploying fully against Democrats.

After Republicans won control of the Senate in the 1980 elections, conservative GOP senators mounted a six-month frontal assault by trying to kill the FEC outright. They came within one vote of gaining a Senate Appropriations Committee recommendation to cut off all the FEC's funds; the motion by Republican senator Ted Stevens of Alaska failed by a 12–12 vote. Later, the conservatives were defeated soundly when the full Senate rejected 65–31 a motion to give the FEC funding for only six months. The Senate Rules Committee held hearings on a proposal by GOP senator Roger Jepsen of Iowa to abolish the FEC altogether, but the idea got little support.

Conservative Republicans carried forward the fight through other means, however. The party's official platform for 1984, crafted by Reagan loyalists, complained about "the inhibiting role federal election laws and regulations have had," and said flatly, "Congress should consider abolishing the Federal Election Commission." President Reagan remained so personally hostile to the law that even during his eight years in the White House he pointedly refused the choice given to every federal taxpayer of designating $1 of his [sic] income tax liability to fund presidential campaigns, including his own.

GOP conservatives weren't able to kill the FEC, but they did manage to weaken it significantly through appointments and budget. Reagan named to one Republican seat a founder of the business political action committee movement, Lee Ann Elliott. As associate executive director of the American Medical Association Political Action Committee (AMPAC), she had not only helped raise and dispense millions of dollars for the physicians' lobby, but spoke to corporations and other trade and professional associations interested in setting up their own PACs.

Her PAC had also been the focus of one of the most intensive inquiries the FEC ever conducted, one that eventually filled thirty-three file drawers. State medical society PACs were in many cases giving money to candidates who had already received the maximum legal gift from AMPAC. In the commission's view, this was a brazen violation of legislation passed in 1976—the so-called nonproliferation amendment—that required all political action committees established by an international union or a corporation to be treated as a single entity with a single contribution limit.

. . .

AMPAC and the state medical associations eventually agreed to comply with the nonproliferation amendments, but with Elliott on the commission, often voting against staff recommendations that investigations be opened, AMPAC was able to get around the $5,000 limit in other ways. In 1986, AMPAC tried to defeat Representative Pete Stark of California, who as chairman of the subcommittee dealing with Medicaid had not only advanced legislation to restrict doctors' fees but had called the AMA's leaders "troglodytes," an insult some of them found impossible to swallow. AMPAC spent $259,000 supporting Stark's Republican opponent. Stark filed a complaint alleging a violation of law.

. . .

The inquiry was blocked, however, when the Republicans created a 3–3 party-line deadlock. Elliott's vote was especially notable because she still drew a pension of $18,831 per year from the AMA. Stark had called this a conflict of interest and formally requested that she remove herself from the case. She refused, telling Stark she did so "after deep introspection into my ability to fairly and impartially consider your complaint."

. . .

After that, President Reagan appointed Elliott to a second six-year term. Stark testified against her, but the Senate approved her overwhelmingly. A Republican defender, Representative Bill Frenzel, observed, "There isn't anyone we could put on the commission who doesn't carry baggage. In fact, we look for baggage because we want people with political experience."

Indeed, under Reagan political experience was preferred over enforcement experience. One of the most experienced and pro-enforcement commissioners, Republican Frank P. Reiche, had formerly been the first chairman of the New Jersey Election Law Enforcement Commission from 1973 until joining the FEC in 1979. During his six years on the FEC, however, he frequently outraged Republican party lawyers by voting to proceed with investigations that the other two Republicans wanted to block. Reiche had been appointed by President Carter and retired in 1985 rather than seek reappointment. Reagan replaced him with Thomas J. Josefiak, a former lawyer for the National Republican Congressional Committee and a more dependable vote for blocking investigations and new regulations.

. . .

Reagan also purged the only Democratic commissioner who had served continuously since the formation of the FEC, Thomas Harris. The commissioner was a persistent voice favoring tight constraints on corporate political action committees and against opening loopholes through which corporate and union money could flow into national politics. He also sometimes reminded the other commissioners in stark language how far they were veering from the original intent of the campaign finance laws.

Harris wrote:

> This is just plain ridiculous. . . . Disbursements for these [PAC] activities are made for the purpose of influencing an election. They are contributions and expenditures under the act. . . . Only persons just alighting from a UFO can doubt that activities of these sorts . . . will promote the candidacy of the [PAC's] founding father.

Reagan refused to reappoint Harris despite the commissioner's backing from Senate Democratic leader Robert Byrd of West Virginia. The senator in turn refused to recommend anyone else, creating a standoff that delayed the choice of a successor for more than a year. Under law, Harris continued to serve until a successor was selected. The eventual compromise choice was Scott Thomas, a former FEC lawyer who was Harris's deputy.

Reagan's appointments reflected the GOP's hostility to government restrictions on political money. "I find the whole idea of regulating this stuff repugnant," said Jan Baran, general counsel both for the Republican National Committee and for Bush's 1988 presidential campaign. "To the extent that we have decided that government ought to regulate this, I want to keep the intrusion to a minimum."

The appointments resulted in an increase in party-line deadlocks on the commission. "Most of us who are close to the process can attest to the fact that there has been an increase in bipartisan splits in recent years," election lawyer Kenneth Gross remarked in early 1989. "Important issues are not being resolved because of party-line splits."

Republicans, in short, had accomplished their aim of blocking much FEC enforcement and regulation.

THE LAW OF THE JUNGLE

. . .

While Republicans were turning against the FEC, House Democrats reacted by pushing for even more partisan appointments of their own. During the impasse over Harris's reappointment, House Speaker O'Neill tried to recruit a Democratic wheel-horse, former representative Joe Minish of New Jersey, to fill the seat. Minish was widely criticized, however, for keeping a hoard of leftover campaign funds after his 1984 reelection defeat with the apparent intent of converting the political donations to personal use. And indeed, he eventually pocketed $200,000 of the money in January 1989.

Amid all of this, political operatives came to view the commission with contempt, as little more than a nuisance. "People take the attitude that the commission is never going to get four votes, and so they can do anything they want," said Daniel Swillinger, a Republican lawyer who had been an assistant general counsel at the FEC during its earlier days. "It is undercutting what was anyway a rather weak enforcement system and making it even more toothless." Even Republican lawyer Jan Baran, despite his preference for minimal regulation, has complained for years that light penalties cause political operatives to mock the law. He said in the midst of the 1984 presidential campaign: "Everybody wanted to be as clean as Caesar's wife when the Watergate hearings were going on. Now, the attitude has changed tremendously. People aren't threatened with going to jail."

Representative Tony Coelho of Califonia, when he was chairman of the Democratic Congressional Campaign Committee, railed against the FEC in a 1986 interview. "Do away with the whole damn thing," he said. "It's a farce what happens. It's used for cover when you want it, and you abuse it when you want to. The public is not benefiting from the damn thing at all." He said that junking the FEC would shock the public into insisting on starting over with an effective enforcement agency. "I think you go back to the law of the jungle and the public would demand that something else be put in its place," he said.

To a large degree, however, the law of the jungle had already returned.

Federal Election Commission v. *NRA Political Victory Fund,* 6 F.3d 821
(D.C. Cir. 1993)

After the *Buckley* Court ruled unconstitutional the congressional appointment of commissioners and the FEC was reconstituted with its six voting members nominated by the president and confirmed by the Senate, the Clerk of the House and the Secretary of the Senate were retained as ex officio members. Seventeen years later, in a case involving a possible illegal transfer of funds from the National Rifle Association to its political action committee, the D.C. Circuit Court of Appeals ruled against the FEC, arguing that it lacked authority in this case because the presence of these two ex officio members violated the Constitution's separation of powers. This decision was left in place when the Supreme Court dismissed the FEC's appeal on the grounds that the FEC lacked standing to independently bring a case under Title 2 (*Federal Election Commission* v. *NRA Political Victory Fund,* No. 93-1151 [U.S. 1994]. As a result of the appeals court decision, the Commission reconstituted itself as a six-member body, all of whose members are appointed by the president.

. . .

OPINION: SILBERMAN, Circuit Judge:

This enforcement action by the Federal Election Commission concerns a transfer of $415,744.72 from the National Rifle Association Institute for Legislative Action (NRA-ILA) to its political action committee, the NRA Political Victory Fund (PVF). The district court held that the transfer was a "contribution" prohibited by the Federal Election Campaign Act (FECA), 2 U.S.C. §§ 431 et seq. (1988), and rejected appellants' various constitutional arguments based on the First Amendment and separation of powers.

We believe that the Commission lacks authority to bring this enforcement action because its composition violates the Constitution's separation of powers. Congress exceeded its legislative authority when it placed its agents, the Secretary of the Senate and the Clerk of the House of Representatives, on the independent Commission as non-voting *ex officio* members. We therefore reverse.

. . .

Appellants claim that the composition of the Commission, particularly its two *ex officio* members, violates the Constitution's separation of powers. In 1974, Congress amended FECA to create the

Commission and charged it with administering the Act. The Commission then, as now, had eight members: the Secretary of the Senate and the Clerk of the House of Representatives (non-voting and *ex officio*), and six voting members whom Congress played varying roles in appointing. In *Buckley* v. *Valeo*, 424 U.S. 1 (1976), the Supreme Court held, inter alia, that the limitations Congress placed on the President's power to nominate voting members of the Commission violated the Appointments Clause. Although the Court mentioned the *ex officio* members, see id. at 113, it never discussed the constitutionality of their status.

After *Buckley,* Congress reconstituted the Commission as follows:

The Commission is composed of the Secretary of the Senate and the Clerk of the House of Representatives or their designees, *ex officio* and without the right to vote, and 6 members appointed by the President, by and with the advice and consent of the Senate. No more than 3 members of the Commission appointed under this paragraph may be affiliated with the same political party.

2 U.S.C. § 437c(a)(1) (1988).

It is argued that the reconstituted Commission still violates separation of powers principles in several respects. First, appellants urge that FECA's requirement that "no more than 3 members of the Commission . . . may be affiliated with the same political party," 2 U.S.C. § 437c(a)(1) (1988), impermissibly limits the President's nomination power under the Appointments Clause. Second, appellants maintain that the President does not exercise sufficient control over the Commission's civil enforcement authority, a core executive function, to satisfy the constitutional mandate that he "take Care that the Laws be faithfully executed." U.S. Const. art. II, § 3. And finally, they assert that Congress exceeded its Article I authority by placing the Secretary and the Clerk on the Commission as *ex officio* members.

. . .

We think the district court's conclusion was erroneous at least with respect to appellants' last two separation of powers arguments—that the independence of the Commission frustrates the President's executive power and that the *ex officio* members unconstitutionally serve on the Commission.

. . .

We turn now to appellants' more substantial claim. It is undisputed that both *ex officio* members are appointed by and are agents of Congress, and it is also settled that Congress may not appoint the voting members of this Commission or, indeed, any agency with executive powers. See *Bowsher* v. *Synar,* 478 U.S. 714 (1986); *Buckley* v. *Valeo,* 424 U.S. 1 (1976). There remains only the question whether *ex officio* non-voting members enjoy a different status for purposes of constitutional analysis.

The Commission would have us conclude that the *ex officio* members are constitutionally harmless. Non-voting members cannot serve as chairman, cannot call or adjourn a meeting, and are not counted in determining a quorum. In short, we are told that the *ex officio* members have no actual influence on agency decisionmaking. If that were so, congressional intent as reflected in the legislative history would seem frustrated. At least certain members of Congress clearly intended that the appointed officers serve its interests while serving as commissioners. See 122 Cong. Rec. 6706 (1976) (statement of Senator

Mansfield agreeing that "as an *ex officio* member, [the Secretary] would not just remain mute, that he could give advice and consent, that he could, in effect, represent the Senate's point of view"); id. (statement of Senator Cannon agreeing with Senator Mansfield with respect to campaign finance matters "as related to the Senate").

Legislative history aside, we cannot conceive why Congress would wish or expect its officials to serve as *ex officio* members if not to exercise some influence. Even if the ex officio members were to remain completely silent during all deliberations (a rather unlikely scenario), their mere presence as agents of Congress conveys a tacit message to the other commissioners. The message may well be an entirely appropriate one—but it nevertheless has the potential to influence the other commissioners. Federal law recognizes in other contexts that non-voting participation can influence a decisionmaking process. For example, Fed. R. Crim. P. 24(c) states: "An alternate juror who does not replace a regular juror shall be discharged after the jury retires to consider its verdict."

. . .

Since "the legislature 'can with the greater facility, mask under complicated and indirect measures, the encroachments which it makes on the co-ordinate departments,'" id. at 2310-11 (quoting *The Federalist* No. 48, at 334), the mere presence of agents of Congress on an entity with executive powers offends the Constitution.

. . .

Indeed, Congress is not even required after our decision, as it was after *Buckley,* to amend the statute. Since what remains of FECA is not "unworkable and inequitable," id. at 252 (Burger, C.J., concurring in part and dissenting in part), the unconstitutional *ex officio* membership provision can be severed from the rest of FECA.

. . .

Federal Election Commission, "Administering and Enforcing the FECA," *Twenty Year Report* (April 1995), pp. 10–19, 38

This selection from the FEC's twentieth anniversary report, while obviously cloaked in the upbeat public relations rhetoric of its genre, presents a useful overview of the functions of the FEC as well as tables documenting the increase in its workload over the last two decades.

The Federal Election Campaign Act (FECA) regulates the financing of elections for federal office. It limits the sources and amounts of funds used to support candidates for federal office, requires disclosure of campaign finance information and—in tandem with the Primary Matching Payment Act and the Presidential Election Campaign Fund Act—provides for the public funding of Presidential elections. . . .

As the agency charged with administering and enforcing the FECA, the Federal Election Commission has four major responsibilities:

—Providing disclosure of campaign finance information;
—Ensuring that candidates, committees and others comply with the limitations, prohibitions and disclosure requirements of the FECA;
—Administering the public funding of Presidential elections; and
—Serving as a clearinghouse for information on election administration.

This chapter highlights the Commission's stewardship of the FECA, focusing on recent improvements the agency has made in carrying out its responsibilities.

CUSTOMER SERVICE

Since its beginning, 20 years ago, the FEC has prided itself in providing outstanding service to the public, the press and the regulated community. Transcending the Commission's prescribed duties, the commitment to customer service is most evident in the Commission's efforts to encourage voluntary compliance with the FECA and to facilitate public access to campaign finance data. This section demonstrates how the agency's outreach and disclosure programs serve the agency's customers.

Outreach

For political committees, outreach begins early. A committee's first contact with the FEC often comes through the agency's toll-free information hotline. Staff from the Information Division explain the requirements of the FECA and send the committee a registration packet that contains forms and publications geared toward its needs.

When a committee submits its registration documents, the Commission's Data staff assign it an identification number and enter the registration information into the FEC database. Microfilm and paper copies of the registration are placed on the public record, and the committee is automatically added to the mailing list for all official notices and correspondence from the Commission, including the agency's award-winning monthly newsletter, the *Record*.

As questions about the FECA arise, committee staff can choose from a variety of FEC services designed to help them understand the law and voluntarily comply with its provisions. (These services are available to anyone interested in learning about the law. . . . Thousands of callers dial the toll-free information hotline for help each year.) Public affairs specialists answer their questions about the law, and reports analysts, who review the actual reports filed by committees, are also available to respond to questions and offer guidance on the law. (The Commission's Audit staff helps Presidential committees comply with the special rules that govern publicly funded campaigns.) Committee staff can also attend instructional workshops and conferences and/or request free FEC publications that explain particular aspects of the law. Should committee staff need a publication or other document quickly, they can call the agency's automated "flashfax" system and receive the document immediately by fax, 24 hours a day, seven days a week. More than 2,500 documents were faxed during the system's first six months of operation (July–December 1994).

If a committee wants official, legally binding guidance from the Commission, it may request an advisory opinion (AO). The Commission responds to these requests within 60 days, or within 20 days if a candidate's committee submits the request just before an election. An AO answers the requesting committee's question and also serves as a precedent for other committees in similar situations. The Commission has issued more than 1,000 AOs since 1975.

To further assist committees, the Commission sends reminder notices along with the necessary reporting forms shortly before reports are due.

Disclosure

Disclosing the sources and amounts of funds used to finance federal elections is perhaps the most important of the FEC's duties. In fact, it would be virtually impossible for the Commission to effectively fulfill any of its other responsibilities without disclosure. The Commission could not, for example, enforce the law without knowledge of each committee's receipts and disbursements. Disclosure also helps citizens evaluate the candidates running for federal office and it enables them, along with the agency, to monitor committee compliance with the election law. Given these facts, the Commission has devoted substantial resources to providing effective access to campaign finance data.

When a committee files its FEC report, the Commission's Public Records Office ensures that a copy is available for public inspection within 48 hours. Simultaneously, the agency's Data staff begins to enter the information disclosed in the report into the FEC computer database. The amount of information disclosed has grown dramatically over the years. By December 1994, more than 12 million pages of information were available for public review.

In the Public Records Office citizens can inspect microfilm and paper copies of committee reports, as well as the FEC's computer database and more than 25 different computer indexes that make the data more accessible. (The G Index, for example, lists individuals who have given more than $200 to a committee during an election cycle. The K and L Indexes offer broader "bank statement" views of receipts and disbursements for PACs, parties and candidates.) Public Records staff assist thousands of callers and visitors every year. (See chart 1.)

On-line computer access to a committee's financial data is also available in a number of state offices through the State Access Program (SAP), and to individual subscribers linked by modem to the Commission's Direct Access Program (DAP). These systems afford access not only to raw financial data, but also to the various categorical indexes mentioned above....

In the near future, computers will play an even larger role in disclosure. The Commission is adding a digital imaging system to permit a user to view a committee's report on a high resolution computer screen (or a paper copy), just as the document appeared in its original form. Further, the Commission plans to develop and implement an electronic filing program within the next few years to expedite disclosure and to ease the data entry burden the agency now faces. (See chart 2.)

Members of the news media may review committee reports using any of the methods described above, and may receive assistance from the Commission's Press Office. Staff answer reporters' questions, issue press releases summarizing campaign finance data and significant FEC actions, and respond to requests under the Freedom of Information Act (FOIA). The press office logs thousands of calls each year....

The Commission also makes available a variety of agency documents, including: advisory opinions, closed enforcement and litigation files, audit reports and both written minutes and audio tapes of Commission meetings.

Chart 1
Persons Served in Public Records

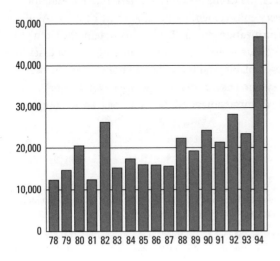

Chart 2
Number of Detailed Contribution and Expenditure Transactions Processed*

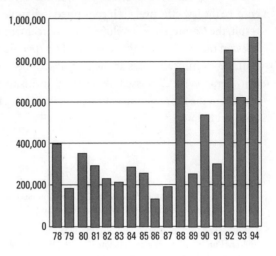

*The Commission lowered its data entry threshold from $500 to $200 in 1989, and began entering soft money transactions in 1991.

ENFORCEMENT

As effective as the Commission's efforts to encourage voluntary compliance with the FECA have been, none would have succeeded without the deterrent provided by the agency's enforcement program. Earlier campaign finance laws were largely ineffectual because no single, independent agency handled enforcement. By contrast, under the current law, the Commission has exclusive jurisdiction over civil enforcement.

Enforcement cases are generated through complaints filed by the public, referrals from other federal and state agencies and the FEC's own monitoring procedures. The Commission's Reports Analysis Division reviews each report a committee files in order to ensure the accuracy of the information on the public record and to monitor the committee's compliance with the law. If the information disclosed in a report appears to be incomplete or inaccurate, the reviewing analyst sends the committee a request for additional information (RFAI). The committee may avoid a potential enforcement action and/or audit by responding promptly to such a request. (Most responses take the form of an amended report.) Although the Commission does not have authority to conduct random audits of committees,[1] it can audit a committee "for cause" when the committee's reports indicate violations of the law.

The agency must attempt to resolve enforcement matters through conciliation. If conciliation fails, however, the Commission (rather than the Justice Department) may take a respondent to court. Likewise, when Commission actions are challenged in court, the Commission conducts its own defensive litigation.[2] The Commission has been involved in more than 350 court cases since 1980.[3]

Prioritization

Until recently, the Commission handled every enforcement matter, regardless of its significance. As the number and complexity of cases increased, a backlog developed, jeopardizing the Commission's ability to effectively enforce the law. Given its limited resources, the Commission recognized that it could not enforce the law effectively if it continued to handle every enforcement matter that came before it. As a result, the Commission developed an enforcement prioritization system. Under this system, the Commission ranks enforcement cases based on specific criteria, and assigns only the more significant cases to staff. Less significant cases are held until staff becomes available, and those that do not warrant further consideration are dismissed. While the prioritization system ensures that the agency devotes its resources to the more significant cases on its docket, the Commission continues to pursue a wide range of cases at all times.

---

1. In its legislative recommendations, the Commission has asked Congress to reinstate the agency's authority to conduct random audits. Congress revoked that authority as part of the 1979 amendments to the FECA [document 2.12].

2. With regard to cases that are appealed to the Supreme Court, however, the high Court ruled, in December 1994, that the FEC could not unilaterally bring cases before it, except those involving the Presidential public funding program. Instead, the Commission must ask the Justice Department either to represent the agency or to grant approval for the Commission to represent itself before the Court. *FEC* v. *NRA Political Victory Fund* [6 F.3d 821 (D.C. Cir. 1993); document 8.2].

3. The Commission has won 90 percent of those cases (excluding cases that were dismissed).

The Commission introduced the prioritization system in 1993. At the same time, the Commission began to seek higher civil penalties when it found serious violations of the law. The agency believes that this combination of prioritization and higher penalties will help deter future violations of the law. (As shown in chart 3, the agency's new approach has had a significant impact.)

Chart 3
Conciliation Agreements and Civil Penalties by Calendar Year*

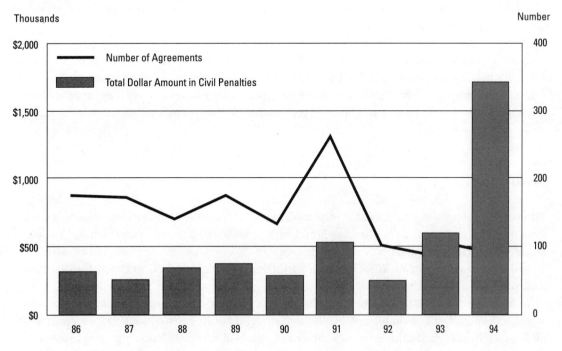

Thousands

Number

— Number of Agreements

▮ Total Dollar Amount in Civil Penalties

*An enforcement case may include several respondents. Because some respondents enter into conciliation agreements more quickly than others, agreements calling for civil penalties in a single enforcement case may be concluded in different years. The figures in this chart represent the total penalties included in all conciliation agreements entered into during the calendar year specified, whether or not the case itself was concluded during that year.

Note that conciliation agreements for a given case are not made public until the entire case closes.

PRESIDENTIAL PUBLIC FUNDING

Every Presidential election since 1976 has been financed with public funds. While the concept of public funding dates back to the turn of the century, a public funding program was not implemented until the early 1970s.

Congress designed the program to correct the problems perceived in the Presidential electoral process. Those problems were believed to include:

—The disproportionate influence (or the appearance of influence) of the wealthiest contributors;

—The demands of fundraising that prevented some candidates from adequately presenting their views to the public; and

—The increasing cost of Presidential campaigns, which effectively disqualified candidates who did not have access to large sums of money.

To address these problems, Congress devised a program that combines public funding with limitations on contributions and expenditures. The program has three parts:
—Matching funds for primary candidates;
—Grants to sponsor political parties' Presidential nominating conventions; and
—Grants for the general election campaigns of major party nominees and partial funding for qualified minor and new party candidates.

Based on statutory criteria, the Commission determines which candidates and committees are eligible for public funds, and in what amounts. The U.S. Treasury then makes the necessary payments. Later, the Commission audits all of the committees that received public funds to ensure that they used the funds properly. Based on the Commission's findings, committees may have to make repayments to the U.S. Treasury.

Audits

Ensuring the proper use of public funds requires Commission auditors to review thousands of transactions involving millions of dollars for each Presidential candidate who receives public funds. The time required for these audits, and the campaigns' response to the Commission's conclusions, can extend several years after the election. These delays have frustrated everyone involved, including the Commission, the candidates and the public.

To minimize these frustrations, the Commission recently introduced a number of innovations to expedite the presidential audit process. In 1991 and 1992, the agency revised its regulations, amended its audit procedures, expanded its use of technology and increased staffing to hasten the completion and disclosure of Presidential audits. The new methods have paid off. The agency issued the final audit reports of all the 1992 Presidential candidates by the end of 1994. In past elections, some reports had taken up to four years to complete.

Tax Checkoff

The public funding program is exclusively funded by the dollars that taxpayers designate for the Presidential Election Campaign Fund on their 1040 tax forms. Beginning in 1980, fewer and fewer taxpayers designated a dollar to the Presidential Fund, even as Fund payments to candidates increased with inflation. . . .

The Commission warned Congress of an impending shortfall in the Fund and launched a public education program, urging taxpayers to "make an informed choice" regarding the checkoff.

In August 1993, Congress preserved the Fund in the short run by increasing the checkoff amount from $1 to $3. The legislation did not, however, index the checkoff amount to inflation. Since payments from the Fund will continue to increase with inflation, a shortfall at some future point remains inevitable. Should a shortfall occur, current law requires the U.S. Department of Treasury to allocate remaining funds, giving first priority to the conventions, second priority to the general election and third priority to the primaries.

. . .

Chart 4
FEC Budget and Staffing History

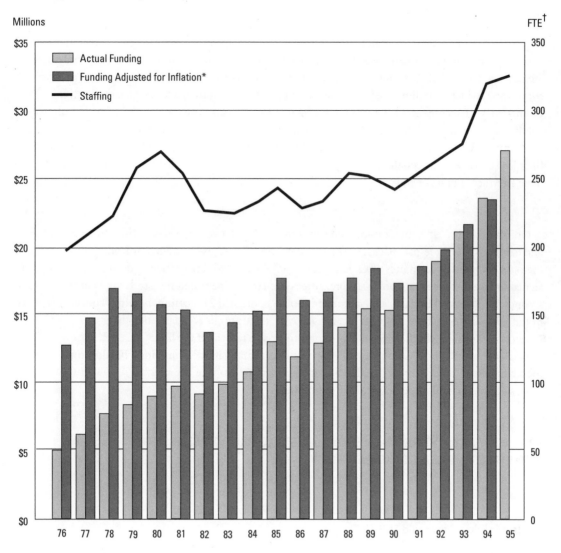

*Activity is expressed in 1994 dollars. This means the values in earlier years have been increased to account for inflation between that year and 1994.

† Full-time equivalent employees.

As part of its annual reporting requirements, the FEC routinely forwards to Congress recommendations for changes in campaign finance law that arise from experiences administering the present system. Some are perennials—such as restoring the Commission's authority to conduct random audits of political committees, which was eliminated by Congress in the 1979 amendments to the Federal Election Campaign Act (document 2.12). Other recommendations—such as giving the FEC explicit authority to conduct its own litigation before the Supreme Court—are made to counter new constraints placed on the Commission by other actors. A careful reading of the explanations offered by the Commission for their legislative recommendations conveys the complexity of the technical, legal, and political environment in which it must operate.

On February 19, 1997, the Commission submitted 57 legislative recommendations to the President and Congress in a three-part package. The first part, entitled "Legislative Recommendations to Improve the Efficiency and Effectiveness of Current Law," contained 23 administrative recommendations designed to ease the burden on political committees and streamline the administration of current law. The second part, "General Legislative Recommendations," contained 24 recommendations concerning areas of the law which have been problematic. In each case, the Commission described the problem and asked Congress to consider clarification or more comprehensive reform of the law.

Finally, the third part, "Conforming Legislative Recommendations," contained 10 additional recommendations that seek to correct outdated or inconsistent portions of the law.

[A sampling of these] recommendations follows. . . .

PART I: LEGISLATIVE RECOMMENDATIONS TO IMPROVE EFFICIENCY AND EFFECTIVENESS OF CURRENT LAW

Disclosure

Electronic Filing Threshold (1997)

Section: 2 U.S.C. Sec. 434(a)

Recommendation: The Commission recommends that Congress give the FEC authority to require committees with a certain level of financial activity to file FEC reports electronically.

Explanation: Public Law 104-79, effective December 28, 1995, authorized the electronic filing of disclosure reports with the FEC. Starting January 1997, political committees (except for Senate campaigns) may opt to file FEC reports electronically.

The FEC has created the electronic filing program and is moving towards providing software to committees in order to assist committees that wish to file reports electronically. To maximize the benefits of electronic filing, Congress should consider requiring committees that meet a certain threshold of financial activity to file reports electronically. The FEC would receive, process and disseminate the data from electronically filed reports more easily and efficiently, resulting in better use of Commission resources. Moreover, information in the FEC's database would be standardized for committees at a certain threshold, thereby enhancing public disclosure of campaign finance information. In addition, committees, once participating in the electronic filing program, should find it easier to complete and file reports.

. . .

Commission as Sole Point of Entry for Disclosure Documents (revised 1997)

Section: 2 U.S.C. Sec.432(g)

Recommendation: The Commission recommends that it be the sole point of entry for all disclosure documents filed by federal candidates and political committees. This would affect Senate candidate committees only. Under current law, those committees alone file their reports with the Secretary of the Senate, who then forwards microfilmed copies to the FEC.

Explanation: The Commission has offered this recommendation for many years. Public Law 104-79, effective December 28, 1995, changed the point of entry for reports filed by House candidates from the Clerk of the House to the FEC. However, Senate candidates still must file their reports with the Secretary of the Senate, who then forwards the copies on to the FEC. A single point of entry is desirable because it would conserve government resources and promote public disclosure of campaign finance information.

For example, Senate candidates sometimes file reports mistakenly with the FEC, rather than with the Secretary of the Senate. Consequently, the FEC must ship the reports back to the Senate. Disclosure to the public is delayed and government resources are wasted.

Public Law 104-79 also authorized the electronic filing of disclosure reports with the FEC. Starting January 1997, political action committees, political party committees, House campaigns and Presidential campaigns all may opt to file FEC reports electronically. This filing option is unavailable to Senate campaigns, though, because the point of entry for their reports is the Secretary of the Senate.

In addition, Public Law 104-79 eliminated the requirements for a candidate to file copies of FEC reports with his or her State, provided that the State has electronic access to reports and statements filed with the FEC. In order to eliminate the State filing requirement for Senate candidates, it would be necessary for a State to have electronic access to reports filed with the Secretary of the Senate, as well as to reports filed with the Federal Election Commission. In other words, unless the FEC becomes the point of entry for reports filed by Senate candidates, either the States will need to have the technological and financial capability to link up electronically with two different federal offices, or Senate candidates must continue to file copies of their reports with the State.

We also reiterate here the statement we have made in previous years because it remains valid. A single point of entry for all disclosure documents filed by political committees would eliminate any confusion about where candidates and committees are to file their reports. It would assist committee treasurers by having one office where they would file reports, address correspondence and ask questions. At present, conflicts may arise when more than one office sends out materials, makes requests for additional information and answers questions relating to the interpretation of the law. A single point of entry would also reduce the costs to the federal government of maintaining two different offices, especially in the areas of personnel, equipment and data processing.

. . .

Contributions and Expenditures

Election Period Limitations for Contributions to Candidates

Section: 2 U.S.C. Sec. 441a

Recommendation: The Commission recommends that limits on contributions to candidates be placed on an election cycle basis, rather than the current per election basis.

Explanation: The contribution limitations affecting contributions to candidates are structured on a "per election" basis, thus necessitating dual bookkeeping or the adoption of some other method to distinguish between primary and general election contributions. The Commission has had to adopt several rules to clarify which contributions are attributable to which election and to assure that contributions are reported and used for the proper election. Many enforcement cases have been generated where contributors' donations are excessive vis-à-vis a particular election, but not vis-à-vis the $2,000 total that could have been contributed for the cycle. Often this is due to donors' failure to fully document which election was intended. Sometimes the apparent "excessives" for a particular election turn out to be simple reporting errors where the wrong box was checked on the reporting form. Yet, substantial resources must be devoted to examination of each transaction to determine which election is applicable. Further, several enforcement cases have been generated based on the use of general election contributions for primary election expenses or vice versa.

Most of these complications would be eliminated with adoption of a simple "per cycle" contribution limit. Thus, multicandidate committees could give up to $10,000 and all other persons could give up to $2,000 to an authorized committee at any point during the election cycle. The Commission and committees could get out of the business of determining whether contributions are properly attributable to a particular election, and the difficulty of assuring that particular contributions are used for a particular election could be eliminated.

It would be advisable to clarify that if a candidate has to participate in more than two elections (e.g., in a post-primary runoff as well as a primary and general), the campaign cycle limit would be $3,000. In addition, because at the Presidential level candidates might opt to take public funding in the general election and thereby be precluded from accepting contributions, the $1,000/5,000 "per election" contribution limits should be retained for Presidential candidates.

A campaign cycle contribution limit may allow donors to target more than $1,000 toward a particular primary or general election, but this would be tempered by the tendency of campaigns to plan their fundraising and manage their resources so as not to be left without fundraising capability at a crucial time.

. . .

Enforcement

Fines for Reporting Violations (1997)

Section: 2 U.S.C. Sec. 437g

Recommendation: The Commission recommends that Congress consider granting the Commission authority to assess fines on a published schedule for straightforward violations relating to the reporting of receipts and disbursements.

Explanation: In maintaining a regulatory presence covering all aspects of the Act, even the most simple and straightforward strict liability disclosure violations, e.g., the late filing or non-filing of required reports, may be addressed only through the existing enforcement process at 2 U.S.C. Sec.437g. The enforcement procedures provide a number of procedural protections, and the Commission has no authority to impose penalties. Instead, the Commission can only seek a conciliation agreement, and without a settlement can only pursue a *de novo* civil action in federal court. This process can be unnecessarily time and resource consuming for all parties involved when applied to ministerial-type civil violations that are routinely treated via published fines by many other states and federal regulatory agencies. Non-deliberate and straightforward reporting violations would not have to be treated as full blown enforcement matters if the Commission had authority to assess fines for such violations under a published fine schedule, subject to a reasonable appeal procedure. Congress could authorize the Commission to promulgate a fine schedule that would consider a number of factors (e.g., the election sensitivity of the report and the previous compliance record of the committee). Addition of such authority would introduce greater certainty to the regulated community about the consequences of noncompliance with the Act's filing requirements, as well as lessen costs and lead to efficiencies for all parties, while maintaining the Commission's emphasis on the Act's disclosure requirements. The Commission would attempt to implement this on a trial basis.

. . .

Ensuring Independent Authority of FEC in All Litigation

Section: 2 U.S.C. Sec. 437c(f)(4) and 437g

Recommendation: Congress has granted the Commission authority to conduct its own litigation independent of the Department of Justice. This independence is an important component of the statutory structure designed to ensure nonpartisan administration and enforcement of the campaign financing statutes. The Commission recommends that Congress make the following four clarifications that would help solidify the statutory structure:

1. Congress should clarify that the Commission is explicitly authorized to petition the Supreme Court for *certiorari* under Title 2, i.e., to conduct its Supreme Court litigation.

2. Congress should amend the Act to specify that local counsel rules (requiring district court litigants to be represented by counsel located within the district) cannot be applied to the Commission.

3. Congress should give the Commission explicit authorization to appear as an *amicus curiae* in cases that affect the administration of the Act, but do not arise under it.

4. Congress should require the United States Marshal's Service to serve process, including summonses and complaints, on behalf of and at no expense to the Federal Election Commission.

. . .

[*Editorial Note: The Supreme Court has held that only the Department of Justice may represent the FEC before the Court under the statutes as currently drafted.*]

Enhancement of Criminal Provisions

Section: 2 U.S.C. Sec. 437g(a)(5)(C) and (d)

Recommendation: The Commission recommends that it have the ability to refer appropriate matters to the Justice Department for criminal prosecution at any stage of a Commission proceeding.

Explanation: The Commission has noted an upsurge of Sec.441f contribution reimbursement schemes, that may merit heavy criminal sanction. Although there is no prohibition preventing the Department of Justice from initiating criminal FECA prosecutions on its own, the vehicle for the Commission to bring such matters to the Department's attention is found at Sec.437g(a)(5)(C), which provides for referral only after the Commission has found probable cause to believe that a criminal violation of the Act has taken place. Thus, even if it is apparent at an early stage that a case merits criminal referral, the Commission must pursue the matter to the probable cause stage before referring it to the Department for criminal prosecution. To conserve the Commission's resources, and to allow the Commission to bring potentially criminal FECA violations to the Department's attention at the earliest possible time, the Commission recommends that consideration be given to explicitly empower the Commission to refer apparent criminal FECA violations to the Department at any stage in the enforcement process.

Random Audits

Section: 2 U.S.C. Sec. 438(b)

Recommendation: The Commission recommends that Congress consider legislation that would require the Commission to randomly audit political committees in an effort to promote voluntary compliance with the election law and ensure public confidence in the election process.

Explanation: In 1979, Congress amended the FECA to eliminate the Commission's explicit authority to conduct random audits [document 2.12]. The Commission is concerned that this change has weakened its ability to deter abuse of the election law. Random audits can be an effective tool for promoting voluntary compliance with the Act and, at the same time, reassuring the public that committees are complying with the law. Random audits performed by the IRS offer a good model. As a result of random tax audits, most taxpayers try to file accurate returns on time. Tax audits have also helped create the public perception that tax laws are enforced.

. . .

Public Financing

State Expenditure Limits for Publicly Financed Presidential Primary Campaigns (revised 1997)

Section: 2 U.S.C. Sec. 441a

Recommendation: The Commission recommends that the state-by-state limitations on expenditures for publicly financed Presidential primary candidates be eliminated.

Explanation: The Commission has now administered the public funding program in five Presidential elections. Based on our experience, we believe that the limitations could be removed with no material impact on the process.

Our experience has shown that, in past years, the limitations have had little impact on campaign spending in a given state, with the exception of Iowa and New Hampshire. In most other states, campaigns have been unable or have not wished to expend an amount equal to the limitation. In effect, then, the administration of the entire program has resulted in limiting disbursements in these two primaries alone.

. . .

[T]he Commission decided to revise its state allocation regulations for the 1992 Presidential election. Many of the requirements, such as those requiring distinctions between fundraising and other types of expenditures, were eliminated. However, the rules could not undo the basic requirement to demonstrate the amount of expenditures relating to a particular state. Given our experience to date, we believe that this change to the Act would still be of substantial benefit to all parties concerned.

. . .

PART II: GENERAL LEGISLATIVE RECOMMENDATIONS

Disclosure

. . .

PACs Created by Candidates

Section: 2 U.S.C. Sec. 441a(a)

Recommendation: The Commission recommends that Congress consider whether PACs created by candidates should be deemed affiliated with the candidate's principal campaign committee.

Explanation: A number of candidates for federal office, including incumbent officeholders, have created PACs in addition to their principal campaign committees. Under current law, such PACs generally are not considered authorized committees. Therefore, they may accept funds from individuals up to the $5,000 limit permitted for unauthorized committees in a calendar year and may make contributions of up to $5,000 per election to other federal candidates once they achieve multicandidate status. In contrast, authorized committees may not accept more than $1,000 per election from individuals and may not make contributions in excess of $1,000 to other candidates.

The existence of PACs created by candidates can present difficult issues for the Commission, such as when contributions are jointly solicited with the candidate's principal campaign committee or the resources of the PAC are used to permit the candidate to gain exposure by traveling to appearances on behalf of other candidates. At times the operations of the two committees can be difficult to distinguish.

If Congress concludes that there is an appearance that the limits of the Act are being evaded through the use of PACs created by candidates, it may wish to consider whether such committees are affiliated with the candidate's principal campaign committee. As such, contributions received by the committees would be aggregated under a single contribution limit and subjected to the limitations on contributions to authorized committees. The same treatment would be accorded to contributions made by them to other candidates.

. . .

Contributions and Expenditures

Issue Advocacy Advertising (1997)

Sections: 2 U.S.C. Sec. 431(8)(A)(i) and (9)(A)(i); 441d

Recommendation: The Commission recommends that Congress consider when "issue advocacy" advertising by corporations, labor organizations, political parties, and other organizations is an in-kind contribution because it is coordinated with a candidate or a candidate's campaign.

Explanation: The 1996 election cycle saw an explosion in "issue advocacy" advertising. Such advertising explores an officeholder's, a party's or a candidate's stand on a particular issue, but does not expressly advocate the election or defeat of a clearly identified candidate or party. Courts have ruled that the Act's prohibition on expenditures by corporations and labor organizations does not extend to issue advocacy that does not contain express advocacy.

The Act defines the term "contribution" to include funds that are spent "for the purpose of influencing an election." Although advertisements devoted solely to issue advocacy do not contain express advocacy, such advertising may benefit or harm a candidacy and consequently influence the election process, particularly if the communication is coordinated with a candidate or his/her campaign. In a series of cases, the Supreme Court has viewed public communications coordinated with campaigns as in-kind contributions. As contributions, such communications were subject to the Act's limitations and prohibitions, but were not subject to the same level of First Amendment protection as expenditures.

In accordance with these rulings, Congress should stipulate when coordination of an issue advocacy advertisement with a candidate or campaign would be considered an in-kind contribution. Additionally, Congress should state that coordination of such a public communication with a corporation or a labor organization would be prohibited activity. Such a prohibition would help the Commission address the public's concern about the use of soft money—funds that are raised or spent outside the prohibitions of the Act (such as corporate or union treasury funds)—to influence federal elections.

. . .

Contributions from Minors

Section: 2 U.S.C. Sec. 441a(a)(1)

Recommendation: The Commission recommends that Congress establish a presumption that contributors below age 16 are not making contributions on their own behalf.

Explanation: The Commission has found that contributions are sometimes given by parents in their children's names. Congress should address this potential abuse by establishing a minimum age for contributors, or otherwise provide guidelines ensuring that parents are not making contributions in the name of another.

. . .

Enforcement

Audits for Cause

Section: 2 U.S.C. Sec. 438(b)

Recommendation: The Commission recommends that Congress expand the time frame, from 6 months to 12 months after the election, during which the Commission can initiate an audit for cause.

Explanation: Under current law, the Commission must initiate audits for cause within 6 months after the election. Because year-end disclosure does not take place until almost 2 months after the election, and because additional time is needed to computerize campaign finance information and review reports, there is little time to identify potential audits and complete the referral process within that 6-month window.

Modifying Standard of "Reason to Believe" Finding

Section: 2 U.S.C. Sec. 437g

Recommendation: The Commission recommends that Congress modify the language pertaining to "reason to believe," contained at 2 U.S.C. Sec.437g, so as to allow the Commission to open an investigation with a sworn complaint, or after obtaining evidence in the normal course of its supervisory responsibilities. Essentially, this would change the "reason to believe" standard to "reason to open an investigation."

Explanation: Under the present statute, the Commission is required to make a finding that there is "reason to believe a violation has occurred" before it may investigate. Only then may the Commission request specific information from a respondent to determine whether, in fact, a violation has occurred. The statutory phrase "reason to believe" is misleading and does a disservice to both the Commission and the respondent. It implies that the Commission has evaluated the evidence and concluded that the respondent has violated the Act. In fact, however, a "reason to believe" finding simply means that the Commission believes a violation may have occurred if the facts as described in the complaint are true. An investigation permits the Commission to evaluate the validity of the facts as alleged.

It would therefore be helpful to substitute words that sound less accusatory and that more accurately reflect what, in fact, the Commission is doing at this early phase of enforcement.

In order to avoid perpetuating the erroneous conclusion that the Commission believes a respondent has violated the law every time it finds "reason to believe," the statute should be amended.

. . .

PART III: CONFORMING LEGISLATIVE RECOMMENDATIONS

. . .

Contributions and Expenditures

. . .

Nonprofit Corporations and Express Advocacy

Section: 2 U.S.C. Sec. 441b

Recommendation: In light of the decision of the U.S. Supreme Court in *FEC* v. *Massachusetts Citizens for Life, Inc.* (*MCFL*) [document 7.4], the Commission recommends that Congress consider amending the provision prohibiting corporate and labor spending in connection with federal elections in order to incorporate into the statute the text of the court's decision. Congress may also wish to include in the Act a definition for the term "express advocacy."

Explanation: In the Court's decision of December 15, 1986, the Court held that the Act's prohibition on corporate political expenditures was unconstitutional as applied to independent expenditures made by a narrowly defined type of nonprofit corporation. The Court determined, however, that these nonprofit corporations had to disclose some aspect of their financial activity—in particular, independent expenditures exceeding $250 and identification of persons who contribute over $200 to help fund these expenditures. The Court further ruled that spending for political activity could, at some point, become the major purpose of the corporation, and the organization would then become a political committee. The Court also indicated that the prohibition on corporate expenditures for communications is limited to communications expenditures containing express advocacy.

Since the Court decision and subsequent related decisions (e.g., *Austin* v. *Michigan [State] Chamber of Commerce,* 494 U.S. 652 (1990)) [document 3.3], the Commission has concluded a rulemaking proceeding to implement changes necessitated by the current case law. See 60 FR 35293 (July 6, 1995). However, the Commission believes that statutory clarification would also be beneficial.

Congress should consider whether statutory changes are needed: (1) to exempt independent expenditures made by certain nonprofit corporations from the statutory prohibition against corporate expenditures; (2) to specify the reporting requirements for these nonprofit corporations; and (3) to provide a definition of express advocacy.

. . .

| DOCUMENT 8.5 | Kenneth A. Gross, "The Enforcement of Campaign Finance Rules: A System in Search of Reform," *Yale Law and Policy Review,* vol. 9, no. 2 (1991), pp. 279–300 |

A former associate general counsel in charge of enforcement at the FEC, Kenneth A. Gross discusses the limitations of the civil and criminal procedures in place for enforcing campaign finance law and suggests a number of reforms designed to strengthen due process protections, enhance the ability of the Commission to deter violations of the law, and make criminal sanctions apply to a broader class of violations. This excerpt deals only with civil procedures.

. . .

   While there have been many proposals to make substantive changes to the campaign finance laws, historically, these proposals have overlooked the need to improve procedures for enforcement of these laws. If this round of reforms is to be effective, particular attention must be devoted to the enforcement provisions in light of the critical inadequacies of the current enforcement scheme.

   The current enforcement mechanism is flawed in three fundamental ways. First, individuals and campaigns accused of Federal Election Campaign Act (FECA) violations do not enjoy many of the due process protections available to the accused in other administrative contexts. Second, the statutory enforcement scheme under the FECA constrains the ability of the Federal Election Commission (FEC) to adequately deter FECA violations—a daunting task in the face of entities that aggressively seek creative ways to evade the laws. Finally, despite the existence of a number of criminal statutes prohibiting elected officials from accepting campaign contributions for improper purposes, the criminal law has been of limited value in regulating campaign finance activity. While the criminal law plays a critical role in protecting the integrity of political campaigns and government processes, as currently written and enforced, it regulates only a relatively narrow class of the most egregious conduct. As a result, prosecutors now must either proceed with the difficult task of proving a criminal case or do nothing due to the lack of a civil enforcement alternative for violations of the law involving the electoral process outside of the jurisdiction of the FEC.

   This article suggests reforms that Congress should adopt in order to address these flaws and improve the enforcement of federal campaign finance laws. Both deterrence and due process protections would be enhanced significantly by reforming the enforcement mechanisms of the FECA. Essential reforms included establishing the use of Administrative Law Judges (ALJs), reinstituting random audits, opening

Reprinted by permission of the Yale Law and Policy Inc. from *Yale Law and Policy Review,* vol. 9, no. 2 (1991), pp. 279–80, 283–91.

the enforcement process to the public, and establishing and publicizing penalty guidelines. Moreover, vigorous criminal enforcement of the FECA and other laws, particularly the bribery and conflict-of-interest statutes, would enhance public trust that elected officials will act in the best interest of their constituents and the nation, rather than for selfish gain. Finally, the addition of a civil penalty provision to the conflict-of-interest statute would provide prosecutors with greater flexibility in identifying sanctions to address appropriately the severity of improper conduct.

. . .

THE CIVIL ENFORCEMENT OF CAMPAIGN FINANCE LAWS—THE FEDERAL ELECTION COMMISSION

A. Overview

. . .

Under the FECA scheme, an enforcement proceeding, called a Matter Under Review (MUR), may be initiated in two ways—either on the basis of (1) a complaint filed with the Commission, often by opposing candidates or by the opposing political party (complaint-generated), or (2) information ascertained by the Commission in the normal course of its business (internally-generated). In either case, the Office of General Counsel (OGC), the Commission's lawyers, prepares an analysis and a recommendation as to whether there is "reason to believe" a violation has occurred or is about to occur. The Commission votes on the recommendations in a closed meeting. If four of the six Commissioners vote to find reason to believe a violation has occurred, the Commission initiates an investigation. If the Commission deadlocks, then it must prepare a statement explaining its disagreements.

The findings of the Commission, deadlocks included, are subject to judicial review in the United States District Court for the District of Columbia. Such a deadlock was challenged when the Commission split along party lines in a case involving a National Republican Senatorial Committee effort to funnel $2.7 million in excessive contributions to Senatorial candidates in twelve states. The Democratic Senatorial Campaign Committee sought judicial review of the FEC's failure to reach a decision. The Court agreed with the FEC's legal staff and the Democrats on the Commission that the method used to funnel contributions, sometimes called "bundling," was illegal, and remanded the case to the FEC to order the prohibition of the bundling activities and award appropriate penalties.

After the Commission has found "reason to believe," it may exercise broad investigative powers. The FEC has the authority to take depositions of witnesses, subpoena documents and answers to questions, and enforce the subpoenas in U.S. District Court. Upon completion of its investigation, the OGC makes its recommendation to the Commission. The respondent has an opportunity to respond in writing only. The FEC then attempts to settle the matter through a conciliation agreement, which routinely includes a detailed recitation of the facts, conclusions of law, an admission of a violation, and a civil penalty. If the respondent does not voluntarily enter into a conciliation agreement with the FEC, the Commission may bring an action on a trial *de novo* basis in a United States district court.

...

The Commission has consistently taken the position that every conciliation agreement must include a full recitation of the facts, an admission of a violation, and a civil penalty, regardless of whether the agreement is entered into before or after probable cause is found. The Commission will retreat from those requirements only in rare instances and, while it will negotiate the "admission language," the Commission is averse to entering into an agreement that contains "neither admit nor deny" language.

If a case cannot be resolved through conciliation, the Commission will sue the respondent and seek the statutory maximum penalty, which is 100% of the amount in violation or $5,000, whichever is higher. If the Commission alleges that the violation is knowing and willful, it will ask the court to impose a penalty of 200% of the amount in violation or $10,000, whichever is higher. Respondents have a significant incentive to settle; once the matter is in litigation, there is a substantial risk that the court will impose a higher penalty than what the Commission offered to settle the matter during the administrative conciliation process.

The Commission is generally successful in getting respondents to admit to violations in conciliation agreements. Most respondents prefer to quietly settle through the MUR process rather than subject themselves to litigation, its related publicity, and the potentially higher civil penalties. Generally, the Commission files suit in less than ten percent of the MURs and in some years, in less than five percent of the MURs. This small percentage reflects the belief of many respondents that litigation should be avoided at all cost.

B. Problems with the Enforcement Process

The complexities and eccentricities of the FECA impede the effective enforcement of the law. Regardless of how stringent the substance of new campaign finance reform may be, certain basic enforcement problems must be addressed if the goals of reform are to be realized. The FECA's enforcement procedures have been criticized by the press and other commentators since the creation of the Commission. Most of the criticisms relate to two problems: lack of due process for respondents (i.e., the political committees and individuals who are subjected to an investigation) and lack of deterrence for violators of the law.

First, several aspects of the enforcement process impinge upon the due process rights of respondents. For instance, respondents are not permitted to address the Commission in person; instead, the respondents may only provide written responses to the OGC, which then provides the Commission with summaries of those responses. Furthermore, respondents are unable to see all of the evidence against them or to challenge the OGC's final recommendations to the Commission.

Second, the FECA as currently written does not adequately deter violations of the statute. Many participants in the political process believe that the election laws need not be heeded. The chance is slim that violations will be detected, party-line deadlocks reduce the chance that the Commission will investigate violations of the law, and any resulting penalty will probably come long after the election.

...

C. Reforms To Enhance Enforcement

Five reforms could help alleviate many of these problems and facilitate the enforcement of the campaign finance laws.

1. Use Administrative Law Judges. Congress could ameliorate the problems of insufficient due process protections, lack of judicial supervision and duplicative fact-finding processes by amending the FECA to provide for adjudicatory proceedings conducted by ALJs. Under such a plan, cases would first be brought before an ALJ and handled under adjudicative procedures, rather than through the investigative procedures described above. In this way, the cumbersome "reason to believe" stage would be eliminated in complaint initiated actions. Moreover, the Commission would serve an appellate function thereby alleviating its involvement in details of the compliance process. For example, the Commission would not be involved in the formulation and approval of interrogatories propounded under subpoena.

Using ALJs to preside over the investigation and briefing process is a common method that enforcement agencies use to adjudicate facts, in accordance with the Administrative Procedure Act. An FEC ALJ would oversee the development of an accurate and complete record of the facts relevant to the proceeding and render a fair and equitable decision on the merits and on the record.

. . .

Under the above plan, ALJs would not make final agency determinations; all decisions would be appealable to the Commission. Because the ALJ proceeding would create a record for review by the Commission and the court, the duplicative nature of the current system would be reduced. Given the availability of a record of the administrative proceedings, Commission decisions based on those proceedings would be appealable to the United States Court of Appeals for the District of Columbia Circuit. *De novo* review by a trial court would be unnecessary. Nothing in this proposed procedure would prevent the respondent from settlement through the conciliation process.

. . .

The use of ALJs would also eliminate deadlocks in initiating and conducting investigations. The disturbing trend toward an increased number of party-line deadlocks has, in some instances, stymied the Commission's ability to investigate cases that appear to involve serious violations of law.

2. Open the Process to the Public. The entire FEC enforcement process is currently closed to the public until a case is dismissed, a conciliation agreement is entered into between the parties, or a suit is filed. The complainant can make public his complaint, but the Commission can say nothing about an action that may be pending for years, and likely will not be resolved prior to the next election. In 1976, when it added a confidentiality requirement to the FECA, Congress had a specific objective, namely, protecting candidates from groundless complaints and adverse publicity arising from FEC investigations.

Maintaining the secrecy of the Commission's deliberations on complaint generated cases does not protect candidates from harm as a result of a groundless complaint. In fact, open deliberations may provide a great disincentive to filing complaints with little or no substance. If a frivolous complaint is filed on the eve of an election, it will quickly become apparent that the complaint has no substance even before the election occurs. Similarly, if Congress adopts the ALJ approach, the ALJ proceedings should be held in open session.

3. Use Summary Procedure for Routine Cases. Even without making a statutory change in the enforcement process, which would be required to adopt the ALJ approach, the Commission could implement its own reforms to improve its efficiency and effectiveness. For instance, the processing of routine cases could be accelerated if the Commission revised its procedures to expand the use of preprobable cause conciliation. If the Commission finds reason to believe a violation has occurred in a case involving a readily apparent violation—found, for example, in a review of the public record or on the face of a document—it should offer a proposed conciliation agreement along with the "reason to believe" notice. Cases that would be suitable for this expedited process are matters which do not raise factual disputes. Examples include late-filings, failure to include proper disclaimers in campaign materials, and excessive corporate contributions.

. . .

4. Conduct Random Audits. Until the 1980s, the FEC conducted audits of randomly-selected campaigns. This practice proved useful, albeit overzealous in some cases, in monitoring FECA compliance. Congress should reinstate the FEC's authority to conduct such random audits.

Congress took action in the 1970s to curtail this FEC power. . . . With the demise of random audits, the FEC now audits only "for cause." A "for cause" audit is based on a review of campaign finance reports filed by a political committee that reveal systematic reporting violations. Unfortunately, the present "for cause" audit provision, implemented by Congress in the 1979 Amendments to the FECA, does not necessarily result in audits of the committees that are most likely to have serious compliance problems. As long as its FEC filings are complete and in order, a political committee could be engaging in serious misconduct and never be audited. The less sophisticated committees that lack the resources to ensure that their reports do not have careless errors are the committees most likely to be audited. This is unfair.

5. Penalties. Random audits can only provide part of the incentive needed to assure compliance with the law. In order to create an effective deterrent, an increased likelihood of being caught must be coupled with higher penalties for serious offenses.

Of course, the FEC could be criticized for unfairly departing from past practices if it dramatically increased its civil penalties without proper notice and justification. Therefore, in raising penalties, the FEC should publish civil penalty guidelines for most violations as well as the criteria for calculating the penalties. The guidelines could allow for adjustments depending on aggravating and mitigating factors.

. . .

Brooks Jackson, "Fixing the FEC: Suggestions for Change: Fulfilling the Promise," in *Broken Promise: Why the Federal Election Commission Failed*, a Twentieth Century Fund Paper (New York : Priority Press, 1990), pp. 59–73

In the concluding chapter of his Twentieth Century Fund study of the Federal Election Commission, Brooks Jackson outlines an ambitious agenda of reform. This includes replacing the current commissioners with a five-member panel headed by a strong chair and including as the tie-breaking vote a public commissioner not aligned strongly with either major party; increasing and protecting the FEC budget; enhancing its resources and strengthening its procedures for investigations and audits; allowing citizens with election-law grievances to sue alleged violators directly if the FEC has failed to act within the specified time; and improving the disclosure of information on contributions and expenditures.

The Federal Election Commission fails for two reasons: the weak structure that Wayne Hays crafted for it, and the sympathy the commissioners feel toward the politicians who hold them captive. The agency lacks both means and will. Can anything be done? What *should* be done?

. . .

REPLACE OR REMODEL?

The FEC requires radical surgery. It suffers not just from a weak structure, but from an institutional culture that has decayed over the years to a degree that is probably irreversible. The commissioners see Congress and the parties, not the public, as their constituency. Like persons held hostage too long, they have identified with their kidnappers.

It shouldn't be necessary to replace the entire agency, however. The staff, which processes literally millions of pages of public disclosure documents, is universally praised for its work. The tiny, but experienced, audit division does a commendable job with the resources available. And the commission has been more than competent in its handling of hundreds of millions of dollars in subsidies to presidential candidates and political party nominating conventions. Even the legal staff, which must plod along burdened by cumbersome procedures, nevertheless has long experience and often shows more vigor than the reluctant commissioners.

What is needed isn't a new agency, but new commissioners with a new spirit, a new and stronger structure, and some streamlined rules and procedures. The blueprint offered here calls for replacing the current commissioners with a five-member panel headed by a strong chair and including as the tie-

---

breaking vote a non-partisan "public" commissioner not aligned strongly with either major party. It also would give the FEC a bigger budget. As a goad to action, it would restore to citizens the right to sue alleged election-law violators directly if the FEC still couldn't act.

A NEW STRUCTURE

Strong Chair

The FEC needs what other independent agencies have, a strong chair to provide leadership. Currently, the six commissioners take one-year turns as chairman. The post is largely ceremonial; the chairman presides at meetings, signs documents, and exerts some small influence over the agenda, but doesn't hire or fire staff or direct operations. In all matters, each of the six commissioners has an equal voice. Drift and deadlock are built in.

Indeed, the FEC's structure makes it possibly the weakest of all federal agencies. The only other six-member panel is the U.S. International Trade Commission (ITC), which also has a weak chairman and no more than three members from either party. But where the FEC requires four votes for action, at the ITC the built-in bias is in favor of action; it requires only three affirmative votes to produce a finding that a U.S. industry has been harmed by unfair price-cutting on imports.

Ideally, the FEC's chair should serve for several years, select and oversee the staff, authorize routine investigations into such minor infractions as late reports, and issue warning letters or citations for the routine, minor violations that make up the bulk of the FEC's caseload. The other commissioners should vote to set general policies, to authorize subpoenas in more serious cases, and to act as a court of appeal.

The president should nominate as the chair a member of the commission from outside his own party. That would provide an incentive to select carefully and would lessen the danger of partisan abuse by the party in power. The incentive should be to pick a person with a reputation for integrity and fairness. All commissioners would continue to be subject to Senate confirmation, of course.

The chair also should have authority to deal with frivolous complaints or petty infractions by dismissing them with the equivalent of public "warning tickets" (subject to review by the full commission). Such a system would allow the enforcement staff to concentrate on truly important cases.

There would be little danger that even such a strong chair could abuse the commission's civil enforcement power for political ends. A bad chair could cause harassment and expense to his or her political enemies, but little more. Such abuse might even backfire, generating sympathy votes for the victim. Besides, the present structure can also be abused, as when party-line deadlocks block enforcement of laws that might inconvenience the party of some of the commissioners.

Indeed, the current weak arrangement may be the more dangerous. It is now possible for commissioners of one party to block any legal action against their own presidential, House, and Senate candidates when they violate election laws. Theoretically, one party could secretly mobilize illegal money to "buy" critical elections while its commissioners provided cover. That may seem far-fetched, but so does the possibility of a partisan coup by an FEC with a strong chair. It is also important to note that a five-member panel with a strong chair still wouldn't have the power to prosecute criminal cases. Furthermore, even a strengthened FEC couldn't collect a single penny in fines without either proving a civil case in federal court, or negotiating an out-of-court conciliation settlement agreeable to both sides. It would be "strong" mostly by comparison to the current system.

Five Members

To provide a clean break with the discredited past, the current commissioners should all be replaced and the size of the panel reduced from six to five.

New commissioners would allow a fresh start—a chance to replace the present hostage mentality with a more independent spirit. The present commissioners are prisoners not only of Congress, but of the institutional culture they have helped to create. If only because of their toleration of soft money, they have demonstrated themselves to be inadequate regulators.

Furthermore, the six-member structure allows the members of either party to prevent even the gathering of facts by investigators. With an odd number of commissioners, actions could no longer be blocked by tie votes.

Such a commission is already in action on the state level. The California Fair Political Practices Commission (CFPPC) has five members, with a strong chair appointed by the governor. Compared to the FEC, the California commission has been a model of vigor and independence.

Expanding the commission to seven members—as proposed in one Senate bill introduced in 1989—would also end deadlocks, but at the cost of retaining all the current commissioners. A five-member panel would be more lean and economical. It also would give relatively more weight to a nonpolitical, "public" member who could become the tie-breaking vote.

"Public" Commissioner

The FEC needs at least one "public" commissioner, whose essential qualification would be a strong reputation for integrity, civic involvement and political independence. Currently, the two major parties hold a monopoly on the nominations. The fifth commissioner should be a representative of those citizens who don't identify strongly with either major party.

This commissioner would represent the decisive vote if the two Democrats and two Republicans should split along party lines. This also would lessen the danger of one party abusing the FEC for partisan ends.

The ideal public commissioner could be a former university president, a retired judge, a prominent member of the clergy, or the leader of a public interest group. Such a person could bring to the commission the skepticism of entrenched party interests that seems to be shared by non-aligned voters—and those who have ceased voting entirely. One reason much of the public feels alienated from their government is the idea—widely held and not entirely baseless—that moneyed interests hold sway in both parties. A public commissioner could represent that viewpoint.

Such a public member should not be a strong partisan, and ideally should be politically independent. At a minimum, he or she should not have held any party office or partisan elective post. (Merely registering to vote in a partisan primary wouldn't be an automatic disqualification, however.)

Staggered Terms

Congress should end the bad practice of confirming the commissioners in pairs, which encourages selection of partisans. Under the current system, an unspoken bargain is sealed: "We'll give you yours if we get ours." The system thus seeks out commissioners burdened by political baggage, as Representative Bill Frenzel noted.

Each commissioner should undergo a separate confirmation, and the Senate should examine each on his or her record and individual merits. This could be accomplished by appointing the commissioners to five-year terms staggered so that one expires each year. Also, because unexpected vacancies could occur, there should be a statutory requirement that each commissioner face confirmation alone.

. . .

INVESTIGATION AND AUDIT

Budget

The FEC's budget should be protected from political retaliation. There is precedent for this at the state level: the California Fair Political Practices Commission has an inflation-adjusted budget that by law the legislature may only increase, but not cut. The FEC needs the same thing.

The FEC also needs an increase in funds. To enforce the current law, a modest increase will provide for additional auditors and investigators and for their travel during their work. And if new duties are heaped upon the commission, such as enforcement of spending limits in 435 House races and thirty-three or thirty-four Senate races every two years, the commission's budget will need to double or triple. The cost in any case won't be a great drain on the Treasury; the FEC now spends only about $15 million a year, one of the smallest budgets of any federal agency.

Investigators

The FEC should reestablish a field staff trained in conducting financial investigations. Candidates might be drawn from such agencies as the Internal Revenue Service, the Federal Deposit Insurance Corporation, or the General Accounting Office, which excel at such tasks. It is clearly inadequate to conduct inquiries with desk-bound lawyers in Washington.

Presently, those lawyers are restricted mainly to a passive role, evaluating statements sent in by complainants and accused violators. When they want to ask questions, they generally must do so through written questionnaires, called interrogatories. But, under current procedures, the commissioners themselves insist on screening each question—a most cumbersome procedure. Written questions make it easy for respondents to give vague or artfully worded, misleading answers. Asking follow-up questions is difficult. Sometimes the FEC probes more deeply by calling in witnesses for full-blown legal depositions, where their words are transcribed as they are cross-examined in the presence of their lawyers. But for the most part, the FEC accepts on faith the factual assertions of lawyers for the defense.

Investigators would be able to track down reluctant respondents more quickly than the FEC's lawyers [have done in the past]. They also could question potential witnesses informally and even take confidential statements when warranted, probing more deeply for facts.

Automatic Warnings and Fines

Well over half the commission's enforcement work involves routine, clear-cut cases such as tardy disclosure reports, or campaign literature that doesn't properly identify its sponsor. Yet even such simple cases go through much the same elaborate process as major violations. The general counsel writes reports, the commissioners vote on whether to proceed with an investigation, FEC lawyers send notices and await replies from lawyers for the accused. Then the FEC counsel writes another report and the full commission votes again, this time on whether to accept whatever fine has been negotiated. While the commission now processes such routine cases in batches, each still can generate a thick file, causing legal expenses and wasted time for everyone.

Under a strong chair, the staff could be delegated the responsibility to process routine cases in the same way that traffic police issue parking citations or speeding tickets. The warning tickets, mentioned earlier, should suffice for first violations. However, repeat offenses should draw escalating fines, which would be assessed automatically by the staff but subject to appeal to the full commission and, ultimately, to the federal courts.

The laws need simplifying in other ways, too. The unenforceable state-by-state spending limits for presidential candidates should be abolished, for example. This would free the FEC's resources for more important matters. The law also should be amended to make clear that bank loans to candidates require collateral equal to the value of the loan, clarifying an area where the FEC has found ambiguity.

Threshold for Investigation

With its docket cleared of the most routine cases, the FEC should be given unequivocal discretion to investigate dubious situations. Currently, the law requires that at least four of the six commissioners must vote to find "reason to believe" that a law has been violated before the staff can proceed with an investigation. Although the FEC's legal staff has declared this to be a rather low threshold, three commissioners have been able to block staff recommendations to proceed in some important cases. This has the effect of killing a case before the staff has even interviewed witnesses or requested documents on a voluntary basis.

Congress should make it clear that the FEC's chair may conduct a preliminary investigation when the chair sees facts that present a "reasonable suspicion" of a violation. Ample safeguards against abuse would still exist. A majority of commissioners still would have to approve issuance of any subpoenas, and the commission's ultimate weapon still would be the power to bring a civil lawsuit in federal court.

Whistleblower Protection

Congress should restore the FEC's ability to investigate anonymous complaints. Indeed, it should go further and allow the FEC to protect the identity of anonymous sources who blow the whistle on violations. FEC lawyers sometimes encounter persons who say, "I can't talk to you, because I'm afraid." For example, when businessmen force employees to make contributions and reimburse them illegally with corporate funds, the workers are usually reluctant to speak for fear that they will be fired. The successful California Fair Political Practices Commission investigates anonymous complaints and protects confidential sources. As a result, according to former CFPPC director Robert Stern, staff employees of politicians have sometimes given information about possibly illegal activities by their employers.

The FEC still would have to prove any violation with public testimony and documentary evidence, of course. But without confidential leads, it can be impossible to find such proof.

Random Audits

Congress should restore the authority of the FEC to conduct audits on a random sample of congressional candidates after each election. Currently the public has no practical assurance that candidates aren't hiding donations or misstating their spending.

The FEC itself annually recommends reinstating random audits. It is time for Congress to accept this basic, common-sense safeguard. It is clear that the honor system just won't do.

Cooperation with Prosecutors

The FEC consciously avoids referring possibly criminal cases for prosecution, an unusual stance for an independent agency. "Everybody else refers cases to us," says Craig Donsanto, the Justice Department's election-crimes prosecutor. Indeed, sometimes the FEC has denied requests from government prosecutors for information from its own investigations, maintaining that they legally must remain secret—even from other federal agencies—until the commission is finished with them.

Congress should amend the law to allow the FEC to share information with sister federal agencies during an investigation.

Access to Courts

In one important sense, the public is now worse off than if there were no FEC at all. The Supreme Court has held that those with complaints must bring them to the FEC and are barred by law from suing the alleged violators directly. If the FEC can't or won't act, then complainants may sue the commission. But there's a catch: under other prevailing court decisions, judges may interfere with the workings of any federal agency only if convinced that it is acting in an arbitrary and capricious manner, contrary to the law it is supposed to administer. And even then, judges typically require the agency merely to reconsider or to provide a better rationale. As the U.S. Court of Appeals in Washington said in a case involving the FEC, "We are not here to run the agencies."

Congress should allow those with election-law grievances to sue alleged violators directly if the FEC has failed to act within the specified time. Corporate stockholders may sue corporate officers, and any citizen may bring a lawsuit alleging environmental or civil rights violations. But the law makes the FEC the only place that citizens may seek relief when they believe the process of government itself is being tainted with illegal money. "Only a bureaucrat can take care of that? It's outrageous," says Roy Schotland, a professor at Georgetown University Law Center.

Since the expense is great, few complainants would actually sue. But the possibility of citizen lawsuits could keep the commission from dawdling. In California, any citizen can bring an election-law suit and, if successful, collect half of any award. Not one has been successful, but former CFPPC director Stern recalls, "When I was there it put tremendous pressure on us to file the right suits." He said it would have been "mortifying" for a citizen to win a suit that the commission refused to pursue.

Senators Mitch McConnell and Harry Reid, in their bill, would grant such a right to sue only to candidates, but this is not enough. Political parties, public interest groups, and ordinary citizens also should have recourse to the courts. The McConnell-Reid bill also provides that the loser reimburse the winner for attorney's fees and costs, which would deter all but the richest candidates from suing. If anything, the law should provide encouragement for such private lawsuits, as is the case in California.

DISCLOSURE

Computerized Disclosure

Nearly everyone agrees that the most important campaign finance reform was accomplished in 1971, before the creation of the FEC, when Congress enacted the first serious requirement that candidates, parties, and political committees at the federal level disclose their incomes and expenses [document 2.8]. The FEC is generally praised for its handling of this public information, but even here improvements could be made.

Congress should require the FEC to track both donor and spending data by computer, and to make this information available on-line to the public. At present, the FEC enters all donations given by PACs to candidates, and enters donations from individuals (as reported by the recipients) of $200 or more. But for several years it didn't attempt to track individual donations of less than $500, citing budget constraints. And during a budget squeeze in 1986, it ceased entering individual donor data altogether, saying it wasn't legally required to computerize anything.

The FEC's data are kept on several hundred reels of microfilm, containing several million pages of campaign finance reports. Since individual donors aren't required to report what they give, a thorough search for any one person's gifts would require looking through every one of those pages filed by all possible recipients. Without use of a computer it is a practical impossibility for anyone to find, for example, all the donations made by a lobbyist seeking to open a loophole in the tax code, or to discover how much was given by the executives of a high-flying savings-and-loan association seeking to influence federal legislation. Congress should require the FEC to make maximum practicable use of modern technology to aid the public in tracking donations and expenditures.

Repeal of "Commercial Use" Ban

Congress should also make clear that the raw disclosure data at the FEC may be computerized, processed, and resold by private groups. The FEC should be encouraging wide dissemination of data, not trying to prevent it. The "commercial use" prohibition should be repealed, or at least narrowed to bar only the solicitation of money from donors whose names are disclosed.

Political committees already have a powerful tool for keeping their donor lists out of the hands of competitors. They are allowed by law to "salt" each report with as many as ten names of nonexistent persons. Anyone illegally sending appeals for money to such pseudonyms then betrays himself automatically. Giving complainants the right to sue alleged violators directly would provide an even stronger deterrent to pirating those lists.

In any event, the business interest that political committees have in their donor lists is far outweighed by the public's right to timely, useful, comprehensible information about who is paying for the election of their lawmakers.

Donor Information

In a similar vein, campaigns should be prohibited from accepting any donation over $200 until they have determined the occupation and employer of the giver.

Many campaigns claim to be unable to discover this basic information about a large fraction of their givers, keeping the public in the dark about their real economic interests. At one time, the FEC was somewhat strict about requiring such information, but Congress in 1979 enacted a standard by which campaigns may omit employer and occupation information if they can show "best efforts" were made to get it. The FEC's regulations state that this requirement is met if the donor is sent a single postcard requesting the information and saying it is required by law.

Donations of under $200 don't have to be disclosed at all under current law. It is hardly asking too much for candidates to obtain employer and occupation information about all the rest.

ALTERNATE IDEAS: INCREMENTAL CHANGE

The ideas outlined here constitute an ambitious goal that is unlikely to be attained soon. Congress, if it acts at all, will surely be reluctant to fire the current six commissioners, most of whom won their jobs through congressional friends in the first place. Others will object to giving more money, power, and discretion to an agency—even such an ineffectual one as the FEC—that regulates the sensitive business of electing the nation's leaders.

A more modest approach would be to expand the commission by adding a seventh, public member, and strengthening the chair. That would break the party-line deadlocks and allow a strong, multiyear chair a chance to work. But leaving the current commissioners in place simply will not change the anti-enforcement culture that has grown up over the years. A stronger alternative would be to make this seventh member the chair, effectively demoting the current commissioners. Such a move also would send a strong message that the FEC's institutional mores are unsatisfactory.

The weakest alternative, of course, would be to keep the present structure and allow complainants to sue alleged violators directly when the FEC fails to act, or when it deadlocks on a tie vote. This approach could encourage marginally better enforcement, but it amounts to an admission that the commission itself can't or won't do its job. The prohibitive cost of lawsuits would also limit the amount of such private policing.

One flawed but intriguing idea merits mention. Former FEC enforcement chief Kenneth Gross has proposed that the commission handle serious cases as mini-trials, prosecuted by the general counsel before an administrative law judge, as is done at some other regulatory agencies [document 8.5]. The commissioners would base their verdicts upon the administrative judge's findings and the factual record developed at the "trial." Any cases appealed to the courts could be swiftly reviewed on the basis of the facts already in evidence. There would be no need for a judge to try the matter over again.

The problem here is that a four-vote majority of a six-member commission would still be required to decide whether a case should even be investigated. But such a procedure could make sense under a strong chair and an odd-numbered commission. . . .

Trevor Potter, "With Changes, the FEC Can Be Effective," *Roll Call* (January 20, 1997), pp. A-29–A-30

A former chairman of the Federal Election Commission and a coeditor of this book, Trevor Potter reviews reform proposals that strive to balance the desire for stronger enforcement of the law with the fear that a strengthened FEC will harass candidates and parties and threaten political freedom. Among the promising ideas he discusses are proposals for a nonvoting member to serve as permanent chairman of the FEC and its "honest broker"; a private right of legal action (with a "loser pays" standard) when the FEC is unable to act; an express grant of independent litigating authority for the Commission before the Supreme Court; and a two-year budget authority.

Proposals to change the Federal Election Commission's structure or grant the agency additional powers have been called the lightening rod of campaign finance reform.

FEC provisions were actually struck out of the Democratic leadership's 1992 reform bill during the debate on the Senate floor as the price of support from a group of Republicans, and the FEC's role has only grown more sensitive since then. Republicans and Democrats alike charge the FEC with irrelevance and a failure to prevent election law violations, while simultaneously objecting to proposals to give the agency new powers or greater resources.

This dichotomy is not necessarily hypocritical or contradictory. While the FEC's general counsel argues that any campaign finance reform that does not significantly strengthen the commission's ability to enforce the campaign finance laws is nothing less than a fraud on the public, Members of Congress and officials of the political parties fear the FEC will use any new powers to intervene directly in election campaigns and harass candidates and parties. They fear a more powerful government bureaucracy could become a potentially dangerous threat to political freedom. Nonetheless, a number of reform proposals step cautiously into this mine field. What follows is a survey of the most common suggestions for reforming the FEC.

STRUCTURE

Single Terms for Commissioners

Virtually all reform proposals include a recommendation that commissioners serve only one term, with no possibility of reappointment, as a way of insulating commissioners from political pressure.

Under the current process, incumbent commissioners must seek support for their reappointment from the White House and Congressional and party leaders while continuing to decide matters affecting those officials (such as audits of presidential campaigns and questions of election law violations by candidates and parties).

First proposed by the American Bar Association's Election Law Committee, single-term proposals were included in last session's McCain-Feingold (Senate) and Smith-Meehan-Shays (House) bills, and are in the recommendations proposed by the American Enterprise Institute–Brookings Campaign Finance Working Group [document 9.9]. Some proposals recommend a six-year term (the current model), while others opt for eight years in order to obtain greater continuity.

The AEI-Brookings proposal would also ensure that commissioners' terms are staggered rather than "paired" (with two commissioners, one from each party, being nominated at the same time) to encourage greater scrutiny of nominees.

Seventh Commissioner

The FEC currently has six commissioners, of whom not more than three may come from one party. Historically, there have always been three Republicans and three Democrats, which has led on occasion to well-publicized tie votes on controversial matters. Reformers have long sought a tie-breaking vote, and the political parties have just as strongly opposed it, fearing the extra vote would go to someone from the other side.

This year, two new proposals have surfaced in an attempt to deal with this complicated issue. The AEI-Brookings Group proposes a seventh non-voting member, who would serve as the FEC's permanent chairman, using the authority of that office to set the agency's agenda and to attempt to cajole the commissioners into compromise, as a sort of "honest broker." A group of political scientists assembled by Herb Alexander of the University of Southern California is planning to propose that the six commissioners be required to agree on a list of names that would then be recommended to the President for nomination as the seventh commissioner. The proposal rests on the theory that anyone the six could agree on would be as neutral as possible.

Both of these proposals will undoubtedly face an uphill battle in Congress, although reformers argue that the FEC's propensity to deadlock must be addressed in some way.

POWERS

Expedited Procedures and Injunctive Relief

Both McCain-Feingold and Smith-Meehan-Shays included provisions allowing the FEC to adapt expedited procedures immediately prior to the election in important cases, and to seek injunctions from the courts in instances where the commission believes violations of law are imminent, with a potential for irremediable damage.

The difficulty with such proposals is that the FEC is already overloaded and unable to deal with its current case load in a timely manner. It is therefore difficult to see how it could devote the resources necessary to investigate alleged violations in an expedited manner, and then assemble the evidence necessary to convince a court to grant an injunction—all in the few weeks immediately prior to an election.

Private Right of Legal Action

One way to circumvent the FEC's occasional deadlocks is to allow private litigants to go directly to court when the FEC is unable to act.

The AEI-Brookings Working Group proposes that individuals or groups be granted the power to independently seek court enforcement of the election laws when the FEC is unable to act because of a tie vote, or fails to act in matters that are both urgent and important enough to affect the outcome of the election.

In such instances, the AEI-Brookings proposals would allow the individuals to take the matter out of the FEC's hands and seek judicial enforcement (including injunctive relief, where appropriate) on their own. To avoid flooding the courts with frivolous and baseless suits, the proposal would adopt a "loser pays" standard for legal fees.

Random Audits

A number of proposals would give the FEC the authority to randomly select and audit political committees. This power was expressly denied the commission by Congress in 1979, after the FEC audited a number of senior Members as a result of a random selection process.

Again, the problem for the FEC is resources: It now spends almost all of its auditor's time on the publicly funded presidential campaigns, with a few audits of egregious Congressional and party committees added to the mix. It is, therefore, hard to see where it would get the time and personnel to perform the proposed random audits.

Independent Litigating Authority

For nearly 20 years, the FEC argued its own cases before the Supreme Court, and independently decided the cases it wanted to ask the Court to take.

The Supreme Court in *FEC [Federal Election Commission]* v. *NRA* looked more closely at the commission's enabling statute and decided Congress had not given the FEC the authority to represent itself before the Supreme Court [document 8.2]. In the absence of such specific authority, the Supreme Court said, the FEC must be subject to the decisions, and representation, of the Solicitor General at the Department of Justice.

The FEC had argued that this undermines the commission's independence, and could result in politically motivated decisions by the Solicitor General's office. Additionally, especially after the *Colorado Republican* case was argued by the Solicitor General himself, it is apparent that the federal election laws are sufficiently arcane and complicated that it helps to have government lawyers thoroughly versed in their peculiar technicalities. Accordingly, several of the campaign finance bills include an express grant of independent litigating authority before the Supreme Court for the FEC.

FINANCES

Along with the structure and authority of the commission, the other element of the FEC that reformers argue must be addressed is the budget process. The American Bar Association, the AEI-Brookings Working Group, and Larry Sabato at the University of Virginia have all proposed changes in an attempt to provide the FEC with more predictable (if not larger) resources.

Two-Year Budget Authority

The ABA and the AEI-Brookings Working Group both propose a two-year budget cycle for the commission. Currently, the FEC has a bare few months between final enactment of one budget and Congressional hearings on the next, often resulting in budget-induced paralysis at the agency as Congressional priorities change and the staff director and commissioners scramble to respond.

A two-year cycle would provide some time for the agency to carry out one set of Congressional policies, and for Congress to evaluate those programs, before beginning the next budget process. This has been proposed by other groups on a government-wide basis, but, perhaps because of the FEC's relatively minuscule management structure, it might be especially useful to that agency.

Inflation Indexing

Sabato argues that Congress should set a reasonable floor for the FEC's budget, and then index it to inflation. This is similar to the funding mechanism approved some years ago by California's voters as part of that state's initiative establishing the California Fair Political Practices Commission.

Each of these proposals will no doubt be the subject of considerable—if behind-the-scenes—debate on Capitol Hill as campaign finance reform is discussed.

The inevitable tension between the desire of reformers for a truly independent enforcement agency and Congress's political and constitutional interest in maintaining a high level of oversight of the FEC will make it an interesting discussion.

Brent Thompson, "A Flawed Institution Should Not Expand," *Roll Call* (January 20, 1997), pp. A-29–A30

A radically different perspective on the FEC and its reform is provided by Brent Thompson, executive director of the Fair Government Foundation, a group founded by two Republican senators to resist campaign finance law encroachments on the First Amendment. Thompson takes special umbrage at the Commission's efforts to enforce a more expansive definition of express advocacy than is suggested by a literal reading of *Buckley* (document 3.1). He disagrees with those who argue the FEC has had inadequate resources to deal with its expanding workload and resists the provisions in the McCain-Feingold legislation to strengthen the enforcement tools of the Commission. Thompson's spirited challenge to any further regulation of money in politics in no doubt viewed sympathetically by many in Congress.

Although spending limits, soft money, and political action committees receive the bulk of attention and debate in regard to campaign finance reform, there is very little discussion over whether the Federal Election Commission is competent to administer the ambitious regulatory system conceived by Sens. John McCain (R-Ariz) and Russ Feingold (D-Wis).

If its past is an adequate guide, the FEC is not up to the task. Its two-decade history, only now receiving serious scrutiny, reveals an agency that has been indifferent to free speech, dismissive of judicial guidance, and less than satisfactory in discharging its core responsibilities in a timely fashion. The FEC's checkered past severely clouds the wisdom of giving additional powers to what can only be described as a challenged agency.

EXPRESS ADVOCACY AND FREE SPEECH

Conceived in 1975, the FEC quickly matured into a highly motivated and muscular regulator of political speech. It proved incapable of constraining its regulatory impulses or according deference to the Constitution. Lacking meaningful Congressional oversight and getting a free pass from the press, the only constraining influences have been its unique bipartisan structure and the federal judiciary.

While the environment is target rich, the FEC's most conspicuous overreaching has occurred in its deeply flawed administration of the "express advocacy" standard. In the 1976 landmark case *Buckley* v. *Valeo* [document 3.1], the Supreme Court ruled that issue advocacy, in contrast to electoral advocacy, may not be regulated consistent with the First Amendment. The High Court found that only "independent expenditures"—those that "expressly advocate" the election or defeat of a particular candidate—may be regulated.

The Court sought to ensure that issue advocacy would be protected from governmental interference. Thus, "[s]o long as persons or groups eschew expenditures that in express terms advocate the election or defeat of a clearly identified candidate, they are free to spend as much as they want to promote the candidate and his views," wrote the Court.

The Court's decision has not been well received among those who favor government regulation of politics, removing, as it did, an entire class of political advocacy from governmental control.

The FEC, indeed, has resisted the *Buckley* decision and at every turn has sought to achieve a different result. It has been quietly but steadfastly enforcing its own definition of express advocacy, which brings large swaths of ordinary political activity under the FEC's heavy regulatory yoke. In case after case, FEC lawyers have propounded artful legal theories in an effort to overcome *Buckley* and expand its regulatory purview. At last count, in 11 of 12 cases the courts have rejected the commission's importuning, returning again and again to the language of *Buckley*.

The FEC's most recent defeat involved the Christian Action Network. The case concerned television ads aired by the network during the 1992 campaign that were critical of candidate Bill Clinton's position on homosexuality. The FEC claimed the ads were independent expenditures illegally paid for with corporate funds and sought a $1.26 million fine. In August 1996, however, a court of appeals affirmed a district court decision that found the FEC's position "unsupportable" [document 7.7].

Although the commission was rightly rebuffed in those cases that went to court, there is no telling in how many administrative cases it succeeded in enforcing its view. There can be no debate that, until recently, the FEC's quixotic enforcement efforts have "successfully" chilled considerable issue advocacy by grassroots organizations and activists. Some of the commission's targets have included National Right to Life, the Christian Coalition, the National Organization for Women, the National Rifle Association, the American Federation of State, County, and Municipal Workers, and ACT-UP (AIDS Coalition to Unleash Power).

While perhaps unintended, the course the FEC has followed should not be surprising. It merely confirms and illustrates known lessons about the tendencies of power and the culture of bureaucracy. A federal appeals court judge was prescient when he warned in 1980 that "such bureaucracies feed on speech and almost ineluctably come to view unrestrained expression as a potential 'evil' to be tamed, muzzled, or sterilized."

On the FEC's performance, one jurist put it bluntly. The FEC has the "weighty, if not impossible, obligation to exercise its powers in a manner harmonious with a system of free expression. The Commission . . . has failed abysmally to meet this awesome responsibility."

THE FEC HAS FAILED TO STICK TO ITS KNITTING

By eagerly aspiring to the role of political speech police, the FEC has failed to stick to its knitting. These dangerous dalliances have left less time and resources to fulfill the FEC's routine (but decidedly unglamorous) responsibilites.

The result has been that ordinary enforcement cases often drag on for years. In a humiliating admission of failure, the FEC was forced in 1993 to drop more than 130 back-logged cases because they had grown stale and unprosecutable.

And in what has become a house joke, audits, which are required by law of presidential campaigns, are notoriously long, strange journeys. The 1988 Bush campaign audit, for example, lasted longer than George Bush served as president. And the audit of Pat Robertson's 1988 presidential campaign took some eight years, mocking the ideal of speedy justice.

The FEC, moreover, is only now entering the computer age, finally making electronic filing and disclosure a partial reality. It finally took an act of Congress earmarking specific funds to force the Commission to modernize.

These problems can scarcely be attributed to insufficient resources. The FEC has been the beneficiary of substantial budget increases at a time when spending on such matters as military preparedness and drug interdiction have declined. From 1991 to 1996, its budget increased 55 percent, and it saw a 24 percent increase in personnel.

Notwithstanding the budget increases, the FEC (like most agencies) without fail pleads poverty at its annual budget hearings. So skilled at talking a good game, a special report of the House Appropriations Committee labeled the commission a "self-licking ice cream cone."

With such an "abysmal" record, it is therefore a serious question to ask how Congress can responsibly grant more power and greater authority to the FEC. Yet that is precisely what McCain and Feingold propose.

ADDING INSULT TO INJURY

The McCain-Feingold legislation would invest in the FEC enormous additional responsibilities, provide the commission unwarranted enforcement tools, while failing to make any needed institutional reforms. Perversely, Congress would be rewarding the FEC for a job not well done.

The sheer scope of responsibilities the FEC would have to juggle is daunting. It would be required to micromanage 468 Congressional contests (33 Senate and 435 House) involving at a minimum some 936 candidates, assuming every race has a challenger.

The main feature of McCain-Feingold is a system of campaign spending limits in which compliance is induced by offers of "free" and reduced-rate broadcast time and reduced-rate postage. Complying Senate candidates would be prohibited from spending more than $250,000 in personal funds and no more than $5.5 million in the general election. In addition to spending limits, complying candidates would be required to raise 60 percent of their funds from within their state, and political action committees would be criminalized.

The FEC would be center stage in administering this complex web of regulation. Its new duties would encompass "certifying" that a candidate has met the requirements of the act and is thus eligible for free broadcast time and the other inducements. The FEC would monitor the spending and fundraising of nearly 1,000 candidates to ensure spending limits are observed and that contributions are properly allocated between in- and out-of-state donors. If a candidate fails to meet the requirements, the FEC would be required to "revoke" that candidate's certification, rendering them no longer eligible for campaign perks.

If the FEC revokes a candidate's certification, it then must determine the value of the benefits received by the candidate, if any, and see to it that an equal amount is collected from the candidate as a repayment. The commission would be responsible for judging whether any of the benefits were misused, or whether spending limits were exceeded. In either case, the FEC would be required to obtain a repayment in full from the offending candidate.

The FEC would also oversee the allocation of broadcast time and would hear petitions by broadcasters seeking to be exempted from giving away their product. Any broadcaster that could show "significant economic hardship" or whose signal is substantially national would be released from participating.

This scheme ought to give policymakers great pause in view of the FEC's troubled experience with the presidential system. The FEC is supposed to enforce spending limits there as well, but as witnessed last year alone with allegations concerning the Dole campaign, any thought of prompt determination is a pipe dream. The FEC is simply not equipped, nor do campaigns lend themselves, to quick resolution of complaints.

Inevitably, complaints alleging spending limit violations would be addressed after the election, and given their likely great number, would swamp existing resources. And because the FEC will not be empowered to invalidate elections, a repayment order will be a meaningless remedy to losing candidates who observed the spending limits.

Prompt resolution, however, is not an acceptable alternative either. The specter of the election police banging down doors at election headquarters, serving subpoenas, and carting away boxes of records during a campaign is not comforting. Yet the McCain-Feingold bill would give the FEC the power to seek temporary injunctions if "there is a substantial likelihood" that a violation of the act is "occurring."

Apart from the practical limitations on the use of injunction authority, as the ACLU has rightly observed, enjoining a candidate from speaking and campaigning would amount to an unconstitutional prior restraint. It is indeed hard to imagine a set of circumstances where an FEC injunction would not restrain a candidate from engaging in political speech. To endow a government agency with such power over the democratic proces is downright frightening.

MODEST REFORM IDEAS

Here are a few modest reforms that would bring some measure of improvement to the FEC.

—Grant the commission chairman real authority and demand real accountability. Currently, the chairmanship is largely honorific and by law must rotate annually. The chairman should be appointed from among the members for a six-year term, and should have the authority to hire and fire the senior staff and determine the enforcement priorities and program. The success or failure of the FEC—and thus accountability—would be vested in a single individual.

—Commissioners should be permitted to serve only one six-year term and should have actual experience running or working in a campaign. The theoretical here is the enemy of the practical. Significant campaign experience should thus be a job prerequisite.

—Just as the state may not appeal criminal acquittals, the commission should be precluded from appealing enforcement cases it loses in district court. It is unfair to respondents to force them to defend an appeal after having already prevailed in district court, and limiting the FEC to one bite at the apple would bring about better resource allocation.

—A reasonable limitations period should be adopted to force the commission to dispose of cases more expeditiously. Nothing contributes more to an appearance of ineptitude, nor generates greater disrespect for the law, than allowing cases to drag on for years. Quick conciliation of cases is what Congress intended, yet it has remained aspirational at best.

—And finally, for certain minor offenses, respondents should have the statutory right to cure the defect, and, if done promptly, avoid enforcement proceedings or sanctions.

RUNNING WITH THE BULLS

The American public has grown cynical over campaigns and elections, in part because of the overblown rhetoric of "reformers," mismatched expectations, and a flawed sense of the possible. Because McCain-Feingold won't work and is, for all intents and purposes, unadministratable, the electorate is being set up for another fall and yet more dashed expectations. It would thus be worse than nothing.

There is a growing body of opinion that is resigning itself to the proposition that the First Amendment, along with the inherent insufficiency of regulation, has rendered the attempt to manage and control the democratic process a fool's errand. As flawed as it is, perhaps the FEC is as competent and effective as its organic limitations will permit. After all, regulating democracy is a bit like running with the bulls in Pamplona. Try as you might to impose order, chaos reigns.

Trevor Potter, "Enforcing Spending Limits in Congressional Elections: Can the FEC Do the Job?" Brookings Working Group on Campaign Finance Reform, 1996
http://www.brook.edu/gs/campaign/round2.htm

As part of an Internet-based discussion during the 104th Congress of the campaign finance legislation proposed by Senators John McCain (R-Ariz.) and Russell D. Feingold (D-Wisc.), Trevor Potter addressed the question of whether the Federal Election Commission (FEC) had the capacity, authority, and resources to administer congressional spending limits. His answer—an unequivocal no—provides a sobering perspective on the administrative impediments to voluntary spending limits in congressional elections. It also helps one understand why enacting effective reform is so difficult.

Has the McCain-Feingold legislation anticipated and dealt sufficiently with the ways the spending limits might be evaded? Will the FEC have the capacity, authority, and resources to administer congressional spending limits?

The answer to the first part of this question is undoubtedly not. History has shown that no legislation can ultimately anticipate and foil the ingenuity of those determined to engage in political speech beyond the intended bounds of the regulatory structure. The entire history of campaign finance regulation in the United States in the twentieth century is of a slow legislative process struggling to catch up with a much faster and constantly evolving set of political practices.

In the area of campaign finance regulation we know very little for certain, but the little we do know includes the fact that each major attempt to regulate political speech in this country in the last ninety years has ultimately foundered. Portions of these regulatory structures have been thrown out by the courts, or narrowed so that they no longer served their intended purpose. Other portions could not be or were not enforced, and new forms of spending grew up just beyond the reach of the law.

The fact that this bill is a reaction to just such developments does not mean it will be any more successful than its predecessors. The legislation enacted in the 1970s was a reaction to the perceived inadequacy of several other attempts to regulate campaign financing, extending back to the 1907 original ban on corporate contributions to political parties or candidates [see chapter 2]. Yet here we are discussing a proposal ninety years later that once again attempts to ban that same corporate money. Given this historical background, the question of administration of any new law—through regulations, disclosure, and enforcement—should be central to any reform legislation. This is especially so as the Federal Election Commission, the agency that would administer a new law, has been widely criticized for its actions (and inaction) under the current laws.

As for the question of whether the FEC will have the capacity, resources, and authority to administer the regulatory behemoth created by McCain-Feingold (particularly the spending limit provisions), I cannot seriously believe that anyone with even the most minimal familiarity with that agency as currently designed and funded could answer yes, or even maybe. It boggles the mind to think of the FEC as we know it attempting to enforce even a tenth of the new regulations contained in this bill.

To begin with, many of the bill's supporters regularly argue that the FEC is not enforcing the current laws adequately. To the extent that is correct, then any new responsibilities are beyond the FEC, unless something changes first. Further, the budget discussion in Congress for several years now has focused largely either on having the FEC do its job more efficiently with minimum additional resources (from the agency's *supporters*) to having the Commission try to do less with less (from those who believe the FEC has acted beyond its authority or intended role). Neither approach appears likely to lead to additional FEC enforcement resources.

In today's real-world FEC, it takes several years and almost all of the Commission's audit resources to look at fewer than a dozen presidential campaigns. Although it is true that these campaigns are large, they also have cadres of lawyers and accountants, computerized accounts, and experienced professional staff that many congressional campaigns lack. The resulting orderly records make presidential audits easier in some ways than other committee audits usually are. The FEC audits almost no party committees or congressional candidates nowadays—only a handful a cycle. That is true even though others qualify for "for cause" audits, never mind the "random audits" the bill provides for.

Meanwhile, every election year brings a raft of complaints that the current (and in comparison to this bill, rather simple) laws are being violated. The Commission deals with only a portion of these on a substantive basis. It dismisses many complaints (perhaps a majority) because they have grown too stale while awaiting assignment to an available staffer, or because they have grown less important as allegations of even larger violations have been filed. Meanwhile, when the Commission does pursue matters to an end, that conclusion is increasingly a court decision finding that the statute of limitations has already run out or that the matter was not constitutionally within the Commission's reach.

This is not an apologia for the Commission. It undoubtedly has its moments of inefficiency, misjudgements, and just plain mistakes. However, the reality is that it is hard to foresee the FEC as it currently exists enforcing a significantly more complicated and more expansive law. The bill only mentions the Commission's current operations when it proposes to limit Commissioners to one term, and when it bestows a variety of new powers (such as random audits, expedited procedures, and injunctive relief) there is no evidence the FEC would ever have the resources or administrative structure to exercise [them].

Furthermore, the bill flies in the face of much of the criticism of the Commission from Congress and the political parties—specifically, that the FEC is already too intrusive in the political process, too bureaucratic, and too overly regulatory. Leaving aside for the moment the question of the degree to which these criticisms are accurate (in my experience, they could fairly be applied to some extent to almost all such regulatory endeavors), surely it is only sensible to ask whether these critics are likely to give the FEC even a portion of the vast additional resources and powers needed to police this bill's provisions.

My list of these provisions is not exhaustive, but it includes the following:

—Expenditure limitations in all Congressional elections (raising questions of what counts, what doesn't, and which "independent" expenditures were actually coordinated);

—Limits on contributions from individuals who are not in-state or in-district "residents" (as monitored and determined how?);

—Seemingly endless calculations on a percentage basis (contributions in excess of $250 cannot exceed 25 percent of receipts; 60 percent of contributions must be from in state, and 50 percent of that in district; nonparticipants must report when they reach 50, 70, and 120 percent of the expenditure limit);

—Commission certification of eligibility and revocation of same if "relevant information comes to its attention" (in the middle of hundreds of hotly contested campaigns); and

—No state party spending for get-out-the-vote or "generic campaign activity" in a federal election year except with federal funds (thereby federalizing most state party activities). This does not even begin to address the restrictions on conduits, solicitations, and fund-raising in the business sphere, or the prohibitions on certain activities (including solicitations) by lobbyists and foreign agents. Expecting the FEC to do any single one of these things would be optimistic; expecting the Commission to enforce this entire package is unbelievable.

Furthermore, there are some legitimate questions about whether an organization large, powerful, and aggressive enough to intervene in the midst of the election process to enforce all of these provisions would in fact be a benefit to a democracy. I am thinking not only of the dangers of abuse of governmental authority in an area at the core of a democracy (although at some point this issue must be taken seriously), but of whether we want the outcome of our elections affected even more than they are already by the decisions of judges and federal regulatory officials during the campaign process.

In sum, I think it is unrealistic to expect enforcement of this regulatory edifice of limits and prohibitions. A lack of enforcement will lead, sure as the sun rises in the east, to widespread noncompliance. That leads to scandal and public disillusionment—which is how we got into this situation in the first place.

McCain-Feingold would do better to address the appointments process for FEC Commissioners (perhaps an advisory panel, modeled on those used for some judges, to provide names to the president) and then admit that the FEC, even in the best of all possible worlds, will not be able to fulfill the role expected of it by this bill. Instead, why not simplify the bill (expenditure limits have proven impossible to enforce whenever and whereever they have been tried), and then provide for a private right of action when violations occur and the FEC is unable to address them, either because of deadlock or understaffing. That would take some of the pressure off an overburdened FEC, while ensuring that allegations of egregious violations can be pursued by those who think they have been injured. A flood of lawsuits could be avoided by providing an opportunity for the Commission to act first, and perhaps by a loser-pays requirement for cases filed in court under such a provision.

RECENT INNOVATIONS

CONTENTS

INTRODUCTION BY ANTHONY CORRADO AND DANIEL R. ORTIZ

The recent history of campaign finance reform at the federal level has been a tale of frustration. Members of one Congress after another promised reform but failed to adopt a major piece of legislation. In 1992, Congress did finally pass a bill, only to see President George Bush veto it. As a result, there has been no significant change in the law governing the financing of federal campaigns since 1979 (document 2.12), despite an increasingly widespread consensus that the system needs a basic overhaul.

The experience at the state level has been a different story. Since 1990, a majority of states have reformed their campaign finance laws. States have responded to many of the same pressures witnessed in national elections—rising campaign costs, underfunded challengers, the growing influence of large donors, and an increase in independent expenditures—by adopting new campaign finance regulations, including many innovative and interesting schemes. These reforms include proposals often described by federal political observers as "politically infeasible," such as strict contribution limits, spending ceilings, and public financing programs. Consequently, state campaign finance laws are increasingly cast as models for federal reform.

But these state reforms have not gone unchallenged. Many of the most innovative statutes have been taken to court, where judges, following the Supreme Court's lead in *Buckley* v. *Valeo* (424 U.S. 1 [1976]; see document 3.1), have often struck down key provisions as violating the First Amendment. These court decisions have limited the alternatives

for future reform that are available to legislators and have led a number of states to adopt more comprehensive, publicly funded campaign finance systems in an effort to withstand any future judicial scrutiny. The judicial response to state legislation has also led some advocates of reform to search for new innovations, such as proposals to provide free broadcast time to candidates. These proposals have broadened the scope of the campaign finance debate and encouraged new ways of thinking about how to improve political finance.

THE STATES REFORM

State elections have not been immune from the financial patterns and problems that have characterized recent federal elections. Like candidates for federal office, candidates at the state and local level have seen the costs of campaigning climb dramatically since the 1970s. Total spending by candidates for statewide offices and state legislative seats grew from about $120 million in 1976 to an estimated $540 million in 1988, a 450 percent increase over twelve years. The rate of increase in the costs of state elections thus outpaced the increase that occurred in presidential and congressional campaigns during the same period.

Although much of this state spending was concentrated in the most populous states, especially in California and Texas, rapidly rising campaign costs were evident throughout the nation, including smaller states like Idaho and Rhode Island. Consequently, by the late 1980s, campaign finance at the state level shared many of the characteristics and problems commonly associated with the funding of federal campaigns. Legislators were placing greater emphasis on fund-raising, political action committees (PACs) and large donors were playing an increasingly important role as a source of campaign revenue, incumbents were outspending challengers by larger and larger sums, and public perceptions of the undue influence of campaign money were on the rise.

The states responded to these shifting patterns of campaign finance by adopting a variety of diverse reforms. In the 1991 legislative sessions alone, ten states passed laws establishing or reducing campaign contribution limits. From 1992 to 1996, twenty-three states and the District of Columbia revised their laws, including a number of states that passed more than incremental reforms or technical modifications of existing laws. For example, during this period California, Colorado, Kentucky, and Nevada passed comprehensive reform packages. Two other states, Maine and Nebraska, established public financing for state elections, and Minnesota and Hawaii revised their public financing programs.

The most popular reform, however, has been the adoption or revision of contribution limits. In 1980, for example, most of the states had no limits on donations to campaign committees from individuals, PACs, corporations, or labor unions. This had changed significantly by 1996. The number of states with limits on individual contributions increased from twenty-three in 1980 to thirty-four in 1996, while the number limiting PAC contributions doubled from sixteen to thirty-two. Direct union contributions were either prohibited or limited in thirty-eight states by 1996, compared with seventeen in 1980, while the restrictions on direct corporate contributions expanded from thirty-one states to forty-two. Some states also adopted prohibitions on contributions by lobbyists or restricted fund-raising activity when legislatures are in ses-

sion. Others have lowered their ceilings on contributions significantly in an effort to reduce the role of private wealth in legislative elections. In this regard, Missouri, Oregon, Montana, and the District of Columbia enacted the most restrictive legislation, limiting individual contributions to no more than $100.

But states have done far more than strengthen contribution limits or establish public financing. They have shown a noteworthy willingness to experiment with new ideas and proposals, which has led to a significant amount of innovation in their regulatory schemes. For example, Oregon sought to restrict the flow of money into political campaigns by allowing candidates for state office to raise no more than 10 percent of their campaign funds from contributors who lived outside the electoral district. Missouri tried to minimize the financial advantage incumbents often enjoy by preventing candidates from carrying over excess campaign funds from one election to another. Minnesota sought to reduce the influence of independent expenditures by increasing the amounts a publicly funded candidate could spend if funds were spent independently in a race in a way that benefitted an opponent (either against the candidate or on behalf of an opponent). And Rhode Island passed a law that gives candidates an incentive to accept public financing (and the accompanying spending limits) by allowing gubernatorial candidates who accept public subsidies to solicit private donations in larger amounts than those allowed candidates who do not accept public money (see documents 9.1 to 9.5).

THE COURTS RESPOND

States have been open to new regulatory options, but the courts have been hesitant to allow expanded regulation. In general, they have followed the principles established by *Buckley* and affirmed the view that the only regulations that can be admitted under the First Amendment are narrowly tailored solutions designed to prevent corruption or the appearance of corruption. The courts have thus struck down any statutes that fail to meet this standard, except for those limits established as a condition for public financing. A review of the leading cases gives an indication of the wide range of ideas that the courts have rejected and demonstrates the capacious and fatal reach of the *Buckley* decision as a continuing force in efforts to change the ways campaigns are financed.

In 1994, a federal court of appeals issued its decision in *Day* v. *Holahan*, 34 F.3d 1356 (8th Cir. 1994), *cert. denied*, 513 U.S. 1127 (1995), which struck down two Minnesota campaign finance provisions (see document 9.1). The first increased the amount a candidate could spend under voluntary guidelines—and funded half of that increase in certain ways—by the sum of independent expenditures made in opposition to the candidate or on behalf of a major party opponent. The second provision placed a cap of $100 on contributions to political committees. The court reasoned that the variable contribution limit was insufficiently related to the state's asserted interest in encouraging candidate participation in public financing and so overturned the law. It further found that the $100 contribution ceiling was too low "to allow meaningful participation in protected political speech and association." It thus ruled that the limit violated the First Amendment.

One year later in *Carver* v. *Nixon*, 72 F.3d 633 (8th Cir. 1995), *cert. denied*, 116 S. Ct. 2579 (1996), the same court of appeals struck down a provision in Missouri's Ballot Proposition A that limited individual or committee contributions to state candidates to $100–$300, depending on the race (see document 9.2). Although this provision regulated contributions made directly to candidates rather than to political committees, the court followed its analysis in *Day* and invalidated the restriction. In a later case, *Shrink Missouri Government PAC* v. *Maupin*, 71 F.3d 1422 (8th Cir. 1995), *cert. denied*,

116 S. Ct. 2579 (1996), this same court struck down another Missouri law, this one designed to discourage candidates from carrying over "war chests" from one election to another (see document 9.3). By requiring candidates to turn over most leftover campaign funds within ninety days of an election, the law encouraged candidates to spend all of their funds by the end of a campaign. More importantly, it prevented incumbents from using leftover funds as part of a war chest to scare off possible future challengers. The court was unwilling to accept this regulation, finding that there was an insufficient connection between the law and any state interests that might justify such a restriction on candidate spending.

In *Vote Choice, Inc.* v. *DiStefano*, 4 F.3d 26 (1st Cir. 1993), a different federal court of appeals decided a case involving Rhode Island's campaign finance law (see document 9.4). The court's decision at first appears to offer reformers some hope, since it struck down only one of three challenged provisions. On closer look, however, the state's "victory" was slight. The first challenged provision required so-called "first dollar disclosure" of all contributions. Under this rule, all PACs had to disclose the identity and amount given by every contributor no matter how small the contribution. The court struck down the provision because it treated donations to PACs more strictly than donations from individuals to candidates, thus violating the First Amendment by placing an undue burden on a PAC's right of association.

The second regulation challenged in this case was a so-called "cap gap." The law provided that an individual could donate up to $2,000, or twice the standard limit of $1,000, to a gubernatorial candidate if that candidate accepted public funding and abided by certain spending limits. This "gap" in the amount of an allowable contribution was designed to encourage candidates to participate in the public financing program and adhere to spending limits by making it easier for them to raise money if they did so. Although this provision treated privately and publicly funded candidates differently, the court upheld the rule on the ground that it "achieves a rough proportionality between the advantages available to complying candidates (including the cap gap) and the restrictions that such candidates must accept to receive these advantages." The court therefore accepted this reform but did not significantly expand the scope of allowable regulation, since this rule fit comfortably within *Buckley's* narrow public financing exception.

The third provision at issue in *Vote Choice* called for free television time for qualified candidates. Specifically, the law provided free television time to candidates who complied with the state's public financing restrictions. The court found that the state law did not conflict with federal law requiring stations to give "equal opportunities" to all candidates. The state statute, the court said, simply did not prohibit giving equal time to noncomplying candidates, as the federal statute would require. Thus, the statute, as interpreted by the court, effectively gave all candidates—complying and noncomplying candidates alike—free television time, thus offering no incentive to candidates to participate in public financing. As a result, the court upheld the statute, but in a way that essentially nullified the effect of the reform.

Attempts to control out-of-district contributions have also failed to withstand judicial scrutiny. In *Vannatta* v. *Kiesling*, 899 F. Supp. 488 (D. Ore. 1995), a federal trial court considered Oregon's limit on the amount of contributions a candidate could receive from outside of his or her electoral district (see document 9.5). The court struck down the law, ruling that it was insufficiently tailored to serve the state's interest in preventing corruption.

MOVING TOWARD COMPREHENSIVE REFORM

The judicial response to recently enacted state laws has led some advocates of reform to embrace com-

prehensive reform alternatives as the only viable solution to the problems plaguing the campaign finance system. David Donnelly, Janice Fine, and Ellen S. Miller, for example, argue that piecemeal solutions such as contribution limits, improved disclosure, and partial public financing will not resolve many of the issues raised by the role of money in politics (see document 9.6). They further contend that even broader solutions based on current models, like the John McCain-Russell D. Feingold proposal that has been introduced in recent Congresses, will simply alter the flow of money in elections and fail to address their principal concerns regarding the influence of private wealth in the political process. Consequently, they advocate more fundamental reform of the system, specifically voluntary, full public financing of election campaigns.

In recent years, this demand for comprehensive reform has gained strength at the state level and produced complete overhauls of the campaign finance system in a number of states. These changes have largely been accomplished through the initiative and referendum process, which has provided public interest groups and other grass-roots organizations with a means of mobilizing public support behind reform and translating it into public policy without having to gain the support of a majority of incumbent legislators. In 1996 alone, seven states (Arkansas, California, Colorado, Maine, Massachusetts, Montana, and Nevada) had campaign finance proposals on the ballot, and these initiatives were approved in every state. Since 1972, fifty-one campaign finance propositions have been on the ballot, with forty-one obtaining approval.

Three of the most important referenda in 1996 were California's Proposition 208, which enacted a comprehensive state regulatory scheme to replace what was essentially an unregulated process; Colorado's Amendment 15, which established a system of contribution limits and voluntary spending ceilings for state elections; and Maine's Question 3, which established a comprehensive program of public funding for state elections (see document

9.7). Another interesting initiative was passed in Arkansas. Called the Arkansas Clean Government Act, this proposition uses tax credits as a tool for public financing (see document 9.8). It offers each individual a 100 percent tax credit for contributions of up to $50 ($100 for married couples) to a candidate, party committee or other political committee. It thus encourages individuals to make small political contributions in exchange for a dollar-for-dollar reduction on their tax bill or an equivalent increase on their tax refund. The Arkansas law also seeks to strengthen the role of small donors by reducing the overall contribution limits to $300 for statewide office and by providing high contribution limits ($2,500) for small-donor PACs, which are PACs that receive no more than $25 from any contributor.

The Maine initiative, also known as the Clean Elections Act, is the most notable of the initiatives adopted in 1996, since it established the nation's first program of full public funding for state elections. Under this law, which will take effect for the elections of 2000, candidates for governor and state legislative offices can receive full public financing for their campaigns. To qualify, candidates simply have to raise a specified number of $5 contributions from within their district (or statewide in the case of a gubernatorial candidate). Those who qualify will receive a grant equal to the average amount spent in the previous two election cycles for the particular office they are seeking. In exchange, candidates who accept public money cannot raise or spend any additional private money and must abide by established spending limits. The law also requires the disclosure of any independent expenditure of $50 or more and adjusts the amount a publicly funded candidate can spend in response to independent expenditures.

Whether these reforms will prove as effective as their sponsors hope remains to be seen. By June 1997, lawsuits already had been filed against the California and Maine initiatives. In addition, the efficacy of public financing will depend on the ad-

equacy of the program's funding and the level of candidate participation—or, in the case of Arkansas, on the extent to which voters choose to make small contributions to take advantage of the tax benefits. But the promise of these initiatives is great. Consequently, reform groups in other states are already pushing similar propositions. In 1997 a bill modeled on the Maine Clean Elections Act was enacted into law in the state of Vermont; another was introduced in the U.S. Senate.

If passing constitutional muster with the courts is one daunting obstacle facing state reformers, another is ensuring that these new state laws are effectively enforced. A forthcoming study of state efforts to enact and implement campaign finance reform by Thomas Gais and Michael Malbin (*The Day After Reform: Sobering Campaign Finance Lessons from the American States*) concludes that state agencies charged with administering campaign finance law are woefully understaffed for performing even the simplest of tasks given to them by their legislatures. Less than eight full-time-equivalent persons work on campaign finance laws and programs in the typical state, with an average agency budget of approximately $350,000 per year. Moreover, there is no correlation between the complexity of the tasks in their statutes and the resources made available to do the job. According to Gais and Malbin, most states have failed to deliver adequately on the promise of disclosure; taking on more difficult tasks is currently beyond their administrative resources and capabilities.

THE FREE TIME ALTERNATIVE

Though some states have embraced public financing in recent years, Congress has shown little enthusiasm for this reform. In fact, the debate over taxpayer funding and spending limits has been at the center of the congressional impasse over reform, with Democrats generally advocating these changes and Republicans opposing them. This stalemate has led some reformers to search for a subsidy that does not require tax monies, as well as an alternative means of reducing the costs of campaigns. The solution most often discussed in this regard is the notion of providing free broadcast time to candidates.

Free television time has gained prominence as a reform alternative as the debate over escalating campaign costs and the demands of political fund-raising has intensified. The principal reason for these rising costs, at least according to most observers, is the increasing cost of media expenses. Although there is no reliable data on aggregate television spending in elections, recent studies show that broadcast media spending (including radio and television broadcast time, production costs, and consulting fees) is the single largest component of campaign budgets, representing about 27 percent of the total expenses in House races, 40 to 45 percent in Senate races, and at least 50 percent in presidential races (document 9.11). The proportions are even higher in the most competitive elections. For example, in competitive Senate races, up to 60 percent of the total amount of spending is devoted to broadcast media.

Because media spending constitutes such a large share of campaign expenditures, many reformers think that any change that can reduce these costs will have a major effect on the financing of campaigns. More than 160 proposals to provide some amount of free broadcast time to candidates or reduced advertising rates have been introduced accordingly in Congress since 1960. Most recent bills call for broadcasters to provide time to candidates at a significantly reduced cost. These proposals therefore shift the burden of payment from the government (which would involve the expenditure of tax dollars) to the broadcasters themselves. Most of these bills further require that candidates must adhere to voluntary campaign spending limits in exchange for this subsidy.

Congress has failed to act, but individuals and groups have continued to press for free time. These private efforts produced a notable experiment in

1996. In February 1996, Rupert Murdoch, head of the Fox television network, announced that his network would provide free time to the leading presidential candidates during the month before the election. Under this plan, each candidate was offered a free half-hour on election eve and ten one-minute segments in the month preceding the election to address selected issues. Murdoch challenged other networks to follow his lead, but these organizations initially showed little enthusiasm. But Murdoch's notion was championed by journalists Walter Cronkite and Paul Taylor, who formed the Free TV for Straight Talk Coalition, which called on the networks to offer each presidential candidate two to five minutes of free time each night during the final month of the election. Under their plan, this time would be used to allow each candidate to speak directly into a camera on the major issues in the race. The segments would be aired simultaneously on different networks to maximize viewer attention.

The Coalition's plan was not adopted by the networks, yet it did induce them to offer some free time to candidates. But the amount of time offered was quite limited and spread out from September to November. It was allocated in a variety of lengths (ranging from ninety seconds to more than two minutes) using different formats, and the networks aired the segments in varying time slots. As a result, relatively few voters saw the free candidate statements and they had little effect in improving voters' knowledge of the candidates.

After the election, the Free TV for Straight Talk Coalition unveiled a bolder free time proposal. This plan calls for the creation of a political broadcast bank that would provide vouchers to House and Senate general election candidates and to qualifying political parties to purchase broadcast time for political spots. This time could only be used for ads of sixty seconds or more that feature the candidate for the duration of the message. The bank would be established by requiring every television and radio station in the country to donate two hours of time at the start of each election cycle as part of each station's public interest obligation.

This plan for a political broadcast bank is a major component of the reform plan presented by Ornstein, Mann, Taylor, Malbin, and Corrado in document 9.9 and was endorsed by the League of Women Voters Education Fund in 1997. As Paul Taylor explains, a broadcast bank may help reduce the cost of campaigns and enhance the quality of political communication by inducing candidates to use free time to speak directly with voters in longer segments, thus encouraging a move away from short spots and attack ads (see document 9.10). It is also seen as a way to improve competition, since it will in effect create a "communications floor" that will guarantee candidates a minimum level of air time. This should especially benefit challengers, who are traditionally underfunded and often lack the resources needed to communicate effectively with voters.

Other analysts question the efficacy of free time proposals and doubt whether free broadcast opportunities will have a major effect on the campaign finance system. The most common concerns raised by these observers is that free time will simply serve as a supplement to the present system. Although candidates will use any free broadcast time given them, they will continue to spend additional sums on advertising and still use negative ads, so the potentially beneficial effects of such time will be diminished. Others question whether the Federal Communications Commission or Congress has the authority to require broadcasters to provide free time. A wide array of constitutional and legal issues has been raised, ranging from First Amendment considerations to the relevance of the "takings clause" under the Fifth Amendment (see document 9.11).

The debate over free time is likely to be complicated and contentious, as is the debate over other major proposals to significantly change the way we finance campaigns. But it demonstrates how some of the traditional problems associated with campaign finance might be resolved by new ideas and new ways of thinking about political reform. Such bold approaches to reform have been a hallmark of state campaign finance reform in recent years. Similar thinking at the federal level is needed and may be the key to future innovations in federal campaign finance law.

In 1993, Minnesota amended its campaign finance laws to include a variable cap on individual campaign expenditures and to limit contributions to political committees to $100. The variable cap allowed candidates who had voluntarily agreed to limit their spending to spend more money if others made independent expenditures against them or in favor of their major political party opponents. The United States Court of Appeals for the Eighth Circuit struck down both provisions. It found that they implicated core First Amendment interests without being sufficiently well tailored to accomplish the state's asserted goals.

————————————————

BOWMAN, Circuit Judge.

. . .

I.

A.

Among the 1993 changes and additions to the Minnesota campaign finance and ethics laws was this provision directed to independent expenditures:

Independent expenditures; limits increased. (a) The [voluntary] expenditure limits in this section are increased by the sum of independent expenditures made in opposition to a candidate plus independent expenditures made on behalf of the candidate's major political party opponents, other than expenditures by an association targeted to inform solely its own dues-paying members of the association's position on a candidate.

(b) Within 48 hours after receipt of an expenditure report or notice required by [the statute], the board shall notify each candidate in the race of the increase in the expenditure limit for the candidates against whom the independent expenditures have been made.

(c) Within three days after providing this notice, the board shall pay each candidate against whom the independent expenditures have been made, if the candidate is eligible to receive a public subsidy and has raised twice the minimum match required, an additional public subsidy equal to one-half the independent expenditures. The amount needed to pay the additional public subsidy under this subdivision is appropriated from the general fund to the board.

Minn. Stat. § 10A.25 subd. 13 (Supp. 1993).

. . .

Under Chapter 10A of the Minnesota Statutes, an independent expenditure is defined as "an expenditure expressly advocating the election or defeat of a clearly identified candidate," but one made neither with the consent or authorization of the candidate nor at his request or suggestion. Once any individual, political committee, or political fund makes (or becomes obligated to make) an independent expenditure of more than $100 on behalf of any candidate, or against any candidate, the following scenario is mandated by [the statute]:

The candidate whose defeat is advocated (or whose opponent's election is encouraged) by the independent expenditure has her own expenditure limits increased by the amount of the independent expenditure. The Minnesota Ethical Practices Board then must pay her, if she is eligible to receive a public subsidy and has raised two times the minimum amount required for a match, an additional public subsidy equal to one-half the amount of the independent expenditure. Thus, by advocating a candidate's defeat (or her opponent's victory) via an independent expenditure, the individual, committee, or fund working for the candidate's defeat instead has increased the maximum amount she may spend and given her the wherewithal to increase that spending—merely by exercising a First Amendment right to make expenditures opposing her or supporting her opponent. Thus the individual or group intending to contribute to her defeat becomes directly responsible for adding to her campaign coffers. To the extent that a candidate's campaign is enhanced by the operation of the statute, the political speech of the individual or group who made the independent expenditure "against" her (or in favor of her opponent) is impaired.

It is clear that independent expenditures are protected speech. "Discussion of public issues and debate on the qualifications of candidates are integral to the operation of the system of government established by our Constitution. The First Amendment affords the broadest protection to such political expression. . . ." It is equally clear that section 10A.25 subd. 13 infringes on that protected speech because of the chilling effect the statute has on the political speech of the person or group making the independent expenditure. As the potential "independent expenders" allege in their briefs (and as at least one sponsor of the legislation intended), the mere enactment of section 10A.25 subd. 13 already has prevented many if not most potential independent expenditures from ever being made. The knowledge that a candidate who one does not want to be elected will have her spending limits increased and will receive a public subsidy equal to half the amount of the independent expenditure, as a direct result of that independent expenditure, chills the free exercise of that protected speech. This "self-censorship" that has occurred even before the state implements the statute's mandates is no less a burden on speech that is susceptible to constitutional challenge than is direct government censorship.

Our conclusion that the most fundamental of rights is infringed by section 10A.25 subd. 13 does not end our inquiry, however. We now must decide whether the statute is content-neutral or content-based, "not always a simple task." But that determination is critical, as it controls the level of scrutiny we apply in assessing whether the infringement results in a constitutional violation. Having reviewed the teachings of the Supreme Court on this subject and applied them to this statute, we conclude that section 10A.25 subd. 13 is content-based.

Section 10A.25 subd. 13 singles out particular political speech—that which advocates the defeat of a candidate and/or supports the election of her opponents—for negative treatment that the state applies to no other variety of speech. We have no difficulty concluding that this is a statute that "by [its] terms distinguishes favored speech from disfavored speech on the basis of the ideas or views expressed," and thus it cannot be content-neutral. Independent expenditures of any other nature, supporting the expression of any sentiment other than advocating the defeat of one candidate or the election of another, do not trigger the statute's limit-increasing and money-shifting provisions. We are bound to "apply the most exacting scrutiny to regulations that suppress, disadvantage, or impose differential burdens upon speech because of its content."

Notwithstanding the content-based infringement on protected constitutional rights perpetrated by section 10A.25 subd. 13, the statute may be upheld as against constitutional challenge if the state can show that it is narrowly drawn to serve a compelling state interest. We hold that the state has made no such showing.

The state's professed interest "is the goal of enhancing the public's confidence in the political process by ensuring the viability of the legislature's statutory scheme designed to encourage candidates to accept the voluntary campaign expenditures [sic] of section 10A.25 and the accompanying public subsidies." While this may be a noble goal, we are not certain it is a sufficiently "compelling" interest to justify the burden that the statute imposes upon speech. We do not decide that issue, however, because we hold that, with candidate participation in public campaign financing nearing 100% before enactment of section 10A.25 subd. 13, the interest, no matter how compelling in the abstract, is not legitimate.

In 1988, eighty-nine percent of candidates for the Minnesota House of Representatives agreed to spending limits. In 1990, the total for all state candidates was ninety-six percent, and in 1992—still before the enactment of the campaign reform legislation challenged here—ninety-seven percent of the state legislative candidates filing for office agreed to abide by spending limits in order to receive a public subsidy. Clearly, the campaign reform legislation was not necessary to encourage candidates' involvement in public campaign financing, as participation was approaching 100% before the new campaign finance laws were passed in 1993. One hardly could be faulted for concluding that this "compelling" state interest was contrived for purposes of this litigation.

Moreover, it occurs to us that no statute that infringes on First Amendment rights can be considered "narrowly tailored" to meet the state's purported interest in these circumstances. Surely the three percent of non-participants could be brought in by means less burdensome to constitutional rights—assuming that group can be brought in at all. In any event, we have our doubts that this statutory scheme would achieve much success in increasing candidate participation in public campaign financing, when the chances of picking up the "bonus" subsidy are so remote. A candidate cannot qualify for the additional subsidy unless particular speech is made against her (or in favor of her opposition) by others who, as we noted above, are discouraged from exercising their rights to so speak by the very same statutory scheme that provides for the bonus subsidy. We have no doubt that section 10A.25 subd. 13 is assuredly not "necessary to serve the asserted interest."

Even if we were to hold that the statute is content-neutral and thus "poses a less substantial risk of excising certain ideas or viewpoints from the public dialogue," we nevertheless would conclude that it violates the First Amendment even examining it with the less exacting scrutiny required when the infringement on speech is content-neutral.

A content-neutral statute will survive a First Amendment challenge if "it furthers an important or substantial governmental interest; if the governmental interest is unrelated to the suppression of free expression; and if the incidental restriction on alleged First Amendment freedoms is no greater than is essential to the furtherance of that interest." Regardless of whether or not the asserted governmental interest in instilling public confidence in the election process is "substantial," section 10A.25 subd. 13 cannot logically be characterized as "essential" to furthering the state's interest. As discussed above, no more than an additional three percent of all candidates could be brought into the public campaign financing scheme (given that ninety-seven percent already participate). Therefore, even if section 10A.25 subd. 13 were content-neutral, the statute's negative impact on political speech must be a violation of the First Amendment rights of those who wish to make the independent expenditures at issue. The statute's burden on First Amendment rights does not satisfy strict, intermediate, or even the most cursory scrutiny.

. . .

III.

[The question remains whether Minn. Stat. § 10A.27 subd.12 is unconstitutional.] Under that section of the campaign reform law, a political committee or political fund cannot "accept aggregate contributions from an individual, political committee, or political fund in an amount more that $100 a year." We hold that the $100 limit is so low as to infringe upon the citizens' First Amendment right to political association and free political expression.

As emphasized by the Supreme Court's decision in *Buckley* v. *Valeo* [document 3.1], it is clear that state-enforced limits on campaign contributions and expenditures stifle First Amendment freedoms. Here, because the limit applies to contributions both by and to political committees and funds, the limit affects not only free political speech but also free association, the "tradition of volunteer committees for collective action. . . . By collective effort individuals can make their views known, when, individually, their voices would be faint or lost."

It also is well established that Minnesota's declared purpose in enacting its $100 limit—to avoid corruption or the appearance of corruption in the political process that could result from large amounts of special interest money circulating in the system—is a compelling state interest.

But the fighting issue here is whether a $100 limit on contributions to political committees or funds is narrowly tailored to serve the state's interest, given the burden it imposes on political speech. We hold that it is not. "Given the important role of contributions in financing political campaigns, contribution restrictions could have a severe impact on political dialogue if the limitations prevented candidates and political committees from amassing the resources necessary for effective advocacy." And the concern of a political *quid pro quo* for large contributions, which becomes a possibility when the contribution is to an individual candidate, is not present when the contribution is given to a political committee or fund that by itself does not have legislative power.

The *Buckley* Court, eighteen years ago, found that a $1000 limit—ten times the limit at issue here—was sufficiently high to pass constitutional muster as narrowly tailored to serve the state's concern for the integrity of the political system. We realize that the *Buckley* limit was never declared to be a constitutional minimum, but it does provide us with some guidance and a frame of reference in evaluating the constitutionality of Minnesota's $100 limit.

Among the undisputed facts relied upon by the District Court is the fact that a $100 contribution in 1976 would have a value of $40.60 in 1994 dollars, or approximately four percent of the $1000 limit approved in *Buckley*. The undisputed facts also show that one-fourth to one-third of [a particular PAC's] contributions exceeded $100 in the most recent election cycle (presumably the cycle before the one now under way). Based on these facts, we agree with the District Court that a $100 limit on contributions to or by political committees and funds significantly impairs the ability of individuals and political committees and funds to exercise their First Amendment rights. An annual $100 limit on contributions to or by political funds and committees is too low to allow meaningful participation in protected political speech and association, and thus is not narrowly tailored to serve the state's legitimate interest in protecting the integrity of the political system. Accordingly, we hold that the $100 limit violates the protections afforded by the First Amendment for free political speech and free association. . . .

In 1994, Missouri voters approved an initiative limiting individual contributions to candidates to $100–$300, depending on the race and the size of the district. The United States Court of Appeals for the Eighth Circuit extended its holding in *Day* v. *Holahan* (document 9.1) to strike down these limits on candidate contributions.

JOHN R. GIBSON, Circuit Judge.

[Missouri voters approved Proposition A in the November 8, 1994 election. It limited campaign contributions as follows:]

. . .

[The following material is from footnote 1:]

. . . (1) No person or committee shall make a contribution to any one candidate or candidate committee with an aggregate value in excess of: (a) $100 per election cycle per candidate in districts with fewer than 100,000 residents[.]

> [(b)] $200 per election cycle per candidate, other than statewide candidates, in districts of 100,000 or more residents. For purposes of this section "statewide candidates" refers to those candidates seeking election to the office of Governor, Lieutenant Governor, Attorney General, Auditor, Treasurer and Secretary of State.
>
> [(c)] $300 per election cycle per statewide candidate.

(2) No person, entity or committee shall make a contribution to any other persons, entities or committees for the purpose of contributing to a specific candidate which when added together with contributions made directly to the candidate or to the candidate's committee, will have an aggregate value in excess of the limits stated in section 1.

(3) No candidate or candidate committee shall solicit or accept any contribution with an aggregate value in excess of the limits stated in this section.

(4) For purposes of this section the term "candidate" shall include the candidate, the candidate's treasurer, and the candidate's committee and any contribution to the candidate's treasurer or candidate committee shall be deemed a contribution to the candidate.

Mo. Ann. Stat. § 130.100. [end of footnote 1]

. . .

I.

. . .

Strict scrutiny [applies] in this case, and the State must show that the Proposition A limits are narrowly tailored to meet a compelling state interest. "When the Government defends a regulation on speech . . . it must do more than simply 'posit the existence of the disease sought to be cured.' . . . It must demonstrate that the recited harms are real, . . . and that the regulation will in fact alleviate these harms in a direct and material way."

. . .

III.

. . .

C.

Carver[, one of the plaintiffs,] argues that the evidence establishes that the limits in Proposition A violate his right to associate as a contributor. The State responds that Carver has not proved that Proposition A limits his right to contribute at a meaningful level. The State contends that the Proposition A limits do not prevent Carver from effectively speaking on behalf of a candidate or joining with other individuals to express themselves in constitutionally protected independent committees. . . . The State argues that there was no proof that contributors like Carver could not find other outlets for effectively expressing their message in Missouri elections. While the extent of Carver's testimony is at best skeletal, it is sufficient to demonstrate that Carver has contributed, and intends to contribute in the future, amounts in excess of the Proposition A limits to support his interest in "good candidates" and "good government." The State's argument that Carver could continue to exercise his First Amendment rights by joining an independent group does not address whether the limits are so low as to prevent Carver from freely associating with a candidate.

The State points out that *Buckley* [document 3.1] does not require specific proof of the maximum contribution limit, and that we may not use "a scalpel" to invalidate Proposition A. It is true that the Court did not analyze the propriety of the $1,000 limit. Indeed, the Court observed that while Congress could have structured the limits in a graduated fashion for congressional and presidential campaigns, its failure to do so did not invalidate the legislation. The Court reiterated the court of appeals' statement that "a court has no scalpel to probe" whether a different ceiling might not serve as well. Although we certainly are not free to fine tune the limits established by Proposition A, and we generally accept the limits established by the legislature, *Buckley* instructs that we must invalidate that judgment when the "distinctions in degree" become "differences in kind."

. . .

In *Day* [v. *Holahan* (document 9.1)], we dealt with the issues raised by very low contribution limits. We considered the constitutionality of a Minnesota statute imposing a $100 limit on contributions to political committees. Although *Day* did not consider contribution limits to candidates, we compared the $100 limit on contributions to political committees in *Day* to the $1,000 limit on contributions to candidates considered in *Buckley*. After recognizing that the $1,000 limit in *Buckley* was not a "constitutional minimum," we nevertheless concluded that the $100 limit significantly impaired the ability of contributors to exercise their First Amendment rights. We held that the limit was "too low to allow meaningful participation in protected political speech and association," and we concluded that the law was "not narrowly tailored to serve the state's legitimate interest in protecting the integrity of the political system." In reaching this conclusion, we relied on the fact that about 25 to 33 percent of the contributions to political committees in the most recent election exceeded the $100 limit, and that after adjusting for inflation, the limit was about 4 percent of the $1,000 limit in *Buckley*. Our observation in *Day* about the effect of inflation applies with equal force in this case.

. . .

The Proposition A limits, ranging from $100 to $300 per election cycle, are dramatically lower than the $2,000 limit per election cycle approved in *Buckley*. Not only are the Proposition A limits much lower than the federal limits, they are lower than the limits in any other state. Two states, Montana and Oregon, have limits for state senate races that equal those in Proposition A, but their limits for statewide offices and state representatives are greater than those in Missouri.

The question thus becomes whether Missouri must adopt the lowest contribution limits in the nation to remedy the corruption caused by large campaign contributions. The State presented testimony at trial about a $420,000 contribution from a Morgan Stanley political action committee to various races in north Missouri, and about the "Keating Five" scandal.

None of these examples prove that the Proposition A limits are narrowly tailored. A $420,000 contribution is a far cry from the limits in Proposition A, and the other examples involve individual conduct leading to criminal prosecution. We cannot conclude that the limits in Proposition A are in any way narrowly tailored or carefully drawn to remedy such situations.

. . .

Further, the State's exhibits show that 27.5 percent of the contributors in the 1994 Auditor's race gave more than the $300 Proposition A limits. In the State Senate race, 23.7 percent of the contributors gave more than the $200 Proposition A limit. Finally, in the State Representative race, 35.6 percent of the contributors gave more than the $100 Proposition A limit.

The State made no showing as to why it was necessary to adopt the lowest contribution limits in the nation and restrict the First Amendment rights of so many contributors in order to prevent corruption or the appearance of corruption associated with large campaign contributions. Proposition A substantially limits Carver's ability to contribute to candidates and will have a considerable impact on many contributors besides Carver. The State simply argues that limits which are nearly four times as restrictive as the limits approved in *Buckley* are narrowly tailored. The State argues we may not fine tune the specific dollar amount of the limits, but fails to demonstrate that the Proposition A limits are not a "difference in kind." We hold that the Proposition A limits amount to a difference in kind from the limits in *Buckley*. The limits are not closely drawn to reduce corruption or the appearance of corruption associated with large campaign contributions. Thus, the State has failed to carry its burden of demonstrating that Proposition A will alleviate the harms in a direct and material way, or is closely drawn to avoid unnecessary abridgement of associational freedoms. Accordingly, we conclude that the Proposition A contribution limits unconstitutionally burden the First Amendment rights of association and expression.

. . .

Shrink Missouri Government PAC v. *Maupin,* 71 F.3d 1422 (8th Cir. 1995), *cert. denied,* 116 S. Ct. 2579 (1996)

Through an initiative Missouri voters passed a "spend-down" provision. It required candidates to return to contributors or to turn over to the state all but a little money left unspent from their campaigns. Its aim was to prevent candidates from amassing war chests in one election for use in another. The United States Court of Appeals for the Eighth Circuit struck the provision down as insufficiently related to the state's asserted goals.

BOWMAN, Circuit Judge.

. . .

II.

. . .

C.

In Proposition A the citizens of Missouri adopted a measure designed to address the practice of carrying over "war chests" of campaign funds for future elections. Under the ballot initiative measure, within ninety days of an election a candidate must turn over any excess funds, "except for an amount no greater than ten times the individual contribution limit" for the office sought, to the Missouri Ethics Commission or to contributors. This is popularly known as a "spend-down provision" because candidates will most likely choose to spend all of their funds during the last days of the campaign rather than returning funds to contributors or turning them over to the state. The ability of a candidate to retain contributions for future elections is thus substantially limited.

The District Court held that the spend-down provision imposes a substantial burden on political speech by requiring that funds raised during a particular campaign be spent during the campaign. The court rejected the state's assumption that "blind support" in the form of a contribution that can be used in the current campaign or any future campaign "must constitute an impermissible attempt at improper *quid pro quo* influence." The state, on the other hand, argues that the spend-down provision does not limit speech but encourages it by requiring candidates "to do precisely what the contributors intend: to speak." In our opinion, the state's argument makes an unwarranted assumption about the intention of campaign contributors and badly misrepresents reality. Some contributors undoubtedly do intend to give a candidate "blind support," and they do so without any hope of gaining improper influence with that candidate. Beyond that, we believe the state's characterization of the provision confirms the District Court's decision that it infringes the First Amendment. From the state's perspective, the provision is intended to require the candidate to speak in the current election. We note that "the right of freedom of thought protected by the First Amendment against state action includes both the right to speak freely and the right to refrain from speaking at all." From the appellees' perspective, the provision limits the quantity of a candidate's speech in future elections. We note that this effect is identical to the effect of the expenditure limits addressed earlier in this opinion except that the impact of the provision is postponed to future elections. Whether we accept the state's or the appellees' characterization of the spend-down provision is irrelevant. Either way, we conclude that rights protected by the First Amendment are implicated and that the provision must be subjected to strict scrutiny.

While strict scrutiny may not always be fatal to a challenged restriction on speech, it is in this case. The state has not demonstrated that the spend-down provision is narrowly tailored to serve a compelling government interest. The state argues that this provision serves three interests.

First, it attacks corruption and its appearance by (1) preventing the kinds of *quids pro quo* that occur when money is given to candidates in uncontested races, and (2) ensuring that the [state's] contributions limits . . . have a measurable effect on the political system. . . . Second, it preserves the integrity of the electoral process by (1) counterbalancing any discriminatory effects against challengers and in favor of incumbents that are created by [the state's] contribution limits, (2) ensuring the opportunity of all citizens, not just those who have amassed large war chests in noncompetitive races, to participate in the political process as candidates, and (3) protecting the free speech interests of contributors. Third, it promotes speech and fairness, thus sustaining the active, alert responsibility of the individual citizen in our democracy.

At the outset, we note that any interest related to the effective operation of [the state's] contribution limits fails to qualify as compelling because we have held [in *Carver* v. *Nixon* (document 9.2)] that those limits are unconstitutional. We further note that any interest defined by reference to funds raised in "noncompetitive" or "uncontested races" is unhelpful because the spend-down provision applies to funds raised in all campaigns; thus the provision is not narrowly tailored to serve such an interest. The sole remaining interests asserted by the state are that the provision "preserves the integrity of the electoral process by . . . protecting the free speech interests of contributors" and that it "promotes speech and fairness, thus sustaining the active, alert responsibility of the individual citizen in our democracy." Assuming that the state has articulated compelling interests, we conclude that the state has failed to demonstrate that the spend-down provision is narrowly tailored to do either of the things that the state asserts it will do. Although the state asserts that the provision protects the free speech interests of contributors, it is just as likely that the provision infringes those interests. Surely the contributor's political free speech interests are not well served if a candidate is compelled (1) to waste campaign contributions on unnecessary speech (in order to spend down the campaign's accumulated assets) or (2) to turn over those contributions to the Missouri Ethics Commission or return them to contributors. With respect to the provision's impact on the "active, alert responsibility of the individual citizen," the state's arguments are broad and conclusory. The state makes no attempt to show how the spend-down provision is narrowly tailored to serve that interest, saying only that "citizens now may decline to participate in a particular race . . . because of the overwhelming advantage carried over from another day" and that the "carryover restriction may well be the difference between having noncompetitive races, in which there is little or no speech, and having active campaigns in which there is uninhibited, robust, and wide-open debate on public issues." These statements fall far short of a showing that the spend-down provision is narrowly tailored to promote "the active, alert responsibility of the individual citizen in our democracy." We conclude that [this measure] cannot withstand strict scrutiny and that it violates freedoms that the First Amendment protects.

Rhode Island strengthened its PAC disclosure requirements and offered public funding to gubernatorial candidates who voluntarily agreed to restrict their campaign spending. To make public funding more attractive, the law raised the contribution limit for candidates who agreed to the restrictions and provided them some free broadcasting time. The United States Court of Appeals for the First Circuit struck down the disclosure provision because it treated PACs more harshly than individuals and thus burdened the right of association. It did, however, uphold the two provisions affecting publicly funded candidates. It thought that allowing them to receive bigger contributions "achieves a rough proportionality between the advantages available to complying candidates . . . and the restrictions that such candidates must accept to receive these advantages." And it construed the broadcast provision as not conflicting with federal law requiring stations to give "equal opportunities" to all candidates.

[Cyr] SELYA, Circuit Judge.

[Rhode Island enacted two provisions. The first, a so-called "first dollar disclosure" requirement, required most PACs to disclose the identity of, and the amount given by, every contributor, no matter how small the contribution. The second offered public funding to gubernatorial candidates who agreed to certain restrictions on campaign spending. In order to make the offer more attractive, this provision raised the amount such candidates could receive as a contribution from any single person or PAC in a single calendar year from $1,000 to $2,000—thus creating a "contribution cap gap" between publicly and privately funded candidates—and also granted such candidates free time on community antenna television and on public broadcasting stations. Two PACs, some individuals, and the ACLU sued to enjoin enforcement of the "first dollar" disclosure requirement and an unsuccessful gubernatorial candidate named Elizabeth Leonard who had rejected public funding sued to enjoin enforcement of the contribution cap gap and free-television-time incentives.]

. . .

II. THE STATE'S APPEAL

. . . Our consideration . . . starts with a discussion of whether first dollar disclosure provisions are always repugnant to the first amendment. Concluding . . . that they are not, we then examine whether the particular first dollar disclosure provision here at issue passes the test of constitutionality.

A. The *Per Se* Challenge.

. . .

It is old hat that compelled disclosure of information about a person's political contributions "can seriously infringe on [the] privacy of association and belief guaranteed by the First Amendment." Thus, courts routinely subject statutes mandating revelation of contributors' identities in the arena of political speech to exacting scrutiny. A disclosure statute may survive such scrutiny only if it satisfies a two-part test: (1) the statute as a whole must serve a compelling governmental interest, and (2) a substantial nexus must exist between the served interest and the information to be revealed.

With respect to the test's first prong, no fewer than three governmental interests have proven sufficient, in varying circumstances, to justify obligatory disclosure of contribution-related information. Thus, forced disclosure may be warranted when the spotlighted information enhances voters' knowledge about a candidate's possible allegiances and interests, inhibits actual and apparent corruption by exposing large contributions to public view, or aids state officials in enforcing contribution limits. Because [the law], read as part of an integrated whole, plainly satisfies this prong of the test—indeed, the Rhode Island statute appears to advance the three interests we have mentioned in much the same fashion as did the statute before the *Buckley* [document 3.1] Court—we proceed directly to the difficult question of whether a substantial relationship exists between the precise modicum of information required to be disclosed and some compelling state interest.

We agree with the plaintiffs that, in certain respects, the fit required to meet the test's second prong is lacking. As the disclosure threshold drops toward zero, the bond between the information revealed and the governmental interests involved becomes weaker and, therefore, more tenuous. Common sense suggests that information about the source of a $1 contribution does not advance the state's interest in deterring actual or apparent corruption because such a donation has a limited (perhaps nonexistent) potential to exact an illegal or unethical *quid pro quo*. Similarly, such information bears little discernible relation to the state's interest in enforcing contribution limits that dip no lower than $1,000: few persons will donate $1 to a PAC on more than 1,000 separate occasions—and those that try will likely grow arm-weary in the process.

But, viewed from another, equally proper, angle, the fit is quite comfortable: signals are transmitted about a candidate's positions and concerns not only by a contribution's size but also by the contributor's identity. Since the identity of a contributor is itself informative, quite apart from the amount of the contribution, a candidate's ideological interests may often be discerned as clearly from a $1 contribution as from a $100 contribution. Hence, we conclude that there is a substantial link between data revealed by first dollar disclosure and the state's compelling interest in keeping the electorate informed about which constituencies may command a candidate's loyalties.

. . .

We hold that first dollar disclosure is not, in all cases, constitutionally proscribed. . . . We turn, then, to the plaintiffs' next theory—a theory that shifts from an exclusive focus on whether first dollar disclosure provisions are ever permissible to a more holistic focus on whether Rhode Island's disclosure requirement, considered in light of the state's overall campaign finance law, withstands constitutional scrutiny.

B. The Contextual Challenge.

It is apodictic that courts, when passing upon the constitutionality of a statutory provision, must view it in the context of the whole statutory scheme. Here, plaintiffs' contextual challenge centers on the disparity between the first dollar disclosure threshold applicable to those who choose to pool money by making contributions to PACs and the $100 disclosure threshold applicable to those who choose to act alone by making direct contributions and expenditures. Plaintiffs say that this disparity not only burdens PAC contributors' first amendment rights of association but also undermines Rhode Island's boast that first dollar disclosure of PAC contributions represents a rationally selected device geared toward achieving a compelling state interest. We find plaintiffs' analysis to be convincing.

The first amendment frowns upon laws which burden associational rights, particularly in the sphere of political speech. The more lopsided the burdens, the more probable it is that a constitutional infirmity looms. Thus, in [*Citizens Against Rent Control* v.] *Berkeley*, the Supreme Court struck down a limitation on contributions to PACs, resting its holding not on the impermissibility of the limits *per se*, but, rather, on the disparity between those limits and the limits applicable to persons who, for one reason or another, preferred not to pool their resources:

To place a Spartan limit—or indeed any limit—on individuals wishing to band together to advance their views on a ballot measure, while placing none on individuals acting alone, is clearly a restraint on the right of association. [Laws which] do not seek to mute the voice of one individual . . . cannot be allowed to hobble the collective expressions of a group.

Berkeley, 454 U.S. @296.

We believe that this passage enunciates three fundamental precepts. First, any law that burdens the rights of individuals to come together for political purposes is suspect and must be viewed warily. Second, burdens which fall exclusively on those who choose to exercise their right to band together, leaving individual speakers unbowed, merit heightened scrutiny. Third, measures which hinder group efforts to make independent expenditures in support of candidates or ballot initiatives are particularly vulnerable to constitutional attack. The first two precepts derive in part from the importance of group expression as a method of amplifying the voices of those with meager means. The last precept derives in part from the fact that independent expenditures, because they have a more attenuated connection with a particular candidate, are a less likely source for *quid pro quo* corruption and a questionable indicator of candidate loyalties.

In *Berkeley*, these three precepts coalesced to scuttle a contribution cap. The case at bar is a fair congener. Here, as in *Berkeley*, the challenged enactment hobbles collective expression by mandating that groups disclose contributors' identities and the extent of their monetary support, no matter how tiny. This, in itself, is a red flag. Here, as in *Berkeley*, the statute has a much less stringent rule for those who prefer individual expression to collective expression. Here, as in *Berkeley*, the statute imposes its one-sided burden regardless of whether a group's members have banded together to contribute directly to a candidate or to make independent expenditures concerning a candidate or referendum. We think that these three points of comparison accurately foretell that here, as in *Berkeley*, the statute cannot stand.

. . .

This imbalance [between PAC and individual contribution disclosure requirements] does not cater to any cognizable government interest. It does not serve the state's interest in combating corruption because corruption can as easily spring from direct contributions to candidates as from contributions that flow through PACs. And, if the danger that tiny contributions will foment corruption is not great enough to justify significant inroads on first amendment rights, it is certainly not great enough to justify disparate treatment of PACs. Similarly, the unevenness does not serve the state's interest in enforcing its contribution limits; after all, the district court found no evidence that PAC contributors might try to subvert the $1,000 cap by an endless stream of $1 donations.

Finally, the interest in an informed citizenry cannot justify the disparity at issue here. To be sure, when contributors' identities are made public, the name of a PAC, standing alone, could in some states have little meaning to a large segment of the electorate. But, Rhode Island has guarded against this contingency by requiring that PACs reveal a wide array of information about their goals and purposes. The obvious result of Rhode Island's legislative mosaic is that when a candidate discloses that a particular PAC has given to his or her cause, state law ensures that this fact will signify more about the candidate's loyalties than the disclosed identity of an individual contributor will ordinarily convey. We think this circumstance is properly considered, and it weighs heavily in our conclusion that the claimed justification for the added (first dollar disclosure) burden that Rhode Island imposes on PACs and PAC contributors is more illusory than real.

In sum, [the first dollar disclosure requirement] has at least three grave weaknesses. First, by mandating public revelation of all PAC contributors, it burdens the rights of individuals to band together for the purpose of making either independent election expenditures or direct political contributions. Second, by imposing this burden on PACs and PAC contributors while regulating candidates and certain of their financial backers (viz., individuals who contribute directly to candidates rather than to PACs) more loosely, the statute compounds the unfairness of the burden. Finally, the disparity between the two disclosure thresholds (one for PACs and the other for individuals), and, hence, the net burden imposed solely on associational rights, bears no substantial relation to the attainment of any important state interest. Their cumulative effect compels the conclusion that the statute abridges the first amendment.

. . .

III. [THE PUBLIC FINANCING PROVISIONS]

. . .

B. The Contribution Cap Gap.

Leonard[, an unsuccessful gubernatorial candidate who rejected public funding,] has questioned several different provisions of the statute. We turn initially to her claim that the contribution cap gap is inimical to the first amendment. In reaching this issue, we stress that Leonard assails only the disparity between the two caps; she voices no *in vacuo* challenge to the $1,000 cap applicable to candidates, such as herself, who eschew public funding.

Leonard's serenade has two themes. Her major theme is that regulatory disparities of this type are inherently impermissible. Her minor theme is that the cap gap burdens her first amendment rights without serving a corresponding governmental interest. We consider these asseverations sequentially. . . .

1. The *Per Se* Challenge. Leonard's *per se* challenge to the contribution cap gap boils down to the assertion that, whenever government constructs incentives for candidates to accept fundraising limits, it departs from its required role as an umpire and becomes a player in the electoral process, much like, say, a referee who eases the rules for one team and not the other. The most immediate barrier to the success of this argument is that the Supreme Court has upheld a very direct and tangible incentive: the provision of public funds to candidates who agree to place decreased reliance on private campaign contributions.

. . .

Leonard also proffers a difference-in-degree distinction. Even if some regulatory incentives may be permissible, she says, Rhode Island's incentives are so strong that they destroy the voluntariness of the public financing system and, therefore, cannot be condoned.

We agree with Leonard's main premise: voluntariness has proven to be an important factor in judicial ratification of government-sponsored campaign financing schemes. Coerced compliance with fundraising caps and other eligibility requirements would raise serious, perhaps fatal, objections to a system like Rhode Island's. Furthermore, there is a point at which regulatory incentives stray beyond the pale, creating disparities so profound that they become impermissibly coercive. It is, however, pellucid that no such compulsion occurred here.

Rhode Island's law achieves a rough proportionality between the advantages available to complying candidates (including the cap gap) and the restrictions that such candidates must accept to receive these advantages. Put another way, the state exacts a fair price from complying candidates in exchange for receipt of the challenged benefits. While we agree with Leonard that Rhode Island's statutory scheme is not in exact balance—we suspect that very few campaign financing schemes ever achieve perfect equipoise—we disagree with her claim that the law is unfairly coercive. Where, as here, a non-complying candidate suffers no more than "a countervailing denial," the statute does not go too far.

To sum up, the implication of the public funding cases is that the government may legitimately provide candidates with a choice among different packages of benefits and regulatory requirements. Rhode Island has done nothing more than implement this principle. We see no sign that the state has crossed into forbidden territory; the contribution cap gap, as structured by the Rhode Island General Assembly, neither penalizes certain classes of office-seekers nor coerces candidates into surrendering their first amendment rights. In short, Leonard has identified no inherent constitutional defect in the state's voluntary, choice-increasing framework.

. . .

C. The Free-Television-Time Provisions.

We now examine Leonard's remonstrance against Rhode Island's offer of free television time to candidates who comply with the eligibility criteria for public financing. . . .

1. Setting the Stage. To understand the free-television-time incentives that have raised Leonard's hackles, a further exegesis is helpful. Under this heading, Leonard attacks two different grants of in-kind assistance to gubernatorial candidates who accept public financing. One such incentive . . . entitles a complying candidate to "free time on community antenna television" pursuant to rules to be formulated by the state Division of Public Utilities (DPU). The second such incentive . . . entitles a complying candidate to "free time on any public broadcasting station" operating under the jurisdiction of the Rhode Island Public Telecommunications Authority (PTA).

2. Preemption. Leonard's attack on the free-television-time provisions proceeds on two fronts. Initially, she contends that the Federal Communications Act (FCA) preempts conflicting state laws, and that [the community antenna television provision] comes within this proscription. We find no such irreconcilable conflict.

The FCA reads in relevant part:

If any licensee shall permit any person who is a legally qualified candidate for public office to use a broadcasting station [or CATV system], he shall afford equal opportunities to all other such candidates for that office in the use of such broadcasting station [or CATV system].

47 U.S.C. § 315(a), (c). . . .

Whether this federal guarantee preempts Rhode Island's free-television-time provisions depends upon how one interprets state law. Leonard argues that in explicitly guaranteeing state-controlled television time to qualifying candidates at no cost, the state intends to exclude all other (non-publicly-funded) candidates from receiving comparable treatment. Any alternate interpretation of the statute, she claims, would render it purposeless.

We think Leonard's argument is deeply flawed. When a statute provides a benefit to some, it does not necessarily bar receipt of the benefit by others. Put in concrete terms applicable to this case, the Rhode Island statute grants free television time to candidates who embrace public funding—but it does not purport to prevent privately financed candidates from reaping the same benefit if some other law—here, the FCA—requires equal treatment.

. . .

3. Excessive Entanglement. Leonard has one last shot in her sling. She urges that the provision of in-kind benefits, such as free television time, has a dangerous tendency to entangle government in the internal workings of political campaigns.

The electoral process is guided by legislatively articulated rules designed to ensure fairness. A fine, but important, line exists between this salutary rulemaking and meddlesome interference in the conduct of elections. There is a point where government involvement in the operation of political campaigns may become so pervasive as to imperil first amendment values. Were a state to loan out its workers as campaign consultants, for example, voters and candidates might legitimately complain that it had gone beyond laying down general rules for office-seekers and begun tampering with, or even manipulating, the electoral process. Such entanglement could conceivably prevent the first amendment from accomplishing its fundamental mission in respect to political speech: "to secure the widest possible dissemination of information from diverse and antagonistic sources, and to assure unfettered interchange of ideas for the bringing about of political and social changes desired by the people." In short, entanglement of this insidious stripe runs too great a risk of creating a convergence of pro-government voices.

Mindful of these concerns, courts must carefully review legislative enactments that potentially entangle government in partisan political affairs. In-kind incentives carry the seeds of potential overinvolvement, especially when they implicate access to state-run organs of communication. Nevertheless, the first amendment does not rule out all in-kind offerings simply because some of them may be too entangling. Legislative bodies (and, ultimately, courts) must separate wheat from chaff, recognizing that, while some in-kind benefits may be excessively entangling, others represent valid and innovative attempts to confront new concerns in the ever-changing world of democratic elections.

. . .

In this case, Leonard has advanced no concrete reason for believing that the free-television-time provisions will excessively entangle the state in the day-to-day details and decisions of the campaign. Because applicable federal laws and regulations require equal time and treatment for all competing candidates insofar as the electronic media are concerned, there is no appreciable danger of lopsided state involvement in the intricate process of scheduling television appearances. By like token, there is no demonstrable risk that state power will influence candidates' speech in a way that undermines first amendment values. Accordingly, there is no excessive entanglement.

IV. CONCLUSION

In its journey to ensure the integrity of the electoral process, a state legislature must march across the hallowed ground on which fundamental first amendment rights take root. The terrain must be negotiated with circumspection and care: disparities, in whatever guise, are not casually to be condoned.

Here, the Rhode Island General Assembly traversed the minefield with mixed results. The disclosure threshold for PAC contributors, as contrasted with the different disclosure threshold for contributors to candidates, creates an impermissible disparity violative of associational rights. A second claimed disparity, involving the contribution cap gap is, in part due to its relatively small size, non-penalizing, non-coercive, justifiable, and, hence, constitutional. For all intents and purposes, the third claimed disparity is virtually non-existent: given the imperatives of extant federal law, the free-television-time provisions of the state statute do not produce significant differences in the benefits available to various candidates for the same office. Thus, we . . . find that [the first dollar disclosure requirement] is unconstitutional, but that the plaintiffs' challenges to other portions of Rhode Island's campaign finance law are bootless.

. . .

In 1994, Oregon voters passed the "Freedom from Special Interests" initiative, which limited the amount of contributions candidates could receive from outside their districts. The law, the district court found, was insufficiently related to the state's interest in preventing corruption. It both limited non-corrupt out-of-district contributions and failed to address in-district corruption.

[Robert E.] JONES, Judge:

. . .

FACTUAL BACKGROUND

On November 8, 1994, Oregon voters passed Measure 6 which essentially limits the amount of campaign contributions that candidates may accept from out-of-district donors. The Measure is comprised of four sections:

(1) Section 1 allows candidates to "use or direct only contributions which originate from individuals who at the time of their donation were residents of the electoral district of the public office sought by the candidate . . . ;"
(2) where more than ten percent of a candidate's total campaign funding is in violation of Section 1, Section 2 punishes the candidate by either (a) forcing the elected official to forfeit the office and to not hold a subsequent elected public office for a period equal to twice the tenure of the office sought, or (b) forbidding the unelected candidate from holding an elected public office for a period equal to twice the tenure of the office sought;
(3) Section 3 prohibits "qualified donors" (i.e., in-district residents) from contributing funds to a candidate on behalf of an out-of-district resident;
(4) Section 4 labels a violation of Section 3 as an "unclassified felony."

Entitled the "Freedom From Special Interests" initiative, Measure 6 is intended to prevent out-of-district individuals and organizations from buying influence in elections, thus allowing "ordinary people [to] secure their rightful control of their own government."

. . .

DISCUSSION

. . .

In the present action, Measure 6 burdens a contributor's political speech and right to associate by limiting the amount of the donated funds that may be used by the candidate. Campaign contributions may, in some cases, be restricted because of the greater potential for political "*quid pro quo*" corruption. Nonetheless, Defendants must still demonstrate in this case that the contribution limitation is narrowly tailored to serve a compelling state interest. At least both parties agree that the state has a compelling interest in preventing "corruption or the appearance of corruption." The issue then is whether the Measure 6 contribution limitation is narrowly tailored to prevent corruption.

I find that Measure 6 campaign limitations are not narrowly tailored to preventing political corruption for several reasons. First, the Measure prohibits non-corrupt, out-of-district contributors from politically associating with candidates running for state offices. Elected officials in state offices impact all state residents, not just the candidate's constituents within his election district. Therefore, the Measure impairs out-of-district residents from associating with a candidate for state office who, if elected, will have a real and direct impact on those persons.

Secondly, the Measure fails to thwart any in-district corruption. The candidate could be wholly funded by one or more wealthy "in-district" individuals who seek to further their own "special interests" by contributing huge amounts of money.

Lastly, the Measure fails to prevent large out-of-district contributions, so long as they do not exceed 10% of the candidate's total campaign expenditures. Therefore, the more money the candidate receives from in-district contributions, the larger the contributions the candidate may accept from out-of-district donors. If the purpose of the Measure is to discourage outside special interests, then the Measure should not be designed to allow out-of-district contributors to increase their donations based upon in-district funding.

In sum, I find that Measure 6 is not narrowly tailored to serve the state's interest in preventing corruption. [The measure therefore] contravenes the First Amendment. . . .

David Donnelly, Janice Fine, and Ellen S. Miller, "Going Public," *Boston Review*, vol. 22, no. 2 (April/May 1997), pp. 3–7

DOCUMENT 9.6

The authors evaluate six models of campaign finance reform proposals in view of five basic principles they believe should guide reform efforts: competition, accountability, fairness, responsibility, and deliberation. They deny that efforts to lower contribution limits, raise contribution limits and improve disclosure, tinker around the edges, institute partial public financing or matching funds, and challenge the *Buckley* decision (document 3.1) honor these basic principles. Rather, they advocate voluntary full public financing, similar to the Maine Clean Elections Act of 1996, as a model that reflects these basic values.

There are only two important things in politics. The first is money and I can't remember the second.

—Mark Hanna

On November 7, 1995, more than a thousand volunteers in Maine collected 65,000 signatures to put the Maine Clean Elections Act on the 1996 ballot. It was the country's most sweeping campaign finance reform proposal, and promised to blunt the domination of special interest money in Maine politics by establishing a system of full public financing of state elections. One year later, by a 56–44 margin, Maine voters enacted this fundamental change. In crisp and decisive terms, they stated that private money would no longer dominate their political life.

The situation in other states, however, remains at least as bad as it was in Maine, and at the federal level matters are much worse. The American people realize that money is eating away at the core of our democracy, and voters seem willing to take decisive action to stop it. But they need a model for reform. Maine's full public financing solution, [Clean Money Campaign Reform], provides that model. . . .

What role should private money play, and how can we correct the current imbalance? The field is now crowded with competing answers to these questions. To explain the advantages of the Maine strategy over the leading alternatives, we will start by setting out some basic principles that should guide reform efforts, and then describe the deficiencies of the alternatives in light of these principles.

Principles

Broad principles should inform the proposals for campaign finance reform. We suggest five:

Competition. Reform must enhance electoral competition. It must encourage qualified Americans of diverse backgrounds and points of view, regardless of their economic means, to seek public office.

Accountability. Reform must increase government accountability and restore public confidence in government. It must eliminate the conflicts of interest created by privately financing the campaigns of our public officials.

Fairness. Reform must guarantee fairer and more equal representation for all citizens. The views of all Americans must be taken into account in the public policy making process irrespective of the ability to make campaign contributions.

Responsibility. Reform must stop the perpetual money chase. Elected officials should be attending to the people's business—meeting with constituents, attending important meetings, researching current policy options—not lounging with large donors.

Deliberation. Reform must begin the process of reinvigorating public participation in our democracy. It must reinstate public elections and legislative debate as forums for deliberation about how best to address the most pressing issues of the day.

Alternatives

While it would be impossible to develop an exhaustive list of proposals to address the money in politics problem, six models dominate public discussion: lowering contribution limits; raising the contribution limits and enhancing disclosure; making lots of modest changes around the edges (like the [John] McCain-[Russell D.] Feingold legislation in the Senate); instituting partial public financing or matching funds; challenging the Supreme Court's 1976 *Buckley* v. *Valeo* decision [document 3.1], which substantially limited the measures that government can use to regulate campaign finance; and full public financing.

Lower contribution limits. A first strategy of reform is to cut into the flow of money as it passes from contributors to candidates—to limit the size of the checks written to candidates for elective office, while not regulating the overall size of spending. Pursuing this strategy, voters in several states have passed proposals to limit contributions to $100 (or some other level). But these proposals have run into legal trouble. Although the Supreme Court has permitted limits on contributions to candidate campaigns—both because such contributions threaten corruption and because potential contributors remain free to spend their money to influence politics without giving it to candidates—the Court confined its concerns to "large" contributions. And lower courts have recently struck down $100 limits in DC, Missouri, and Oregon as too stringent and therefore incompatible with First Amendment speech rights.

Because of these legal troubles, we do not have much experience with more stringent contribution limits. Still, we can make some informed judgments about their effectiveness on the basis of evidence gathered in a few election cycles. Thus, although it appears that the overall money given to candidates went down, there was a corresponding increase in money spent outside the system through independent expenditures. Moreover, these measures may have the perverse effect of encouraging candidates to spend even more time courting contributors because a large number of contributions are needed to wage a serious campaign. Furthermore, it is easier for incumbents to find the numbers of contributors needed to mount strong campaigns than it is for challengers. If reduced contribution limits lead to increased independent expenditures, more candidate time on fundraising, and a playing field tilted toward incumbents, then they do not fare well on grounds of fairness, responsibility, and competitiveness, even if they help on accountability.

Raising contribution limits/more disclosure. A second strategy of reform would put increased weight on full disclosure of support, while raising contribution limits or eliminating them entirely. Pursuing this strategy would, we believe, put the financing of our elections even more securely in the hands of wealthy economic interests and cause an even more dramatic skewing of public policy in favor of the big campaign contributors. Raising the limits would skew the current imbalance in contributions even more. Business interests already contribute seven times as much as labor and ten times as much as ideological groups. For example, in 1996, energy interests gave $21 million in congressional races, whereas environmental groups gave just $2 million. As the principles of accountability, fairness, and deliberation imply, the issue isn't simply how much money is being spent and how much time it takes to raise it, but where it comes from, who provides it and who doesn't, what obligations and conflicts of interest result, and how the political debate itself gets skewed.

At the same time, the remedy of full disclosure falls short. Mere documentation does not correct the problems just noted. We already know that economic interests influence, skew, and control the political process. As Representative Barney Frank (D-MA) has commented, "We are the only human beings in the world who are expected to take thousands of dollars from perfect strangers on important matters and not be affected by it." Assuming a reliable source of information, disclosure may inform the public of how skewed the process is, but it won't shield our elected officials, nor will it correct for the unfair influence that contributors have over the political process. Citizens are like battered women: they already know who is hurting them, and how much. They need a way out, not more information about the source and extent of the damage.

Modest changes around the edges. A third strategy aims to control the flow of money—rather than simply providing greater information about it—but differs from contribution limits in the target of the controls. The leading such proposal at the federal level is the McCain-Feingold bill, which includes voluntary spending limits for US Senate candidates, a ban on PAC [Political Action Committee] contributions to federal candidates, and regulations of "soft money," and would require candidates to rely substantially on in-state contributions. Candidates who agree to the spending limits will receive free television time and reduced postage rates.

Though not without merit, these changes would only bring slight advantages on the reform principles. The voluntary spending limits in McCain-Feingold, for example, are only slightly lower than the current average. The House companion bill ([Christopher] Shays-[Marty] Meehan) sets these voluntary spending limits at higher than the current average for House candidates. More fundamentally, though, we would achieve at best limited gains in fairness and accountability. That's because the current problems are not principally a result of PACs or out-of-state state contributions. PACs are now responsible for only 25 percent of funding for congressional campaigns. And because PACs are not the exclusive vehicle for wealthy donors, a PAC ban might further slant the playing field: it would disarm labor unions and other interest groups that raise their money from a large number of small contributions from their members. Business interests do not now rely on PACs for their political contributions. If PACs were banned tomorrow, business would simply channel all, rather than most, of its money through large individual contributions. A PAC ban, if constitutional, would take us back to the days when there were no PACs and most of the money came from wealthy business executives.

Furthermore, the great majority of funds for these races already comes from in-state: For Senators, 63 percent of their funds came from within their home states, and 78 percent of House candidates' funds were raised from within their home states. Big contributors will continue to have an insurmountable advantage when it comes to gaining access and influence with elected officials; they will just be closer to home.

Partial public financing. The fourth strategy adopts a different angle on reform: Instead of looking for the optimal restrictions on private money, it aims to increase the role of public money as a supplement to private resources, perhaps by using public funds to match small contributions. Although the Maine proposal embraces the principle of public financing, we think that schemes of partial public financing are worst-of-both-worlds hybrids: they couple the most troubling effect of private financing with the most problematic aspects of public financing.

Consider the best-known case of partial public financing: the system of financing our presidential elections. Candidates must first raise lots of special interest money; after they have become indebted to those private contributors, the candidates then receive their public money. So we are asked to pay twice. First, through public financing, we support presidential candidates who are already obligated to private economic interests. Then we finance the tax breaks, subsidies, and other forms of corporate welfare granted to corporate sponsors as payback. But even systems of matching funds that—unlike the presidential scheme—attempt to amplify small contributions by providing a high ratio of public money to private money don't change the fundamental calculus, because they don't outlaw very large private contributions from wealthy special interests that, matching funds or no matching funds, are enormously influential.

Challenging "money equals speech." A fifth line of approach is less a reform strategy in its own right than an effort to set the stage for substantial reform by challenging the Supreme Court's claim that money equals speech. In its 1976 decision in *Buckley* v. *Valeo,* the Court determined that political spending was protected by the First Amendment. Though the Court agreed, as was indicated earlier, that contribution limits are legal, it also held that governments cannot impose overall spending limits on campaigns, or regulate candidates' spending from their own pockets, or limit independent expenditures (money spent by a private group or individual without coordinating with a party or candidate). Because of *Buckley,* there can be no mandatory spending limits, and any system of public financing must be optional.

Thus some reformers argue that the first order of business is to challenge *Buckley,* perhaps through a constitutional amendment that would restrict First Amendment protections of campaign spending. But this cannot be the entire solution to the growing problem of private money in our political system. Even if we could limit spending, we would still have not dealt directly with the corrosive element—the private sources of money that produce a conflict of interest. Moreover, as advocates of the Equal Rights Amendment and the Balanced Budget Amendment would argue, a Constitutional amendment effort takes years and marshaling the forces to enact it in two-thirds of the states is daunting.

. . .

Clean Money

Our preferred alternative—what we call [Clean Money Campaign Reform]—is a system of voluntary full public financing that cuts the cord of dependency between candidates and their special interest contributors. While no solution closes off all channels of influence, [Clean Money Campaign Reform] blocks the path that creates most trouble for the reform principles: the donations of large sums of money by special interests to candidates who, should they win, may be able to influence policy in areas of interest to these donors. This is the proposal that Maine voters enacted [, that Vermont passed into law] and that legislatures and citizens in, for example,] Connecticut, North Carolina, Illinois, Massachusetts, Missouri, Idaho, Washington, and Wisconsin, will consider in the coming months and years.

The law that Maine voters passed was based on model legislation drafted by the Working Group on Electoral Democracy in the late 1980s for federal elections. The model legislation called for full public financing of campaigns for candidates who agree to spending limits, no private money, and a shorter campaign season. Over several years, Maine activists rewrote this model to fit the political reality of running for office in Maine, and running a state-wide referendum campaign to pass the legislation.

The Maine Clean Elections Act was drafted to go as far as possible in the public financing direction while remaining within the confines of *Buckley*. The construction of the Act makes as many changes as possible on the private side and it creates a public financing option. The measure sets lower, but not restrictive, contribution limits for candidates who continue to exercise their right to privately finance their campaigns, and, at its center, the Act established the "Clean Elections Option" to publicly finance candidates who agree to spending limits and to neither seek nor spend any private money.

For the first time, office seekers will have the option of qualifying for and accepting only public money for their election campaigns. Here is how it works: Candidates who choose to enter into the Clean Elections Option must agree to limit spending to the amount provided in public money and to refuse all private contributions once the public money comes in. They must also agree to a shorter campaign season. These candidates don't get something for nothing. To qualify for public funds, they must collect a specified number of $5 qualifying contributions from voters in their district (or state-wide in the case of governor). A small amount of private money can be raised as start up "seed money," but these contributions are limited to $100 and there is an overall cap. The key difference from matching funds schemes is that they can neither raise nor spend any private money once they receive public money. Moreover, this law covers primaries as well as general elections. "Clean Elections" candidates would also receive supplementary public funds if they are outspent by privately-financed opponents, or independent expenditures, or a combination of the two. These funds would be capped at twice the original amount provided to the candidate.

Returning to our five principles, then, what are the advantages of [Clean Money Campaign Reform]?

By providing an alternative to the special interest system for financing elections, [Clean Money Campaign Reform] will level the playing field for candidates, thus enhancing electoral competition. At the same time, public money will lower the economic barriers now faced by citizens who might consider running for office and, by reducing the role of private money, increase the importance of the political activities available to all citizens. In both ways, Clean Money should mean a more fair political system, with greater equality in opportunities for political influence. Unlike any other proposals, [Clean Money Campaign Reform] also strengthens accountability by eliminating political contributions as a way of impacting legislative deliberation and policy making. In addition, . . . [c]lean [m]oney . . . would establish greater responsibility by freeing our elected officials from the perpetual money chase, and allowing them to use their time to engage important issues of the day free of the undue influence of special interest money. Finally, while the implications for political deliberation are uncertain, the same can be said for any of the other proposals. And there is no reason to think that public financing will produce even greater distraction from important public issues than the current system provides.

. . .

| Kenneth R. Mayer, "Campaign Finance Reform in the States: A Report to the Governor's Blue Ribbon Commission on Campaign Finance Reform" (Madison, Wisc., February 6, 1997), pp. 4–11 | DOCUMENT 9.7 |

Although Congress has not passed a campaign finance reform bill since 1979 (document 2.12), states and localities have approved forty-one ballot propositions since 1972. Kenneth R. Mayer discusses three of the most important referenda from the 1996 election: California's Proposition 208, Maine's Question 3, and Colorado's Amendment 15. Together they provide a useful sample of the varied state-level efforts to reform campaign finance.

. . .

RECENT REFORM EFFORTS

. . .

Many of the recent changes to campaign finance law have originated through ballot initiatives and referenda, rather than through legislatively enacted statutes. In the 1996 elections alone, seven states (Arkansas, California, Colorado, Maine, Massachusetts, Montana, and Nevada) had campaign finance reform proposals on the ballot, and initiatives were approved in every state. According to the Citizens Research Foundation, there have been fifty-one campaign finance reform ballot propositions on state or local ballots since 1972, with 41 obtaining approval.

Three of the most important 1996 referenda were California's Proposition 208, which enacted a comprehensive campaign finance reform system to replace what was essentially an unregulated process; Maine's Question 3, which established public financing of state elections; and Colorado's Amendment 15, which established contribution and voluntary spending limits.

California: Proposition 208

Until November 1996, campaign finance in California was largely unregulated. Individuals, PACs, corporations, and labor unions could make unlimited contributions to state political candidates. A legislative attempt to establish public financing failed in 1984, and a 1988 initiative effort resulted in contradictory proposals that were largely invalidated in the courts after a single election cycle.

In 1996, however, California voters approved Proposition 208, a comprehensive reform initiative encompassing contribution limits, voluntary spending limits, regulation of independent expenditures, restrictions on campaign contributions from lobbyists, bans on candidate to candidate transfers, control of campaign war chests, and tighter disclosure.

The centerpiece of Proposition 208 is a combination of contribution and spending limits. Candidates can now voluntarily agree to spending limits for statewide and legislative races as follows:

Spending Limits in California

	Primary	General
Governor	$6 million	$8 million
Other Statewide	$1.5 million	$2 million
State Senate	$300,000	$400,000
State Assembly	$150,000	$200,000

These limits are imposed separately for each election, so a candidate for governor who runs in a primary could spend up to $14 million over the entire election cycle. The limits double for statewide offices and triple for legislative offices when (a) a candidate faces a "non complying" opponent—i.e., a candidate who does not agree to spending limits—who raises or spends 75% of the spending limit; or (b) when independent expenditures opposing the complying candidate, or supporting the non-complying candidate, total 25% (for statewide races) or 50% (for non-statewide races) of the applicable spending. Primary spending limits will increase by 50% in the event that California moves to an "open primary" system. Complying candidates receive a free statement in a voter education ballot pamphlet mailed to all registered voters (noncomplying candidates are charged the costs of printing and distribution) and have their compliance noted on ballots.

Proposition 208 also imposed the following individual, PAC, corporate, and labor union contribution limits, per election. The limits double for candidates who agree to spending limits:

Contribution Limits in California

	Candidate Does Not Agree to Spending Limits	Candidate Agrees to Spending Limits
Statewide	$500	$1,000
Legislative Races, and Local Races in Districts with ≥ 100,000 residents	$250	$500
Local Races with < 100,000 residents	$100	$250

Contributions to PACs are limited to $500 per calendar year, and no individual or organization other than a political party (meaning PACs, corporations, and labor unions) can contribute more than

$25,000 to all candidates and political parties during an election cycle. Corporations and labor unions are still permitted to make campaign contributions, but candidates cannot accept in aggregate more than 25% of the applicable spending limit from such groups, in combination with PAC money.

Proposition 208 established much more lenient limits on political party activity. Unlike the contribution limits set out above, political parties are allowed to contribute up to 25% of the applicable spending limit to any candidate (for both the primary and general elections). In a general election, therefore, parties can contribute up to $2 million to gubernatorial, $100,000 to state Senate, and $50,000 to state Assembly candidates, respectively.

Proposition 208 contains four other noteworthy reforms. First, it establishes a new form of political action committee called a "Small Contributor Committee," which can accept contributions from individuals totaling less than $50 per individual per year. Contribution limits for small contributor PACs are doubled, and such contributions do not count against the 25% aggregate ceiling applicable to overall PAC, corporate, and union contributions.

Second, California now requires all candidates to dispose of surplus campaign funds within ninety days of an election. Elected candidates may use up to $10,000 for their office expense account, but all other funds must be turned over to a political party, returned to contributors, or transferred to the state's general fund. The intent is to prevent candidates from accumulating large reserves of campaign funds that may discourage future challengers.

Third, Proposition 208 sharply restricts the window in which candidates can accept contributions. Statewide candidates may neither solicit nor accept contributions until twelve months before a primary or general election, while Senate and Assembly candidates must wait until six months before an election. All candidates must stop accepting contributions within 90 days of an election. This time limitation is one of the most restrictive in the country. While a number of states prohibit contributions to incumbent legislators during legislative session, only Alaska imposes a similar time-window.[1]

Fourth, Proposition 208 indirectly regulates independent expenditures by restricting on how groups making such expenditures can raise money, and also by defining independent expenditures as contributions under certain circumstances. Groups that spend more than $1,000 on independent expenditures in support of or opposing any candidate are prohibited from accepting contributions of more than $250 per election. Spending on behalf of a candidate by political parties, other candidate committees of the same legislative body and party, and by individuals who have contributed more than $100 per election to that candidate, are not to be considered independent expenditures, and count against the normal contribution limits.

Maine: Ballot Question 3

Also in the 1996 elections, Maine voters instituted a comprehensive system of public finance of state campaigns, to take effect in 2000. Unlike other public finance systems—such as Minnesota's or Wisconsin's—which use public funding to reduce reliance on private contributions, Maine's system attempts to completely replace all private funding of state elections.

---

1. In Alaska, candidates may not raise campaign funds before January 1 of an election year, and must stop raising funds within 45 days after an election. Illinois, Indiana, and Michigan, have windows that apply only to judicial candidates. Candidates in Kentucky may not accept contributions within 30 days before an election, and must end fundraising immediately after an election.

The Maine Clean Election Act created the nation's first total public finance system. Candidates for Governor and the state legislature who accept public funding will receive a grant equal to the average spending level for the office in the previous two election cycles.[2] In order to qualify, candidates must raise a qualifying amount in contributions of between $5 and $100 from voters within the applicable election district, and once they receive a grant are barred from accepting any private contributions. Publicly funded candidates are allowed to advertise their acceptance of public funds. The Act institutes relatively low thresholds for candidates wishing to qualify for public funds: a candidate for the state House of Representatives could qualify for a full public grant after raising a total of $500 in contributions from 50 individuals.[3]

Non-publicly funded candidates face decreased contribution limits, as follows:

Contribution Limits for Privately Funded Candidates in Maine

	Previous Limit	New Limit, Governor	New Limit, Other State Office
Individuals	$1,000	$500	$250
Corporations	$5,000	$500	$250
PACs	$5,000	$500	$250

Question 3 also requires registration of all groups exceeding a $50 threshold for independent expenditures; limits the amount of independent expenditures a group can make to $5,000 per candidate; and sets time limits on when candidates can solicit qualifying contributions.

A broad spectrum of groups—ranging from The Maine Civil Liberties Union to the National Right to Life Political Action Committee—has already announced intentions to challenge the law. The lawsuits will argue that the public grants and spending limits are not truly voluntary, and that the lowered contribution limits for candidates who forego public funding interfere with First Amendment guarantees. Apart from legal questions, adequate funding is also an issue since the law did not by itself create a self-executing funding mechanism to pay for the public grants. Instead, it relies on annual transfers from state revenues (which the legislature can change), a $3 income tax check-off (which has not yet been established), and a doubling of lobbyist registration fees.

Colorado: Amendment 15

Like California before Proposition 208, prior to 1996 Colorado law left state campaign finance largely unregulated: individuals, PACs, corporations, and labor unions could make unlimited contributions to

---

2. There are separate calculations for primary and general elections, as well as for contested and uncontested elections. Public funded candidates who face opponents not accepting the funds, will have their grants increased by the amount they are outspent, up to twice the level of the original public grant.

3. Tony Corrado, a political scientist at Colby College, argues that this may undermine public support by encouraging "fringe" candidates to run with public funds.

candidates. Legislation adopted in 1996 established contribution limits, but the law was superseded in November 1996 by a ballot initiative, Amendment 15.

Amendment 15 imposed a comprehensive system of contribution limits and voluntary spending limits. It significantly reduces the amount that individuals and PACs can contribute ... to candidates, prohibits corporate and union contributions, bans conduits, and prohibits candidate transfers. The new limits established by Amendment 15 are:

Contribution Limits in Colorado

Office	Individual Contributions (per election)	PAC Contributions (per election)	Aggregate PAC Contributions (per cycle)	Political Party Contributions (per cycle)
Governor	$500	$500	$400,000	$400,000
Lt. Governor	$500	$500	$20,000	$20,000
Other Statewide	$500	$500	$80,000	$80,000
State Senate	$100	$100	$15,000	$15,000
State Rep.	$100	$100	$10,000	$10,000

The voluntary spending limits are:

Spending Limits in Colorado

Office	Spending Limit
Governor	$2 million
Lt. Governor	$100,000
Other Statewide	$400,000
State Senate	$75,000
State Rep.	$50,000

Candidates who accept the limits are allowed to advertise their compliance in their political messages; those who refuse must include a disclaimer that indicates their non-compliance. Ballots will clearly identify whether or not candidates have agreed to or refused to abide by spending limits. Contribution limits double for candidates who agree to spending limits, when they face an opponent who refuses the limits and who raises 10% or more of the applicable spending limit.

Amendment 15 also changes the way candidates must handle unspent campaign funds. Under the new law, any leftover balances are counted under the aggregate contribution limit for PACs in the next election cycle, no matter where the funds originated. For example, a State Senator who had $15,000 left after an election would be unable to accept any PAC funds in the new election cycle, as the carryover balance would count toward the aggregate $15,000 PAC contribution limit. The law is retroactive, so candidates who now have "war chests" face the new restrictions in the 1997–1998 cycle.

. . .

DOCUMENT 9.8 Zach Polett, "Empower Citizens," *Boston Review,* vo. 22, no. 2 (April/May 1997), p. 12

The Arkansas Clean Government Act, passed in November 1996 by a large margin, instituted a comprehensive reform of the system. Most notable of its provisions are reduced contribution limits, a 100% tax credit for small individual contributions, a small-donor Political Action Committee (PAC) provision to encourage small contributions, and a limit on independent expenditures. In this article, Zach Polett, director of Political Operations for the ACORN family of organizations, recognizes its deficiencies but maintains that it will improve candidate accountability and empower small donors while limiting the influence of wealthy individuals.

On the same day that 313,581 Maine voters were passing the Maine Clean Elections Act by a 56% to 44% margin, 487,432 Arkansas voters were passing the Arkansas Clean Government Act by nearly double that margin—66% to 34%—a greater margin, in fact, than that by which they supported native son Bill Clinton's reelection as president.

. . .

The Arkansas initiative does the following:

1. Contribution Limits: Reduces the $1000 contribution limit per candidate per election to $300 for statewide office and $100 for other offices.

2. Tax Credit Public Financing: Provides public financing by allowing a 100% annual tax credit of $50 for individuals and $100 for married couples for contributions to a candidate committee, a political party or a political committee.

3. Small-Donor PACs: Sets up a new class of committees that may receive no more than $25 from any contributor but may contribute up to $2500 to a candidate.

4. Independent Expenditure Committees: Requires disclosure of the contributions they receive and limits these contributions to $500.

5. Disclosure: Tightens disclosure requirements to $50 for candidates and for the first time in Arkansas requires disclosure of contributions to political parties.

6. Local Government: Allows local governments to enact their own stricter campaign finance laws.

In the first few months since the passage of the Arkansas Clean Government Act, we have already seen results. Republican Governor Mike Huckabee had to cut back his December gala $1000 per plate fundraiser down to the new $300 limit. Candidates who played under the new rules in a January 1997 special legislative election reported in the local press that they spent much more time in door-to-door campaigning because "the new rule lessens lobbyist influence and makes the process more accessible to average people." And the City of Little Rock has introduced and is likely to pass a New Party–sponsored ordinance, made possible by the new state law, that severely restricts when city council members can fundraise, helping to reduce conflicts of interest.

Need for Accountability. As the campaign finance reform community moves forward in its efforts to fundamentally change the financing system of American politics, we think it's important to develop a system that encourages and empowers the participation of organized everyday voters in the process— and through this the accountability of candidates and politicians to organized groups of voters. We believe that politics in America is already too candidate-centered, as opposed to being issues- and values-centered. We definitely want a system that decreases the dependence of politicians on wealthy individuals and well-financed corporate interests, but not by strengthening the power of politicians and weakening organized groups of "regular" voters.

As we often say in the campaign finance reform movement, "follow the money." We are concerned that if we create a public financing system that provides all the money to politicians and none to organized groups of citizens, then we will inadvertently create a system that encourages candidates and elected officials to be even less accountable than they are now. By getting all the legal political money "magically," that is straight from the government, they will have the funds to speak more and listen less.

Ross Perot provides an instructive example. He has the political money "magically"—in his case first through his own wealth and then through the presidential public financing funds he received for the 1996 general election. Thus he doesn't need to be accountable to any organized groups of voters—and he isn't.

If public funding goes only to candidates—and all other money is kept out of the process—then candidates will be greatly empowered vis-à-vis voters. We're not convinced that this is such a good thing.

As we change the campaign finance system in America, we want to change who the politicians have to listen to, but we don't want to make them independent actors who don't need to listen to anyone— except the pollsters. Therefore, as we develop public funding mechanisms for political campaigns, we need to make sure that all the cash doesn't go directly to candidates.

Tax Credits as a Public Financing Tool. The Arkansas initiative uses tax credits as its public financing tool. The way it works is that every Arkansan effectively has $50 of political public financing dollars from the state government ($100 for a married couple) that s/he can allocate as s/he deems fit. Individuals can direct their piece of public financing to a candidate, to a political party, or to a political committee. Voters can send it all to one, or divide it up any way they choose. They can invest their piece of public financing in a candidate's campaign or in a political group with which they agree. They can even decide not to invest it at all—in which case the state, not the individual, keeps the money.

The mechanism for this contribution is that individuals make the contribution or contributions and then get the funds back from the state as a dollar-for-dollar reduction of their state income tax bill or as an addition to their annual state income tax refund.

Candidates, parties, and organized groups (political committees) will thus compete with each other for these public funds, by working to convince voters that they should direct their share of public financing in that candidate's or group's direction. All Arkansans will be equal in this process, since all will have the same $50 to allocate. And non-Arkansans will not be able to make an allocation since they are not Arkansas taxpayers.

Small Donor Political Action Committees. The Arkansas initiative sets up and defines a new kind of political action committee called a "small-donor political action committee." These committees are restricted to accepting small contributions of no more than $25 from individuals. Thus they are nearly equally accessible to "lean cats" as they are to "fat cats"—and the fat cats' contributions need to be pretty lean, no more than $25.

What makes the small-donor PAC particularly effective as a campaign finance reform tool is its combination with the contribution limits of the initiative. Under the initiative, regular PACs and individuals can contribute no more than $100 per election to a candidate (or $300 for a statewide race) while small-donor PACs are allowed to contribute up to $2500. Thus small-donor PACs empower small donors while decreasing the power of traditional, large-donor PACs. They also have the advantage of putting more money into the system, thus answering one of the objections raised to relatively low contribution limits.

Reality Check. Let's be real. The rich and powerful, both corporations and individuals, will always have more political influence than the rest of us, and especially than those of us who are poor. Money talks. The Maine and Arkansas initiatives, for example, don't restrict private money expenditures by, or contributions to, independent expenditure campaigns or political parties. No campaign finance reform law can ever totally level the playing field—not Maine, not Arkansas, not a constitutional amendment. But we don't need to oversell the reforms we're promoting. The current system is broken and everyone knows it. The best we can do is to change the rules of the game in ways that help empower voters and promote candidate accountability, while decreasing somewhat the overriding influence of wealthy contributors.

. . .

Norman J. Ornstein, Thomas E. Mann, Paul Taylor, Michael J. Malbin, and Anthony Corrado, "Reforming Campaign Finance," Issued December 17, 1996, Revised May 7, 1997, Brookings Campaign Finance Reform Website, http://www.brook.edu/gs/newcfr/reform.htm, Presented as *5 Ideas For* Practical *Campaign Reform* by the League of Women Voters Education Fund, July 21, 1997

DOCUMENT 9.9

Broadcasting, one of the larger costs of most campaigns, represents an attractive target for reform. Many recent reform proposals would provide free or reduced-rate television advertising to candidates. The following reform plan, which also deals with soft money, issue advocacy, small donations and enforcement, outlines one such proposal. It is of interest, among other reasons, because it would (1) use vouchers in order to subsidize campaigns while distorting the broadcasting market as little as possible, (2) regulate the form of subsidized advertising, and (3) grant the political parties a large role in deciding how much subsidy individual candidates receive.

The campaign finance system in America has been a problem for some time. But in 1996, it went from the political equivalent of a low-grade fever to Code Blue—from a chronic problem needing attention sooner or later to a crisis, with a system clearly out of control. The system needs both an immediate fix in a few important areas, and some sustained attention to the broader problems. We need an approach that breaks us out of the unproductive framework—Democrats insisting on a bottom line of tough spending limits and public financing, Republicans insisting on a bottom line of no spending limits and no public financing—that has doomed any constructive change for decades. It must instead use constructive ideas to help reduce existing problems without creating large unanticipated new ones.

And any proposal must accommodate the Supreme Court's rulings, from *Buckley* v. *Valeo* [document 3.1] to last year's *Colorado [Republican]* decision [document 3.4], that give wide leeway to individuals and groups independently to raise and spend resources in public and political debate under the First Amendment. If a Constitutional Amendment to alter the impact of the Court's decisions were desirable (and it is not clear that amending the First Amendment is the appropriate course of action), it is not practical in the near term. So other ways must be found to reform the system within the existing constitutional context—ways that will achieve the objectives of placing huge donations to candidates or parties off limits; leveling the playing field for outside groups and candidates in political communications in campaigns; enhancing political discourse and dialogue in the campaign; strengthening enforcement and disclosure; and encouraging small individual contributions.

We propose changes in five key areas.

1. "Soft" Money

The idea of "soft" money, spending by parties outside federal regulation, emerged in the reforms of the 1970s, as a way to enhance the role and status of party organizations [see chapter 6]. Unlike the hard money that goes to campaigns, soft money can come directly from corporate coffers and unions, and in unlimited amounts from wealthy individuals. It is harder to trace, less systematically disclosed, and less accountable.

Over time, soft money contributions for "party-building and grass roots volunteer activities" (the language of the law) came to be used for broader purposes, and evolved into a complex system of parties setting up many separate accounts, sometimes funneling money from the national party to the states or vice versa, or back and forth in dizzying trails. But soft money was a comparatively minor problem in campaign funding until 1992. Parties sharply increased their soft money fundraising and spending for a wide range of political activities, including broadcast ads, both in and out of election season. The escalation increased alarmingly in 1996. Both parties sought and received large sums of money, often in staggering amounts from individuals, companies, and other entities, and poured unprecedented sums of soft money into the equivalent of party-financed campaign ads. There is now evidence that some of this money came illegally from foreign sources.

The original limited role of soft money, as a way to enable funds to be used to enhance the role and capability of the parties, especially the state parties, has been mangled beyond recognition. Still, any change in law must recognize that state parties are governed by state laws; that traditional party-building activities, from voter registration and get-out-the-vote drives to sample ballots, have an inevitable overlap between campaigns for state and local offices and campaigns for federal office; and that the goal of enhancing the role of parties is a laudable and necessary one.

What to do? We propose the following:

—Prohibit national party committee soft money by eliminating the distinction in law between nonfederal and federal party money for funds raised by national party committees or their agents. In other words, create one pot of national party money that has similar fund-raising qualifications to the money raised for candidates, namely, no corporate and union funds and limits on sums from individuals. Money may only come from individuals and registered political committees, which are given specific limitations.

—Give parties freedom to allocate the hard resources they are able to raise among their candidates for office as they choose and not subject to existing restrictions, in order to provide a robust role for political parties even as they lose the soft money resources; this in turn will move the parties away from the subterfuge, encouraged by the *Colorado [Republican]* decision, that they can operate independently of their own candidates.

——Expand the existing limits on individual contributions to parties. Currently, individuals can give a total of $25,000 per year in hard money to federal candidates and/or parties, with a sublimit of $20,000 to a party (and with no limits on soft money donations.) Change the limits so that individuals can give the current limit of $25,000 per year to candidates, but create a separate limit of $25,000 per year to political parties. Index both figures to inflation.

—Stiffen party disclosure requirements. Currently, parties can transfer unlimited sums to state parties or related entities for use as they wish, without any federal disclosure of the state party expenditure. We propose that any monies transferred from a federal party to a state party or state and local entity be covered by federal disclosure laws, including the source and the nature of any expenditure of the funds, and that any transfers from state parties to federal committees come only from federal accounts. We also encourage states to continue their own trend of strong state-based disclosure requirements.

Issue Advocacy

1996 saw an explosion of political ads both by outside groups, such as the AFL-CIO and business entities, and by both political parties, with unlimited (i.e., unregulated) contributions and outlays because they were classified not as campaign-related independent expenditures but as "issue advocacy" ads [see chapter 7]. The Court in *Buckley* v. *Valeo* defined political ads as those that explicitly advocate the election or defeat of a candidate. This very narrow definition has allowed groups to employ television and radio ads that were political ads in every sense except that they avoided any explicit candidate advocacy. Thus, huge numbers of campaign ads aired that were thinly disguised—at best—as issue ads. They praised or—more frequently attacked—specific candidates but ended with the tag line "Call Congressman _____ and tell him to . . . " (stop raising taxes, stop cutting Medicare, etc.).

The Supreme Court has appropriately stated that issue advocacy is protected under the First Amendment, as are independent expenditure campaigns. However, funding for independent expenditure campaigns can be regulated as are candidate and party funding for elections. We believe that there is room for Congress to define with more clarity what is meant by issue advocacy and political campaigning without running afoul of the Court's real intent. Thus we propose:

Any paid communication with the general public that uses a federal candidate's name or likeness within ninety days of a primary or of a general election—the same times used by Congress to limit lawmakers' postal patron mass mailing communications—be considered a campaign ad, not an issue advocacy message, and be covered by the same rules that govern independent expenditure campaigns, meaning among other things that they cannot be financed by corporate or union funds, but can use publicly disclosed voluntary contributions in a fashion similar to funds raised by political action committees. (An exemption would apply, as it does in current law, for candidate debates and press coverage.)

This change would not limit in any way groups' ability to communicate in a direct targeted fashion with their own members or constituents. Nor would it limit advertising campaigns or the freedom of parties or independent groups to get their issue-oriented messages out. What it would do is change the funding basis of campaigns that include actual federal candidates to conform to other comparable election-related efforts. The AFL-CIO or the Chamber of Commerce, the Christian Coalition, or the Sierra Club, for example, could run whatever ads it wanted, funded as it wished, whenever it wanted that mentioned or referred to no specific candidate for office. It could run ads that mentioned candidates or lawmakers in a similar fashion except during the ninety days before a primary or general election. During the two ninety-day periods, ads could run that mentioned a candidate or used the candidate's likeness—but *those* ads would have to be funded in the same fashion as other independent expenditure campaigns—in other words, by publicly disclosed money raised on a voluntary basis by a political committee.

Broadcast Bank

No campaign finance reform will be effective unless it ensures adequate means for candidates and parties to get their messages across. A positive and constructive campaign finance reform proposal will channel resources in the most beneficial ways, empowering parties and candidates (including challengers) and encouraging small individual contributions, while removing as much as possible the unfair advantages and subsidies available to independently wealthy, self-financed candidates. At the same time, a constructive reform will try to encourage better debate and deliberation in campaigns by encouraging more candidate-on-screen discourse. In that spirit we propose:

—Creation of a "broadcast bank" consisting of minutes of television and radio time on all broadcast outlets. Drawing on this bank, the FEC will dispense vouchers to purchase time for political spots. One half of all vouchers will go directly to general election candidates for U.S. House and Senate who have raised over a threshold amount in contributions from small donors in their district or state. The other half will go to major (and qualifying minor) parties, which will be free to distribute the vouchers to general election candidates of their choice for local, state or federal office. This distribution system is designed to allow parties to decide where additional time will have the greatest competitive impact. It will also allow candidates who do not wish to use their broadcast vouchers to trade them into their party for other campaign resources, such as phone banks or direct mail.

—Such time can now be used for ads, provided that no message is less than sixty seconds, and provided that the candidate appear on screen for the duration of all television messages, and the candidate's voice be used for the duration of all radio communication.

—In order to establish the bank, every television and radio station in the country will contribute at least two hours of prime spot time at the beginning of each two-year election cycle, in fulfillment of its public interest obligations. The time will be assigned a monetary value, based on market rates where it originated. The bank will distribute vouchers denominated in money, not time. Candidates and parties can use the vouchers at any station they wish. At the end of every election, the bank will reimburse stations that redeemed more than two hours worth of free time with proceeds it will collect from stations that redeemed fewer. Thus, the time bank will insure that all stations bear an equitable burden, but that the political marketplace has the flexibility to use the time where it will have the greatest impact. The market value of the time placed in the bank should be pegged at $500 million per two-year election cycle—the estimated value of all political time sold in 1995–96. (The two-hour time obligation can be adjusted up or down to meet this target.) This target figure will be indexed to rise with inflation. The cost to the broadcast industry will be partially offset by the elimination of the existing lowest unit rate charge requirement on paid political advertising.

—Candidates who want to purchase time outside of the broadcast bank system may do so, but must do so at market rates (lowest unit rates would no longer be mandated for such time).

Small Individual Contributions

Over the past several years, campaigns for Congress have seen sharp changes in the nature of contributions. A shrinking share of campaign resources have come from small donations from individuals, while steadily increasing shares have come from both larger contributions ($500 to $1,000) and political action committees. Of all the sources of private monies that go into our political campaigns, the most desirable and least controversial is that contributed by in-state individuals in small amounts. The more citizens are involved in the campaign process, the more stake they have in the political system; a small contribution is a positive way, with no direct link to a legislative product, to enhance the political process.

One of the most significant goals of campaign finance reform, then, is to find ways to encourage small individual contributions, especially in-state, and to encourage candidates to raise more of their funds in this fashion. The key to doing so is [to]:

—Create a 100% tax credit for in-state contributions to federal candidates of $100 or less. The credit would apply to the first $100 an individual gave to candidates—in other words, $25 given to each of four candidates would result in a $100 credit. It would not apply to large contributions; it would be phased out if an individual gave more than $200 to the candidate.

—Consider funding the tax credit for small contributions by assessing campaigns a 10 percent fee for large contributions ($500 or $1,000 or more.) Consider further the trade-off of raising the individual contribution limit of $1,000 to $2,500 or $3,000 to take into account inflation in the two decades since it was instituted while simultaneously assessing the fee for large contributions to pay for the tax credits.

Enforcement

The lack of strong enforcement of campaign laws has been a serious problem in the past, but escalated sharply in 1996. The Federal Election Commission is poorly and erratically funded, hampering its ability to gather information, disseminate it in a timely fashion, and use it to investigate and act on complaints of violations of the laws or regulations [see chapter 8]. The Commission's structure, with six commissioners, three of each major party, makes inevitable frequent deadlock along partisan lines. Little if any penalty results from blatant violations of the campaign laws. Elections are not overturned, and if there are subsequent financial penalties, they are rarely commensurate with the severity of the violations and in any case are of little importance if the violations made the difference between winning and losing. Candidates and parties knowingly take advantage—and never more openly than in 1996.

It would be desirable to change the structure of the FEC, including changing the selection of its membership. Given the *Buckley* decision and the attitudes of lawmakers from both parties, major structural changes are probably not practical. But there are other ways to create a more viable disclosure and enforcement regimen. We recommend [doing the following]:

—Move from the current practice of voluntary electronic filing to a mandatory one, with a *de minimus* threshold.

—Move from annual appropriations for the FEC to two-year or even longer-term funding, with a bipartisan mechanism in Congress to maintain adequate funding for the Commission. Congress should also consider an independent funding source for the FEC, such as a modest filing fee for campaigns and related committees.

—Allow a private cause of legal action directly against the alleged wrongdoer where the FEC is a) unable to act by virtue of a deadlock; or b) where injunctive relief would be necessary and appropriate (a high standard requiring a showing of immediate, irreparable harm). In order to deter frivolous actions, a "loser pays" standard should apply to requests for injunctive relief. Streamline the process for allegations of criminal violations, by creating more shared procedures between the FEC and the Justice Department, and fast-tracking the investigation from the FEC to Justice if any significant evidence of fraud exists.

—Put into legislation a requirement that until a campaign has provided all the requisite contributor information to the FEC, it cannot put a contribution into any account other than an escrow account where the money cannot be spent. In turn, the current ten-day maximum holding period on checks would have to be waived.

—Adopt a single eight-year term for Commissioners, with no holding over upon expiration. Commissioners' terms should be staggered, so than no two terms expire in the same year. Congress should explore ways to strengthen the office of chairman, including considering creating a new position of nonvoting chairman and presiding officer, as the Commission's Chief Administrator.

These reforms are not top-to-bottom comprehensive changes in the federal campaign financing system. Comprehensive proposals do exist—although they include radically different approaches. But no comprehensive proposal is practical at the moment, or could in fact "cure" the problems in the system once and for all. Nor would any two of us agree on all or even most of the elements that might be included in a comprehensive package. The changes we propose are doable and sensible, and if enacted, would make a very positive difference in American campaigns.

In the following excerpt, one of the authors of the broadcast bank proposal reprinted in document 9.9 explains its aims and operations more fully. He also defends two of its more controversial provisions: requiring the candidate to appear on screen and be the only speaker in subsidized commercials and giving half the vouchers to the political parties for distribution as they see fit to candidates.

Objectives

The objectives of The National Political Time Bank are to reduce the cost of political campaigns; to cut down on special interest influence; to distribute communication resources more equitably between challengers and incumbents; to insure that candidates are the most robust communicators in their own campaigns; to strengthen political parties; to enhance political discourse; and to increase candidate accountability.

How It Would Work

At the beginning of each election cycle, every television and radio station will contribute two hours of prime spot time to a national political time bank administered by the Federal Election Commission [FEC].

Drawing on this time bank, the FEC will dispense vouchers to candidates to purchase time for political spots. One half of all vouchers will go directly to general election candidates for the U.S. House and Senate who have raised contributions from a threshold number of small donors in their districts. The other half will go to major (and qualifying minor) parties, which will be free to distribute them to general election candidates of their choice for local, state, or federal office.

Candidates can spend the vouchers on any station they wish, at any time they wish.

Vouchers can only be used to buy blocks of time of one minute or more. Candidates must agree to appear on screen and be the only speakers in all spots bought with vouchers.

After every election, the FEC time bank will reimburse stations that redeemed more than an hour's worth of free time vouchers (for example, stations in districts with competitive races) with proceeds it will collect from stations that redeemed fewer. Thus, the time bank will insure that all stations bear an equal burden, but that the political marketplace has the flexibility to use the free time where it will have the greatest impact.

Cost

The market value of the time to be distributed by this bank will be pegged at $500 million per two year election cycle—the estimated value of all political time sold in the 1995–1996 cycle. (The two-hour time obligation can be adjusted up or down to meet the target). This target figure will be indexed to rise with inflation. The $500 million figure equals less than half of 1 percent of the biannual gross advertising revenues of the television and radio industry. The cost to the industry will be partially offset by the elimination of the existing lowest unit charge requirement on paid political advertising.

Congress will appropriate sufficient funds to the FEC to handle its new responsibility.

More Accountability, Better Discourse

It makes little sense to provide a free time subsidy for political communication if that political communication winds up discouraging citizens from voting. Unfortunately, much paid political advertising on television does just that. In the typical attack ad, the candidate paying for the ad does not appear—a format that diminishes accountability, facilitates distortion, heightens cynicism, and shrinks turnout.

The candidate-on-screen format requirement is not meant to dull the thrust-and-parry of political campaigns. Rather, it is meant to foster a campaign discourse that favors words over images, substance over sound bites, fair comment over blind broadsides. The hope is that over time, campaigns conducted in this manner will attract citizens to the public square, rather than drive them away.

Candidates can still resort to traditional attack advertising, paid for with privately raised funds. The paid spots will tend to be crowded out by the voucher spots, however, because the voucher spots will have first claim on time sold in the final 90 days of a campaign.

More Competition, Stronger Parties, Cleaner Politics

This time bank will create a communications "floor" for Senate and House candidates. A floor will work to the advantage of challengers, who tend to be underfunded and thus have greater need for seed resources to get their message out.

Challengers also stand to benefit from the allocation of vouchers to the parties. Given their goal of maximizing the number of electoral offices they win, parties will tend to allocate these vouchers disproportionately to challengers who are underfunded but within competitive striking range.

To be sure, there will be circumstances when parties will serve their interest by allocating vouchers to incumbents—for example, to incumbents who are targets of self-financed millionaire challengers or of negative ad campaigns by independent groups. Vouchers will help insure that the most robust voices in campaigns belong to candidates (who can be held accountable on election day) rather than outside groups (who cannot).

This new bank of communication resources will help parties become more vital sources of political cohesion at a time when atomizing forces in our political and media culture induce candidates to behave like independent contractors and interest groups to behave like surrogate parties.

If a time bank is enacted as part of a broader package of campaign finance reforms, these party vouchers could serve as a replacement for party soft money. Better than soft money, however, the vouchers will not come from interested givers—thus, they should help restore public confidence in electoral politics. And unlike soft money, the vouchers can be transferred to the party's candidates without violating the letter or spirit of the law.

Joseph E. Cantor, Denis Steven Rutkus, and Kevin B. Greely, "Free and Reduced-Rate Television Time for Political Candidates," CRS Report for Congress 97-680 GOV (Congressional Research Service, July 7, 1997), pp. 22–29

The following excerpt from a recent report by the Congressional Research Service looks at many of the arguments on both sides of the television-time proposals. Its conclusions are mixed. On the one hand, it finds that the various television-time proposals might not effectively promote the reformers' twin goals of reducing the importance of money in politics and of raising the quality of political debate. On the other hand, it finds that the opponents' primary legal arguments against such provisions—that the FCC cannot implement them without specific statutory authorization and that they would violate the broadcasters' free speech rights and constitute an unconstitutional taking of the broadcasters' property—are weak.

Policy Issues: A Pro/Con Discussion

Judging from the number and diversity of voices registering their opinion in editorial pages, in public policy forums and coalitions, and in bills introduced in Congress, public discussion of the concept of free or reduced-rate broadcast time for political candidates has long been led by those favoring the idea. To the extent opposition has been voiced, it has usually come from the broadcasting industry. Aside from an obvious concern for the financial impact on themselves, broadcasters have raised legitimate policy concerns. Several of the major arguments on each side are discussed below.

Reducing the Role of Money in Politics. The driving force behind free and reduced-rate proposals has been the desire to decrease the level of money in politics. While such proposals would seem to promote that objective, opponents raise the question whether candidates are not likely to react by simply purchasing more time at lower rates. Candidates with easy access to financial resources may well seek to maximize their advantage. The possibility of lowering the aggregate levels of money in elections would increase if workable, enforceable spending limits accompanied the free or discounted air time (assuming limits could be so designed).

While it is difficult to be certain of the impact on aggregate money levels, it is possible that free or lower-cost advertising would also result in increased electoral competition. Candidates who now lack adequate resources to buy television time would be better able to afford it and possibly make lopsided contests into more genuine ones. Some who favor free or reduced-rate proposals make this "level playing field" argument. Many observers, however, are not persuaded that money plays too great a role in our elections. These individuals see the level of money as consistent with the costs of other goods and services and as part of the price we pay for debate in a modern, democratic society.

Importance of Television in Campaigns. While proponents focus on television because of the importance of broadcasting in reaching large numbers of people, opponents point to recent aggregate data that show TV's importance to have been exaggerated in anecdotal accounts. Recent, better documented aggregate data show that TV and radio costs account for 27% of House campaign and 42% of Senate campaign budgets; this includes production and consultant costs as well as air time. Even the aggregate data, however, show broadcast advertising to be the single biggest expenditure category in both Senate and House elections. The more competitive races and the larger states show a much greater role for broadcast advertising: Senate campaign expenditures of 60% or more on broadcast advertising are common. In the absence of official data such as those formerly compiled by the FCC, even today's improved estimates and data compilations are not definitive in this area.

Obligation of Broadcasters. Proponents insist that it is not only constitutional but appropriate for broadcasters to provide free and discount air time that would advance the public interest. They assert that the public, not the broadcasters, own the airwaves. Broadcasters respond that they are already giving political candidates discounted time under the lowest unit rate requirements, which they estimate saves candidates 30% off regular commercial rates. . . .

Broadcasters also contend that they already voluntarily provide free air time to candidates in the form of debate time and news coverage. Furthermore, they note that many candidates refuse to avail themselves of the free debate time. There is, of course, a difference between broadcast candidate debates and broadcast candidate ads. Only in the latter does the candidate have full control over how his or her message is presented, and for that reason the spot ads have come to play the major role they do in our elections.

Thus, broadcasters argue that they are already providing substantial public service at their own expense and that it is unfair to ask them to do substantially more. Opponents also raise the concern that broadcast advertising rates might have to be raised if these proposals were enacted, with commercial advertisers then passing on the higher costs to the consumers. Proponents justify their demands on broadcasters by the billions of dollars worth of digital spectrum licenses that broadcasters will soon receive at no cost from the government. Furthermore, some 105th Congress proposals have provided for exemption procedures for broadcasters who might suffer "significant economic hardship" from the free and reduced-cost requirements. Notable examples are S.25 (the [John] McCain-[Russell D.] Feingold bill) and its House counterpart, H.R. 493 (the [Christopher] Shays-[Marty] Meehan bill).

Quality of Political Debate. Improving the level of discourse in elections is a goal invariably cited by proponents of free broadcast time. While it is often raised as a secondary objective, many supporters place particular emphasis on it. They base their hopes not on the reduced costs of advertising but on the conditions which invariably accompany these proposals—conditions that may avoid constitutional objection because they are voluntarily agreed to in exchange for a specified benefit. Supporters believe that lengthier advertisements and such format requirements as candidate appearance would work toward a more rational discussion of issues and a greater sense of accountability, thus reversing the perceived trend toward "negative" advertisements in recent years.

Opponents of free broadcast time observe that negative campaigning has always been a part of our elections and that the age of television only makes it more visible. They note that "negative" ads may simply be comparisons of candidates sharply defined in ways that may make one of those candidates uncomfortable. Rather than a blight on the electoral system, they point out that such communication can have a useful function. "Negative" ads are not inherently mudslinging or character attacks. Even advertisements that do not use the "talking heads" format can contribute to the debate on significant policy issues.

Methods of election communications are chosen based on their presumed effectiveness. While opinion survey respondents overwhelmingly express disapproval of the negative tone of political ads, political consultants insist they are effective. Supporters of free broadcast time may be responding to what citizens claim to want, rather than what experience indicates they are moved by, and many believe it is worth taking a first step toward the kind of political debate so widely espoused.

Policy Conclusions

Regardless of how dominant television is in today's politics, there is little doubt that its role is sufficiently great to be prominent in any discussion of issues pertaining to both campaign financing and the tone of debate in U.S. elections today. Whether as part of a comprehensive legislative package or as an incremental step in a larger process, decreasing the cost and increasing the quality of candidates' TV advertisements continue to loom large among reform goals. While the potential effects of the proposals discussed in this report are subject to debate, they have garnered considerable support across the political spectrum.

If Congress decided to require free or lower-cost broadcast time, a fundamental question, arguably more basic than those discussed above, would have to be answered: How far-reaching should the new rules be? In other words, should the benefits be an *addition* to the existing system, thus injecting an element of a "better" method; or should they be a *replacement* for the current system, with all candidate advertising to be conducted under the proposed price and format requirements? The extent of benefits will have a critical impact on all subsequent policy decisions.

LEGAL AND CONSTITUTIONAL CONSIDERATIONS

Current FCC Authority to Require Provision of Free Air Time

While the Communications Act of 1934 does not confer specific authority upon the FCC to require the provision of free air time for political advertising, the statute may implicitly grant the commission discretionary authority to impose such a condition on prospective and existing broadcast licensees. In granting broadcast licences and license renewals under the act, sections 307 and 309 direct the FEC to determine "whether the public interest, convenience and necessity will be served."[1] In addition, section 303 authorizes the commission to, "as public convenience, interest or necessity requires . . . [m]ake such rules and regulations and prescribe such restrictions and conditions . . . as may be necessary to carry out the provisions of [the] Act."[2]

---

1. *See* 47 U.S.C. §§ 307(a), 309(a).

2. 47 U.S.C. § 303(r).

In carrying out its mandate to ensure that broadcasters operate in the "public interest," the agency has consistently been found by reviewing courts to possess broad discretion to impose technical, structural *and* program related conditions to the grant and retention of a broadcast license. Most notable on this issue is *Red Lion Broadcasting Co.* v. *Federal Communications Commission,* where the Supreme Court upheld components of the FCC's "fairness doctrine," which required broadcasters to devote air time to opposing viewpoints on issues of public importance.[3] There, the Court held that the agency's public interest mandate provided adequate authority to impose such a requirement and noted the breadth of the FCC's authority under the standard.[4] In addition, reviewing courts have upheld past FCC regulations, encouraging the access of independently produced programming to network owned and affiliated stations, as a valid exercise of the agency's discretion under the public interest mandate.[5]

Given the breadth of discretion provided the agency under this standard, it could be argued that the public interest mandate would provide the FCC sufficient authority to require broadcasters to provide free air time for political advertisements. Such a requirement would arguably constitute a valid exercise of the FCC's discretion if it finds that the public benefits that flow from a "free air time" requirement would outweigh the encroachment on broadcast licensees' editorial discretion.[6]

First Amendment Validity of Free Air Time Proposals

In requiring broadcasters to set aside time for the broadcast of political advertisements, free air time proposals raise concerns regarding their validity under the First Amendment to the Constitution. In examining relevant Supreme Court precedent on the issue, however, it appears that such a requirement might well withstand constitutional scrutiny, as applied to broadcasters.

Throughout its First Amendment jurisprudence, the Court has generally afforded more limited First Amendment protection to broadcasters than to other media of expression and has analyzed content-based restrictions imposed upon them under a more lenient standard of review. In *National Broadcasting Company* v. *United States,* the Court addressed the distinction drawn between broadcasters and other media of expression for First Amendment purposes. Responding to arguments that the FCC was without authority to issue substantive content-based regulations and that such requirements violated broadcasters' First Amendment rights, the Court noted the physical limitations inherent to the electro-magnetic spectrum as a scarce public resource that could not accommodate all who wished to utilize it. The Court concluded that because of the radio spectrum's limited physical characteristics, the government has a legitimate interest in developing a licensing scheme that ensures its most efficient and effective use in the public interest. Accordingly, the FCC is not limited under either its governing statute or

---

3. 395 U.S. 367 (1969).

4. *Id.* At 380 ("This mandate to the FCC to assure that broadcasters operate in the public interest is a broad one, a power 'not niggardly' but expansive.") *See also National Broadcasting Co.* v. *United States,* 319 U.S. 190 (1943).

5. *See Mt. Mansfield Television, Inc.* v. *Federal Communications Commission,* 442 F.2d 470 (2nd Cir. 1971) (upholding the FCC's prime time access and financial interest and syndication rules); *National Association of Independent Television Producers and Distributors* v. *Federal Communications Commission,* 516 F.2d 526 (2nd Cir. 1975) (prime time access rule).

6. The commission might find, for example, that such a requirement furthers goals and principles underlying the First Amendment such as the promotion of greater citizen awareness of and debate on issues of public importance and the encouragement of greater participation in the electoral process.

the Constitution to regulating the technical aspects of the broadcast industry but may impose some forms of content-based regulation in furtherance of this goal.[7]

The notion that "physical scarcity" justifies a greater degree of government regulation of the broadcast medium was reiterated in *Red Lion*. There, the Court noted that "[b]ecause of the scarcity of radio frequencies, the Government is permitted to put restraints on licensees in favor of others whose views should be expressed on this unique medium. . . ."[8] More recently, the Court reaffirmed the validity of the "scarcity rationale," despite widespread questions about its continued necessity given the emergence of new mediums of expression such as cable and direct broadcast satellite.[9]

In addition to Supreme Court precedent supporting more governmental leeway in regulating the content of broadcasters, other decisions indicate that regulations designed to foster access for politically motivated speakers would be constitutionally permissible. In *Columbia Broadcasting System* v. *Federal Communications Commission*, the Court held that the statutory right of access for political candidates set out in section 312(a)(7) did not violate the First Amendment. The Court found that the provision "properly balances the First Amendment rights of federal candidates, the public and broadcasters."[10] In addition, the Court noted that the requirement promoted First Amendment principles by "enhancing the ability of candidates to present, and the public to receive, information necessary for the effective operation of the democratic process."[11] The Court distinguished the provision from previous attempts to provide a general right of access to the public, which it invalidated in an earlier opinion.[12] Moreover, in *Buckley* v. *Valeo* [document 3.1], the Court stressed the importance of providing candidates the "opportunity to make their views known" and of the electorate to "make informed choices among candidates for office. . . ."[13]

In applying the line of reasoning utilized by the Court, it appears that a requirement that broadcasters provide free air time for political advertisements might well withstand a First Amendment challenge. Similar to the provision at issue in *CBS* v. *FCC*, such a proposal would provide a limited right of access to enable political candidates to present and the public to receive their views on important public issues. In addition, a free air time proposal would arguabl[y] promote free speech principles by facilitating a better informed electorate and the more effective operation of the democratic process. Given the status accorded to "political speech," a reviewing court could find a strong governmental interest in requiring access to broadcast stations for such purposes.

---

7. *Id.* at 226–227. Commonly referred to as the "scarcity rationale," this line of reasoning has been the touchstone for government regulation of the broadcast media and has been applied to justify other content-based regulatory requirements. *See Red Lion Broadcasting Company* v. *FCC*, 395 U.S. 367 (1967) ("physical scarcity" used to justify FCC fairness doctrine and personal attack and political editorial rules); but *see Telecommunications Research and Action Center* v. *FCC*, 801 F.2d 501 (D.C. Cir. 1986), *cert. denied*, 107 S.Ct. 3196 (1987), where the court called into question the continued validity of the assumptions underlying the "scarcity rationale."

8. *Red Lion,* supra. at 390. *See also Columbia Broadcasting System, Inc.* v. *FCC*, 453 U.S. 367 (1981) (spectrum scarcity used to affirm statutory requirement that broadcast stations grant reasonable access to legally qualified candidates for Federal office.).

9. *See Turner Broadcasting System* v. *Federal Communications Commission*, 512 U.S. 622 (1994).

10. 453 U.S. at 397.

11. *Id.* at 396.

12. *See Columbia Broadcasting System, Inc.* v. *Democratic National Committee*, 412 U.S. 94 (1973).

13. *See generally,* 424 U.S. 1 (1976).

Note however that, given the fact that cable operators apparently enjoy a much greater degree of First Amendment protection than do broadcasters, such requirements as applied to cable television operators would be subject to more intense judicial review. In *Turner,* the Court responded to the argument that regulations governing cable television should be analyzed under the First Amendment standards applied to broadcasters. The Court noted that "the rationale for applying a less rigorous standard of First Amendment scrutiny to broadcast regulation . . . does not apply in the context of cable regulation."

Thus, as applied to cable, a free air time requirement would apparently be analyzed under the more exacting standard of review normally applied to content-based regulations, under which the government must show a "compelling governmental interest" and that the particular regulation is "narrowly tailored" to achieve the government's objective.[14]

While it appears that the government's interest in promoting greater citizen awareness of public issues and encouraging greater participation in the electoral process might be sufficiently "compelling" to justify a free air time requirement, the constitutional validity of the regulation would ultimately depend upon whether the particular regulatory scheme is the "least burdensome" means available to achieve the government's objective. Relevant to the issue of "least burdensome" alternatives would be any congressional hearings or other factfinding activities undertaken prior to the enactment of any free air time proposal applicable to cable.

Fifth Amendment "Takings" Questions

In addition to First Amendment issues associated with free air time proposals, such initiatives also raise questions regarding whether conditioning a broadcast license on compliance with the requirement would constitute a "taking" of property without just compensation, in violation of the Fifth Amendment. In making the "takings" argument, broadcasters essentially contend that a requirement to provide free air time for political advertisements would deprive them of air time that could be sold to commercial advertisers and thus diminish the advertising revenues that could be realized from the use of the license.

However, relevant statutory provisions and Supreme Court precedent on the issue indicate that a Fifth Amendment "takings" challenge to a free air time requirement would not be actionable, as broadcasters have no right to the grant of a license or "property interest" in the use of a frequency. Under section 304 of the Communications Act of 1934, applicants for a broadcast license are expressly required to waive "any claim to the use of any particular frequency or of the electromagnetic spectrum as against the regulatory power of the United States because of previous use of the same. . . ."[15] In *Federal Communications Commission* v. *Sanders Bros. Radio Station,* the Court interpreted this provision as a clear expression of congressional intent that "no person is to have anything in the nature of a property right as a result of the granting of a license."[16] Since broadcasters do not have a "property right" as a result of the license, it appears that no "taking" would occur in connection with a free air time requirement. . . .

---

14. *See e.g. Boos* v. *Barry,* 485 U.S. 312 (1987). With regard to whether a particular regulation is sufficiently "tailored," the Court has required that the government choose the "least restrictive means [of regulating the speech]" available to accomplish the government's objective "without unnecessarily interfering with First Amendment freedoms." *See Sable Communications of California* v. *Federal Communications Commission,* 492 U.S. 115 (1989).

15. 47 U.S.C. § 304.

16. *See* 309 U.S. 470, 475 (1940); *see also Ashbacker Radio Corp.* v. *Federal Communications Commission,* 326 U.S. 327, 331–32 (1945).